Learning
RED HAT
LINUX

Related titles from O'Reilly

Learning Debian GNU/Linux

Learning Red Hat Linux

Linux Device Drivers

Linux in a Nutshell

Linux Network Administrator's Guide

LPI Linux Certification in a Nutshell

Running Linux

Understanding the Linux Kernel

Also available

The Linux Web Server CD Bookshelf

Learning
RED HAT
LINUX

SECOND EDITION

Bill McCarty

O'REILLY®

Beijing · Cambridge · Farnham · Köln · Paris · Sebastopol · Taipei · Tokyo

Learning Red Hat Linux, Second Edition
by Bill McCarty

Copyright © 2002, 1999 O'Reilly & Associates, Inc. All rights reserved.
Printed in the United States of America.

Published by O'Reilly & Associates, Inc., 1005 Gravenstein Highway North, Sebastopol, CA 95472.

O'Reilly & Associates books may be purchased for educational, business, or sales promotional use. Online editions are also available for most titles *(safari.oreilly.com)*. For more information contact our corporate/institutional sales department: 800-998-9938 or *corporate@oreilly.com*.

Editor:	Chuck Toporek
Production Editor:	Leanne Clarke Soylemez
Cover Designer:	Hanna Dyer
Interior Designer:	David Futato

Printing History:

September 1999:	First Edition.
January 2002:	Second Edition.

Nutshell Handbook, the Nutshell Handbook logo, and the O'Reilly logo are registered trademarks of O'Reilly & Associates, Inc. The association between the image of a man wearing a wide-brimmed hat and the topic of Red Hat Linux is a trademark of O'Reilly & Associates, Inc.

Red Hat, RPM, and all Red Hat–based trademarks are trademarks or registered trademarks of Red Hat, Inc. The screenshots from Red Hat Linux are copyright © Red Hat, Inc., and are reprinted by permission. Netscape Communications Corporation has not authorized, sponsored, endorsed, or approved this publication and is not responsible for its content. Netscape and the Netscape Communications corporate logos are trademarks and trade names of Netscape Communications Corporation.

Many of the designations used by manufacturers and sellers to distinguish their products are claimed as trademarks. Where those designations appear in this book, and O'Reilly & Associates, Inc., was aware of a trademark claim, the designations have been printed in caps or initial caps.

While every precaution has been taken in the preparation of this book, the publisher assumes no responsibility for errors or omissions, or for damages resulting from the use of the information contained herein.

ISBN: 0-596-00071-5
[M]   [11/02]

Table of Contents

Preface . . . . **ix**

1. Why Run Linux? **1**
What Is Linux?   1
Reasons to Choose or Not Choose Linux   10

2. Preparing to Install Red Hat Linux **13**
Minimum Hardware Requirements   13
Collecting Information About Your System   14
Installation Types   22
Preparing Your Hard Disk   23

3. Installing Red Hat Linux **30**
Installing the Operating System and Applications   30
Start the Installation   31
Logging In   62
Getting Help   65

4. How Linux Works **68**
User Accounts   68
How Linux Organizes Data   68
Using X   75

5. Using the GNOME Desktop **81**
Using GNOME   81
Configuring GNOME   90
GNOME Office   95
GNOME Resources   98

6. Using the KDE Desktop **100**
Using KDE   100
KDE's Desktop   100
Configuring KDE   107
KOffice   111
KDE Resources   114

7. Conquering the bash Shell **116**
Issuing Shell Commands   116
Correcting Commands   117
Working with the Linux Command Prompt   119
Useful Linux Programs   136

8. Using the RPM Package Manager **139**
Packages   139
The rpm Command   139
Finding Packages   141
Querying the RPM Database   142
Installing a Package   143
Uninstalling a Package   146
Updating a Package   147
Advanced RPM Techniques   147
Gnome RPM   148
The Red Hat Network   154

9. Configuring and Administering Linux **155**
Configuring a Printer   168
Configuring Sound   173

10. Connecting to the Internet **176**
Configuring Your Modem Using rp3   176
Using wvdial   182
Web Browsers   183
gFTP FTP Client   188
Configuring Linux to Use a Cable or DSL Modem   189

11. Setting Up a Networked Workstation **191**
Networking Overview   191
LAN Administration Using Neat   192

Samba 201
Samba Client Configuration and Use 215
Setting Up a DHCP Server 218

12. Setting Up Internet Services **224**
Running an FTP Server 224
Running Apache 227
Configuring a Mail Server 233
The Secure Shell 235
Configuring DNS 239
Implementing a Basic Firewall 240
Network Security Tips 243

13. Advanced Shell Usage and Shell Scripts **245**
The Power of the Unix Shell 245
Filename Globbing 246
Shell Aliases 248
Using Virtual Consoles 249
X and the Shell 250
Shell Scripts 251
Understanding Shell Scripts 260

A. Linux Directory Tree **269**

B. Principal Linux Files **271**

C. Managing the Boot Process **275**

D. Installing and Configuring X **292**

E. Linux Command Quick Reference **312**

Glossary **323**

Index **327**

Preface

You've probably heard about Linux from a magazine, radio or TV program, or a friend. You're wondering what Linux is about and whether you should give it a try. If so, particularly if you currently use Microsoft Windows, this book was written for you.

When the first edition of this book was being written, Linux was a much talked about novelty. Today, Linux has invaded corporate information technology departments, becoming a popular technology used by hobbyists and professionals alike.

As predicted in the first edition of this book, Linux is becoming easier to use. Every day brings a new tool or feature designed for ease of use. If you work with Microsoft Windows and have dabbled a bit in MS-DOS or are curious about what happens inside Windows, you can install and configure Linux. Thousands of people from all walks of life—even journalists, who are notorious for their technical ineptitude—have already done so.

This book is based on Red Hat Linux, the most popular Linux distribution. It includes two CDs that contain everything you need to install and configure your own Red Hat Linux system. This book will make your Linux journey easier by giving you the big picture, providing you with step-by-step procedures, and getting you started doing useful or fun activities, such as word processing or games. This book focuses on the needs of the new Linux user and on desktop Linux applications. You'll learn about networks and servers, but the details of those topics are left for more advanced books.

Organization of This Book

This book contains 13 chapters and 5 appendixes:

Chapter 1, *Why Run Linux?*
> This chapter is designed to introduce you to Linux and help you determine whether Linux is appropriate for you.

Chapter 2, *Preparing to Install Red Hat Linux*

This chapter helps you understand what's involved in installing Red Hat Linux and guides you through the process of gathering information about your system necessary to successfully install Linux.

Chapter 3, *Installing Red Hat Linux*

This chapter takes you step-by-step through the installation of Red Hat Linux.

Chapter 4, *How Linux Works*

Before you can effectively use a desktop environment, you need to know some Linux fundamentals. This chapter explains basic Linux concepts that underlie graphical and nongraphical system use.

Chapter 5, *Using the GNOME Desktop*

This chapter explains how to configure and use the GNOME desktop environment and GNOME Office, GNOME's desktop application suite.

Chapter 6, *Using the KDE Desktop*

This chapter explains how to configure and use the K Desktop Environment (KDE) and introduces you to KOffice, KDE's desktop application suite.

Chapter 7, *Conquering the bash Shell*

This chapter digs deeper into the *bash* shell, the Linux command-line interface. You'll learn how to use the Linux command-line interface, which resembles MS-DOS but is much more powerful and sophisticated. Here you'll see firsthand just how powerful and easy to use Linux can be.

Chapter 8, *Using the RPM Package Manager*

This chapter explains the Red Hat Package Manager, which helps you manage programs and applications.

Chapter 9, *Configuring and Administering Linux*

Administering a multiuser operating system such as Linux is somewhat more complicated than administering a single-user operating system, but Linux includes tools that simplify the work. This chapter shows you how to configure your Linux system, including how to configure sound and printers.

Chapter 10, *Connecting to the Internet*

This chapter shows you how to connect to the Internet via your Internet service provider (ISP). Once connected, you can use your Linux system to surf the Web and access other familiar Internet services.

Chapter 11, *Setting Up a Networked Workstation*

This chapter shows you how to connect your Linux system to other systems on your Local-Area Network (LAN).

Chapter 12, *Setting Up Internet Services*

This chapter shows you how to set up servers that users around the world can access via the Internet. For example, you'll learn how to install and configure Apache, the world's most popular web server.

Chapter 13, *Advanced Shell Usage and Shell Scripts*

This chapter shows how to use advanced shell features and how to create shell scripts that extend the capabilities of Linux.

Appendixes to the book help you locate important files and directories, manage the way your system boots, and use common Linux commands. In particular, you may need Appendix D for instructions on what to do in case the X Window System doesn't configure properly during the installation process.

Sources of Information

If you are new to the world of Linux, there are a number of resources to explore and become familiar with. Having access to the Internet is helpful, but not essential.

Red Hat's Web Site

Your primary resource for information on Red Hat Linux is Red Hat's web site at *http://www.redhat.com*. Red Hat's web site includes more resources than can be mentioned here. Among the most important are:

The Red Hat Linux 7.2 support page
http://www.redhat.com/support/docs/howto/rhl72.html

At this site, you'll find:

- The Official Red Hat Linux Installation Guide
- Hardware Compatibility Lists
- The Official Red Hat Linux Getting Started Guide
- Red Hat Linux 7.2 Gotchas and Workarounds
- Red Hat Linux 7.2 All Errata
- Red Hat Linux FAQ
- Red Hat Linux 7.2 Reference Guide
- Red Hat Linux 7.2 Customization Guide

The redhat-install-list mailing list
http://www.redhat.com/mailing-lists

On this list, you can obtain installation assistance from members of the Red Hat Linux community.

Bugzilla
http://bugzilla.redhat.com

Bugzilla is a database that lists possible bugs affecting Red Hat Linux. The database often gives fixes or workarounds for bugs.

Linux Documentation Project Guides

The Linux Documentation Project (LDP) is a group of volunteers who have worked to produce books (guides), HOWTO documents, and manual pages on topics ranging from installation to kernel programming. The LDP works include:

Linux Installation and Getting Started
> By Matt Welsh et al. This book describes how to obtain, install, and use Linux. It includes an introductory Unix tutorial and information on systems administration, the X Window System, and networking.

Linux System Administrators Guide
> By Lars Wirzenius and Joanna Oja. This book is a guide to general Linux system administration and covers topics such as creating and configuring users, performing system backups, configuring major software packages, and installing and upgrading software.

Linux System Adminstration Made Easy
> By Steve Frampton. This book describes day-to-day administration and maintenance issues of relevance to Linux users.

Linux Programmers Guide
> By B. Scott Burkett, Sven Goldt, John D. Harper, Sven van der Meer, and Matt Welsh. This book covers topics of interest to people who wish to develop application software for Linux.

The Linux Kernel
> By David A. Rusling. This book provides an introduction to the Linux kernel, how it is constructed, and how it works. Take a tour of your kernel.

The Linux Kernel Module Programming Guide
> By Ori Pomerantz. This guide explains how to write Linux kernel modules.

More manuals are in development. For more information about the LDP, consult their World Wide Web server at *http://www.linuxdoc.org* or one of its many mirrors.

HOWTO documents
> The Linux HOWTOs are a comprehensive series of papers detailing various aspects of the system, such as installation and configuration of the X Window System software or how to write in assembly language programming under Linux. These are generally located in the *HOWTO* subdirectory of the FTP sites listed later, or they are available on the World Wide Web at one of the many Linux Documentation Project mirror sites. See the file *HOWTO-INDEX* for a list of what's available.
>
> You might want to obtain the *Installation HOWTO*, which describes how to install Linux on your system; the *Hardware Compatibility HOWTO*, which contains a list of hardware known to work with Linux; and the *Distribution HOWTO*, which lists software vendors selling Linux on diskette and CD-ROM.

Linux Frequently Asked Questions
> The *Linux Frequently Asked Questions with Answers* (FAQ) contains a wide assortment of questions and answers about the system. It is a must-read for all newcomers.

Documentation Available via FTP

If you have access to anonymous FTP, you can obtain all the previously listed Linux documentation from various sites, including *http://www.ibiblio.org/pub/Linux/docs* and *http://tsx-11.mit.edu/pub/linux/docs*.

These sites are mirrored by a number of sites around the world.

Documentation Available via WWW

There are many Linux-based WWW sites available. The home site for the Linux Documentation Project can be accessed at *http://www.linuxdoc.org*.

The Open Source Writers Guild (OSWG) is a project whose scope extends beyond Linux. The OSWG, like this book, is committed to advocating and facilitating the production of open source (*http://www.opensource.org*) documentation. The OSWG home site is at *http://www.oswg.org:8080/oswg*.

Both of these sites contain hypertext (and other) versions of many Linux-related documents.

Documentation Available Commercially

A number of publishing companies and software vendors publish the works of the Linux Documentation Project. Two such vendors are:

Specialized Systems Consultants, Inc. (SSC)
> *http://www.ssc.com*
> P.O. Box 55549 Seattle, WA 98155-0549
> Phone: (206) 782-7733
> Fax: (206) 782-7191
> Email: *sales@ssc.com*

Linux Systems Labs
> *http://www.lsl.com*
> 18300 Tara Drive
> Clinton Township, MI 48036
> Phone: (810) 987-8807
> Fax: (810) 987-3562
> Email: *sales@lsl.com*

Both companies sell compendiums of Linux HOWTO documents and other Linux documentation in printed and bound form. O'Reilly & Associates, Inc., publishes a series of Linux books, including:

Running Linux
> This installation and user guide to the system describes how to get the most out of personal computing with Linux.

Linux in a Nutshell
> Another in the successful "in a Nutshell" series, this book focuses on providing a broad reference text for Linux.

LPI Linux Certification in a Nutshell
> While this book is geared toward junior-level system administrators who want to take the Linux Professional Institute's exams for Level 1 Certification (LPIC-1), this book is also a great resource for new users, such as yourself.

Linux Journal and Linux Magazine

Linux Journal and *Linux Magazine* are monthly magazines for the Linux community, written and published by a number of Linux activists. They contain articles ranging from novice questions and answers to kernel programming internals. Even if you have Usenet access, these magazines are a good way to stay in touch with the Linux community.

Linux Journal is the older magazine and is published by SSC, Inc., for which details were listed previously. You can also find the magazine on the World Wide Web at *http://www.linuxjournal.com*.

Linux Magazine is a newer, independent publication. The home web site for the magazine is *http://www.linuxmagazine.com*.

Linux Usenet Newsgroups

If you have access to Usenet news, the following Linux-related newsgroups are available:

Red Hat–specific lists

linux.redhat.announce
> Announcements by Red Hat.

linux.redhat.devel
> For software developers using Red Hat Linux.

linux.redhat.install
> Issues related to installation of Red Hat Linux.

linux-redhat.list
> General Red Hat Linux issues.

linux.redhat.misc
General Red Hat Linux issues and advocacy.

linux.redhat.rpm
For Red Hat Package Manager (RPM).

General Linux topics

comp.os.linux.redhat
linux.redhat
Dedicated to addressing general questions related to Red Hat Linux.

comp.os.linux.admin
Administering Linux systems.

comp.os.linux.advocacy
Arguing the benefits of Linux in comparison to other operating systems.

comp.os.linux.announce
Moderated. Announcements of new software, distributions, bug reports, and goings-on in the Linux community. All Linux users should read this group. Submissions may be mailed to *linux-announce@news.ornl.gov*.

comp.os.linux.development
Discussions about developing the Linux kernel and system itself.

comp.os.linux.development.apps
Writing Linux applications and porting applications to Linux.

comp.os.linux.development.system
Linux kernels, device drivers, and modules.

comp.os.linux.embedded
Writing embedded systems using Linux.

comp.os.linux.hardware
Hardware compatibility with the Linux operating system.

comp.os.linux.help
Help in installing and using Linux.

comp.os.linux.misc
Topics not covered by other groups.

comp.os.linux.networking
Networking and communication.

comp.os.linux.portable
Linux on laptops and other portable computers.

comp.os.linux.questions
Questions and answers concerning Linux.

comp.os.linux.security
Security issues concerning Linux.

comp.os.linux.setup
Linux installation and system administration.

comp.os.linux.x
X servers, clients, libraries, and fonts.

There are also several newsgroups devoted to Linux in languages other than English, such as *fr.comp.os.linux* in French and *de.comp.os.linux* in German.

Linux Mailing Lists

There are a large number of specialist Linux mailing lists on which you can find many people willing to help with questions you might have.

The best known of these are the lists hosted by Rutgers University. You may subscribe to these lists by sending an email message formatted as follows:

```
To: majordomo@vger.rutgers.edu
Subject: anything at all
Body:

subscribe listname
```

Some of the available lists related to Linux networking are:

linux-net
Discussion relating to Linux networking

linux-ppp
Discussion relating to the Linux PPP implementation

linux-kernel
Discussion relating to Linux kernel development

Online Linux Support

There are many ways of obtaining help online, where volunteers from around the world offer expertise and services to assist users with questions and problems.

The OpenProjects IRC Network is an IRC network devoted entirely to open projects—open source and open hardware alike. Some of its channels are designed to provide online Linux support services. IRC stands for Internet Relay Chat, a network service that allows you to talk interactively on the Internet to other users. IRC networks support multiple channels on which groups of people talk. Whatever you type in a channel is seen by all other users of that channel.

There are a number of active channels on the OpenProjects IRC network where you will find users 24 hours a day, 7 days a week who are willing and able to help you solve any Linux problems you may have or just chat. You can use this service by installing an IRC client like *irc-II*, connecting to *servername irc.openprojects.org: 6667*, and joining the *#linpeople* channel.

Linux User Groups (LUGs)

Many Linux user groups around the world offer direct support to users, and many engage in activities such as installation days, talks and seminars, demonstration nights, and other completely social events. Linux user groups are a great way of meeting other Linux users in your area. There are a number of published lists of Linux user groups. Some of the better-known ones are:

Groups of Linux Users Everywhere
  http://www.ssc.com/glue/groups

LUG list project
  http://www.nllgg.nl/lugww

LUG registry
  http://www.linux.org/users

Other Web Sites

The following are useful Linux-related web sites. Check them out to get the latest information about Linux. Perhaps the most useful is the home page of the Linux Documentation Project (LDP). There, you can find almost anything you want to know about Linux. The Linux Documentation Project web site includes a search engine that makes it easy to find what you need.

Eric S. Raymond's Linux Reading List HOWTO
  http://www.linuxdoc.org/HOWTO/Reading-List-HOWTO/index.html

Linux Documentation Project
  http://www.linuxdoc.org

Linux Gazette
  http://www.linuxgazette.com

Linux Today
  http://www.linuxtoday.com

Linux Web Ring
  http://nll.interl.net/lwr

  The Linux Web Ring offers a convenient way to explore a variety of Linux-related web sites. Participating web sites present links to one another; by following these links, you can circumnavigate the entire ring or you can use the Web Ring's home page to seek exactly the sort of page you're interested in.

Linux Weekly News
  http://www.lwn.net

O'Reilly & Associates Linux DevCenter
  http://linux.oreilly.com

Slashdot

http://www.slashdot.org

The motto of the Slashdot web site is "News for nerds. Stuff that matters." You'll find a great deal of interesting news and information there, concerning not only Linux, but the open source community and computing generally.

Conventions Used in This Book

The following typographical conventions are used in this book:

Bold

Used for commands, programs, and options. All terms shown in bold are typed literally.

Italic

Used to show arguments and variables that should be replaced with user-supplied values. Italic is also used to indicate new terms, URLs, filenames, file extensions, and directories, and to highlight comments in examples.

`Constant width`

Used to show the contents of files or the output from commands.

`Constant width bold`

Used in examples and tables to show commands or other text that should be typed literally by the user.

`Constant width italic`

Used in examples and tables to show text that should be replaced with user-supplied values.

#, $

Used in some examples as the root shell prompt (#) and as the user prompt ($) under the Bourne or *bash* shell.

 Signifies a tip, suggestion, or general note.

 Indicates a warning or caution.

A final word about syntax: in many cases, the space between an option and its argument can be omitted. In other cases, the spacing (or lack of spacing) must be followed strictly. For example, **–wn** (no intervening space) might be interpreted differently from **–w** *n*. It's important to notice the spacing used in option syntax.

Path Notation

I use a shorthand notation to indicate paths. Instead of writing "From the Start menu, choose Find, then Files or Folders," I write: Start → Find → Files or Folders. I distinguish menus, dialog boxes, buttons, or other GUI elements only when the context would otherwise be unclear. Simply look for the GUI element whose label matches an element of the path.

Keyboard Accelerators

In a keyboard accelerator (such as **Ctrl-Alt-Del**), a dash indicates that the keys should be held down simultaneously, whereas a space means that the keys should be pressed sequentially. For example, **Ctrl-Esc** indicates that the Control and Escape keys should be held down simultaneously, whereas **Ctrl Esc** means that the Control and Escape keys should be pressed sequentially.

Where a keyboard accelerator contains an uppercase letter, you should not type the Shift key unless it's given explicitly. For example, **Ctrl-C** indicates that you should press the Control and C keys; **Ctrl-Shift-C** indicates that you should press the Control, Shift, and C keys.

How to Contact Us

Please address comments and questions concerning this book to the publisher:

O'Reilly & Associates, Inc.
1005 Gravenstein Highway North
Sebastopol, CA 95472
(800) 998-9938 (in the United States or Canada)
(707) 829-0515 (international/local)
(707) 829-0104 (fax)

We have a web page for this book, where we list errata, examples, or any additional information. You can access this page at:

http://www.oreilly.com/catalog/redhat2/

To comment or ask technical questions about this book, send email to:

bookquestions@oreilly.com

For more information about our books, conferences, Resource Centers, and the O'Reilly Network, see our web site at:

http://www.oreilly.com

Acknowledgments

Thanks to my editor, Chuck Toporek, who undertook the sometimes exasperating task of looking at this book through the eyes of a reader. Chuck pointed out many errors, clarified many obscure sentences, and suggested many improvements. Also, many thanks to David Chu, Chuck's editorial assistant, for handling all the logistics of getting my book out for review and into production on time.

Thanks also to Margot Maley of Waterside Productions, Inc., who brought this authorship opportunity to my attention.

Several reviewers, some working for O'Reilly & Associates and some working elsewhere, commented on the manuscript and suggested helpful corrections and improvements. In particular, I'd like to thank the following people for taking time away from their busy schedules to review this latest edition: Jonathan Blandford, Greg Dickerson, Joe Johnston, Dave Mason, Andy Oram, Randy Russell, Mary Jane Caswell-Stephenson, and Laurie Lynne Tucker. I greatly appreciate their assistance and readily confess that any errors in the manuscript were added by me after their reviews and so are entirely my responsibility.

My family—Jennifer, Patrick, and Sara—provided compassion and assistance during this latest authorship experience. Their efforts are worthy of special note, because we sold two houses and purchased a new one during the preparation of the first edition this book. They generously undertook more than their share of work on our turn-of-the-(twenty-first-)century home so that I could focus on writing. Thanks, guys.

I also acknowledge the love, concern, and support of my savior, Jesus Christ. His perfect love is entirely undeserved.

## CHAPTER 1

Why Run Linux?

Welcome to Linux, the operating system that everyone's talking about. Unlike the weather—which proverbial wisdom says you can't do anything about—you *can* do something about Linux. You can run it on your own PC, so that you can see first-hand what the talk is about. This chapter is the first leg of your journey into the land of Linux. Here, you'll learn whether this particular journey is right for you and what you can expect down the road. If you're impatient to get started, you can jump ahead to the next chapter, which helps you prepare your PC for installing Linux. But if you'd like to know more about the history and capabilities of Linux, read on.

What Is Linux?

Linux is an *operating system*, a software program that controls your computer. Most PC vendors load an operating system—generally, Microsoft Windows—onto the hard drive of a PC before delivery; so, unless the hard drive of your PC has failed, you may not understand the function of an operating system.

An operating system solves several problems arising from hardware variation. As you're aware, no two PC models have identical hardware. For example, some PCs have an IDE hard drive, whereas others have a SCSI hard drive. Some PCs have one hard drive; others have two or more. Most PCs have a CD-ROM drive, but some do not. Some PCs have an Intel Pentium CPU, whereas others have an AMD Athlon, and so on. Suppose that, in a world without operating systems, you're programming a new PC application—perhaps a new multimedia word processor. Your application must cope with all the possible variations of PC hardware. As a result, it becomes bulky and complex. Users don't like it because it consumes too much hard drive space, takes a long time to load, and—because of its size and complexity—has more bugs than it should.

Operating systems solve this problem by providing a standard way for applications to access hardware devices. Thanks to the operating system, applications can be more compact, because they share the commonly used code for accessing the hardware.

Applications can also be more reliable, because common code is written only once—and by expert programmers rather than by application programmers.

GNU/Linux

Properly speaking, the name *Linux* applies to the Linux kernel, the most basic and fundamental part of a computer operating system. Some people prefer to refer to the "Linux operating system" as "GNU/Linux." Doing so emphasizes the contribution of the GNU project—which is described later in this chapter—to the development of the Linux operating system. However, Red Hat calls its operating system Red Hat Linux, not Red Hat GNU/Linux. Therefore, in this book we refer to both the kernel and operating system as Linux. Context will help you understand whether the entire operating system or only the kernel is meant.

Pronouncing Linux

Internet newsgroup participants have long debated the proper pronunciation of Linux. Because Linus Torvalds originated the Linux kernel, his pronunciation of the word should reign as the standard. However, Linus is Finnish and his pronunciation of Linux is difficult for English speakers to approximate. Consequently, many variations in pronunciation have arisen. The most popular pronunciation sounds as though the word were spelled *Linnucks*, with the stress on the first syllable and a short *i*.

If your computer has a sound card, you can hear how Linus Torvalds pronounces Linux at *http://www.ssc.com/lj/linuxsay.html*. Linus's personal opinion is that how you pronounce Linux matters much less than whether you use it.

As you'll soon learn, operating systems do many other things as well; for example, they generally provide a filesystem so you can store and retrieve data and a user interface so you can control your computer. However, if you think of a computer's operating system as its subconscious mind, you won't be far off the mark. It's the computer's conscious mind—applications such as word processors and spreadsheets—that do useful work. But, without the subconscious—the operating system—the computer would cease breathing and applications would not function.

Desktop and Server Operating Systems

Now that you know what an operating system is, you may be wondering what operating systems other PC users are using. According to the market research firm IDC, Microsoft products account for about 92 percent of sales of desktop operating systems. However, bear in mind that, because Linux is a free operating system, Linux sales are a mere fraction of actual Linux installations. Unlike most commercial oper-

---

ating systems, Linux is not sold under terms of a per-seat license; a company is free to purchase a single Linux CD-ROM and install Linux on as many systems as they like.

Later in this chapter you'll learn how Linux is distributed, but notice that Linux was termed a *free* operating system. If you have a high-speed Internet connection, you can download, install, and use Linux without paying anyone for anything (except perhaps your Internet service provider, who may impose a connection fee). It's anyone's guess how many people have downloaded Linux, but estimates indicate that between 7 and 10 million computers now run Linux.

Linux is primarily run as a server platform—not as a desktop system. Linux servers can be powered up and online 24/7, connected (at least occasionally) to the Internet, and ready to provide services to requesting clients. For example, many Linux users run web servers, but the number of desktop Linux users—those who power on their computers and then power them off when they're done—is rising.

This book focuses on how Linux can be used on the desktop. However, if you're unfamiliar with Linux and Unix, this book is right for you even if you plan to set up a Linux server. This book will take you through the basics of setting up and using Linux as a desktop system. After you've mastered what this book offers, you should consult *Running Linux,* by Matt Welsh, Matthias Kalle Dalheimer and Lar Kaufman (O'Reilly & Associates, Inc.), a more advanced book that focuses on setting up and using Linux servers. You might also enjoy *Linux in a Nutshell*, by Ellen Siever, Stephen Spainhour, Jessica P. Hekman, and Stephen Figgins (O'Reilly); this book puts useful Linux reference information at your fingertips. *LPI Linux Certification in a Nutshell* by Jeffrey Dean (O'Reilly) is a concise summary of Linux system administration information and procedures that's useful whether or not you're interested in seeking certification.

How Linux Is Different

Linux is distinguished from other popular operating systems in three important ways:

- Linux is a cross-platform operating system that runs on many computer models. Only Unix, an ancestor of Linux, rivals Linux in this respect. In comparison, Windows 95/98 runs only on CPUs with the Intel architecture. Windows NT runs only on CPUs with the Intel architecture or the Compaq Alpha. And Windows 2000 runs only on CPUs with the Intel architecture, although Microsoft originally announced that Windows 2000 would be available for the Compaq Alpha as well.

- Linux is free, in two senses. First, you can pay nothing to obtain and use Linux. On the other hand, you may choose to purchase Linux from a vendor that bundles Linux with special documentation or applications or that provides technical support. However, even in this case, the cost of Linux is likely to be a fraction of what you'd pay for another operating system. So, Linux is free or nearly free in an economic sense.

Second, and more important, Linux and many Linux applications are distributed in source form. This makes it possible for you and others to modify or improve them. You're *not* free to do this with most operating systems, which are distributed in binary form. For example, you can't make changes to Windows or Office—only Microsoft can do that. Because of this freedom, Linux is being constantly improved and updated, far outpacing the rate of progress of any other operating system. For example, Linux was the first operating system to support Intel's Itanium 64-bit CPU.

- Linux has more attractive features and performance. Free access to Linux source code lets programmers around the world implement new features and tweak Linux to improve its performance and reliability. The best of these features and tweaks are incorporated in the Linux kernel or made available as kernel patches or applications. Not even Microsoft can mobilize and support a software development team as large and dedicated as the volunteer Linux software development team, which numbers in the hundreds of thousands, including programmers, code reviewers, and testers.

The Origins of Linux

Linux traces its ancestry back to a mainframe operating system known as Multics (Multiplexed Information and Computing Service). Multics was one of the first multiuser computer systems and is still in use today. Participating in its development, which began in 1965, was Bell Telephone Labs, along with the Massachusetts Institute of Technology (MIT) and General Electric.

Two Bell Labs software engineers, Ken Thompson and Dennis Ritchie, worked on Multics until Bell Labs withdrew from the project in 1969. One of their favorite pastimes during the project had been playing a multiuser game called Space Travel. Without access to a Multics computer, they found themselves unable to indulge their fantasies of flying around the galaxy. Resolving to remedy this, they decided to port the Space Travel game to run on an otherwise unused PDP-7 computer. Eventually, they implemented a rudimentary operating system they named *Unics*, as a play on *Multics*. Somehow, the spelling of the name became *Unix*.

Their operating system was novel in several respects, most notably its portability. Most previous operating systems had been written for a specific target computer. Just as a tailor-made suit fits only its owner, such an operating system could not be easily adapted to run on an unfamiliar computer. In order to create a portable operating system, Ritchie and Thompson first created a programming language called C. Like assembly language, C let a programmer access low-level hardware facilities not available to programmers writing in a high-level language such as FORTRAN or COBOL. But, like FORTRAN and COBOL, a C program was not bound to a particular computer. Just as a ready-made suit can be altered here and there to fit a purchaser, writing Unix in C made it possible to easily adapt Unix to run on computers other than the PDP-7.

As word of their work spread and interest grew, Ritchie and Thompson made copies of Unix freely available to programmers around the world. These programmers revised and improved Unix, sending word of their changes back to Ritchie and Thompson, who incorporated the best improvements in their version of Unix. Eventually, several Unix variants arose. Prominent among these was BSD (Berkeley Systems Division) Unix, written at the University of California, Berkeley, in 1978. Bill Joy—one of the principals of the BSD project—later became a founder of Sun Microsystems, which sold another Unix variant (SunOS) to power its workstations. In 1984, AT&T, the parent company of Bell Labs, began selling its own version of Unix, known as System V.

Free Software

What Ritchie and Thompson began in a distinctly noncommercial fashion ended up spawning several legal squabbles. When AT&T grasped the commercial potential of Unix, it claimed Unix as its intellectual property and began charging a hefty license fee to those who wanted to use it. Soon, others who had implemented Unix-like operating systems were distributing licenses only for a fee. Understandably, those who had contributed improvements to Unix considered it unfair for AT&T and others to appropriate the fruits of their labors. This concern for profit was at odds with the democratic, share-and-share-alike spirit of the early days of Unix.

Some, including MIT scientist Richard M. Stallman, yearned for the return of those happier times and the mutual cooperation of programmers that then existed. So, in 1983, Stallman launched the GNU ("GNU's Not Unix") project, which aimed at creating a free, Unix-like operating system. Like early Unix, the GNU operating system was to be distributed in source form so that programmers could read, modify, and redistribute it without restriction. Stallman's work at MIT taught him that, by using the Internet as a means of communication, programmers could improve and adapt software at incredible speed, far outpacing the fastest rate possible using traditional software development models, in which few programmers actually see one another's source code.

As a means of organizing work on the GNU project, Stallman and others created the Free Software Foundation (FSF), a nonprofit corporation that seeks to promote free software and eliminate restrictions on the copying, redistribution, understanding, and modification of software. Among other activities, the FSF accepts tax-deductible charitable contributions and distributes copies of software and documentation for a small fee, using this revenue to fund its operations and support development activities.

If you find it peculiar that the FSF charges a fee—even a small fee—for "free" software, you should understand that the FSF intends the word *free* to refer primarily to freedom, not price. The FSF believes in three fundamental software freedoms:

- You can copy GNU software and give it away to anyone you choose.

- If you're a programmer, you can modify GNU software any way you like, because you have access to the source code. In return, your modified code should be available for others so they can enjoy the privileges of learning from and modifying it.

- You can distribute improved versions of GNU software. However, you cannot charge anyone a fee for using your improved version (although you can charge a fee for providing a user with a physical copy of your software).

Copyleft

Commercial software vendors protect their proprietary rights to software by copyrighting the software. In contrast, the FSF protects software freedom by *copylefting* its software under the GNU General Public License (GPL). To copyleft software, the FSF uses the same legal instrument used by proprietary software vendors—the copyright—but the FSF adds special terms that guarantee freedom to users of the software. These terms give everyone the right to use, modify, and redistribute the software (or any software derived from it), but only if the distribution terms are unchanged. Thus, someone who attempts to transform FSF software into a proprietary product has no right to use, modify, or distribute the product.

If the FSF placed its software in the public domain, others would be free to transform it into a proprietary product, denying users the freedom intended by the original author of the software. For example, a company might distribute the software in binary rather than source form and require payment of a license fee for the privilege of making additional copies.

As the FSF puts it: "Proprietary software developers use copyright to take away the users' freedom; we use copyright to guarantee their freedom. That's why we reverse the name, changing *copyright* into *copyleft*."

The Linux Kernel

By the early 1990s, the FSF had obtained or written all the major components of the GNU operating system except for one: the kernel. About that time, Linus Torvalds, a Finnish computer science student, began work on a kernel for a Unix-like system. Linus had been working with Minix, a Unix-like operating system written by Andrew Tannenbaum primarily for pedagogical use. Linus was disappointed by the performance of the Minix kernel and believed that he could do better. He shared his preliminary work with others on Internet newsgroups. Soon, programmers around the world were working together to extend and improve his kernel, which became known as *Linux* (for *Linus's Minix*). As Table 1-1 shows, Linux grew rapidly. Linux was initially released on October 5, 1991, and as early as 1992, Linux had been integrated with GNU software and other open source software to produce a fully functional operating system, which became known as Linux after the name of its kernel.

Table 1-1. The History of Linux

Year	Version	Estimated users	Kernel size (Kbytes)	Milestone(s)
1991	0.01	100	63	Linus Torvalds writes the Linux kernel.
1992	0.99	1000	431	GNU software is integrated with the Linux kernel, producing a fully functional operating system.
1993	0.99	20,000	938	High rate of code contributions prompts Linus to delegate code review responsibility.
1994	1.0	100,000	1,017	First production kernel is released.
1995	1.2	500,000	1,850	Linux is ported to non-Intel processors.
1996	2.0	1,500,000	4,718	Linux supports multiple processors, IP masquerading, and Java.
1999	2.2	7,500,000	10,593	Linux growth rate exceeds that of Windows NT.
2001	2.4	10,000,000	19,789	Linux invades the enterprise as major companies begin using it.

However, work on Linux did not cease. Since the initial production release, the pace of development has accelerated as Linux has been adapted to include support for non-Intel processors and even multiple processors, sophisticated TCP/IP networking facilities such as IP masquerading, and more. Versions of Linux are now available for such computer models and architectures as the PowerPC, the Compaq/DEC Alpha, the Motorola 68k, the Sun SPARC, the MIPS, and many others. Moreover, Linux does not implement an obscure Unix variant: it generally complies with the POSIX (Portable Operating System Interface) standard that forms the basis of the X/Open specifications of The Open Group.

The X Window System

Another important component of Linux is its *graphical user interface* (GUI, pronounced "gooey"), the *X Window System*. Unix was originally a mouseless, text-based system that used noisy teletype machines rather than modern video monitors. The Unix command interface is very sophisticated and, even today, some power users prefer it to a point-and-click graphical environment, using their video monitors as though they are noiseless teletypes. Consequently, some remain unaware that Unix long ago outgrew its text-based childhood and now provides users a choice of graphical or command interfaces.

The X Window System (or simply *X*) was developed as part of MIT's Project Athena, which it began in 1984. By 1988, MIT released X to the public. MIT has since turned development of X over to the X Consortium. The XFree86 Project, Inc., in cooperation with the X Consortium, distributes a version of X that runs on Intel-architecture PCs.

X is a unique graphical user interface in three major respects:

- X integrates with a computer network, letting users access local and remote applications. For example, X lets you open a window that represents an application running on a remote host: the remote host does the heavy-duty computing; all your computer needs do is pass the host your input and display the resulting output.

- X lets you configure its look and feel to an amazing degree. To do so, you run a special application—called a *window manager*—on top of X. A variety of window managers are available, including some that closely mimic the look and feel of Microsoft Windows.

- X is optional. Systems used as servers are often configured without a GUI, saving resources to serve client requests.

Linux Distributions

Because Linux can be freely redistributed, you can obtain it in a variety of ways. Various individuals and organizations package Linux, often combining it with free or proprietary applications. Such a package that includes all the software you need to install and run Linux is called a *Linux distribution*. Table 1-2 shows some of the most popular Linux distributions.

Table 1-2. Popular Linux Distributions and Their Home Pages

Distribution	Home page
Debian GNU/Linux	*http://www.debian.org*
Linux-Mandrake	*http://www.linux-mandrake.com*
Red Hat Linux	*http://www.redhat.com*
Slackware Linux	*http://www.slackware.com*
SuSE Linux	*http://www.suse.com*

Red Hat, Linux-Mandrake, SuSE, and Slackware are packaged by commercial companies, which seek to profit by selling Linux-related products and services. However, because Linux is distributed under the GNU GPL, you can download these distributions from the respective companies' web sites or make additional copies of a Linux distribution you purchase. (Note, however, that you cannot necessarily make additional copies of proprietary software that these companies may distribute with their Linux distribution.) Debian GNU/Linux is the product of volunteer effort conducted under the auspices of Software in the Public Interest, Inc. (*http://www.spi-inc.org*), a nonprofit corporation. This book is bundled with a copy of Red Hat Linux, which you can install and run on your PC and redistribute freely under the terms of the GPL.

Linux Features and Performance

The origins of Linux and the availability of its source code set it apart from other operating systems. But most users choose an operating system based on features and performance—and Linux delivers these in spades.

Linux runs on a wider range of hardware platforms and runs adequately on less costly and powerful systems than other operating systems. Moreover, Linux systems are generally highly reliable.

But this impressive inventory of selling points doesn't end the matter. Let's consider some other technical characteristics of Linux that distinguish it from the pack. Foremost in the minds of many is the low cost of Linux. Comparable server operating systems can cost more than $100,000. On the other hand, the low cost of Linux makes it practical for use even as a desktop operating system. In that mode, it truly eclipses the competition.

Many desktop systems are employed as servers. Because of its design and heritage, the features and performance of Linux readily outshine those of desktop operating systems used as makeshift servers. Moreover, Microsoft's software license for Windows NT/2000 restricts the number of authenticated client connections; if you want your Windows NT/2000 server to be able to handle 100 authenticated clients, you must pay Microsoft a hefty license fee. However, Linux imposes no such restriction; your Linux desktop or server system is free to accept as many client connections as you think it can handle.

Again, because of its design and heritage, Linux provides more reliable data storage than competing desktop operating systems. Most Linux users store their disk data using the *ext2* and *ext3* filesystems, which are superior in performance and reliability to filesystems (partition types) provided by Microsoft operating systems, including FAT, FAT32, and NTFS. Of course, Microsoft claims that its NTFS filesystem is so reliable that you'll probably never need special software tools to recover lost data—truth is, Microsoft provides no such tools. Despite Microsoft's ambitious claims, some Windows NT users report that NTFS reliability is less than satisfactory. Here's a case in point:

> When my Windows NT workstation crashed a little over a year ago, I discovered that its NTFS filesystem was damaged. I searched the Microsoft web site for recovery instructions and tools and found nothing that helped. So I went to my local software store and purchased a third-party disk recovery tool for Windows NT. When I opened the box, I was angered to discover that it supported recovery of FAT and FAT32 data, but not NTFS data.
>
> Eventually, I recovered 95 percent of my data by using a free Linux utility that was able to open the damaged NTFS partition and copy its files. If I'd been without Linux, I'd be without my data.

Like other server operating systems such as Windows NT/2000, Linux supports advanced disk management, known as a Redundant Array of Inexpensive Disks (RAID), which makes it possible to automatically duplicate stored data on several hard drives. This greatly improves the reliability of data storage; if one hard drive fails, the data can be read from another. Competing desktop operating systems, such as Windows 95/98, do not support this capability (though several third parties sell drivers or hardware devices that let you add this capability to your desktop operating system).

If you're an old computer dog who remembers the days of MS-DOS, you may have a fondness for what's now called the MS-DOS Prompt window or the Command Line Interface (CLI). However, if you've worked exclusively within the Windows point-and-click environment, you may not fully understand what the MS-DOS Prompt window is about. By typing commands in the MS-DOS Prompt window, you can direct the computer to perform a variety of tasks.

For most users, the MS-DOS Prompt is not as convenient as the GUI offered by Windows. That's because you must know the commands the operating system understands and must type them correctly if you expect the operating system to do your bidding.

However, the MS-DOS Prompt window lets you accomplish tasks that would be cumbersome and time-consuming if performed by pointing and clicking. Linux comes with a similar command interface, known as the *shell*. But, the word *similar* fails to do justice to the Linux shell's capabilities, because the MS-DOS Prompt provides a fraction of the capabilities provided by the Linux shell.

You may have used the MS-DOS Prompt and, finding it distastefully cumbersome, forever rejected it in favor of pointing and clicking. If so, you'll be pleasantly surprised to see how easy it is to use the Linux shell. You'll certainly be pleased—perhaps amazed—by the enormous power it offers. Moreover, you can customize the operation of the Linux shell in an almost limitless number of ways and even choose from among a variety of shells. You'll learn more about the Linux shell in Chapter 7.

If you're a programmer, you'll also admire the ease with which it's possible to develop portable, Unix-compliant software. Linux comes with a suite of software development tools, including an assembler, C/C++ compilers, a *make* application, and a source code librarian. All of these are freely distributable programs made available under the terms of the GNU GPL.

Reasons to Choose or Not Choose Linux

Notwithstanding its high points, Linux is not for everyone. You should approach your decision to use Linux as you'd approach any decision, by evaluating the pros and cons. Here are several reasons to run Linux:

You want a stable and reliable computing platform.
> No popular operating system is more stable and reliable than Linux. If you're tired of crashes and hangs and the lost time and data they entail, you're a candidate for Linux.

You want a high-performance computing platform.

Linux can coax blazingly fast performance out of hardware below the minimum required to load and run other popular operating systems. And, with ample memory and a fast CPU, Linux goes toe-to-toe with anything Microsoft or other vendors offer. If speed is your thing, Linux is your hot rod.

You need a low-cost or free operating system.

If you're on a budget or if you need to set up many systems, the low cost of Linux will let you reserve your hard-earned capital for hardware or other resources. Linux is the best operating system value on the planet.

You're a heavy network or Internet user.

If you use networks, especially the Internet, Linux's advanced support for TCP/IP may light up your life. Linux makes it easy to construct firewalls that protect your system against hackers or routers that let several computers share a single network connection.

You want to learn Unix or TCP/IP networking.

The best way—perhaps the only way—to learn more about Unix or TCP/IP networking (or computers generally) is through hands-on experience. Whether you're interested in such experience owing to personal curiosity or career ambition (system administrators are often handsomely paid), Linux affords you the opportunity to gain such experience at low cost, without leaving the comfort of your home.

You seek an alternative to Microsoft's vision of computing's future.

If you're tired of marching to the relentless drumbeat of the Redmond juggernaut, Linux offers a viable way to cut the umbilical cord and set about creating a new, open source computing destiny for yourself and others.

You want to have fun.

Hopefully, you've discovered that one of the best reasons for doing anything is that it's fun. Many Linux users report that they've never had so much fun with a computer. There's no better reason for running Linux than that.

To be frank, some folks shouldn't run Linux. If one or more of the following are true of you, you should run Linux *only* if you have a good friend who's knowledgeable about Linux, available by phone at odd hours, and works cheap:

You're scared of computers.

If you're scared of computers, you should spend more time working with Windows 98/2000 before venturing into the Linux world. Linux may indeed be right for you, but it's not right just yet.

You don't like to learn.

Setting up and running Linux will require you to learn new concepts and skills. None of these are especially difficult, but if you don't like to learn, setting up and running Linux will stress you out. Instead, you should stick with the familiar.

You're married to certain Windows applications.

You can run some Windows applications under Linux's WINE emulation; however, this isn't true of every Windows application. Before putting your toe in the Linux waters, you should obtain up-to-date information on the status of WINE emulation of your favorite Windows applications (see *http://www.winehq.com*). Alternatively, you can purchase the commercial products VMware (see *http://www.vmware.com*) or Win4Lin (see *http://www.netraverse.com*).

Rather than convert your desktop system to run Linux, you may prefer to install Linux on a second system or to set up your computer as a dual-boot system, running both Windows and Linux on separate partitions of a single hard drive. That way, you have your choice of running your favorite Windows applications or Linux whenever you desire.

## CHAPTER 2

Preparing to Install Red Hat Linux

Before installing Linux, you must first gather some information about your system. This chapter presents information you need to know and tasks you need to perform before installing Linux. It helps you make certain that your IBM-compatible PC meets the minimum hardware requirements for Linux. It shows you how to document your Windows operating system configuration so you can respond to questions presented by the Red Hat Linux install procedure. It also describes the four types of Red Hat Linux installations. Finally, this chapter shows you how to prepare your hard disk for installing Linux.

Minimum Hardware Requirements

Linux supports a wide range of PC hardware, but not even Linux supports every known device and system. Your PC must meet certain minimum requirements in order to run Linux. The following sections present these minimum requirements; however, for the latest and most complete information, you should check Red Hat's hardware compatibility web site, *http://hardware.redhat.com*. Red Hat's web site will also help you determine whether Linux supports the devices installed in your system. If you're not familiar with PC hardware, check out Robert and Barbara Thompson's *PC Hardware in a Nutshell: A Desktop Quick Reference* (O'Reilly & Associates, Inc.), an excellent introduction and reference to PC hardware.

Central Processing Unit (CPU)

Red Hat Linux 7.2 fully supports the Intel i486, Pentium, Pentium Pro, Pentium II, and Pentium III processors; however, it does not support the Intel i386 and earlier processors. Red Hat Linux also supports non-Intel processors such as the Cyrix 6x86 and the AMD K5, K6, and Athlon. However, a few problems are unique to non-Intel processors. For example, Red Hat reports that some AMD K6 systems freeze during the Linux install. Similarly, some users have also reported installation problems with AMD Athlons, which were solved by updating their system BIOS or replacing their system motherboard.

Motherboard

The motherboard is the main part of a PC. It holds the CPU, RAM, and other components. The motherboard includes several buses that link the CPU, RAM, and other components. Red Hat Linux supports the standard ISA, EISA, PCI, and VESA (VLB) system buses used on most IBM-compatible PCs, as well as the AGP, USB, and IEEE 1394 (FireWire) auxiliary buses.

Your motherboard should include at least 64 MB of RAM for optimum Red Hat Linux performance. Some very determined and skilled users have managed to coax Linux into working on systems with as little as 4 MB of RAM; however, Red Hat does not recommend or support systems with so little RAM. A handful of motherboards present special problems when installing Red Hat Linux. Generally, the problem stems from a bad BIOS, for which a fix is often available. Check Red Hat's web site, *http://www.redhat.com/apps/support*, for details. You'll find a link to some quick fixes for Red Hat Linux 7.2 on that page as well.

Drives

An anonymous wag once quipped that one can never be too thin, be too rich, or have too much hard disk space. Fortunately, Linux is not extremely hungry for disk space. To install and use Red Hat Linux 7.2, you should have a minimum of 300 MB of free hard disk space. More realistically, you should have at least 1.2 GB of free disk space, particularly if you're planning on running the X Window System.

For convenient installation using the CDs included with this book, your system should include an IDE or SCSI CD-ROM drive. Most recently manufactured PCs can boot from a CD. If your PC can't boot from a CD, you will need to use the floppy drive to create a *boot floppy*, which you can then use to install Red Hat Linux. Instructions for how to create and use the boot floppy are in Chapter 3.

 It's also possible to install Linux from a PCMCIA CD-ROM drive; an FTP, web, or NFS server; or a hard drive. See the Red Hat Linux 7.2 Installation Guide and Reference Guide, available at *http://www. redhat.com/docs/manuals/linux*.

Collecting Information About Your System

Before you launch into the installation process, you should collect some basic information about your system. Generally, Red Hat's installer will successfully probe your system and discover its configuration, but when it fails to do so, you must be prepared to supply the required information. Otherwise, you'll be forced to terminate the installation procedure, obtain the information, and then start all over again.

Information You Need

Table 2-1 specifies the configuration information you need and gives you space to conveniently record the information as you gather it. If your system currently runs Windows, you can obtain much of the needed information by using Windows utilities, as explained in the next section. To obtain the remaining information, you can consult your system documentation and the documentation for any devices installed by you. If your documentation is missing or incomplete, you may need to contact your hardware vendor or manufacturer. Alternatively, you may be able to find the needed information on the manufacturer's web site; use a search engine such as Yahoo! or AltaVista to discover the URL of the web site. Sometimes, you'll need to examine your system's BIOS settings or open your system's case and examine the installed hardware; consult your system documentation to learn how to do so.

Table 2-1. Configuration Information Needed to Install Red Hat Linux

Device	Information needed	Information about your system
Hard drive(s)	The number, size, and model of each hard drive.	
	Which hard drive is first, second, and so on.	
	Which adapter type (IDE or SCSI) is used by each drive.	
	For each IDE drive, whether the BIOS is set for LBA mode.	
	The number and type of each existing partition and the amount of free disk space.	
CD-ROM drive(s)	Which adapter type (IDE, SCSI, or other) is used by each drive.	
	For each drive using a non-IDE, non-SCSI adapter, the make and model of the drive.	
SCSI adapter (if any)	The make and model of the adapter.	
RAM	The amount of installed RAM.	
Video adapter	The make and model of the adapter and the amount of installed video RAM (VRAM).	

Table 2-1. Configuration Information Needed to Install Red Hat Linux (continued)

Device	Information needed	Information about your system
Video monitor	The make and model of the video monitor and the manufacturer's specifications, if available, especially the horizontal and vertical sync (refresh) rates.	
Mouse	The type (serial, PS/2, or bus).	
	The protocol (Microsoft, Logitech, MouseMan, etc.).	
	The number of buttons.	
	For a serial mouse, the serial port to which it's connected (COM1 or COM2).	
Sound adapter (if any)	The make, chipset, and model of the adapter.	
Network adapter (if any)	The make and model of the card.	
IP address	The dotted-quad number, such as 10.1.2.7, that identifies your system to other Internet hosts. Many Internet service providers (ISPs) assign IP addresses dynamically, by using a DHCP server; in that case, you don't need to know the IP address of your system.	
Netmask	A dotted-quad number that identifies the portion of your system's IP address that specifies its network address. The number typically contains one or more instances of the value 255. If your ISP is using DHCP, you don't need to know the netmask.	
Gateway IP address	The IP address of the host that routes traffic between your system and the Internet. If your ISP is using DHCP, you don't need to know the gateway IP address.	
DNS server	The IP address of one or more Internet hosts that provide domain name services (DNS) for your system. If your ISP is using DHCP, you don't need to know the DNS servers.	

Table 2-1. Configuration Information Needed to Install Red Hat Linux (continued)

Device	Information needed	Information about your system
Domain name	The domain name of your system. This generally looks like *xxx*.net or *xxx*.com, with *xxx* identifying your Internet service provider. If your ISP is using DHCP, you don't need to know the domain name.	
Hostname	The hostname of your system. You can generally find the hostname prefixed to the domain name. If your ISP is using DHCP, you don't need to know the hostname.	

Sound Adapter Information

You don't actually need information about your system's sound adapter during installation. However, you will need it when you configure the sound card (see "Configuring Sound" in Chapter 9). It's generally convenient to obtain information about the sound adapter when you obtain the information needed for installation.

Collecting Configuration Information from Windows

If you run Windows 95/98, you can obtain much of the information needed to install Linux by using the Windows System Properties dialog box, which you can launch by using the Control Panel:

1. Click on the Start menu. A pop-up menu appears.
2. Select Settings on the pop-up menu and click on Control Panel in the submenu. The Control Panel appears.
3. Double-click on System. The System Properties dialog box appears. If necessary, click on the General tab, so that the dialog box resembles Figure 2-1.

   The General tab of the System Properties dialog box shows the type of your system's processor and the amount of installed RAM.
4. Click on the Device Manager tab. The appearance of the dialog box changes to resemble Figure 2-2.

   You can double-click on an icon (or single-click on the Plus key adjacent to an icon) to obtain additional information. For example, by double-clicking on the Disk Drives icon, you can determine whether a disk drive uses an IDE or SCSI interface.

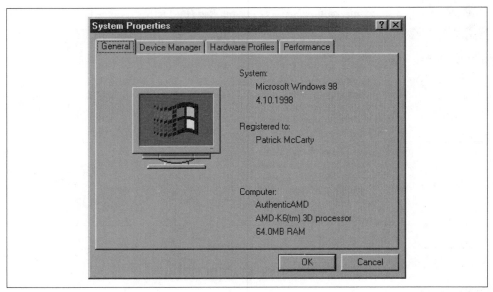

Figure 2-1. The General tab of the System Properties dialog box

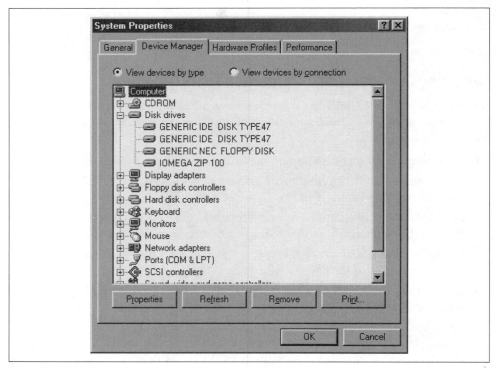

Figure 2-2. The Device Manager tab of the System Properties dialog box

If you have a printer, you can use the Print button to print information about your system's devices.

You can gather the following information from the Device Manager tab:

— The number and type (IDE or SCSI) of your system's hard drives

— The make and model of CD-ROM drives

 Some installed CD-ROM drives do not appear in the Device Manager tab of the System Properties dialog box. Often the *C:\CONFIG.SYS* file will contain clues to help you learn more about such drives.

— The make and model of SCSI adapters, if any

— The make and model of the video adapter

— The type of mouse installed

— The make and model of multimedia adapters, such as sound cards, if any

— The make and model of network adapters, if any

When you've recorded the information provided by the Device Manager tab, click Cancel to exit the System Properties dialog box.

If your computer is attached to a network, you should collect information describing your network adapter:

1. In the Control Panel, double-click Network to launch the Network dialog box, as shown in Figure 2-3.

2. Double-click the TCP/IP entry associated with your network adapter (not the Dial-Up Adapter), launching the TCP/IP Properties dialog box, shown in Figure 2-4. If the IP Address tab is not visible, click it. This dialog box tells you the IP address and subnet mask (netmask) of your system. If the "Obtain an IP address automatically" button is selected, the IP address and subnet mask will be blank. In that case, you don't need to be concerned about them because a DHCP server on your network supplies the network configuration automatically; Red Hat Linux can obtain its network configuration from this same server.

3. Click the DNS Configuration tab. This tab, shown in Figure 2-5, provides the Host (hostname), Domain (domain name), and DNS Server information you'll need during installation. If the Disable DNS button is selected, you don't need to be concerned about this information.

4. Click the Gateway tab. This tab, shown in Figure 2-6, provides the Installed Gateway (gateway IP address). If no gateways are listed, don't be concerned. A DHCP server is likely providing this configuration information automatically.

5. Finally, click Cancel to close the TCP/IP Properties dialog box. Clicking Cancel again closes the Network dialog box.

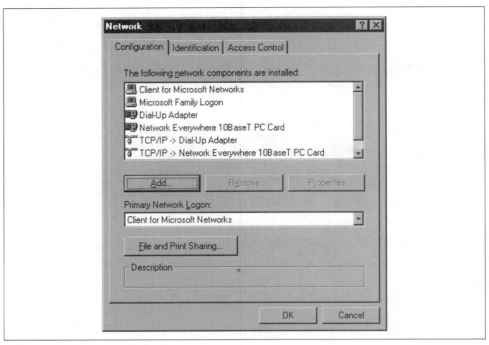

Figure 2-3. The Network dialog box

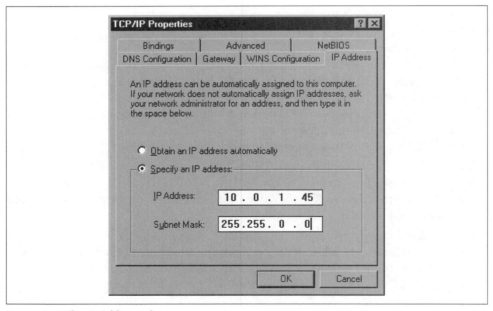

Figure 2-4. The IP Address tab

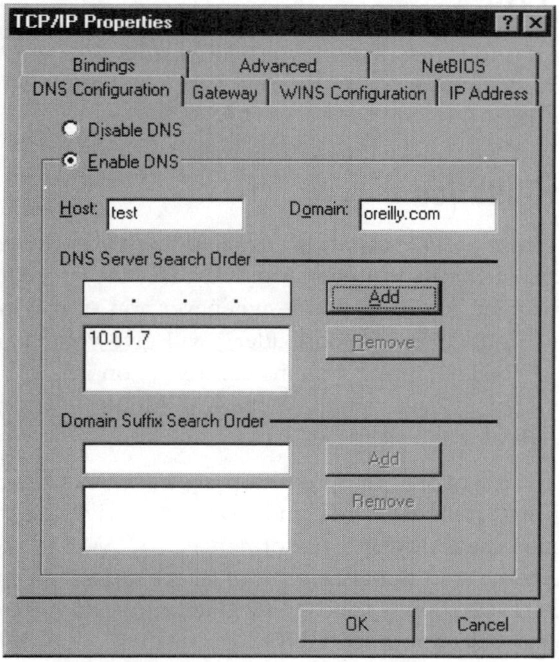

Figure 2-5. The DNS Configuration tab

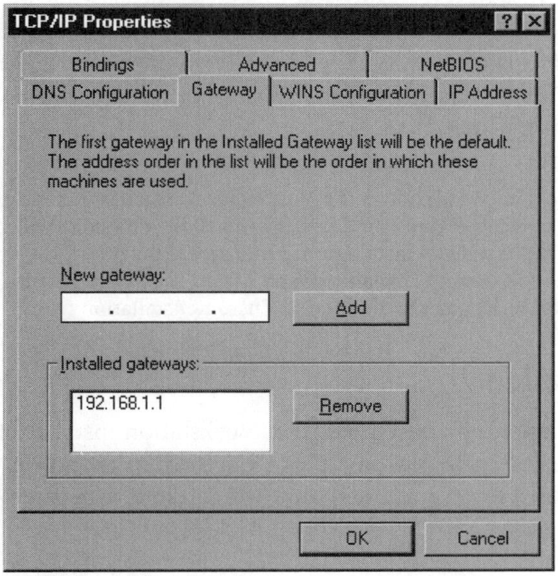

Figure 2-6. The Gateway tab

Installation Types

Red Hat Linux defines four installation types: *Workstation*, *Laptop*, *Server*, and *Custom*. In addition, you can upgrade an existing Red Hat Linux installation by selecting the Upgrade option.*

Workstation Installation

If you're new to Linux, the Workstation installation type is the easiest to perform, especially if you currently run Windows. In that case, the procedure will automatically configure your system to dual boot—whenever you start your system, a Linux utility, GRUB (the Grand Unified Bootloader), will give you the choice of starting Windows or Linux. Both operating systems can reside on a single system as long as you have a large enough hard drive. A typical Linux Workstation installation requires about 1.2 GB of free disk space.

Red Hat Linux provides two primary desktop environments for use as a graphical user interface (GUI) to Linux: GNOME and KDE. These rival desktop managers provide generally similar capability and performance. GNOME is the default desktop option and has been the traditional favorite of Red Hat Linux users. If you've used KDE and like it, then you should choose the KDE option. If you prefer to keep your options open, you can select both the GNOME and KDE options, but you'll need an extra 300 MB or so of disk space to accommodate both options simultaneously. Since this book covers both GNOME and KDE, you should select both desktop environments during the installation process.

Even though the Workstation installation type is generally the easiest, you should choose the Custom installation type, which is explained later. The Custom installation type is more flexible and therefore better able to help you cope with problems that may arise during installation.

 You should not choose the Workstation installation type if your system currently runs Windows NT or 2000; doing so will break your existing Windows installation. You can easily remedy the damage, but this book doesn't explain how to do so. If you are running Windows NT or 2000, you should use the Custom installation type.

Laptop Installation

The Laptop installation type resembles the Workstation installation type. It includes support for devices often found on laptops but seldom found on desktops, such as PCMCIA cards, wireless network adapters, and infrared data interconnection (IRDA)

---

* Upgrading an existing Red Hat system is beyond the scope of this book, so we will not cover the Upgrade installation option in Chapter 3.

---

peripherals. Choosing the Laptop installation type doesn't automatically install applications that use such devices; it merely installs a special kernel that supports common laptop device types and a handful of related utilities. You'll need to install appropriate applications after you've installed and configured Red Hat Linux. Like the Workstation installation type, the Laptop installation type will break an existing Windows NT or 2000 installation. You'll likely find it more convenient to install Red Hat Linux on your laptop by using a Custom installation rather than a Laptop installation.

Server Installation

The Server installation type is appropriate for systems that will be hosting a web server or other services. It does not include a GUI, so it's not suitable for desktop use. You shouldn't set up a system using the Server installation type until you've had significant experience with Red Hat Linux. A typical Server installation requires from 650 MB to 1.2 GB of free disk space.

 The Server installation type *destroys all data* on your hard drive, including any existing Windows and non-Windows partitions. Do not perform a Server installation if you want to preserve the data on your system.

Custom Installation

The Custom installation type gives you complete control over the installation process. You can specify whether to configure your system for dual booting, which software packages to install, and so on. The Custom install is covered in detail in Chapter 3.

To perform a Custom installation, you should have from 300 MB to 2.4 GB of free disk space available. However, 300 MB is an absolute minimum, and 2.4 GB is needed only if you're planning to install everything (including the kitchen sink). More realistically, you should have at least 1.2 GB of free space available. If you have the expertise and patience, you can omit certain packages that would otherwise be installed during a Custom installation so that your Linux system occupies less disk space. The Select Individual Packages option will be covered in Chapter 3.

Preparing Your Hard Disk

To prepare your hard disk for installing Linux, you must allocate the space in which Linux will reside. You'll learn how to do so in this section. First, you'll learn how hard disks are organized; then you'll learn how to view the structure of a hard disk. Finally, you'll learn how to alter, or *partition*, the structure of your hard disk in preparing to install Red Hat Linux.

How Hard Disks Are Organized

Let's start by reviewing facts you've probably learned by working with Windows. Most operating systems, including Windows 95/98, manage hard drives by dividing their storage space into units known as *partitions*. So that you can access a partition, Windows associates a drive letter (such as *C:* or *D:*) with it. Before you can store data on a partition, you must *format* it. Formatting a partition organizes the associated space into what is called a *filesystem*, which provides space for storing the names and attributes of files as well as the data they contain. Windows supports several types of filesystem, such as FAT and FAT32; a newer filesystem type that provides more efficient storage, launches programs faster, and supports very large hard drives.

Partitions comprise the *logical structure* of a disk drive, the way humans and most computer programs understand the structure. However, disk drives have an underlying *physical structure* that more closely resembles the actual structure of the hardware. Figure 2-7 shows the logical and physical structure of a disk drive.

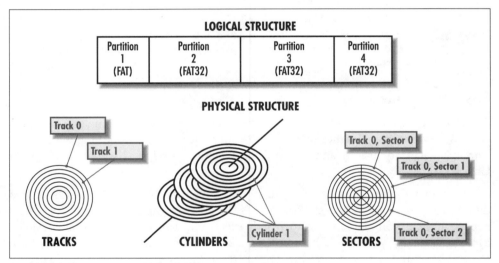

Figure 2-7. The structure of a hard disk

Mechanically, a hard disk is constructed of platters that resemble the phonograph records found in an old-fashioned jukebox. Each platter is associated with a read/write *head* that works much like the read/write head on a VCR, encoding data as a series of electromagnetic pulses. As the platter spins, the heads record data in concentric rings known as *tracks*, which are numbered beginning with zero. A hard disk may have hundreds or thousands of tracks.

All the tracks with the same radius are known as a *cylinder*. Like tracks, cylinders are numbered beginning with zero. The number of platters and cylinders of a drive determines the drive's *geometry*. Some PCs require you to specify the drive geometry in the BIOS setup. Most modern PCs autodetect the drive geometry but let you specify a custom value if you prefer.

Most operating systems prefer to read or write only part of a track, rather than an entire track. Consequently, tracks are divided into a series of *sectors*, each of which holds a fixed number of bytes, usually 512.

To correctly access a sector, a program needs to know the geometry of the drive. Because it's sometimes inconvenient to specify the geometry of a drive, some PC BIOS programs let you specify *logical block addressing* (LBA). LBA sequentially numbers sectors, letting programs read or write to a specified sector without the burden of specifying a cylinder or head number.

Viewing Disk Partitions

The first step in preparing your hard disk is viewing its partition information. Once you know how your hard disk is organized, you'll be able to determine how to reorganize it to accommodate Linux. To view the partitions that exist on your hard disk drives, you can use the *fdisk* utility:

1. Click on the Windows Start menu. The Start pop-up menu appears.
2. Select Programs. The Programs submenu appears.
3. From the Programs submenu, click on MS-DOS Prompt. An MS-DOS Prompt window appears.
4. Type **fdisk** and press **Enter**. The *fdisk* menu appears, as shown in Figure 2-8.

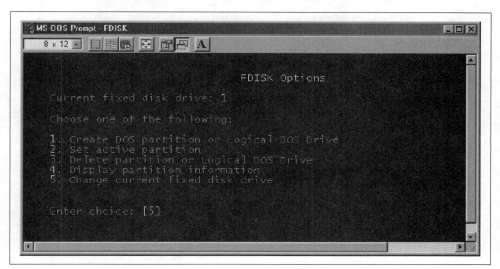

Figure 2-8. The fdisk Options screen

The *fdisk* menu may not appear immediately. Instead, Windows may ask if you want to enable large disk support; if this occurs, type **N** and press **Enter**. You don't need to enable large disk support to view partition information.

5. If your system has only one hard drive, you won't see option 5, titled "Change current fixed disk drive." If option 5 is available, type **5** and press **Enter**. This takes you to a screen, resembling the one shown in Figure 2-9, that lets you specify the current fixed disk drive.

   If option 5 is not available, type the number associated with the Display Partition Information option and press **Enter**. The screen will resemble the one shown in Figure 2-9, though its arrangement will be somewhat different.

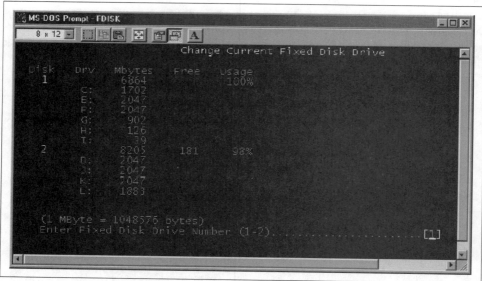

Figure 2-9. The fdisk "Change current fixed disk drive" screen

The screen shows each hard drive and its size, numbering the drives beginning with 1. If a drive contains free space not allocated to a partition, the screen shows the amount of space available. The screen also shows how much of the drive's space has been allocated to partitions, as a percentage of the total drive space.

Under the information describing a drive, the screen shows the size of each partition that resides on the drive. The screen also shows the associated drive letter, if any.

6. When you're done viewing partition information, press **Esc** twice to exit *fdisk* and return to the MS-DOS prompt. You can then close the MS-DOS Prompt window by clicking on the Close icon in the upper-right corner of the window or by typing **exit** and pressing **Enter**.

Obtaining Sufficient Disk Space

Red Hat Linux, as of the 7.2 release, no longer supports a *partitionless installation,*[*] which was an option in previous versions that allowed you to install Linux without dedicating a partition for it. This is a good thing, because Linux doesn't run particularly fast or reliably in a partitionless mode.

This means that you will have to devote at least three partitions to Linux during the installation process. By viewing the partitions on your hard drive, you can determine which of the following two cases best describes your system:

- You have available free (unpartitioned) disk space large enough to accommodate Linux (300 MB to 2.4 GB, depending on the type of installation you want and the number of packages you want to install).

  In this case, make a note of the drive that holds the free disk space. You can then begin the installation process described in Chapter 3. However, see the tip on PC BIOS limitations, later in this section.

- You don't have enough free (unpartitioned) disk space to accommodate Linux. If you don't have sufficient disk space, you have several options:

  — If your system has room for an additional disk drive, you can install a new drive and use it to hold Linux. The next section, titled "Installing a new disk drive," offers some considerations and tips on installing a new drive. This is generally the best option, because it sidesteps problems arising due to PC BIOS limitations.

  — If you have one or more unused partitions, you can delete them and use the space you gain to hold Linux. The later section titled "Identifying an unused partition" shows how to identify an unused partition.

  — If you have one or more partitions that are larger than needed, you can shrink them and use the space you gain to hold Linux. The later section titled "Shrinking a partition" shows you how to determine whether a partition is larger than needed and how to free the excess space.

---

[*] However, according to the release notes for Red Hat Linux 7.2, only upgrades to previous partitionless installations are still supported.

The BIOS of many PCs cannot access more than two hard drives and cannot access data on or beyond cylinder 1023 of a hard drive. In order to boot Linux, the installation program must create a 16 MB (or larger) boot partition (*/boot*) in an area accessible by the BIOS. If your available free space does not satisfy these criteria, you must obtain additional free space as described in the following sections.

Red Hat Linux supports LBA32, which can work around this problem, but many systems sold as supporting LBA32 do not actually do so. Moreover, enabling LBA32 support requires that you manually partition your system during installation. Therefore, you should partition your system as described to maximize the likelihood that it will work properly.

If you're unsure whether your free space satisfies these criteria, simply begin the installation; the installation program will notify you if it is unable to proceed. In that case, you can return to this chapter to learn how to gain or add additional disk space.

Installing a new disk drive

Often, the easiest way to install Linux is to install a new disk drive. If your system has only a single hard drive, you can probably install a second drive and place Linux on the new drive. Before purchasing a drive, you should make sure that the system provides room to mount the new drive and that you have the proper data and power cables. Be sure to install both disk drives on the primary disk controller so they can be booted; if you have an IDE CD-ROM drive, you should move it to the secondary controller.

If your system already has two disk drives, you probably can't simply add a third disk drive: the BIOS of most PCs let you boot the system from only the first or second hard drive on the primary controller. In such a case, you can probably replace one of your existing drives with a larger drive adequate to support your existing needs and Linux.

Identifying an unused partition

You can use the drive letter information provided by *fdisk* to examine the contents of a partition in Windows Explorer. If you can find a partition that holds no useful data but is large enough to accommodate the type of Linux installation you want, you can delete the partition and use the free space to hold Linux. At least 16 MB of the unused partition should reside within the first 1023 cylinders of the drive; otherwise, you will have to use a boot floppy to load Linux.

The easiest way to delete a partition is to use the Red Hat install utility. Make note of the partition you wish to delete in Table 2-1 and then begin the installation process described in Chapter 3.

Shrinking a partition

Even if all of your partitions contain useful data, one or more partitions may be larger than required. In that case, you can reduce the size of each such partition and reorganize the drive to include contiguous unused space to hold Linux. Again, at least 16 MB of the unused space should reside within the first 1023 cylinders of the disk drive; otherwise, you'll have to use a boot floppy to load Linux.

You can use the Windows Explorer to determine the amount of free disk space in a partition. To do this, right-click on the drive icon and click on Properties in the pop-up menu. The Properties dialog box shows the amount of used and free disk space associated with the drive.

If you are able to find one or more partitions that have sufficient free space for a Linux installation, you can use a special utility to split the used and unused portions of a partition into separate partitions. Disc 1 of Red Hat Linux includes the *fips* utility, which can split FAT and FAT32 partitions. For information on using *fips*, see the documentation in the *dosutils* directory of the CD-ROM.

 If you make a mistake while attempting to shrink a partition, or if the software malfunctions, you may lose all data in one or more partitions. You should not attempt to shrink a partition until you've completely backed up your system and made sure that your backup is usable.

Many Linux users find PowerQuest's *PartitionMagic* utility helpful. Unlike *fips*, PartitionMagic is commercial software; however, it is relatively inexpensive (approximately $60 to $70) and supports partition types and operations not supported by *fips*. For example, PartitionMagic can split NTFS, HPFS, and Linux *ext2* partitions. This is important, because you may not initially create Linux partitions of exactly the right size. Using *fips*, you'd be stuck, but using PartitionMagic, you can change your system's partition structure as many times as you like until you get it just right. For information on PartitionMagic, see the PowerQuest web site at *http://www.powerquest.com/partitionmagic*.

 Use of PartitionMagic is beyond the scope of this book. I mention it here because I feel that—although it isn't free—PartitionMagic is a valuable, timesaving tool for partitioning your hard drive. Instructions on how to install and use PartitionMagic are included with PartitionMagic.

CHAPTER 3

Installing Red Hat Linux

This chapter shows you how to install Red Hat Linux by following a simple, step-by-step procedure. During the installation, you'll need to refer to the information you collected in Table 2-1 of Chapter 2. Most users will be able to complete the installation procedure without difficulty; however, this chapter includes a section that describes how you can obtain help if you encounter installation problems. Once you successfully complete the installation procedure, you'll have your own working Red Hat Linux system.

Installing the Operating System and Applications

To install Red Hat Linux, follow this simple step-by-step procedure:

1. Start the installation.
2. Select installation options.
3. Create partitions.
4. Configure the boot loader.
5. Configure networking.
6. Configure the system time.
7. Configure language support.
8. Configure user accounts and authentication.
9. Select packages.
10. Configure X.
11. Install packages.
12. Create a boot disk.
13. Complete the video configuration.
14. Complete the installation.

Although the Linux installation procedure is generally trouble-free, errors or malfunctions that occur during the installation of an operating system can result in loss of data. You should not begin the installation procedure until you have backed up all data on your system and determined that your backup is error-free.

Start the Installation

To begin installing Linux, you must boot your system from the installation media. Most recently manufactured PCs can boot from the Disc 1 Red Hat Linux CD-ROM. However, unless you generally boot from a CD-ROM—which is quite unlikely—you'll need to reconfigure your PC's BIOS so your PC is able to boot from a CD-ROM. To do so, enter your PC's BIOS screen and look for a configuration item titled something like Boot Order or Boot Priority. Change the configuration so that the CD-ROM drive has the highest boot priority. Consult your PC's documentation for details on entering and using its BIOS configuration screens.

Creating a Boot Floppy

If your PC can't boot from a CD-ROM, you must create a boot floppy disk. Creating a boot floppy requires some special measures; you can't simply copy files onto a disk and then boot from it. To create a Red Hat Linux installation boot floppy by using a PC that runs Microsoft Windows, perform the following steps:

1. Format a floppy.
2. Insert Disc 1 of Red Hat Linux into your system's CD-ROM drive.
3. Start an MS-DOS Prompt window by clicking on Start → Run, typing **command**, and pressing **Enter** (Windows 9*x* or NT) or Start → Programs → Accessories → Command Line Interface (Windows 2000).
4. In the command window, change to the drive letter that corresponds to your CD-ROM drive, for example, *d:*, *e:*, or some other letter (see Figure 3-1).
5. In the command window, type **cd \dosutils\rawrite** to switch to that directory on the CD and press **Enter**.
6. When prompted, specify the filename of the disk image source as **images\boot. img** and press **Enter**.
7. When prompted, specify the drive letter of your floppy drive, for example, **a**, and press **Enter**.
8. As instructed by the program, make sure the formatted floppy diskette is still in your floppy drive and press **Enter**. It takes perhaps a minute or so for the *rawrite* utility to create the floppy diskette.

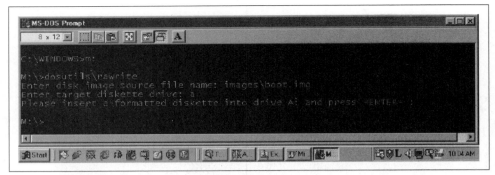

Figure 3-1. Using rawrite to make a boot diskette

 If your PC requires one or more PCMCIA or unusual SCSI devices during boot up, you must follow a somewhat more complicated procedure. See Appendix E of the *The Official Red Hat Linux x86 Installation Guide*, available at *http://www.redhat.com*, for details.

Boot the Installation Program

To start the installation process, insert Disc 1 of Red Hat Linux into your system's CD-ROM drive. If your system cannot boot from a CD-ROM, insert the boot floppy you created and reboot your PC.

When the system reboots, you should see a welcome screen featuring a *boot:* prompt and a series of messages explaining various installation options, as shown in Figure 3-2. This prompt lets you enter special parameters to work around a variety of installation problems. Generally, it's not necessary to do so. Simply press **Enter** or wait about a minute and the installation program will start.

For perhaps a minute, you'll see text flashing by as the system boots. Then, you'll see the Red Hat Linux splash screen, soon followed by the System Installer screen. Click Next to proceed.

Understanding the Installer's User Interface

Like other modern Linux distributions, Red Hat Linux includes a graphical installation program that simplifies the installation and initial configuration of Linux. Figure 3-3 shows a typical screen displayed by the installation program. You won't see this particular screen until later in the installation process. The screen includes the following elements:

A main window

The installation program runs in a full-screen window that contains one or more child windows within it. The upper-left corner of each child window displays the name of the window. You cannot minimize or change the size of the installation program's main window.

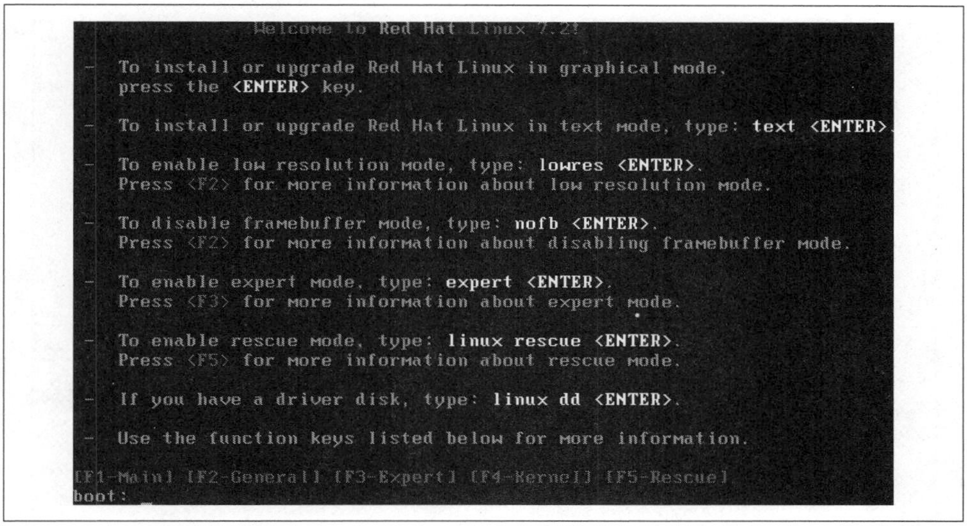

Figure 3-2. The installation welcome screen

Graphical Install...What Graphical Install?

If you don't see the Red Hat Linux splash screen but instead see a screen with red and blue text areas over a black background such as that shown in Figure 3-2, your system is not compatible with the Red Hat Linux graphical install. Perhaps your system lacks sufficient RAM or has an unsupported video adapter.

In that case, you can use a text-based installation procedure. To do so, reboot your system and respond to the *boot:* prompt by typing **linux expert** and pressing **Enter**. Because this special installation procedure is text-based, you won't be able to use a mouse. Instead, use **Tab** to move from field to field, use **Space** to select fields, and press **Enter** to click a selected button.

If you need additional help using the text-based installation procedure, see Chapter 5 of *The Official Red Hat Linux x86 Installation Guide*, available at *http://www.redhat.com/docs/manuals/linux/RHL-7.2-Manual/install-guide*.

The cursor

The installation program also has an on-screen cursor. The location of the cursor is called the input focus. At any time, exactly one control has the input focus, which lets it respond to keyboard input. The control that has the input focus has a rectangle outlining it. In Figure 3-3, the OK button has the input focus.

Dialog boxes

The installation program uses dialog boxes to obtain user input. In Figure 3-3, an untitled dialog box is visible. You can recognize it by the controls it contains,

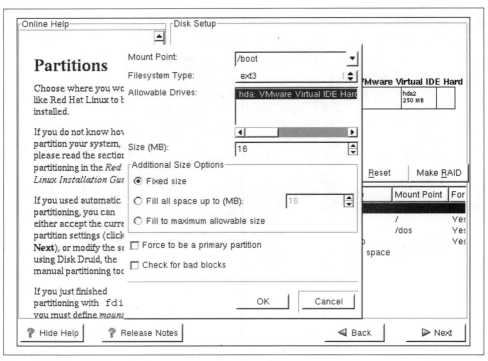

Figure 3-3. A typical installation screen

such as Mount Point and Size (MB). You dismiss a dialog box by using its OK or Cancel button. You cannot minimize or move an installation dialog box.

Text boxes

Text boxes let you type text that is sent to the installation program when you dismiss the dialog box by using the OK button. In Figure 3-3, the field labeled Size (MB) is a text box.

Checkboxes and radio buttons

Checkboxes and radio buttons let you specify that an option is enabled or disabled or select a specific option from a list. A dark area indicates an enabled option; a light area indicates a disabled option. You can click a checkbox to toggle the checkbox between its enabled and disabled states. In Figure 3-3, the field labeled "Force to be a primary partition" is a checkbox; the item labeled Fixed Size is a radio button.

List boxes

List boxes let you choose an item from a predefined list. If a list box has many items, it will have an associated scrollbar that lets you page through the list. The selected item, if any, is indicated by the item's dark background. In Figure 3-3, the item *hda* is the active item of the list box titled Allowable Drives. You click a list box item to make the item active or click the list box's scrollbar to page through the list of items contained in the list box.

Buttons

When you click a button, the installation program performs a corresponding action. For example, clicking the OK button of a dialog box tells the installation program to accept the dialog box contents and proceed to the next step. Similarly, clicking the Cancel button of a dialog box tells the installation program to ignore the dialog box contents. Many installation screens include a helpful Back button that lets you return to the previous installation step. Most installation screens include a Next button that takes you to the next installation step.

Online Help

The Online Help panel lets you view information that helps you understand what the current installation screen does and how to use it. If you don't understand the installation procedure or if you're curious to learn more, read the information in the Online Help panel.

Use Virtual Consoles to Monitor the Installation

A console is a combination of a keyboard and a display device, such as a video monitor. A console provides a basic user interface adequate to communicate with a computer: you can type characters on the keyboard and view text on the display device.

Although a home computer system seldom has more than one console, Linux systems provide several virtual consoles. By pressing a special combination of keys, you can control which console your system's keyboard and monitor are connected to.

Table 3-1 describes the virtual consoles used by the installation program. The main installation dialog appears in virtual console number 7. If you like, you can use the indicated keystrokes to view a different virtual console.

The contents of virtual consoles 1 through 5 can be useful in monitoring and troubleshooting; generally you will not need to switch from one virtual console to another. Nevertheless, you may find it interesting to view the contents of the virtual consoles during the installation procedure.

Table 3-1. Virtual Consoles Used by Red Hat's Installation Program

Console	Keystroke	Contents
1	Ctrl-Alt-F1	Installation dialog
2	Ctrl-Alt-F2	A shell prompt that lets you enter commands to be processed by Linux
3	Ctrl-Alt-F3	The installation log, containing messages from the install program
4	Ctrl-Alt-F4	The system log, containing messages from the Linux kernel and other system programs
5	Ctrl-Alt-F5	Other messages, including those concerning the creation of filesystems
7	Ctrl-Alt-F7	The graphical window, which is the main window used by the installation program

Choose the Installation Language

Figure 3-4 shows the Language Selection screen, which asks you to specify what language should be used during the installation process. Click the desired language and then click Next. The Keyboard Configuration screen appears.

Figure 3-4. The Language Selection screen

Select the Keyboard Type

The Keyboard Configuration screen, shown in Figure 3-5, lets you specify the type of keyboard attached to your system. The preselected choices are appropriate for most U.S. users. If you prefer another keyboard configuration, click the desired model or layout. If you like, you can type text in the box labeled Test Your Selection Here to see if it appears appropriately. Then, click Next to proceed. The Mouse Configuration screen appears.

 You can change the keyboard configuration after completing the installation by using the **kbdconfig** command.

Select the Mouse Type

The Mouse Configuration screen, shown in Figure 3-6, lets you specify the type of mouse attached to your system. The installation program generally determines the

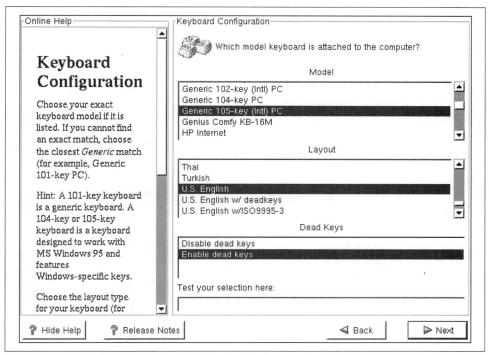

Figure 3-5. The Keyboard Configuration screen

type of mouse automatically. If you prefer a different mouse configuration, click the desired mouse type.

Many graphical Linux programs are designed to use a three-button mouse. If your mouse has only two buttons, you should generally enable the Emulate 3 Buttons checkbox. Click Next to proceed. The Welcome screen appears. Click Next to proceed to the Install Type screen.

You can change the mouse configuration after completing the installation by using the **mouseconfig** command.

Select the Installation Type

The Installation Type screen, shown in Figure 3-7, lets you choose whether to perform any of four types of fresh installations or an upgrade of your existing Red Hat system. The Install options—Workstation, Server, Laptop, and Custom—were described in Chapter 2. As explained, the appropriate choice for most users is Custom. Therefore, click the radio button next to Custom and click Next to proceed.

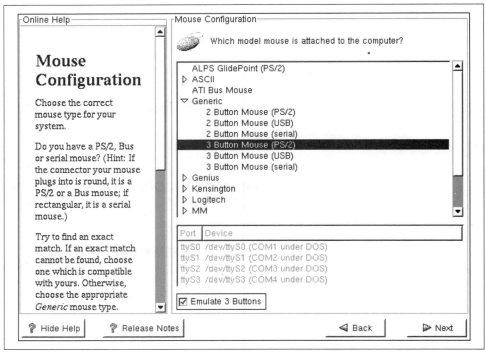

Figure 3-6. The Mouse Configuration screen

The step-by-step procedure given in this chapter describes only the Custom option. The procedures required for other options are similar, and you can probably complete a non-Custom installation with the help of this chapter. However, if you want a more detailed procedure for performing a non-Custom installation, see *The Official Red Hat Linux x86 Installation Guide*.

Create Partitions

In the next phase of installation, you use Red Hat's Disk Druid program to establish Linux partitions on your hard disk drive. Figure 3-8, the Disk Partitioning Setup screen, appears. Disk Druid can usually create the necessary partitions automatically, so you can generally click Automatically Partition and click Next to proceed.

Before the Disk Partitioning Setup screen appears, an untitled dialog box may appear, announcing that Disk Druid has found a problem with the partition table of one of your system's hard drives. The dialog box tells you how to resolve the problem. Generally, you need to restart the installation and specify the geometry of your hard drive in response to the *boot:* prompt. Appendix C describes the most common options. If you plan to erase all the data on your hard drive, you can click Skip Drive and continue with the installation.

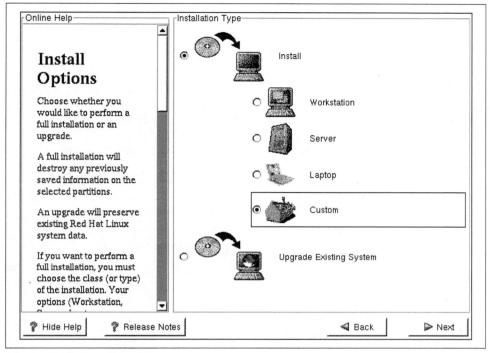

Figure 3-7. The Installation Type screen

You may prefer to create Linux partitions by using Disk Druid manually. If so, follow the instructions in the next section; otherwise, skip ahead to the "Configure the Boot Loader" section.

> The installation program provides a third partitioning method, manual partitioning via *fdisk*. However, as the Disk Partitioning Setup screen suggests, this program is suitable only for experts. Unlike Disk Druid, *fdisk* does not check that your partitions have been properly defined. Unless you're familiar with *fdisk*, it's best to avoid using it until you gain more experience with Linux.

Use Disk Druid

You use Disk Druid to add, edit, and delete Linux partitions. Figure 3-9 shows the Disk Setup screen. The top part of the screen contains a list box that describes each existing partition. The bottom part of the screen contains a list box that describes each disk drive. The middle part of the screen contains buttons that control the operation of Disk Druid.

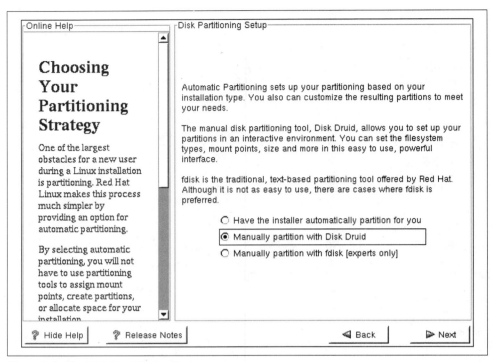

Figure 3-8. The Disk Partitioning Setup screen

Adding a partition

Whereas Windows associates drive letters, such as *D:*, with filesystems, Linux associates directories—known as mount points—with filesystems. At a minimum, you should establish the following three Linux partitions on your system's hard drive:

- A Linux native partition to hold the Linux kernel. This partition, which has the mount point */boot*, should be at least 50 MB in size. However, there's no advantage to making it larger than 50 MB.

- A Linux native partition to hold the Red Hat Linux operating system. This partition, known as the root partition, has the mount point /. It should be as large as you can afford.

- A Linux swap partition to provide a work area used by Red Hat Linux to efficiently manage your system's RAM memory. This partition, which has no mount point, should have a size two times the amount of your PC's installed RAM. However, the swap partition should not be smaller than 190 MB or larger than 2000 MB. This partition is not mounted by Linux and therefore has no associated mount point.

To add a partition, click New, and the dialog box shown in Figure 3-10 appears.

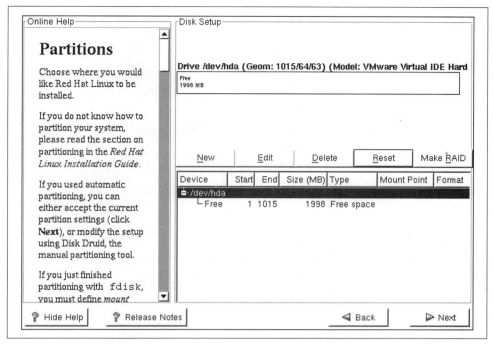

Figure 3-9. The Disk Setup screen

Create the /boot partition

To add the required Linux native partition with the mount point */boot*, enter the following values:

Mount Point
Select */boot* from the drop-down menu. The mount point specifies the directory name by which the partition will be known to Linux.

Filesystem Type
Select *ext3* as the filesystem type.[*]

Allowable Drives
Choose one or more hard disk drives on which to place the partition. If you select more than one hard disk drive, Disk Druid chooses a drive from among those you specify; Disk Druid never creates a partition that spans multiple disk drives.

Size (MB)
Specify the size in megabytes of the */boot* partition, which should be 50 MB.

Additional Size Options
Specify Fixed Size.

---

[*] See Chapter 4 for more information about the *ext3* filesystem type.

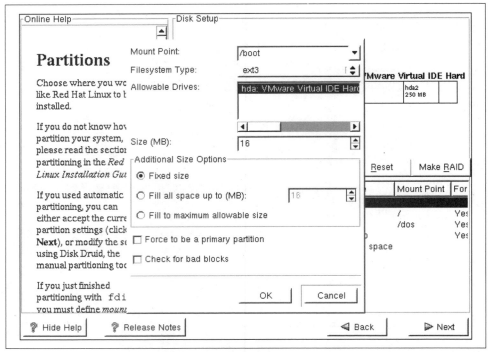

Figure 3-10. The untitled dialog box used to create a partition

Click OK to accept the input values, or if you don't want to create the partition, click Cancel. The untitled dialog box disappears.

If you enter an inappropriate value, Disk Druid may be unable to create the requested partition. In such a case, it displays a dialog box that explains the reason the partition could not be created. Study the dialog box to determine what you did wrong and try again.

Create the / partition

To add the required Linux native partition with the mount point /, click Add to launch the new partition dialog box and then enter the following values:

Mount Point
Type a forward slash (/) to denote the root directory.

Filesystem Type
Select *ext3* as the partition type.

Allowable Drives
Choose one or more hard disk drives on which to place the partition.

Size (MB)
Specify the size in megabytes of the / partition, which should be at least 300 MB. More realistically, the size of the partition should be at least 1.2 GB.

Additional Size Options
> Specify "Fill to maximum allowable size," so the Linux native partition will be as large as possible. If you prefer to restrict the size of the partition, select "Fill all space up to (MB)" and specify the maximum desired size in the immediately following text box.

Click OK to accept the input values. The untitled dialog box disappears.

Create the swap partition

To add the required Linux Swap partition, click New to launch the new partition dialog box. Enter the following values:

Mount Point
> Leave this field blank.

Filesystem Type
> Select Swap.

Allowable Drives
> Choose one or more hard disk drives on which to place the partition. If you select more than one hard disk drive, Disk Druid chooses a drive from among those you specify; Disk Druid never creates a partition that spans multiple disk drives.

Size
> Specify twice the amount of RAM in your system. However, do not specify less than 190 MB or more than 2000 MB.

Additional Size Options
> Specify Fixed Size.

Click OK to accept the input values. The untitled dialog box disappears.

Editing a partition

If you wish to change one or more values associated with a partition, highlight the partition you wish to change and click Edit. Disk Druid launches a dialog box that you can use to change the mount point of a previously existing partition or other options of a partition you've just created.

You cannot use this dialog box to change the size, grow option, or type of a previously existing partition; instead, you must delete such a partition and re-create it.

Deleting a partition

If you wish to delete a partition, highlight it and click Delete. Disk Druid presents a dialog box that asks you to confirm the operation.

Deleting a partition destroys all the data it contains. Exercise great care to delete only unneeded partitions.

Starting over

If you determine that you've made mistakes and want to abandon the changes you've specified, simply click Reset. Disk Druid resets all partitions to their original state.

Save your changes

When you're done, the Disk Setup window should look similar to the one shown in Figure 3-11. If you had existing MS-DOS or other partitions, these would be shown as well. To save your changes and proceed with the installation, click Next.

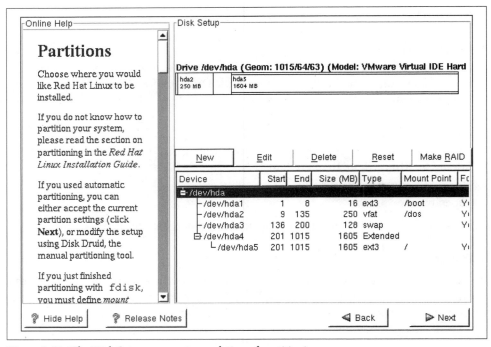

Figure 3-11. The Disk Setup screen at completion of partitioning

Configure the Boot Loader

Next, the installation program presents the Boot Loader Configuration screen, shown in Figure 3-12. GRUB, the Grand Unified Bootloader, is a special program used to start Linux—or another operating system—when you boot your system. This screen lets you choose an alternative boot loader (LILO) or omit installation of a boot loader altogether. You can also specify the location where GRUB will be installed.

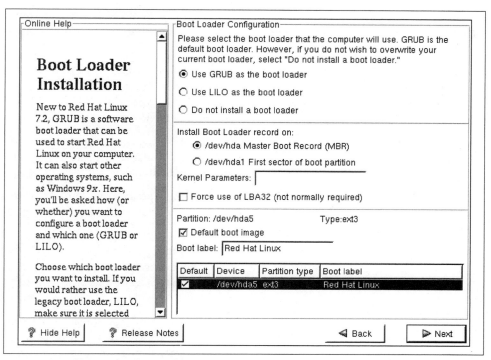

Figure 3-12. The Boot Loader Configuration screen

Most Linux users install GRUB on the Master Boot Record (MBR) of their PC's primary hard drive. However, doing so poses some risk. For example, if your PC boots using System Commander, the OS/2 Boot Manager, or the Windows NT/2000 loader, installing GRUB on the MBR will prevent you from booting any operating system other than Linux until you specially configure GRUB. Moreover, some antivirus applications detect changes to the MBR and roll them back. The bottom line is that, for a few Red Hat Linux users, GRUB can present some headaches.

You can easily avoid GRUB in either of two ways. First, you can boot Linux by using the boot floppy prepared near the end of the installation procedure. Linux won't boot as quickly as it might, but you won't face the prospect of disabling your other operating system if you're running a dual-boot system. If booting from a floppy seems antediluvian, you can use *loadlin*, an MS-DOS program that can start Linux. Appendix C explains how to use *loadlin* to boot Linux.

If you're running Windows NT/2000 or using special boot software, specify that GRUB should be installed on the first sector of the Linux boot partition (*/boot*) rather than on the MBR. Then you can boot from a Linux boot floppy or configure your special boot software to start GRUB, which will boot Linux. If you're not running Windows NT/2000 or using special boot software, specify that GRUB should be installed on the MBR.

The Force Use of LBA32 checkbox is disabled by default. Some SCSI drives require this option. Most non-SCSI drives can boot—and will boot faster—if this option is disabled.

You can also specify kernel parameters. Generally, no special kernel options are needed. However, if you discover that a kernel option is required (for example, to access a CD-ROM drive with a proprietary interface), you can specify it here. At boot time, GRUB will pass to the kernel any options you specified.

The Boot Loader Configuration screen also lets you select the operating systems that GRUB will be able to boot. When it boots your PC, GRUB displays a screen that lets you select from among the configured operating systems.

The installation program preselects Linux as the default operating system. To specify a different default operating system, highlight the corresponding partition and click Default.

If you like, you can change the label associated with an operating system by highlighting the corresponding partition and typing the desired label in the text box labeled Boot Label. When you've completely specified the desired boot loader configuration, click Next to proceed.

The GRUB Password screen appears. If you want to prevent unauthorized persons from using your Linux system, you can use the GRUB Password screen to prevent someone from passing information to the Linux kernel that overrides security checks; however, this level of protection is rarely necessary. If you decide to create a GRUB password, check the Use a GRUB Password? box and enter a password in the space provided; then click Next to proceed.

Configure Networking

After you've configured the boot loader, the installation program probes for a network card. If it finds one, the installation program presents the Network Configuration screen, shown in Figure 3-13. If your computer is attached to a local area network (LAN), you can use the Network Configuration screen to configure networking. If your computer is not attached to a LAN, click Next.

If your computer is part of a LAN, your networking situation falls into one of two categories: you connect to the Internet via a dialup connection or you're on a LAN with a permanent connection to the Internet via a gateway. The Red Hat Linux network configuration procedure isn't so different from that of Windows, which has a Control Panel that lets you identify and configure your network hardware. Windows has a separate utility, Dial-up Networking, for making actual modem connections. In Linux, you configure networking much the same way.

First you need to specify what kind of network connections you'll be making (Ethernet and/or modem) and provide some basic information about the type of network

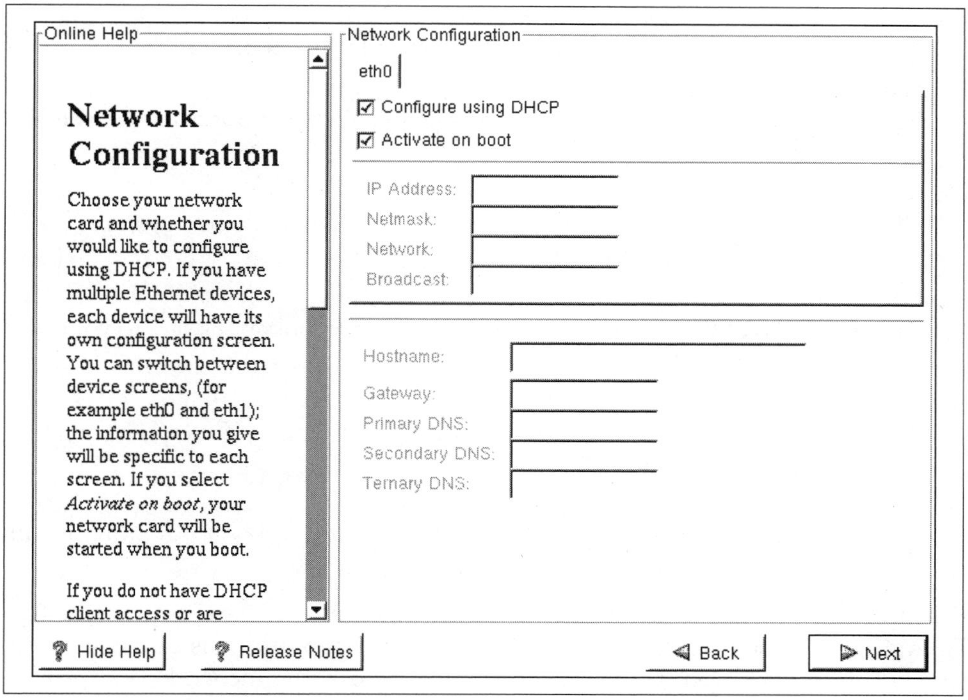

Figure 3-13. The Network Configuration screen

you're connecting to. Later, after you've set up your Linux system, you'll use a separate program to actually make a dialup modem connection.

If your computer connects to a DHCP server, Red Hat Linux can automatically determine its network configuration when your PC boots. To specify automatic network configuration, simply enable the Configure Using DHCP checkbox.

You should generally enable the Activate on Boot checkbox. Doing so specifies that your computer's network card should be activated when the system boots.

If no DHCP server is available or if you prefer to manually enter the network configuration, disable the Configuring Using DHCP checkbox and fill in the network configuration text boxes, using the information you recorded in Table 2-1 of Chapter 2:

IP Address
> The host address of your system (for example, 192.168.1.2)

Netmask
> A bitmask that specifies the portion of your system's network address that uniquely identifies the network (for example, 255.255.255.0)

Network
> The network address of your system (for example, 192.168.1.0)

Broadcast

> The broadcast address of your system (for example, 192.168.1.255)

Hostname

> The hostname of your system, including the domain name (for example, *newbie. redhat.com*)

Gateway

> The host address of the router your system uses to send packets beyond its local network (for example, 192.168.1.1)

Primary DNS

> The IP address of the system that provides hostname lookup services to your system (for example, 192.168.1.1)

Secondary DNS

> The IP address of the system used to look up host names if the primary name server is unavailable (optional)

Ternary DNS

> The host address of the system used to look up hostnames if the primary and secondary name servers are unavailable (optional)

When you've entered the desired network configuration, click Next to proceed. The Firewall Configuration screen, shown in Figure 3-14, appears. This screen lets you specify protection against threats originating across the network. Chapter 12 explains the firewall capabilities of Red Hat Linux in more detail. If you are not concerned about network security, you should select the Medium security option; otherwise, you should select High security. Make your choice and click Next to proceed.

After installation, you can use the *lokkit* or *gnome-lokkit* program to change your firewall settings, as explained in Chapter 12.

Configure the Language

Next, the installation program presents the Additional Language Support screen, shown in Figure 3-15. You earlier selected the language used during the installation procedure; however, this screen has a different function. It doesn't select the language in which system messages will appear during system operation; it merely lets you install support—including X fonts and spelling dictionaries—for one or more languages that you will use in working with your installed Red Hat Linux system. As the screen explains, multiple languages consume significant disk space, so select a single language unless you have extra room on your drive and intend to use other languages on your system. After you've made your choice or choices, click Next to proceed.

Online Help

Firewall Configuration

Red Hat Linux also offers you firewall protection for enhanced system security. A firewall sits between your computer and the network, and determines which resources on your computer remote users on the network are able to access. A properly configured firewall can greatly increase the out-of-the-box security of your system.

Choose the appropriate security level for your system.

Firewall Configuration

Please choose your security level:

○ High   ⦿ Medium   ○ No firewall

⦿ Use default firewall rules

○ Customize

Trusted devices: ☐ eth0

Allow incoming: ☑ DHCP
☐ SSH
☐ Telnet
☐ WWW (HTTP)
☐ Mail (SMTP)
☐ FTP

Other ports:

[Hide Help]   [Release Notes]   [◁ Back]   [▷ Next]

Figure 3-14. The Firewall Configuration screen

Configure the System Clock

After you bypass or complete the Network Configuration screen, the installation program presents the Time Zone Selection screen, shown in Figure 3-16.

Select a time zone by clicking on the map or by clicking an entry in the list box that appears below the map. By default, the map shows North America. Click the list box labeled View to choose a different region.

If you want to set your system's clock to UTC (Universal Coordinated Time), enable the System Clock Uses UTC checkbox. However, you should not enable this checkbox if your PC is set up to boot an operating system, such as Microsoft Windows 9*x*, that does not support setting the system clock to UTC.

After making your selections, click Next to proceed.

After completing the installation, you can change the time zone setting by using the *timeconfig* command.

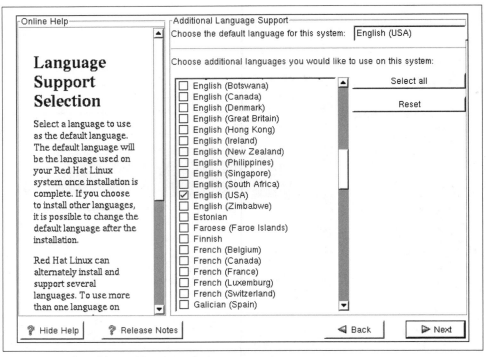

Figure 3-15. The Additional Language Support screen

Configure User Accounts and Authentication

The user who administers a Linux system is known as the root user, or simply *root*. To protect your system against mischief and misadventure, you should protect the root user's login with a password. To enable you to do so, the installation program presents the Account Configuration screen, shown in Figure 3-17.

Simply choose a password for the root user and type it twice: in the text field labeled Root Password and the nearby text field labeled Confirm.

 Be sure to make a mental note of the password, because you'll need it in order to log in once system installation is complete. If you must, write down the password, but if you do so, make sure the password is kept safe from anyone who might use it to compromise your system.

You should create at least one additional user account during system installation. You can use this account when not performing system administration, thereby avoiding unnecessary use of the root account, which might lead to a breach of system security or integrity. To create an additional user account, click the Add button. The Add a New User dialog box appears, prompting you to enter a user name, the user's

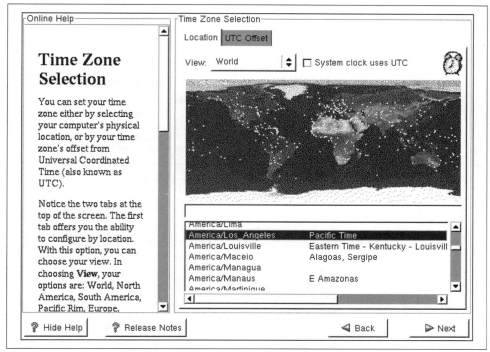

Time Zone Selection

You can set your time zone either by selecting your computer's physical location, or by your time zone's offset from Universal Coordinated Time (also known as UTC).

Notice the two tabs at the top of the screen. The first tab offers you the ability to configure by location. With this option, you can choose your view. In choosing **View**, your options are: World, North America, South America, Pacific Rim, Europe,

Online Help

Location · UTC Offset

View: World · □ System clock uses UTC

America/Lima
America/Los_Angeles · Pacific Time
America/Louisville · Eastern Time - Kentucky - Louisvill
America/Maceio · Alagoas, Sergipe
America/Managua
America/Manaus · E Amazonas
America/Martinique

? Hide Help · ? Release Notes · ◁ Back · ▷ Next

Figure 3-16. The Time Zone Selection screen

full name, and a password for the new user. You need to enter the password twice to confirm that it has been entered correctly. You can establish additional user accounts during system installation if you like, but it's generally easier to establish them after system installation is complete.

Once you've specified the password for the root account and have set up an additional user account, click Next to proceed. The installation program shows the Authentication Configuration screen, shown in Figure 3-18.

Generally, the default options are appropriate: both Enable MD5 Passwords and Enable Shadow Passwords should be selected. MD5 lets you use passwords longer than eight characters; specifying shadow passwords hides encrypted passwords from ordinary users. Only in special circumstances would it be necessary or appropriate to disable either option.

Unless your PC is part of a network that uses NIS, LDAP, Kerberos 5, or SMB, you don't need to specify options associated with these tabs. Otherwise, consult your network administrator to determine the appropriate settings. Click Next to proceed; the Package Group Selection screen appears.

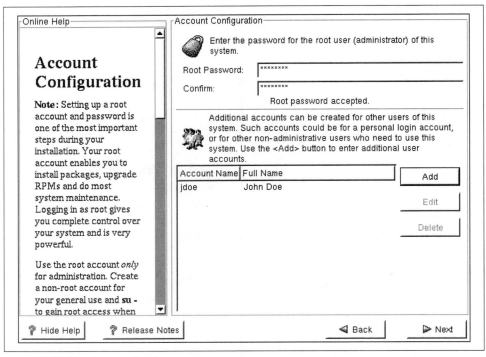

Figure 3-17. The Account Configuration screen

Selecting Packages

To install an application under Red Hat Linux, you generally install a package that contains all the files needed by the application. If you like, you can specify the individual packages you want to install; however, the large number of available packages makes it tedious to specify them one at a time. Instead, the installation program lets you specify package groups you want (or need) to install. A *package group* is simply a group of related packages.

The Package Group Selection screen, shown in Figure 3-19, lets you specify which packages should be installed. Simply enable the checkbox associated with each desired package group. The installation program has preselected several package groups for you.

Generally, you should select the following package groups, some of which may have been preselected for you:

Printing Support
    Lets you print to a local or remote printer (selected by default).

Classic X Window System
    A minimal graphical user interface (GUI) suitable for occasional use (selected by default).

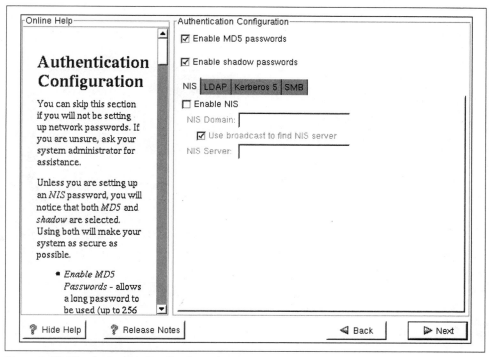

Figure 3-18. The Authentication Configuration screen

X Window System

The GUI used with Red Hat Linux (selected by default).

Laptop Support

Kernel support for PCMCIA and IRDA and related utilities and tools; you should select this package group if you will be running Linux on a laptop.

GNOME

The GNOME desktop, the default Red Hat Linux desktop (selected by default).

KDE

The KDE desktop, an alternative to GNOME, which can coexist with GNOME.

 Since this book covers use of both GNOME and KDE (see Chapters 5 and 6, respectively), you should select the KDE package group to be installed.

Sound and Multimedia Support

Support for audio cards, CD burning, and other multimedia functions (selected by default).

Network Support

A variety of applications and tools useful when a system is attached to a network (selected by default).

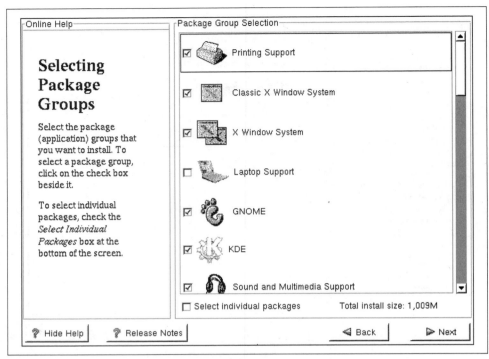

Figure 3-19. The Package Group Selection screen

Dialup Support

> A variety of applications and tools useful when a system connects to a network via a dialup modem (selected by default).

Messaging and Web Tools

> Applications for sending and receiving mail, browsing the web, and reading and posting Internet newsgroup messages.

In addition, you can choose from among the following package groups, according to your interests and the characteristics of your system:

Graphics and Image Manipulation

> The GIMP (GNU Image Manipulation Program) lets you perform graphic operations similar to those supported by Adobe Photoshop and several other graphics programs.

News Server

> Support for serving Internet news articles (recommended only for Linux experts).

NFS File Server

> Support for sharing files via the Network File System (NFS).

Windows File Server

> Lets you share files and printers via your Windows LAN.

Anonymous FTP Server
An FTP (File Transfer Protocol) server (*not recommended for beginners*).

SQL Database Server
The PostgreSQL database management system.

Web Server
Lets you serve web pages to clients on your LAN or the Internet; this package group installs the Apache web server.

Router/Firewall
Programs and utilities useful when using a Linux system as a router or firewall.

DNS Name Server
Support for a DNS server (*not recommended for beginners*).

Network Managed Workstation
Support for Simple Network Management Protocol (SNMP) utilities (*not recommended for beginners*).

Authoring and Publishing
Includes DocBook SGML/XML, TeX, and other authoring and publishing tools.

Emacs
Support for the Emacs text editor.

Utilities
Several utilities that help you manage a system.

Legacy Application Support
Libraries needed by old versions of Linux software.

Software Development
Support for programming in C and other languages.

Kernel Development
Source code for the Linux kernel and utilities required to build the kernel.

Windows Compatibility/Interoperability
Lets you run native Windows applications or access MS-DOS files stored on your PC's hard drive if you're running Linux in a dual-boot configuration. In particular, this package group installs WINE, which is a Unix implementation of the Win32 libraries (*http://www.winehq.com*) that allows you to run Windows applications from within Linux.

Games and Entertainment
Includes a variety of games, including X-based games if you choose to install the X Window System.

Everything
This will install all available packages on your system.

The Package Group Selection screen also shows the approximate size of the selected package groups in its lower-right corner.

If you don't know which components to select, don't worry; you can install additional components after setting up your Red Hat Linux system. If, on the other hand, you want to be able to select individual packages as well as components, enable the Select Individual Packages checkbox. When you're satisfied with your choices, click Next to proceed. If you checked the Select Individual Packages checkbox, the Individual Package Selection screen appears. Select any desired packages. Then, click Next to proceed.

If you requested installation of individual packages, the Unresolved Dependencies screen may appear. You should generally accept the preselected option, "Install packages to satisfy dependencies." Click Next to proceed.

Configure Video

Next, the installation program displays the Graphical Interface (X) Configuration screen, shown in Figure 3-20, which helps you configure X, the Linux graphical user interface. If the installation program was able to determine the type of video card associated with your computer, it will highlight the appropriate item in the X Configuration list box. If you prefer to specify a different video card, click the desired item.

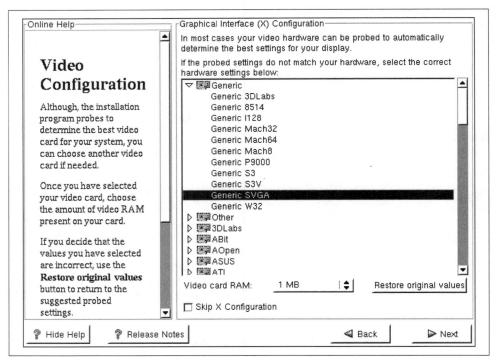

Figure 3-20. The Graphical Interface (X) Configuration screen

If your video card is not listed, you may be able to use the Generic SVGA compatible entry. This will yield a basic, working X configuration. Later, you can follow the instructions given in Appendix D to achieve a better configuration.

You should specify the amount of video memory installed on your video card. Specifying a value that is too large will probably prevent X from starting. If you followed the procedure given in Chapter 2, you should have learned the amount of video memory installed on your card; otherwise, consult your video card's documentation to determine the proper value. If you can't locate the information, select a conservatively low value; choosing a value that's too low will prevent you from using high-resolution video modes but won't damage your monitor.

Installing the Packages

When the installation program is ready to begin installing packages, it presents the About to Install screen, shown in Figure 3-21. Up to this point, the installation program has made no changes to your system's hard drive. This is your last chance to terminate the installation procedure before any data is written. To abort the installation procedure, press **Ctrl-Alt-Delete** or press your system's hardware reset button.

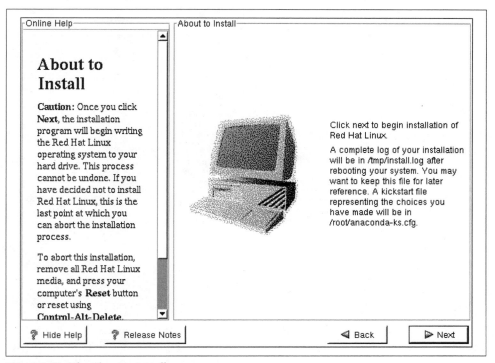

Figure 3-21. The About to Install screen

The installation program now formats any partitions you earlier specified for formatting. Depending on the size of your system's hard drive, this step may take several minutes to complete. When formatting is done, the Installing Packages screen, shown in Figure 3-22, appears, and the installation program begins installing packages. This screen displays the name of each package as it is installed and presents a progress bar that shows the status of the installation process. When all the packages have been installed, you're ready to create a boot diskette. Click Next to proceed.

 Depending on the number of packages you've selected to install, and the speed of your system, it can take 30 minutes or more to install all of the packages on your system. Don't go too far away after you start to install Red Hat, as you will need to insert Disc 2 at some point.

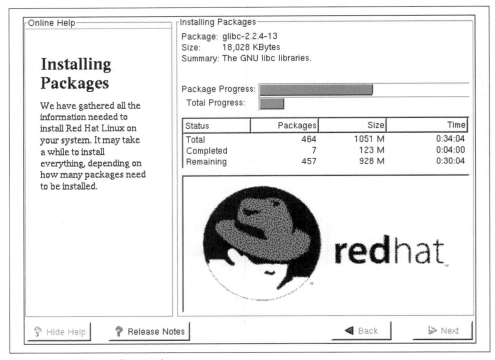

Figure 3-22. The Installing Packages screen

Create a Boot Floppy

The installation program next gives you the opportunity to create a boot floppy, by presenting the Boot Disk Creation screen, shown in Figure 3-23. This floppy is not the same as the one you may have created and used to start the installation procedure. You should take the opportunity to create the boot floppy, because it may enable you to boot your Linux system even if the boot loader fails to install properly or the system boot information is damaged. You must create a boot floppy if Windows NT/2000 is installed on your system; in that case, you won't be able to boot your system without the boot floppy.

To create a boot floppy, click Next. The installation program will prompt you to insert a blank floppy in your system's floppy drive. Insert the diskette and click OK. The installation program may take several minutes to create the boot floppy.

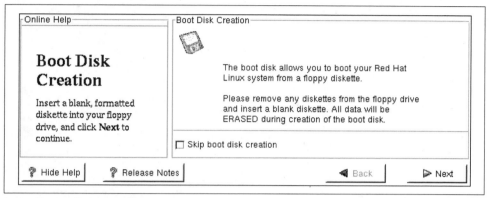

Figure 3-23. The Boot Disk Creation screen

Complete the Video Configuration

Earlier in the installation, you specified the make and model of your system's video card. The next two screens guide you in completing the video configuration.

Identifying your system's monitor

The installation program next presents the Monitor Configuration screen, shown in Figure 3-24. The Monitor Configuration screen includes a list of supported video monitors. If the installation program was able to determine the type of monitor associated with your PC, it highlights the appropriate item in the Monitor Configuration list box. If you prefer to specify a different monitor, click the desired item.

 Don't select a monitor that has an identifier merely similar to that of your monitor. Similarly identified models often have quite different characteristics. Failing to select the appropriate monitor may result in permanent damage to your monitor, particularly if your monitor is an older, fixed-frequency model. If your monitor displays a scrambled image, turn it off promptly and recheck your configuration.

If you can't find your monitor listed, don't despair: you can select the Unprobed Monitor entry or a monitor type from the Generic hierarchy. If you do so, the installation program suggests horizontal and vertical sync (also known as *vertical refresh*) rates or ranges. You should compare these with the characteristics of your monitor,

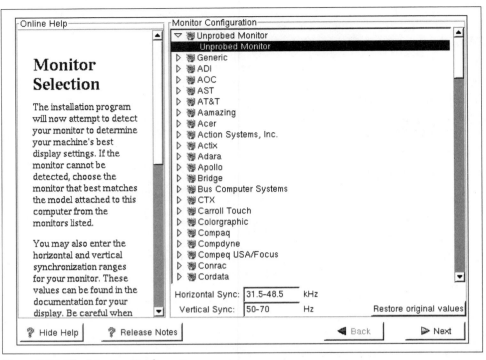

Figure 3-24. The Monitor Configuration screen

which you can generally obtain from the owner's manual or from the manufacturer's web site; adjust the rates of ranges if necessary. If you fail to find information describing your monitor, you can try some conservative values that are unlikely to damage all but the oldest of monitors. Low values are safer than high values. For example, try setting the horizontal sync range to 50–70 kHz and the vertical sync rate to 60 Hz.

Once you've selected your monitor or specified its sync rates, click Next to proceed. The Custom Graphics Configuration screen appears.

Selecting custom graphics options

The Customize Graphics Configuration screen, shown in Figure 3-25, lets you specify several X-related options. You can choose the color depth, which determines the number of colors your system will display. You can also choose the screen resolution, which determines the number of pixels your system will display. Larger resolutions result in greater detail; however, your system's video adapter and monitor may not operate with all possible settings. Moreover, specifying a high resolution consumes additional system resources, such as RAM. You can click the Test Setting button to see that a given setting works and what it looks like. When testing a setting, a small, untitled dialog box appears asking whether you can read its text; if so, click Yes to accept the current setting or No to reject it and try another setting.

When X Fails

Sometimes, the installation program can't configure X to work properly. Generally, this is due to video hardware that's not compatible with X. If you find yourself in this situation, you can skip the configuration of X by using the dialog box that appears when the X configuration fails. The installation will then proceed, but X will not be configured. You can try to achieve a working X configuration after Linux has been installed by following these steps.

First, read the following chapters:

- Chapter 4, *How Linux Works*
- Chapter 7, *Conquering the bash Shell*
- Appendix D, *Installing and Configuring X*

Then, perform the following steps:

1. Reboot your system. Since X hasn't been configured, you will enter Linux in text mode (runlevel 3), so you won't see a graphical interface.
2. Log in as *root* and enter the password.
3. Next, you need to configure X on your system, which will allow you to boot into Graphical mode (runlevel 5) rather than Text mode (runlevel 3). To do this, you will use the *Xconfigurator* command to attempt to configure X on your system; type **Xconfigurator** at the command line and press **Enter** to start the process.

From here, follow the steps detailed in the "Configuring X" section of Appendix D.

If, as suggested, you installed either the GNOME or KDE desktop, use the proper radio button to select the desired default desktop. You shouldn't select a default desktop other than one you specified for installation. For example, if you selected to install only GNOME, don't select KDE as your default desktop, because it won't be available. If you're uncertain about which desktop environment to choose, select GNOME. Also check the Graphical radio button, which specifies that your Linux system will start in graphical mode. Selecting Graphical mode will start X when you boot Linux, allowing you to use one of the desktop environments (GNOME or KDE), as well as your mouse. If you're not familiar with the Linux command line, you should select graphical mode as your login type. When you've completed the X configuration, click Next to proceed.

Complete the Installation

The installation program then presents its final screen, shown in Figure 3-26, which explains that Red Hat Linux has been successfully installed. If you installed GRUB on your system's MBR, follow the instruction to remove the installation media before rebooting your system. However, if you installed GRUB on the first sector of the Linux boot partition, you must boot from a Linux boot floppy until you configure your boot manager to boot Linux.

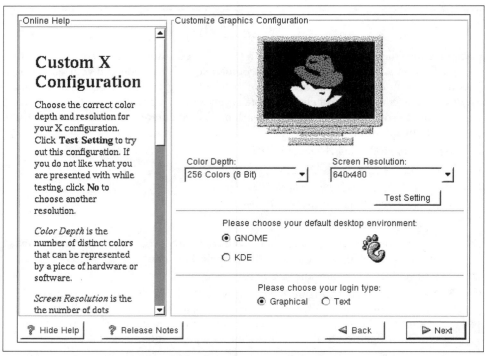

Figure 3-25. The Customize Graphics Configuration screen

Try booting your system from its hard drive or a Linux boot floppy, as appropriate. If your system successfully boots Linux, you're ready to log in to your Red Hat Linux system.

Logging In

Depending on which desktop environment you specified as the default (GNOME or KDE), the appearance of your login screen will vary. If you see a screen similar to that shown in Figure 3-27, you're ready to log in via the GNOME display manager. If you see a screen with a letter *K* and several gears at the right of a dialog box like that shown in Figure 3-29, you're ready to log in via the KDE display manager.

Logging into GNOME

If you configured GNOME as your default desktop, the login screen should resemble that shown in Figure 3-27. To log in, type **root** in the text box labeled Login and press **Enter**. The field goes blank, and you are prompted to verify the password by entering it again. Type the password and press **Enter** to log in.

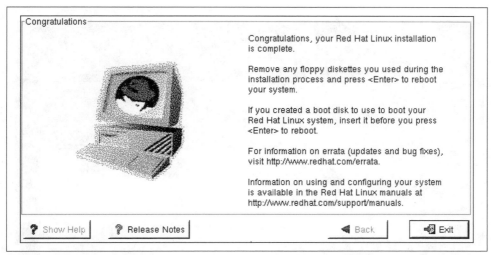

Figure 3-26. The Congratulations screen informs you that you've successfully completed installing Red Hat Linux

Figure 3-27. The GNOME login screen

The GNOME desktop, shown in Figure 3-28, appears. If you like, click around the desktop and see what you can discover. Chapter 5 explains how to use the GNOME desktop; however, you should read Chapter 4 before reading that chapter.

To shut down your system, click the G-shaped foot at the lower-left corner of the desktop panel, and you are taken to another login screen. Instead of entering the username and password, click on the System menu and select Reboot to restart your system or Halt to shut down your computer. Now you're ready to move on to Chapter 4 to learn more about how Linux works.

Logging into KDE

If you configured KDE as your default desktop, the login screen should resemble that shown in Figure 3-29. To log in, type **root** in the text box labeled Login and type the password you earlier assigned to the root user in the text box labeled Password. Then click Go!

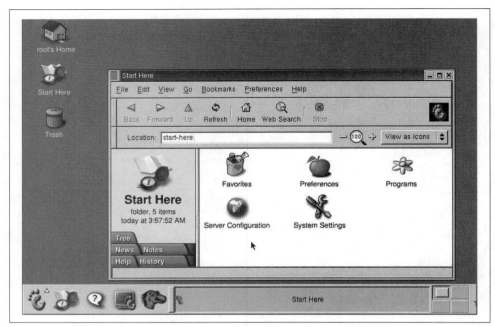

Figure 3-28. The GNOME desktop

Figure 3-29. The KDE login screen

The KDE desktop, shown in Figure 3-30, appears. Chapter 6 explains how to use the KDE desktop; however, you should read Chapter 4 before reading that chapter.

To close the dialog box in the foreground, click its Close button. If you like, click around the desktop and see what you can discover.

To shut down your system, click the *K* icon at the lower-left corner of the desktop's panel. A smaller window saying "End KDE Session?" appears, with the option to Logout or Cancel; click Logout and you are returned to the login window shown in Figure 3-29. To shutdown your system, click on the System menu and select the Halt option. You are asked to confirm (Yes or No) whether you really want to shutdown your computer; click Yes to shutdown your computer. Now you're ready to move on to Chapter 4 to learn more about how Linux works.

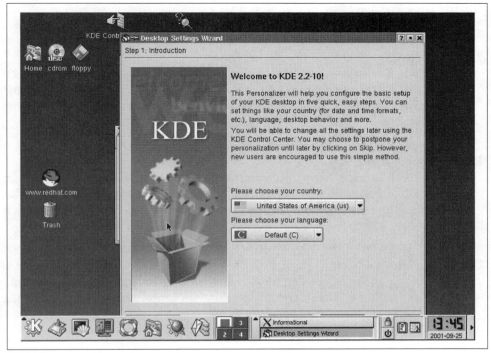

Figure 3-30. The KDE desktop

Getting Help

If your system fails to boot or if you're unable to complete the Linux installation process, don't despair: this section will help you troubleshoot your installation.

Failed Graphical Login

Sometimes, the graphical login fails. This is particularly likely if your system wasn't manufactured recently or if it's a laptop rather than desktop computer.

If you don't see either display manager's screen, your X configuration isn't appropriate for your system's video hardware. It could be that your X configuration needs to be tweaked to make X work properly. In the worst case, your system's video hardware may not be compatible with X; in that event, you will be able to run only nongraphical Linux applications.

 If you see a scrambled image rather than text or images on your monitor, immediately switch off the monitor. If your monitor is an older model, it can be damaged by the incorrect configuration. To reconfigure your system so that it operates properly, follow the procedures in the sidebar "When X Fails," earlier in this chapter.

Additional Resources

The help you need is probably close by, in one of these sources:

The Official Red Hat Linux 7.2 Installation Guide
    This guide is distributed with retail boxed copies of Red Hat Linux, either on CD-ROM or as a printed book. It's also available online. It provides a step-by-step guide to installing Red Hat Linux that includes more details than are given in this chapter.

    http://www.redhat.com/docs/manuals/linux/RHL-7.2-Manual/install-guide

Red Hat Linux 7.2 bug fixes
    The Red Hat Linux 7.2 bug fixes web page describes bugs discovered in Red Hat Linux 7.2 and provides links to updated packages that resolve known problems. Sometimes, the installation media themselves are found to contain bugs. In that case, you may be able to find and download fixes from this web page.

    http://www.redhat.com/support/errata/rh72-errata-bugfixes.html

Linux Installation and Getting Started
    Though somewhat out of date, this resource still gives useful information and hints for installing Linux. Though it addresses Linux generally, much of the material is applicable to Red Hat Linux.

    http://www.redhat.com/mirrors/LDP/LDP/gs/gs.html

Red Hat Linux Frequently Asked Questions
    This FAQ site is maintained by Red Hat. It provides answers to many common questions regarding Red Hat Linux and includes a section on installing it.

    http://www.redhat.com/support/docs/faqs/rhl_general_faq/FAQ.html

The Linux Installation HOWTO
    This HOWTO resembles *Linux Installation and Getting Started*. It too addresses Linux generally rather than Red Hat Linux, but it contains much useful information and is more current than *Linux Installation and Getting Started*.

    http://www.redhat.com/mirrors/LDP/HOWTO/Installation-HOWTO

Red Hat Linux Solutions Database
    This database can be searched online. It contains resolutions and workarounds for many Red Hat Linux problems.

    http://www.redhat.com/apps/support

The Linux on Laptops web page
    Installing Linux on a laptop presents special difficulties, because laptops regularly contain peculiar hardware. Worse, two laptops that have identical model numbers may contain different hardware. The Linux on Laptops web page is an essential resource for those who want to install Red Hat Linux on a laptop.

    http://www.linux-laptop.net

Red Hat Bugzilla FAQ

This searchable database covers problems reported by users of Red Hat Linux. You can use Bugzilla to determine if someone else has had the same problem you're experiencing. Often, the Bugzilla record will include a workaround or fix for your problem.

http://www.redhat.com/bugzilla/redhat-faq.cgi

Usenet newsgroups

Several Usenet newsgroups address Red Hat Linux. You can find a list of these at *http://metalab.unc.edu/linux/intro.html.* If your Internet service provider (ISP) provides access to these newsgroups—as most do—you can read and post messages from and to other Linux users around the world. If necessary, consult your ISP for information on accessing these newsgroups. If you have only web access, you can search Usenet postings via Google, at *http://groups.google.com.*

Don't post blindly to these newsgroups or you may draw angry responses; instead, you should first attempt to find answers to your questions elsewhere. Generally, the Linux community is quite willing to help even those who ask what some consider dumb questions; as a courtesy to all, however, it's best if you do some work on your own before seeking the help of others.

CHAPTER 4

How Linux Works

Before you can effectively use a desktop environment, you need to know some Linux fundamentals. This chapter explains basic Linux concepts that underlie graphical and nongraphical system use. It describes Linux user accounts and how Linux organizes data as filesystems, directories, and files. This chapter also explains how to use the X Window System (often known simply as X). Because both GNOME and KDE are built atop X, an understanding of X is central to using either desktop environment.

User Accounts

Like other multiuser operating systems, such as Windows NT/2000, Linux uses user accounts to identify users and allocate permissions. Every Linux system has a special user, known as the *root* user. The root user is analogous to the Windows NT/2000 user known as Administrator. The root user can perform privileged operations that are forbidden to other users. For instance, most system administration operations can be performed only by the root user. By default, the user ID associated with the root user is *root*.

You should be judicious in your use of the root account. For instance, you should safeguard the associated password, so that no one uses it to compromise your system. Also, you should log in as the root user only when performing privileged operations. Following this advice will help you avoid disasters such as accidentally deleting important files that are protected against access by ordinary, non-root users.

How Linux Organizes Data

In order to make the most effective use of your Linux system, you must understand how Linux organizes data. If you're familiar with Windows or another operating system, you'll find it easy to learn how Linux organizes data, because most operating systems organize their data in similar ways. This section explains how Linux organizes data and introduces you to several important Linux commands that work with directories and files.

Devices

Linux receives data from, sends data to, and stores data on *devices*. A device generally corresponds to a hardware unit, such as a keyboard or serial port. However, a device may have no hardware counterpart: the kernel creates several *pseudodevices* that you can access as devices but that have no physical existence. Moreover, a single hardware unit may correspond to several devices. For example, Linux defines each partition of a disk drive as a distinct device. Table 4-1 describes some typical Linux devices; not every system provides all these devices, and some systems provide devices not shown in the table.

Table 4-1. Typical Linux Devices

Device	Description
atibm	Bus mouse
audio	Sound card
cdrom	CD-ROM drive
console	Current virtual console
fd*n*	Floppy drive (*n* designates the drive; for example, fd0 is the first floppy drive)
ftape	Streaming tape drive not supporting rewind
hd*xn*	Non-SCSI hard drive (*x* designates the drive and *n* designates the partition; for example, hda1 is the first partition of the first non-SCSI hard drive)
inportbm	Bus mouse
lp*n*	Parallel port (*n* designates the device number; for example, lp0 is the first parallel port)
modem	Modem
mouse	Mouse
nftape	Streaming tape drive supporting rewind
nrft*n*	Streaming tape drive supporting rewind (*n* designates the device number; for example, nrft0 is the first streaming tape drive)
nst*n*	Streaming SCSI tape drive not supporting rewind (*n* designates the device number; for example, nst0 is the first streaming SCSI tape drive)
null	Pseudodevice that accepts unlimited output
printer	Printer
psaux	Auxiliary pointing device, such as a trackball or the knob on IBM's ThinkPad
rft*n*	Streaming tape drive not supporting rewind (*n* designates the device number; for example, rft0 is the first streaming tape drive)
scd*n*	SCSI device (*n* designates the device number; for example, scd0 is the first SCSI device)
sd*xn*	SCSI hard drive (*x* designates the drive and *n* designates the partition; for example, sda1 is the first partition of the first SCSI hard drive)
sr*n*	SCSI CD-ROM (*n* designates the drive; for example, sr0 is the first SCSI CD-ROM)
st*n*	Streaming SCSI tape drive supporting rewind (*n* designates the device number; for example, st0 is the first streaming SCSI tape drive)
tty*n*	Virtual console (*n* designates the particular virtual console; for example, tty0 is the first virtual console)

Table 4-1. Typical Linux Devices (continued)

Device	Description
ttySn	Modem (n designates the port; for example, ttyS0 is an incoming modem connection on the first serial port), serial device (such as Palm Pilot), or some PCMCIA devices
zero	Pseudodevice that supplies an inexhaustible stream of zero-bytes

Filesystems

Whether you're using Windows or Linux, you must format a partition before you can store data on it. The installation procedure automatically formats the partitions you create during system installation. When Linux formats a partition, it writes special data, called a *filesystem*, on the partition. The filesystem organizes the available space and provides a directory that lets you assign a name to each *file*, which is a set of stored data. A filesystem also enables you to group files into *directories*, which function much like the folders you create using the Windows Explorer: directories store information about the files they contain.

Every CD-ROM and floppy diskette must also have a filesystem. The filesystem of a CD-ROM is written when the disk is created; the filesystem of a floppy diskette is rewritten each time you format it.

Windows 98 lets you choose to format a partition as a FAT or FAT32. Windows NT/2000 also support the NTFS filesystem type. Linux supports a wider variety of filesystem types; Table 4-2 summarizes the most common ones. The most important filesystem types are *ext3* and *ext2*, which are used for Linux native partitions; *msdos*, which is used for FAT partitions (and floppy diskettes) of the sort created by MS-DOS and Microsoft Windows; and *iso9660*, which is used for CD-ROMs. Linux also provides the *vfat* filesystem, which is used for FAT32 partitions of the sort created by Windows *9x*. Linux also supports reading Windows NT/2000 NTFS filesystems; however, the support for writing such partitions is not enabled in the standard Red Hat Linux kernel.

Table 4-2. Common Filesystem Types

Filesystem	Description
coherent	A filesystem compatible with that used by Coherent Unix
ext	The predecessor of the ext2 filesystem; supported for compatibility
ext2	The standard Linux filesystem
ext3	The new standard journaling filesystem for Red Hat Linux.
hpfs	A filesystem compatible with that used by IBM's OS/2
iso9660	The standard filesystem used on CD-ROMs
minix	An old Linux filesystem, still occasionally used on floppy diskettes
msdos	A filesystem compatible with Microsoft's FAT filesystem, used by MS-DOS and Windows
nfs	A filesystem compatible with Sun's Network File System

Table 4-2. Common Filesystem Types (continued)

Filesystem	Description
ntfs	A filesystem compatible with that used by Microsoft Windows NT's NTFS filesystem
reiserfs	A Linux filesystem designed for high-reliability, large-capacity storage systems
sysv	A filesystem compatible with that used by AT&T's System V Unix
ufs	A filesystem used on BSD and Sun Solaris systems
vfat	A filesystem compatible with Microsoft's FAT32 filesystem, used by Windows 9x
xenix	A filesystem compatible with that used by Xenix
xfs	A filesystem used on SGI systems

The *ext3* filesystem type is a new feature of Red Hat Linux 7.2; previous versions of Red Hat Linux were based on the *ext2* filesystem type. An *ext3* filesystem stores data in the same basic way as an *ext2* filesystem; however, an *ext3* filesystem includes a special *journal* that records changes to the filesystem. If the filesystem becomes corrupted—perhaps because the system was powered off rather than properly shut down—the journal can be used to recover data that might otherwise be lost. Moreover, an *ext3* filesystem can be recovered more quickly than an *ext2* filesystem. The combination of greater reliability and faster recovery is critically important when Linux is used to host a server with one or more large hard disks, but the combination is a convenience even for desktop users.

Directories and Paths

If you've used MS-DOS, you're familiar with the concepts of files and directories and with various MS-DOS commands that work with them. Under Linux, files and directories work much as they do under MS-DOS.

Home and working directories

When you log in to Linux, you're placed in a special directory known as your *home directory*. Generally, each user has a distinct home directory, where the user creates personal files. This makes it simple for the user to find files previously created, because they're kept separate from the files of other users.

The *working directory*—or *current working directory*, as it's sometimes called—is the directory you're currently working in. When you log in to Linux, your working directory is initialized as your home directory.

The directory tree

The directories of a Linux system are organized as a hierarchy. Unlike MS-DOS, which provides a separate hierarchy for each partition, Linux provides a single hierarchy that includes every partition. The topmost directory of the directory tree is the *root directory*, which is written using a forward slash (/), not the backward slash (\) used by MS-DOS to designate a root directory.

Figure 4-1 shows a hypothetical Linux directory tree. The root directory contains six subdirectories: */bin*, */dev*, */etc*, */home*, */tmp*, and */usr*. The */home* directory has two subdirectories; each is the home directory of a user and has the same name as the user who owns it. The user named *bill* has created two subdirectories in his home directory: *books* and *school*. The user named *patrick* has created the single *school* subdirectory in his home directory.

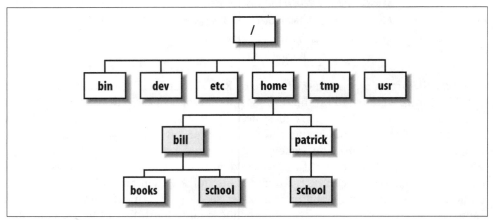

Figure 4-1. A hypothetical Linux directory tree

Each directory (other than the root directory) is contained in a directory known as its parent directory. For example, the parent directory of the *bill* directory is *home*.

 The root user has a special home directory, */root*. This directory is commonly called "slash root" to distinguish it from the root directory, */*.

Absolute and relative pathnames

If you look closely at Figure 4-1, you'll see that two directories named *school* exist: one is a subdirectory of *bill,* and the other is a subdirectory of *patrick*. To avoid the confusion that could result when several directories have the same name, directories are specified using *pathnames*.

There are two kinds of pathnames: *absolute* and *relative*. The absolute pathname of a directory traces the location of the directory beginning at the root directory; you form the pathname as a list of directories, separated by forward slashes (/). For example, the absolute pathname of the unique directory named *bill* is */home/bill*. The absolute pathname of the *school* subdirectory of the *bill* directory is */home/bill/school*. The absolute pathname of the identically named *school* subdirectory of the *patrick* directory is */home/patrick/school*.

When a subdirectory is many levels below the root directory, its absolute pathname may be long and cumbersome. In that case, it may be more convenient to use a relative pathname, which uses the current working directory, rather than the root directory, as its starting point. For example, suppose that the *bill* directory is the current working directory; you can refer to its *books* subdirectory by the relative pathname *books*. Notice that a relative pathname can never begin with a forward slash, whereas an absolute pathname must begin with a forward slash. As a second example, suppose that the */home* directory is the current working directory. The relative pathname of the *school* subdirectory of the *bill* directory would be *bill/school*; the relative pathname of the identically named subdirectory of the *patrick* directory would be *patrick/school*.

Linux provides two special directory names. Using a single dot (.) as a directory name is equivalent to specifying the working directory. Using two dots (..) within a pathname takes you up one level in the current path, to the parent directory. For example, if the working directory is */home/bill*, .. refers to the */home* directory. Similarly, if the current working directory is */home/bill* and the directory tree is that shown in Figure 4-1, the path *../patrick/school* refers to the directory */home/patrick/school*.

File Permissions

Unlike Windows 98, but like other varieties of Unix and Windows NT/2000, Linux is a multiuser operating system. Therefore, it includes mechanisms to protect data from unauthorized access. The primary protection mechanism restricts access to directories and files based on the identity of the user who requests access and on access modes assigned to each directory and file.

Each directory and file has an associated user, called the *owner*. The user who creates a file initially becomes the owner of the file. Each user belongs to one or more sets of users known as *groups*. Each directory and file has an associated group, which is assigned when the directory or file is created.

Access permissions determine what operations a user can perform on a directory or file. Table 4-3 lists the possible permissions and explains the meaning of each. Notice that permissions work differently for directories than for files. For example, permission r denotes the ability to list the contents of a directory or *read* the contents of a file. A directory or file can have more than one permission. Only the listed permissions are granted; any other operations are prohibited. For example, a user who had file permission rw could *read* or *write* the *file* but could not execute it, as indicated by the absence of the execute permission, x.

Table 4-3. Access Permissions

Permission	Meaning for a directory	Meaning for a file
r	List the directory	Read contents
w	Create or remove files	Write contents
x	Access files and subdirectories	Execute

The access modes of a directory or file consist of three sets of permissions:

User/Owner
Applies to the owner of the file

Group
Applies to users who are members of the group assigned to the file

Other
Applies to other users

The *ls* command, which you'll meet in Chapter 7, lists the file access modes in the second column of its long output format, as shown in Figure 4-2. The GNOME and KDE file managers use this same format. The column contains nine characters: the first three specify the access allowed the owner of the directory or file, the second three specify the access allowed users in the same group as the directory or file, and the final three specify the access allowed to other users (see Figure 4-3).

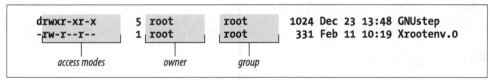

Figure 4-2. Access modes as shown by the ls command

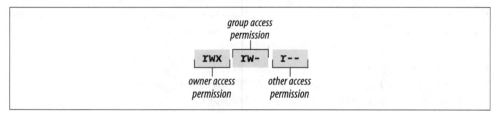

Figure 4-3. Access modes specify three permissions

Mounting and Unmounting Filesystems

You cannot access a hard drive partition, CD-ROM, or floppy disk until the related device or partition is *mounted*. Mounting a device checks the status of the device and readies it for access. Linux can be configured to automatically mount a device or partition when it boots or when you launch a desktop environment. By default, GNOME and KDE automatically mount removable media devices such as CD-ROMs and floppy disks.

Before you can remove media from a device, you must unmount it. You can unmount a device by using a desktop environment or issuing a command. For your convenience, the system automatically unmounts devices when it shuts down. A device can be unmounted only if it's not in use. For example, if a user's current working directory is a directory of the device, the device cannot be unmounted. See

Chapter 7 for more information on mounting and unmounting devices with the *mount* and *umount* commands.

Using X

X is the standard graphical user interface (GUI) for Linux. Like other GUIs, such as Windows and Mac OS, the X Window System lets you interact with programs by using a mouse (or other pointing device) to point and click, providing a simple means of communicating with your computer.

Originally implemented as a collaborative effort of Digital Equipment Corporation (DEC) and the Massachusetts Institute of Technology (MIT), X was first released in 1987. Subsequently, the X Consortium, Inc. (*http://www.x.org*), became responsible for the continued development and publication of X.

Despite its age, X is a remarkable and very modern software system, offering a cross-platform, network-oriented GUI. It runs on a wide variety of platforms, including essentially every flavor of Unix, such as Solaris, Linux, and the BSDs (FreeBSD, Net-BSD, and OpenBSD). X clients are available for use, for example, under Windows 3.*x*, *9x*, NT, and 2000. The sophisticated networking capabilities of X let you run a program on one computer while viewing the graphical output on another computer via a network connection.

Most Linux users run XFree86, a freely available software system compatible with X. XFree86 was developed by the XFree86 software team, which began work in 1992. In 1994, The XFree86 Project, Inc. (*http://www.xfree86.org*) assumed responsibility for ongoing research and development of XFree86.

Keyboard Operations

Using the keyboard with X closely resembles using the keyboard with Windows. X sends your keyboard input to the active window, which is said to have the *input focus*. The active window is usually the window in which you most recently clicked the mouse.

 This chapter refers to your pointing device as a *mouse*. However, like Windows, X supports a variety of pointing devices, such as optical mice and Wacom graphics tablets.

While Windows lets you choose to perform most operations by using the keyboard or mouse, X was designed for use with a mouse. If your mouse isn't functioning, you'll find it quite challenging or even impossible to use most X programs. X allows you to access only a few important functions via the keyboard:

* Switching video modes

- Using virtual consoles
- Abruptly terminating X

Switching video modes

When you configured X, you specified the video modes in which X can operate. Recall that the current video mode determines the resolution and color depth of the image displayed by your monitor—for example 16 bits per pixel color depth and 1024×768 pixels screen resolution.

By pressing **Ctrl-Alt-+** (using the plus key on the numeric keypad), you command X to switch to the next video mode in sequence. X treats the video modes as a cycle: If X is operating in the last video mode, this key sequence causes X to return to the first video mode.

The similar key sequence **Ctrl-Alt--** (using the minus key on the numeric keypad) causes X to switch to the previous video model. If you shift to a video mode that your monitor doesn't support—as demonstrated by an unsteady or garbled image—you can use this key sequence to return to a supported video mode, avoiding the inconvenience of terminating X and reconfiguring your system.

Using virtual consoles

Even while X is running, you can access the Linux virtual consoles. To switch from graphical mode to a virtual console running in text mode, type **Ctrl-Alt-F*n***, where **F*n*** is a function key and *n* is the number of the desired virtual console. X uses virtual console 7, so only virtual consoles 1 through 6 are accessible while running X.

To switch from a virtual console back to X, type **Ctrl-Alt-F7**. Nothing is lost when you switch from X to a virtual console or back, so you can move freely between the graphical and text operating modes.

Terminating X

You can terminate X abruptly by typing **Ctrl-Alt-Backspace**. However, this method of terminating X is appropriate only when X is malfunctioning. Terminating X abruptly closes down running applications, which may result in loss of data.

Terminal Windows and Pop-up Menus

In Windows, you don't need to restart in DOS mode simply to have access to the DOS command line. Similarly, in X you don't need to switch to a virtual console simply to have access to the command line—X enables you to open a terminal window. A terminal window resembles the MS-DOS Prompt window or command-line interface window; like the Linux shell, it lets you type commands and view command output. Various window managers support different ways of accessing a terminal window.

The terminal window is just one example of a frequently used program under X that you'll want to access. Most window managers install with a default set of common programs that can be accessed by right-clicking with the mouse on the desktop. For example, most window managers let you right-click on the desktop and select a terminal window program from the pop-up menu that appears. However, the pop-up menu displayed by a window manager may display program names rather than program functions. In this case, you may have some difficulty determining which entry on the pop-up menu corresponds to a terminal program. Many programs that provide terminal windows have names that include the sequences *xt* or *xterm*. Selecting such an entry launches a terminal window. You'll learn more about window managers later in this chapter.

Mouse Operations

Mouse operations under X are similar to mouse operations under Windows, although you perform them differently. The most common mouse operations are:

- Copying and pasting text
- Using scrollbars

Copying and pasting text

To copy and paste text, you must first mark the text by moving the mouse to the beginning of the text; then click the left mouse button and drag the mouse across the text to be copied. X automatically copies the marked text into a buffer; you don't need to press **Ctrl-C** or perform any other operation. If you find that you need to change the size of the marked text section, you can click the right mouse button and move the mouse to adjust the marked text.

> Some window managers display a pop-up menu when you click the right button, even when the mouse cursor is above text. When using such a window manager, you cannot use the right mouse button to adjust the size of the marked text section.

To paste the text, properly position the insertion point and click the middle mouse button. If your mouse has only two buttons, simultaneously click the left and right buttons to simulate clicking the middle mouse button. You may find that this operation requires a little practice before you get it right, but once you've mastered it, you'll find it works almost as well as having a three-button mouse.

Using scrollbars

Many X programs provide scrollbars that resemble those provided by Windows. However, the operation of scrollbars under X originally differed from that under Windows. Most X programs have been revised to display scrollbars that work like Windows scrollbars, although a few have not.

If you're having trouble using a scrollbar, try using the original X method of working with it. To page forward, click the left mouse button on the scrollbar. Clicking near the top of the scrollbar scrolls forward a short distance, as little as a single line. Clicking near the bottom of the scrollbar scrolls the window by a page. To page backward, click the right mouse button on the scrollbar. Again, clicking near the top of the scrollbar scrolls a short distance, as little as a single line. Clicking near the bottom of the scrollbar scrolls the window by a page.

Virtual Desktop

Under X, your desktop can be scrollable, that is, larger than the size of your monitor. For example, even if your monitor has a maximum resolution of 800 × 600, you might have a desktop of 1600 × 1200 or even 3200 × 2400. Such a desktop is known as a *virtual desktop*. Most desktop environments provide a tool called a *pager*, which lets you move around the virtual desktop. The pager provides a thumbnail view of your virtual desktop; by clicking within the thumbnail, you center your actual desktop on the clicked location. You'll learn more about pagers in the next two chapters.

> Don't confuse the term *virtual desktop* with the term *virtual console*. A virtual console is used to log in and enter commands in text mode; a virtual desktop is used to obtain an oversized desktop in graphics mode.

Window Managers

Using X means interacting with Linux on several different levels. X itself merely provides the graphics facility for displaying components of a GUI: X draws the screen, draws objects on the screen, and tracks user input actions such as keyboard input and mouse operations. To organize the desktop into familiar objects like windows, menus, and scrollbars, X relies on a separate program called a window manager. But even more functionality is required. A window manager alone doesn't provide tight integration between applications of the sort required by drag-and-drop operations; that higher degree of integration comes from what's called a desktop environment. While X itself is a single program, X under Linux supports several popular window managers and two popular desktop environments, GNOME and KDE.

Window managers create the borders, icons, and menus that provide a simple-to-use interface. Window managers also control the look and feel of X, letting you configure X to operate almost any way you desire. Table 4-4 describes the most popular Red Hat Linux window managers. For detailed information about a variety of window managers, see Matt Chapman's *xwinman.org* web site.

Table 4-4. *Popular Window Managers*

Window manager	Description
Enlightenment	A highly configurable, eye candy window manager. Has been in development status for a long time.
KWM	A window manager that sports an accompanying desktop, KDE. The combination of KWM and KDE provides a robust and efficient user interface. Not compliant with GNOME desktop.
Sawfish	Formerly known as Sawmill, Sawfish is the default window manager used with Red Hat Linux GNOME. A rather sparse but fast and reliable window manager.
TWM	A very basic and somewhat dated window manager. At one time, it was the dominant Linux window manager.
WindowMaker	Resembles the user interface of the NeXT computer (NeXTStep). Compatible with KWM.

Desktop Environments

A *desktop environment is* a set of desktop tools and applications. The Windows desktop includes applications such as the Windows Explorer, accessories such as Notepad, games such as FreeCell and Minesweeper, and utilities such as the Control Panel and its applets. Although you can run X without a desktop, having a desktop helps you work more efficiently. The two most popular desktop environments used with Linux are GNOME and KDE.

GNOME

GNOME, which stands for the GNU Network Object Model Environment (pronounced "guh-nome"), is a freely available desktop environment that can be used with any of several window managers, including Sawfish and Enlightenment. One of GNOME's most interesting features is session awareness. When you reenter GNOME after logging out, it reconfigures your desktop to match the state at the time you exited by launching each application that was open when you exited. GNOME even restores each application to its former state by, for example, moving to the page that was open when you exited.

Both GNOME and KDE support a myriad of standard and optional desktop tools and applications, such as:

- Games and amusements such as Fish, Fifteen, gEyes, and Game of Life
- The GNU Image Manipulation Program (GIMP)
- Ghostview, which lets you view PostScript files and print them on non-PostScript printers
- Internet applications such as Netscape Communicator, Mozilla, gFTP, NcFTP, X-Chat, slrn, pine, and elm
- Multimedia applications such as Audio Mixer and CD Player

- General applications such as gEdit, a text editor; Netscape Navigator, a Linux version of the popular browser; and Gnumeric, an Excel-like spreadsheet application
- Utilities for configuring and using GNOME on your Linux system

GNOME is specially associated with the desktop suite known as GNOME Office, which includes the AbiWord word processor, the Gnumeric spreadsheet application, and 15 other applications. Chapter 5 explains how to configure and use GNOME.

KDE

KDE (the K Desktop Environment) is a freely available desktop that includes KWM, the K Window Manager, as an integral component. KDE provides a file manager, a help system, a configuration utility and a variety of accessories and applications, such as:

- Games such as Kmines, Kpoker, and Ktetris
- Graphical applications such as Kfract, a fractal generator, and Kview, an image viewer
- Multimedia applications such as Kmix, a sound mixer, and Kmedia, a media player
- Network applications such as Kmail, a mail client; Knu, a network utility; and Krn, a news client

As with GNOME, new KDE accessories and applications are available almost weekly. Work is underway on a complete open source office suite (KOffice) that runs under KDE. You can learn more about KDE and the status of KOffice by browsing the KDE web site (*http://www.koffice.org*).

At one time, KDE was distributed under a license that suggested that some users owed a fee to developers of an important library used to develop KDE. This inhibited acceptance of KDE within the free software community. Several releases of Red Hat Linux featured only GNOME, despite the popularity of KDE among some users. Currently, KDE is open source and may be freely distributed. Although Red Hat defines GNOME as the default desktop environment, the standard Red Hat Linux distribution includes KDE, giving users a convenient desktop choice. KDE is explained in Chapter 6.

## CHAPTER 5

Using the GNOME Desktop

Red Hat Linux provides a choice of two desktop environments: GNOME and KDE. This chapter explains how to configure and use the GNOME desktop environment and GNOME Office, GNOME's desktop application suite. Chapter 6 explains how to configure and use the KDE desktop environment.

Using GNOME

If you selected GNOME to be the default desktop during the installation process, you will see the GNOME desktop as shown in Figure 5-1 after logging in. The contents of your desktop may be different, of course. If you want to launch a GNOME session, but KDE is configured as the default desktop environment, select Gnome from the Session menu of the KDE login screen. Of course, GNOME must be installed in order for this to work.

To log out of GNOME, left-click on the main menu, which resembles a foot, as shown in Figure 5-2. From the pop-up menu that appears, select the Log Out menu item. A Log Out dialog box, shown in Figure 5-3, appears and asks you to confirm your decision to log out. Clicking Yes terminates your GNOME session. If you enable the checkbox titled Save Current Setup, the GNOME session manager will save the state of your desktop and restore it when you log in again to GNOME. In addition to the Logout button, Halt and Reboot buttons appear on the Log Out dialog box. You can use the Halt button to shut down your system or the Reboot button to restart it.

The GNOME Desktop

The term *desktop* can be used in either of two senses. It can refer to the entire GNOME display or to the empty area of the display where no windows or icons appear, as indicated in Figure 5-4. To keep straight these meanings, *GNOME desktop* will be used when referring to the entire display and *desktop* will be used when referring to the empty area of the display.

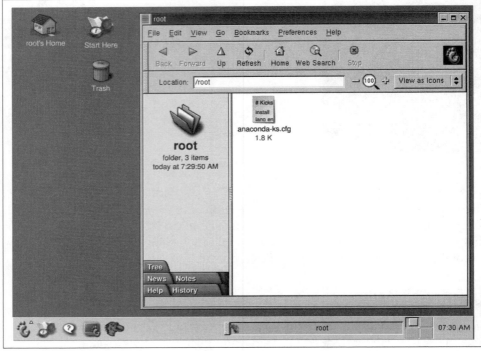

Figure 5-1. The GNOME desktop

Clicking the desktop with the middle mouse button causes a pop-up menu to appear; the menu lets you conveniently launch popular applets and applications. Right-clicking the desktop causes a different pop-up menu to appear; this menu lets you arrange the desktop windows and icons. Figure 5-4 shows the elements of the GNOME desktop, which are described in the following sections.

Home directory icon

The Home Directory icon, which resembles a house, is normally located in the upper-left corner of the display. The icon provides a convenient way to access the file manager: double-clicking the icon with the left mouse button launches Nautilus, GNOME's browser and file manager, which displays the contents of the user's home directory.

Drive icons

If you have permission to mount a CD-ROM or floppy drive, your desktop includes an icon representing the drive. Depending on the type of drive, the icon may resemble a CD-ROM or a floppy. If you right-click on the icon, a pop-up menu appears. The menu lets you mount the device, eject the device's media, or open Nautilus to view the files residing on the device.

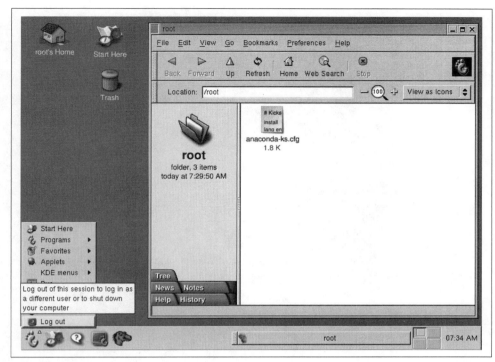

Figure 5-2. Logging out of GNOME

Figure 5-3. The Log Out dialog box

Start Here icon

By double-clicking the Start Here icon, you can launch Nautilus to view a folder that contains several useful icons. Double-clicking any icon in the folder launches a window containing icons that provide convenient access to GNOME facilities:

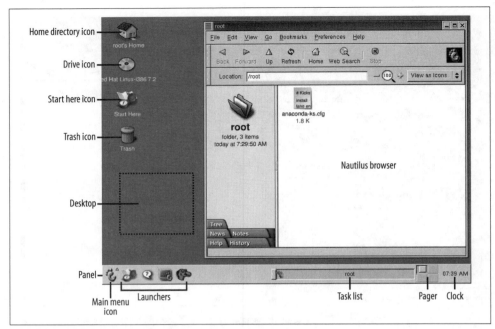

Home directory icon
Drive icon
Start here icon
Trash icon
Desktop
Panel
Main menu icon
Launchers
Task list
Pager
Clock

Nautilus browser

Figure 5-4. Parts of the GNOME desktop

Favorites

> The Favorites icon provides access to a folder in which you can place icons that provide access to GNOME facilities you want to be able to conveniently access.

Preferences

> The Preferences icon provides access to a folder containing icons that enable you to view and modify a variety of preferences, including those for the desktop, document handlers, user interface look and feel, multimedia, peripherals, sessions, and the Sawfish window manager.

Programs

> The Programs icon provides access to a folder containing icons that let you launch programs. Most likely, you'll find it more convenient to use GNOME's menu, described later in this chapter.

Server Configurator

> The Server Configurator icon provides access to tools for configuring servers, such as Apacheconf, a tool for configuring the Apache web server.

System Settings

> The System Settings icon provides access to tools for viewing and modifying the system configuration, including:

> - The system clock
> - Hardware devices

- Internet (dial-up) configuration
- Network configuration
- Printer configuration
- Service configuration
- User accounts

Trash icon

The Trash icon lets you view files that have been deleted by using Nautilus. Files deleted by using the *rm* command are not stored in the trash; they are immediately deleted. Simply double-click the icon, and GNOME launches Nautilus to view the directory where deleted files are stored.

The GNOME Panel

The panel appears along the bottom edge of the display. However, if you prefer a different location, you can move the panel; to do so, click and drag the panel to the desired location. The panel functionally resembles the Windows 9*x* taskbar; you can use it to launch programs, switch from one program to another, and perform other tasks.

 Moving the mouse cursor over an icon in the panel reveals a message informing you of the function of the icon.

The panel can also contain *applets*, programs represented as panel icons. Applets are typically small programs that display information or take action when clicked. For example, a *launcher applet* launches an application when its button in the panel is clicked.

If you select Main Menu → Panel → Panel Manual, GNOME launches Nautilus to view the GNOME Panel Manual. The GNOME Panel Manual explains the function and operation of the GNOME panel in detail.

By default, the GNOME panel contains the following items:

Main menu
   The main menu icon resembles a big foot in the shape of a "G." Left-clicking the main menu icon presents a menu from which you can choose a variety of programs. Several of the menu entries are submenus; selecting such an entry pops up a new menu to the side of the original entry.

Start Here
   The launcher icon for the Start Here folder resembles a compass superimposed on a map. Left-clicking the icon presents the same folder presented by left-clicking the Start Here icon on the GNOME desktop, described earlier in this chapter.

Help viewer

The launcher icon for the GNOME help viewer resembles a question mark; clicking the icon launches Nautilus and points Nautilus to GNOME help documents. You can also launch the help viewer by selecting the Help menu item of a GNOME application or applet or by selecting the Programs → Help menu item from the main menu.

The default home page of the help viewer includes a hyperlink that takes you to the *GNOME User's Guide*. The user's guide will help you discover additional useful GNOME features and capabilities.

GNOME Terminal

The GNOME terminal launcher icon resembles a video monitor. Clicking the icon launches GNOME Terminal, a terminal emulator for X, which you can use to enter shell commands. See the later section titled "Using GNOME Terminal."

Mozilla

The Mozilla launcher icon resembles a red dinosaur. Click the icon launches the Mozilla web browser.

Task list

The task list contains a button for each active task. Clicking a task's button raises the task's window to the front of the screen, so that you can view it.

Pager

Depending on your X configuration, GNOME may provide a virtual desktop larger than your monitor can display. In this case, the Pager lets you switch between pages of the desktop. Figure 5-4 shows that GNOME has provided a virtual desktop with four pages, only one of which is visible at any given time. The highlighted icon shows the page you're currently viewing as your desktop. To view a different page, simply click the icon that represents the desktop page you want to view.

Clock

The clock displays your system's current time. If the clock is not visible, select Panel → Add to Panel → Applet → Clock from the main menu. Once you've added the clock applet to the panel, it will appear automatically the next time you start GNOME. You can use this technique to add a variety of other applets to the panel, including the pager or task list, if either somehow disappears.

Using Nautilus

The new GNOME file manager is called Nautilus. To launch Nautilus, double-click a directory or drive icon or select Programs → Applications → Nautilus from the main menu. Nautilus has two main panes, as shown in Figure 5-5. The left pane may display information about the current directory or a hierarchical directory tree. To switch between these views, click the Tree tab. To select a directory in the left pane, simply left-click it.

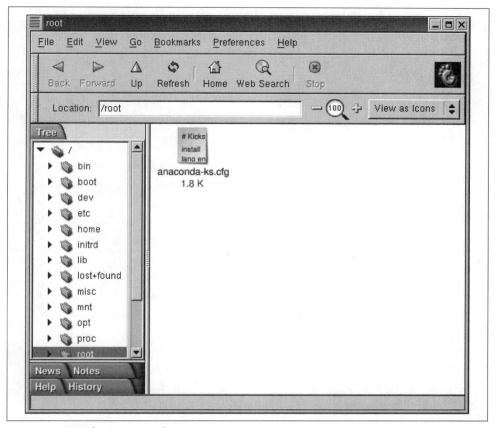

Figure 5-5. Nautilus in icon mode

The right pane can show an icon for each file or detailed information about each file, as shown in Figure 5-6. To switch from icon to detailed mode, left-click the control labeled View as Icons or View as List. You can also select custom mode, which lets you tailor the display appearance according to your own taste.

To view the contents of a folder shown in the right pane, simply double-click the folder's icon. To view the contents of the folder that contains the current folder, click the Up toolbar icon.

Nautilus can be used as a file manager to copy, move, rename, and delete files. To perform one of these operations, you must first select the file (or files) by left-click-ing in the right pane. To select additional files, hold down the **Ctrl** key as you select them. The Edit menu includes a menu item that lets you click on all files that appear in the right pane.

- To move a file, simply drag it to its new location.

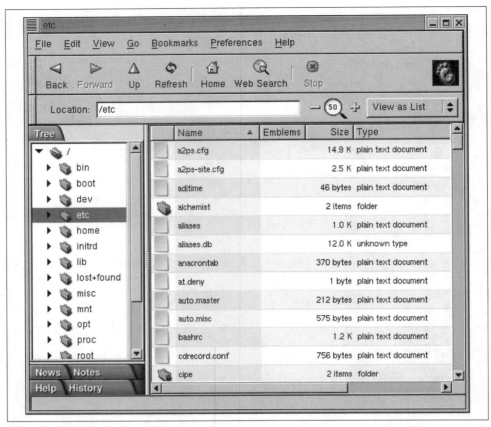

Figure 5-6. Nautilus in list mode

- To copy a file, hold down **Ctrl** while dragging it. Alternatively, you can right-click on a file and use the pop-up menu to specify the action you want to perform. Nautilus then displays a dialog box that lets you specify additional options.

- To rename a file, right-click on the file's icon and select Show Properties from the pop-up menu. Simply type the new name and click on the close icon in the upper right corner of the dialog box.

- To delete a file, right-click on the file and select Move to Trash from the pop-up menu.

Nautilus lets you double-click on a file to launch the application associated with the file. Alternatively, you can right-click on the file and select Open With from the pop-up menu. Nautilus launches a dialog box that lets you specify the application that should be launched.

Many applications are GNOME-compliant, supporting drag-and-drop operations like those supported by Windows. For example, you can open two file manager windows and drag-and-drop files or directories between them.

The Nautilus menus provide additional functions, including the ability to configure the operation of Nautilus. If you're familiar with the Windows Explorer, you'll find most of these functions and capabilities familiar. To learn more about Nautilus, use the Nautilus Help menu to view the Nautilus Quick Reference or the GNOME User's Manual.

Using GNOME Terminal

Similar to the MS-DOS Prompt window, the GNOME terminal, shown in Figure 5-7, provides a window in which you can type shell commands and view their output. To launch GNOME terminal, you can either click the GNOME Terminal icon on the Panel, or select Programs → System → GNOME Terminal from the main menu. You can open multiple GNOME terminal windows if you like.

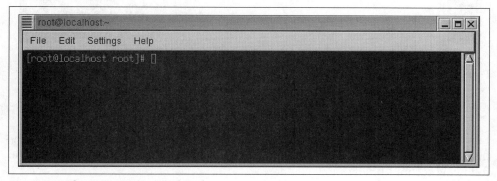

Figure 5-7. The GNOME Terminal application

The Settings menu lets you configure the operation of GNOME Terminal, as shown in Figure 5-8. For example, you may find that the default font is too large or too small for your liking. If so, select Settings → Preferences from the GNOME terminal window. A dialog box pops up. Select the General tab and left-click the Browse button next to the Font field. A second dialog box pops up, from which you can select the font, font style, and font size you prefer.

To exit GNOME terminal, simply type **exit** on the command line and press **Enter**. Alternatively, select Close Terminal from the File menu.

 You can find additional GNOME applets and applications by visiting the GNOME software map at *http://www.gnome.org/applist*.

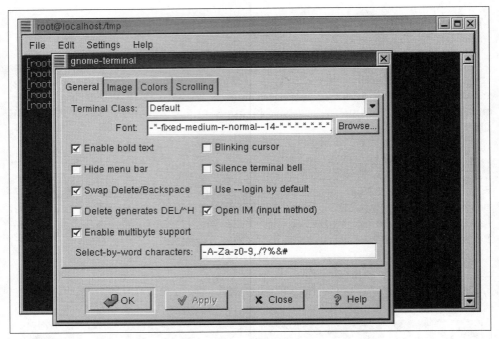

Figure 5-8. Editing terminal settings

Configuring GNOME

Like most GNOME applications, GNOME itself is highly configurable. You can configure GNOME's panel, its main menu, and its overall appearance and function. The following sections briefly show you how.

The GNOME Panel

You can add a launcher to the GNOME panel. Clicking on a launcher launches a predetermined application. To add a new launcher applet, right-click on the panel and select Panel → Add to Panel → Launcher from the pop-up menu. The Create Launcher Applet dialog box, as shown in Figure 5-9, appears.

You can specify a name for the launcher, a comment, and the command that GNOME executes to launch the application. GNOME automatically provides a default icon. If the program to be run is a text-based program, check the Run in Terminal checkbox.

If an application is already on the main menu, you can quickly create a launcher for it. Simply right-click on the application's menu item and select "Add this launcher to panel" or "Add this applet as a launcher to panel" from the pop-up menu.

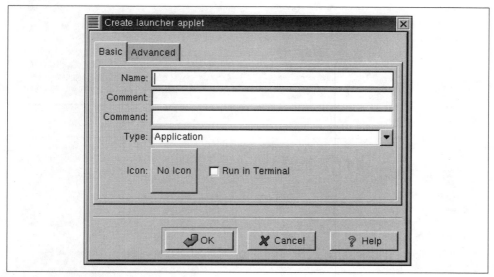

Figure 5-9. Creating a launcher applet

If your panel contains many launchers, it may become crowded and confusing. To remedy this, you can create one or more drawers, like that shown in Figure 5-10. Drawers act like menus; you click on a drawer to open it and view the launchers it contains. Clicking an open drawer closes it and hides its contents.

Figure 5-10. A drawer

To add a drawer, right-click on the panel and select Panel → Add to Panel → Drawer from the pop-up menu. To move a launcher into the drawer, click on the drawer to open it, right-click on the launcher and select Move from the pop-up menu. Next, move the cursor over the open drawer and click the left mouse button.

If you add a launcher or drawer and later decide you don't want it, you can remove it from the panel. Simply right-click on the unwanted applet and select Remove from Panel from the pop-up menu, as shown in Figure 5-11.

Configuring the GNOME Main Menu

You can configure GNOME's main menu by using the menu editor. To launch the menu editor, select Programs → Settings → Menu Editor from the main menu, as shown in Figure 5-12.

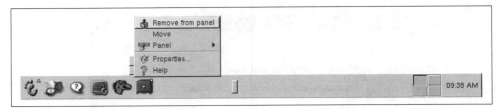

Figure 5-11. Removing a panel item

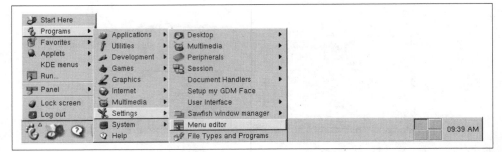

Figure 5-12. Launching the menu editor

The menu editor window, shown in Figure 5-13, has two main panes. Its appearance and operation resemble that of the file manager. The left pane of the menu editor hierarchically displays the menu tree, whereas the right pane shows information pertaining to the currently selected menu item. You can use toolbar buttons to move the current menu item up or down the menu tree, add a new submenu or menu item, or delete the current menu item.

The GNOME Start Here Facility

You can configure the appearance and operation of GNOME and GNOME-compliant applications by using the GNOME Start Here facility, shown in Figure 5-14. The Start Here facility resembles the Windows Control Panel, although it looks and works somewhat differently. To launch the Start Here facility, click the Start Here icon on the desktop or panel.

Like the Windows Control Panel, which uses small programs called *applets* to perform its functions, the GNOME Start Here facility uses small programs called *capplets*; however, the Start Here facility's user interface hides this detail from you. Nautilus serves as the Start Here facility's user interface. You can use the Start Here facility to:

- Select background properties
- Configure a screensaver
- Select a desktop theme
- Select a window manager

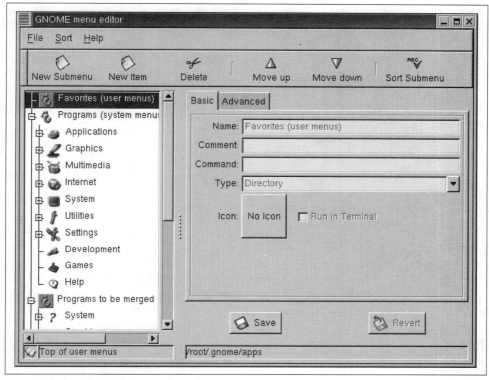

Figure 5-13. Using the menu editor

- Configure the default text editor
- Specify MIME types that control the handling of multimedia files
- Configure the keyboard bell and sounds
- Configure keyboard and mouse properties
- Specify applications that GNOME automatically launches when it starts
- Specify a variety of options governing the appearance of GNOME-compliant applications

Simply select the configuration category by double-clicking the appropriate folder in the Start Here window. The resulting window may contain configuration capplets, folders, or both.

When you double-click on a capplet, a configuration dialog box appears. You can then revise the configuration parameters by specifying the desired values. Many dialog boxes include a Preview button, which lets you experiment without permanently altering the GNOME configuration. The Revert button, if present, lets you restore the original configuration. The Apply or OK button permanently updates the GNOME configuration, whereas the Cancel button discards your changes and leaves your settings as they were.

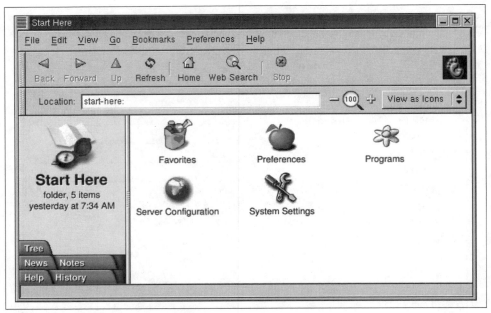

Figure 5-14. The GNOME Start Here facility

Themes

One favorite feature among Linux users is the use of desktop themes to control the way windows and interface elements (such as radio buttons, checkboxes, and buttons) are drawn. You can select from among a variety of themes developed by fellow Linux users by using the GNOME Control Center. If the standard choices aren't adequate to satisfy you, you can visit *http://www.themes.org*, which hosts more than 5000 themes for various window managers, include GNOME. To see only GTK themes compatible with GNOME, go to *http://gtk.themes.org*.

When you find a theme you like, download the tarball and save it to the */tmp* directory.* Don't unpack the file. Instead, launch the Start Here facility and select Preferences → Desktop → Theme Selector. When the Theme Selector appears, click Install New Theme and navigate to the file you downloaded and saved in */tmp*, then click OK. If the theme is compatible, you'll now see it listed in the Available Themes box. To try it, click the theme name and click Preview. If you like the new theme, click OK to adopt it.

---

* The theme is contained in a *.tar.gz* file, which is commonly referred to as a tarball.

GNOME Office

GNOME Office, GNOME's desktop application suite, is made up of more than a dozen components that will eventually comprise a complete suite of desktop applications for GNOME users. The components are in various stages of development; some are mature and usable, whereas others are in initial development. Among the components of GNOME Office are:

- AbiWord, a word processor
- Achtung, a presentation application
- Dia, a diagramming application
- Evolution, an Outlook-like personal information manager including calendar and email
- Eye of GNOME, an image viewer
- Galeon, a web browser
- The GIMP, an image editing application
- Gnucash, a personal finance manager
- Gnumeric, a spreadsheet application

You can learn more about the GNOME Office project by visiting its web site, *http://www.gnome.org/gnome-office*.

AbiWord

GNOME Office applications are available from the GNOME menu. For example, AbiWord is available by selecting Main Menu → Programs → Applications → AbiWord. Figure 5-15 shows AbiWord's main window.

The AbiWord word processor was originally developed by AbiSource, Inc. It runs on Win32 platforms, as well as Linux. It has strong support for localization and has been localized for Chinese, Japanese, Korean, and Slavic languages. AbiWord development is ongoing, so its feature set and performance are subject to rapid improvement.

AbiWord has a variety of import and export filters, and additional filters are planned. For instance, a Palm Pilot import filter is soon promised. At the time of this writing, the filters—like those of other Linux office applications—work imperfectly. For instance, AbiWord terminated when trying to open a Microsoft Word 97 document containing an early version of this chapter. However, AbiWord was able to open a version of the document saved in RTF format.

Gnumeric

The GNOME Office spreadsheet application, Gnumeric, is shown in Figure 5-16. The functionality and user interface of Gnumeric closely resemble those of Microsoft

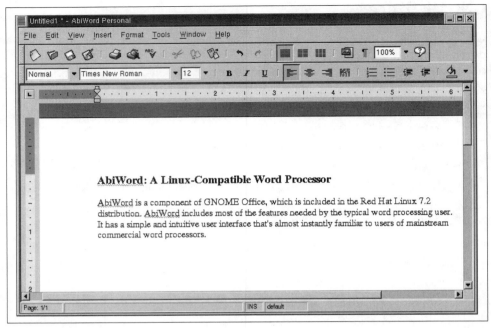

Figure 5-15. AbiWord

Excel. Eventually, GNOME Office developers hope to be able to support Microsoft's Visual Basic for Applications. The GNOME Basic project has already provided code being used in Gnumeric, which already supports about 95 percent of Excel's built-in functions.

The GIMP

The GIMP, which is short for *GNU Image Manipulation Program*, is among the most mature components of GNOME Office. GIMP was originally written by written by Peter Mattis and Spencer Kimball. It lets you work with bitmap graphics data; its functions resemble those of Adobe Photoshop. GIMP is useful for tasks such as image design, image composition, and photo touch-up. Most users find GIMP to be quite functional and reliable.

GIMP supports the PSD format used by Adobe Photoshop and well as BMP, GIF, JPEG, MPEG, PCX, PDF, PNG, PS, TGA, TIFF, XPM, and many other formats. It comes complete with a suite of free plug-ins that rival those available commercially for Adobe Photoshop. Studio users will be amazed at the capabilities of GIMP's Script-Fu, which lets users write simple (or sophisticated) macros that perform GIMP operations. Using Script-Fu, common studio operations such as image transformations and format conversions can be automated so that they run while you relax.

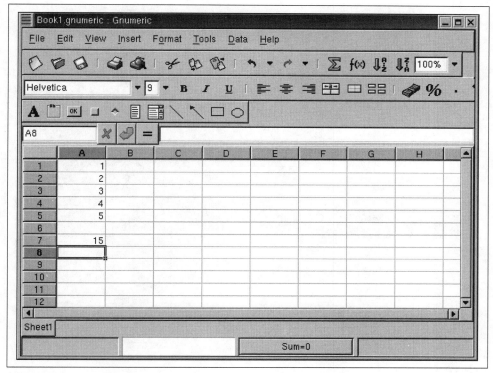

Figure 5-16. Gnumeric

Unlike AbiWord and Gnumeric, GIMP is not automatically installed with GNOME. If you selected Graphics and Image Manipulation during system installation, GIMP was automatically installed; otherwise, you can manually install GIMP by using the RPM package manager, as explained in Chapter 8.

When GIMP is first launched, you will be asked to specify options such as cache size, application swap file directory, and monitor resolution. Generally, the default options presented to you are satisfactory, so just click Continue to skip each dialog box.

When GIMP appears, you'll see five windows, as shown in Figure 5-17:

- The main GIMP toolbox window, where images are created or edited
- Layers, Channels & Paths
- Tool Options
- Brush Selection
- GIMP Tip of the Day

If you're familiar with other bitmapped graphics applications, you'll likely find GIMP so easy to use that you won't need to refer to documentation, except for help in using

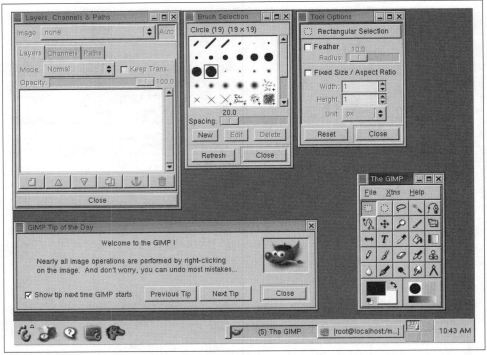

Figure 5-17. The GIMP

GIMP's advanced features. Even if you haven't used a bitmapped graphics application before, don't fret. Many people have written documentation, tutorials, and books on using GIMP, so you won't have trouble figuring out how to use it. One of the most popular helps is Karin and Olaf Kylander's *GIMP User Manual*, known as the *GUM*. To access the GUM and many other GIMP documents, see *http://gimp.org/docs.html*. If you're interested in using GIMP regularly, see Sven Neumann's *GIMP Pocket Reference* (O'Reilly & Associates, Inc.).

GNOME Resources

Several books have been written on GNOME. This chapter has described only a small fraction of what GNOME can do. The following additional resources are available:

GNOME User's Guide
> The official guide to using GNOME, available via the GNOME help system.
>
> *http://www.labs.redhat.com/gug/users-guide/*

GNOME Quick Start

A brief introduction to GNOME's main features.

http://www.labs.redhat.com/gug/users-guide/quickstart.html

The GNOME FAQ

Written by Telsa Gwynne, the GNOME FAQ provides answers to some of the most commonly asked questions concerning GNOME.

http://www.gnome.org/faqs/users-faq/

CHAPTER 6

Using the KDE Desktop

Red Hat Linux provides a choice of two desktop environments: GNOME and KDE. The preceding chapter explains how to configure and use the GNOME desktop environment. This chapter explains how to configure and use the KDE desktop environment and KOffice, KDE's desktop application suite.

Using KDE

Red Hat Linux initially included only GNOME; however, it now supports both GNOME and KDE. Figure 6-1 shows KDE's desktop. If your system is configured to use GNOME and you want to launch a KDE session, select "KDE" from the Session menu of the GNOME login screen. Of course, KDE must be installed in order for this to work.

KDE has a main menu icon in its panel, at the lower left of the screen. The icon features a large letter *K* superimposed on a gear. Clicking the icon reveals a menu that includes a Logout menu item. You can use the Logout menu item to terminate KDE or to switch desktop environments; you must be logged in as *root* to shut down your system.

KDE's Desktop

Figure 6-2 shows the parts of the KDE desktop, which are described in the following subsections.

The KDE Desktop

Clicking the KDE desktop with the middle mouse button causes a pop-up menu to appear; the menu lets you switch virtual desktops or rearrange the current desktop. Right-clicking the desktop causes a different pop-up menu to appear; this menu lets you create desktop shortcuts and perform a variety of other functions. The desktop

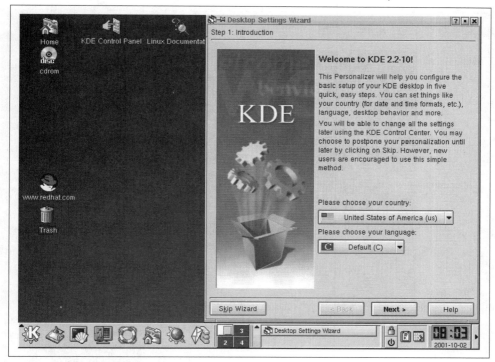

Figure 6-1. The KDE desktop

includes a variety of icons and folders. The specific icons and folders that appear may vary depending on the software installed on your system and your KDE configuration.

KDE Control Panel icon

Clicking the KDE Control Panel icon launches KDE's Control Panel, which lets you configure your system. The functions of the KDE Control Panel resemble those of GNOME's Start Here facility.

Home Directory icon

The Home Directory icon enables you to view your home directory by using KDE's file manager, Konqueror. Konqueror is described in more detail later in this chapter.

Linux Documentation icon

Clicking the Linux Documentation icon launches KDE's browser, Konqueror, to let you view a mirror of the Linux Documentation Project (LDP) web site. The LDP publishes many Linux-related documents including HOWTOs and mini-HOWTOs.

www.redhat.com icon

Clicking the www.redhat.com icon launches KDE's browser, Konqueror, to let you view Red Hat's web site, *http://www.redhat.com*.

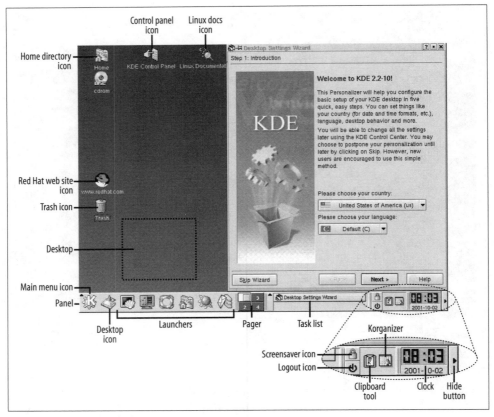

Figure 6-2. The KDE desktop

Trash icon

Clicking the Trash icon lets you view the contents of the directory in which KDE stores files move to the Trash bin by using Konqueror. Files deleted by using Konqueror or the *rm* command are not stored in the trash; they are immediately deleted.

Drive icons

If you have permission to mount a CD-ROM or floppy drive, your desktop includes an icon representing the drive. If you click the icon, a pop-up menu appears. The menu lets you mount the device.

The KDE Panel

KDE's panel appears along the bottom edge of the display. The panel normally contains the main menu icon, launch icons, the pager, the task list, a clock, and a hide button. The icon that resembles a life buoy launches KDE's help system.

Moving your mouse over an icon in the Panel displays a message informing you of the icon's function.

Main menu icon

As mentioned, the main menu icon features a letter *K* superimposed on a gear. Left-clicking the main menu presents a menu from which you can choose a variety of programs. Several of the menu items are submenus; selecting such a menu item pops up a new menu to the side of the original menu item.

Desktop icon

The desktop icon, which is located immediately to the right of the main menu icon, hides any open windows, letting you view the desktop contents that the windows would otherwise obscure. To view the desktop, click the desktop icon. To restore the open windows, click the desktop icon a second time.

Launch icons

The KDE panel contains a variety of launch icons. The specific icons that appear vary, depending on the applications you've installed and the KDE configuration. Among the icons you're likely to see are these:

- KDE Terminal icon, which launches a KDE Terminal
- KDE Control Center icon, which launches the KDE Control Center used to configure KDE
- KDE Help icon, which launches Konqueror to let you view help information
- Home directory icon, which launches Konqueror to let you view your home directory
- Konqueror icon, which launches Konqueror
- KMail icon, which launches the KMail email client

Pager

Like GNOME, KDE features a virtual desktop that's larger than your system's monitor. The pager lets you navigate the virtual desktop. By default, one of four virtual desktop pages is visible. The four pager buttons let you select a different desktop page. The button that shows window contents rather than a numeral indicates the page you're currently viewing as your desktop. To view a different page, simply left-click the button that represents the desktop page you want to view.

Task list

The task list contains a button for each active task. Clicking a task's button raises the task's window to the front of the screen so you can view it.

Clock

The KDE clock gives the current date and time.

Screensaver icon

The screensaver icon lets you lock the console and display a screensaver. To regain access to the console, you must type your password. This function is useful when you leave your computer unattended, because it prevents unauthorized persons from using the computer during your absence.

Logout icon

The shutdown icon enables you to conveniently shutdown your system. To log out of KDE, left-click the icon.

Clipboard tool

The Clipboard tools lets you view the contents of KDE's clipboard.

Korganizer icon

The Korganizer icon launches Korganizer, a KDE application that provides a scheduler and to do list.

Hide button

You can hide and restore KDE's panel by left-clicking the hide button. Hiding the display is useful when you want to make as much of the screen as possible available to an application. Another way to gain more screen space is to right-click the panel and select the Size menu item, which lets you adjust the height of the panel.

Using Konqueror

Konqueror, KDE's browser, is used to view KDE help information. As mentioned, you can launch it by clicking the icon resembling a life buoy. Konqueror can also be used to view web pages; Figure 6-3 shows Konqueror being used to view a web page.

Konqueror is also KDE's file manager. When you click the icon that resembles a small house superimposed on a larger file folder, Konqueror displays the contents of your */home* directory, as shown in Figure 6-4.

By clicking the Tree View icon at the right of Konqueror's toolbar, you can cause Konqueror to display information in a format that resembles the familiar two-pane layout used by the Microsoft Windows Explorer and GNOME's Nautilus. However, Konqueror uses only a single pane to display the directory tree and the files it contains. To select a directory, click it.

You can choose from among several other views by using the View icons or menu. For instance, in addition to its default mode showing files and directories as icons, Konqueror has a detailed mode that shows more information, including file size, modification time, and access modes (permissions). To change modes, click either of the two icons at the far right of Konqueror's icon bar. The rightmost icon selects icon mode; the icon to its left selects detailed mode. Figure 6-5 shows Konqueror's detailed mode in Tree View.

Figure 6-3. KDE's Konqueror

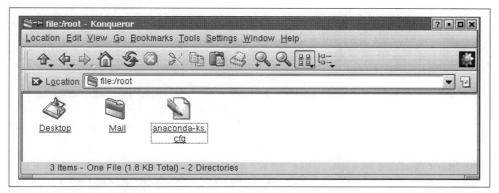

Figure 6-4. Konqueror displaying the contents of a directory

Konqueror can be used to move, copy, rename, and delete files and directories. You can perform these and other file operations in a variety of ways. To rename a file, right-click on the file's icon and select Rename from the pop-up menu. Simply type the new name and press **Enter**. To delete a file, right-click on the file and select Delete from the pop-up menu. A dialog box asks you to confirm your decision. Alternatively, you can send the file to KDE's trash can, which resembles the Windows

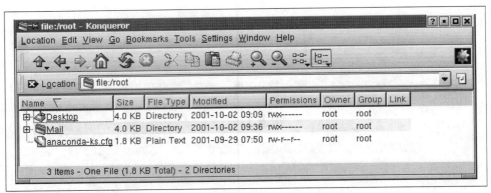

Figure 6-5. Konqueror's detailed mode in Tree View

Recycle Bin. You can retrieve files sent to the trash can, if you do so promptly. Click the trash can to view or move its contents.

You can move, copy, or delete multiple files in a single operation. Select the files by holding down the **Ctrl** key as you select them one at a time by right-clicking them. Alternatively, you can click and drag the cursor around a group of files. To move or copy the selected files, simply drag them to the new location. When you release the mouse, a pop-up menu lets you specify whether you want to move or copy the files.

Rather than move or copy a file, you can use the pop-up menu to create a link. Konqueror lets you click—not double-click—on a link to launch an application on the file associated with the link. Alternatively, you can right-click on the file or link and select Open With from the pop-up menu. KDE launches a dialog box that lets you specify the application that should be launched.

Using KDE Terminal

Similar to the MS-DOS Prompt window, the KDE terminal provides a window in which you can type shell commands and view their output. To launch KDE Terminal, you can click the KDE Terminal icon on the Panel or select System → Terminal from the KDE menu. You can open multiple KDE terminal windows if you like.

The Settings menu lets you configure the operation of KDE Terminal. For example, you may find that the default font is too large or too small for your liking. If so, select Settings → Font from the KDE terminal window. Then simply select the font size you prefer.

To exit KDE Terminal, simply type **exit** on the command line and press **Enter**. Alternatively, select Quit from the File menu.

Configuring KDE

KDE is highly configurable. This section explains how to use the KDE Panel, the KDE Control Panel, the KDE Control Center, and the KDE menu editor.

The KDE Panel

It's simple to add a launcher icon to the KDE Panel. To do so, simply drag the application's icon from Konqueror to the Panel. Alternatively, you can right-click on the Panel, select Add from the pop-up menu, and choose a program from the menu that appears. To remove a launcher from the Panel, right-click the launcher and select Remove from the pop-up menu.

If your panel contains many launchers, it may become crowded and confusing. To remedy this, you can create a child panel, like that shown in Figure 6-6. To do so, right-click the Panel and select Add → Extension → Child Panel. You can move the child panel to a different edge of the screen by dragging it. Launchers can be added to a child panel by dragging and dropping, just as you add them to the Panel. To remove a child panel and its contents, right-click the hide button at the end of the child panel and select Remove from the pop-up menu.

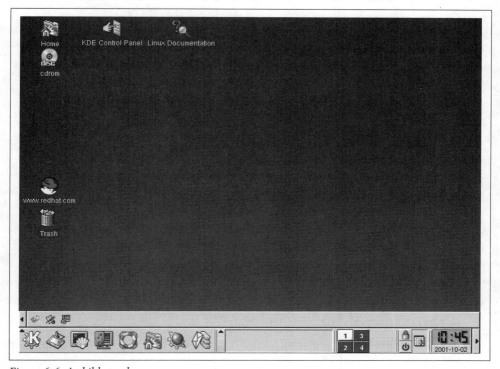

Figure 6-6. A child panel

The KDE Control Panel

To launch the KDE Control Panel, click the KDE Control Panel desktop icon. The Control Panel, as shown in Figure 6-7, appears.

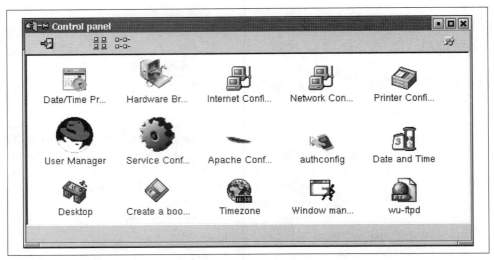

Figure 6-7. The KDE Control Panel

To launch a Control Panel applet, click its icon. The Control Panel applets and their uses include:

Date/Time Properties
Set the current date and time and configure time synchronization

Hardware Browser
View hardware devices and configuration

Internet Configuration
Configure modems and dial-up connections

Network Configuration
Configure networking

Printer Configuration
Configure the printer

User Manager
Configure user accounts

Service Configuration
Configure system and network services

Apache Configuration
Configure the Apache web server

authconfig
Configure NIS, LDAP, and Hesiod authentication

Date and Time
  Set the current date and time

Desktop
  Configure the desktop

Create a boot disk
  Create a diskette capable of booting the system

Timezone
  Specify the time zone

Window manager
  Configure the window manager

wu-ftpd
  Configure the FTP server

Applets that perform system administration functions generally require that you be logged in as *root*; otherwise, they won't operate properly. Most of these functions are also performed by other Red Hat Linux facilities. Therefore, only the Desktop applet is described here. See the sources listed at the end of the chapter for further information about the KDE Control Panel applets.

The KDE Control Center

You can launch the KDE Control Center by clicking the Desktop applet in the KDE Control Panel or by clicking the KDE Panel icon that resembles a terminal with a superimposed circuit board. Figure 6-8 shows the KDE Control Center.

The Control Center user interface features two panes. The left pane presents a hierarchically structured set of configuration categories, and the right pane displays information pertaining to the current choice.

Using Control Center, you can:

- Configure file browsing
- Obtain help in using KDE
- View system information
- Configure KDE's look and feel
- Configure networking
- Configure peripheral devices, such as the keyboard and mouse
- Personalize a variety of system configuration items, including email-related items
- Configure power control
- Configure sound
- Configure Konqueror's web browsing features and other web- and network-related configuration items

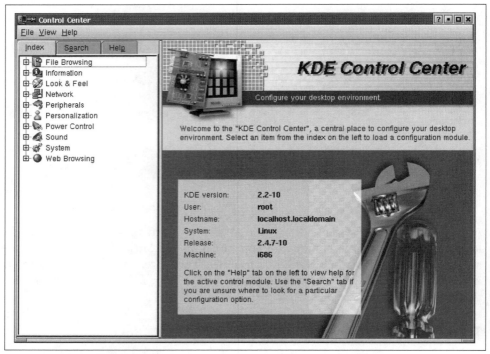

Figure 6-8. The KDE Control Center

Simply select the configuration category by clicking in the left pane. You can then revise the configuration parameters by specifying the desired values in the right pane. The contents of the right pane vary depending on the current selection in the left pane.

KDE Themes

For the benefit of those who enjoy eye candy, KDE supports themes. Visit *http://kde. themes.org* to learn more about and obtain themes for KDE.

When you find a theme you like, download it and save it to the */tmp* directory.* If the file has an extension other than *ktheme*, you must unpack it. To do so, navigate to the file using Konqueror and click it. Click as necessary to open folders and navigate to the *ktheme* file. Then, drag the *ktheme* file to the desktop.

Finally, launch the KDE Control Center and choose Look & Feel → Theme Manager from its menu. When the Theme Selector appears in the right pane, click Add, and navigate to the file you dragged to the desktop, then click OK. If the theme is compatible, you'll now see it listed in the Installer box. To try it, click once on the theme name and click Apply.

---

* The theme is contained in a *.tar.gz* file, which is commonly referred to as a tarball.

The KDE Main Menu

You can configure KDE's main menu by using the KDE menu editor. To launch the menu editor, select System → Menu Editor from the KDE main menu. The menu editor window (Figure 6-9) has two panes. The left pane of the menu editor hierarchically displays the menu tree, and the right pane shows information pertaining to the currently selected menu item. You can drag and drop to reposition menu items and submenus. You can use the New Item or New Submenu icons to create new menu entries.

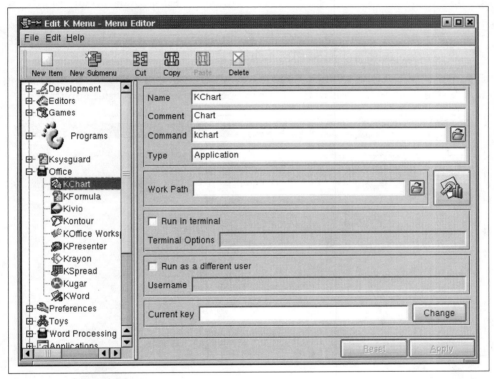

Figure 6-9. The menu editor

KOffice

KOffice, KDE's desktop application suite, is an open source project aimed at producing a complete desktop suite. Some of the most prominent KOffice components are:

- KWord, a word processor
- KSpread, a spreadsheet application
- KPresenter, a presentation graphics application
- KChart, an application for producing charts and graphs

Installing KOffice

If you selected the KDE desktop during system installation, the installation program should have installed KOffice. However, you can install KOffice manually. To do so, use the RPM Package Manager, as explained in Chapter 10.

Using KOffice

The standard KDE panel includes icons that launch popular KOffice applications. KOffice applications also appear on the KDE menu; select Main Menu → Office to view them.

Perhaps the most convenient way to use KOffice is via the KOffice Workspace, which you can launch from the KDE menu.

Figure 6-10 shows the KOffice Workspace, which provides icons for KOffice along its left side. It also supports drag-and-drop operations among KOffice applications.

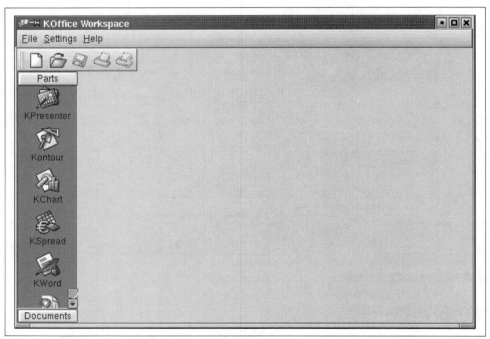

Figure 6-10. The KOffice Workspace

To launch a KOffice application, click the corresponding icon. Figure 6-11 shows KWord's main screen, which appears if you click the KWord icon. Notwithstanding its relatively weak support for import and export, KWord is a sophisticated and easy-to-use word processor.

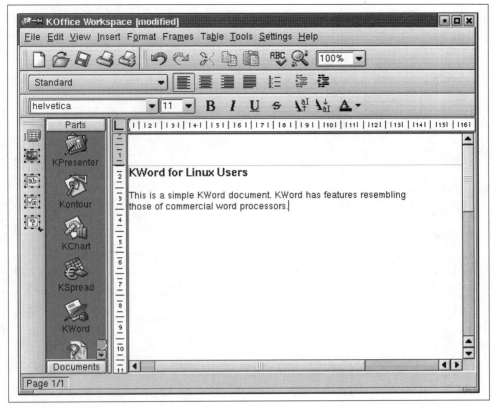

Figure 6-11. KWord

Unlike most word processors, KWord is frame-oriented rather than page-oriented. Adobe PageMaker and some other desktop publishing applications share this characteristic. In a frame-oriented application, text fills frames and can be directed to flow from one frame to another. Frames make it easy to construct multicolumn layouts that contain pictures or graphics that interrupt the flow of text.

KWord also supports familiar word processing features such as numbered paragraphs, indents, page headers and footers, tables, footnotes, and endnotes. Some functions, such as tab settings, are not yet fully operational.

Figure 6-12 shows KSpread, the KOffice spreadsheet application. Like Gnumeric, KSpread's functionality and user interface resemble those of Microsoft Excel. KSpread is in a quite preliminary state of development. Its web page (*http://www.koffice.org/kspread*) does not yet include a description or list of features.

Figure 6-13 shows KPresenter, KOffice's presentation graphics application. The functions provided by KPresenter resemble those of Microsoft PowerPoint. However, KPresenter is still in beta release; therefore, many functions remain to be implemented. For example, it cannot yet import or export PowerPoint files or those of

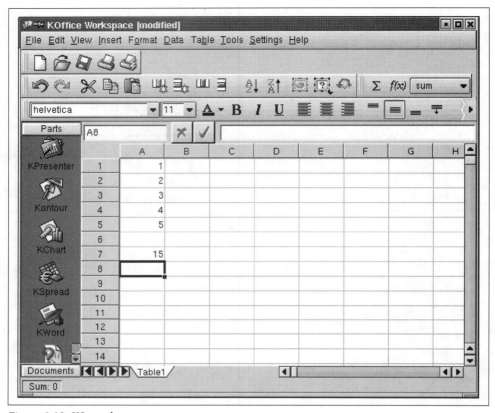

Figure 6-12. KSpread

other popular presentation graphics applications. The program does support text as well as graphics objects in popular formats including BMP, GIF, JPEG, PNG, PNM, WMF, XBM, and XPM. And it can produce an HTML slide show version of a presentation. Based on the capabilities and quality of the beta release, the full release may prove to be a useful application.

KDE Resources

Entire books have been written on using KDE, so this chapter has provided a mere overview of KDE's many features and facilities. The following additional resources are available via KDE's help information function:

Introduction to KDE

A brief overview of how to use KDE is available via Konqueror.

KDE User's Guide

The most comprehensive existing KDE documentation is available via Konqueror or online:

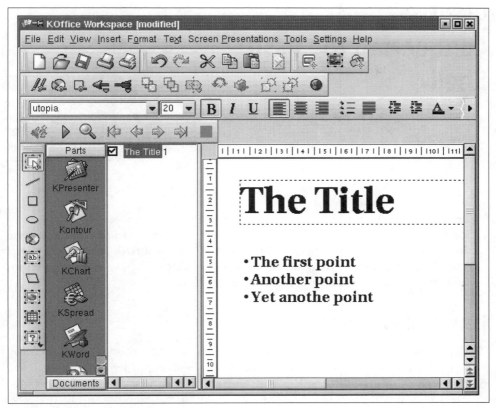

Figure 6-13. KPresenter

http://www.kde.org/documentation/userguide

The KDE FAQ

Answers to some of the most commonly asked questions concerning KDE can be found online:

http://www.kde.org/documentation/faq

Use these resources to learn more about KDE. Also, visit the KDE web site, *http://www.kde.org*. There you'll find more information—and more current information—about KDE and the KDE project.

CHAPTER 7

Conquering the bash Shell

The real power of Linux lies in the shell. So, if you aspire to master Linux, you must conquer the shell. Once you've done so, you'll have the ability to direct your system to do almost anything. This chapter describes the powerful *bash* shell. The chapter also briefly explains shell variables, shell scripts, and shell aliases, preparing you for an in-depth, continuing study of Linux and its shell.

Issuing Shell Commands

The component of Linux that interprets and executes commands is called the *shell*. Usually, you'll access the shell via a terminal window, as explained in Chapters 5 and 6. However, the section "Using Virtual Consoles" later in this chapter explains how to use a virtual console. Linux supports a variety of different shells, but the most popular is the *bash* shell. The Linux *bash* shell presents the user with a *Command Line Interface* (CLI). CLIs are familiar to Windows users who have worked in the MS-DOS window, and indeed the Windows MS-DOS Prompt window is a kind of command-line shell. The Linux *bash* shell works much like the MS-DOS Prompt window; you type text commands and the system responds by displaying text replies. As your first Linux command, type **w** and press **Enter**. Your contents of the terminal window should look something like this:

```
[bill@home bill]$ w
11:12am  up 6 min,  1 user,  load average: 0.00, 0.08, 0.05
USER     TTY      FROM     LOGIN@   IDLE   JCPU   PCPU  WHAT
bill     tty1              11:11am  0.00s  0.20s  0.11s -bash
```

The **w** command tells Linux to display the system status and a list of all system users. In the example, the output of the command tells you that it's now 11:12 a.m., that the system has been up for six minutes, and that only one user—*bill*—is currently logged in. Notice that the command output is very terse, packing much information into a few lines. Such output is typical of Linux commands. At first, you may find Linux output cryptic and difficult to read, but over time you'll grow to appreciate the efficiency with which Linux communicates information.

Linux provides many commands besides the **w** command—so many that you may despair of learning and recalling them. Actually, the number of commands you'll use regularly is fairly small. Soon, these will become second nature to you.

Try a second command, the **date** command:

```
[bill@home bill]$ date
Fri Oct 5 11:15:20 PST 2001
```

The **date** command displays the current date and time.

If you find working with MS-DOS distasteful or intimidating, you may not immediately enjoy working with the Linux command line. However, give yourself some time to adjust. The Linux command line has several features that make it easier to use, and more powerful, than MS-DOS.

Correcting Commands

Sometimes you may type a command incorrectly, causing Linux to display an error message. For example, suppose you typed **dat** instead of **date**:

```
[bill@home bill]$ dat
bash: dat: command not found
```

In such a case, carefully check the spelling of the command and try again. If you notice an error before pressing **Enter**, you can use the **Backspace** key to return to the point of the error and then type the correct characters.

Just as a web browser keeps track of recently visited sites, the *bash* shell keeps track of recently issued commands in what's known as the *history list*. You can scroll back through *bash*'s history by using the Up arrow key, or back down using the Down arrow key, just as you would with the Back and Forward buttons on a web browser. To reissue a command, scroll to it and press **Enter**. If you like, you can modify the command before reissuing it. When typing shell commands, you have access to a minieditor that resembles the DOSKEY editor of MS-DOS. This minieditor lets you revise command lines by typing key commands. Table 7-1 summarizes some useful key commands interpreted by the shell. The key commands let you access a list of the 500 most recently executed commands, saved in the *~/.bash_history* file.

Table 7-1. Useful Editing Keystrokes

Keystroke(s)	Function
Up arrow	Move back one command in the history list.
Down arrow	Move forward one command in the history list.
Left arrow	Move back one character.
Right arrow	Move forward one character.
Backspace	Delete previous character.

Table 7-1. Useful Editing Keystrokes (continued)

Keystroke(s)	Function
Tab	Attempt to complete the current word, interpreting it as a filename, username, variable name, or command as determined by the context.
Ctrl-A	Move to beginning of line.
Ctrl-D	Delete current character.
Ctrl-E	Move to end of line.
Ctrl-L	Clear the screen, placing the current line at the top of the screen.
Ctrl-U	Delete from beginning of line.
Ctrl-Y	Retrieve last item deleted.
Esc .	Insert last word of previous command.
Esc ?	List the possible completions.
Esc b	Move back one word.
Esc d	Delete current word.
Esc f	Move forward one word.
Esc k	Delete to end of line.

One of the most useful editing keystrokes, **Tab**, can also be used when typing a command. If you type the first part of a filename and press **Tab**, the shell will attempt to locate files with names matching the characters you've typed. If something exists, the shell fills out the partially typed name with the proper characters. You can then press **Enter** to execute the command or continue typing other options and arguments. This feature, called either *filename completion* or *command completion*, makes the shell much easier to use.

In addition to keystrokes for editing the command line, the shell interprets several keystrokes that control the operation of the currently executing program. Table 7-2 summarizes these keystrokes. For example, typing **Ctrl-C** generally cancels execution of a program. This keystroke command is handy, for example, when a program is taking too long to execute and you'd prefer to try something else.

Table 7-2. Useful Control Keystrokes

Keystroke	Function
Ctrl-C	Sends an interrupt signal to the currently executing command, which generally responds by terminating itself.
Ctrl-D	Sends an end-of-file to the currently executing command; use this keystroke to terminate console input.
Ctrl-Z	Suspends the currently executing program.

Several other special characters control the operation of the shell, as shown in Table 7-3. The # and ; characters are most often used in shell scripts, which you'll learn about in more detail later in this chapter. The & character is useful for running a command as a background process.

Table 7-3. Other Special Shell Characters

Character	Function
#	Marks the command as a comment, which the shell ignores.
;	Separates commands, letting you enter several commands on a single line.
&	Placed at the end of a command, causes the command to execute as a background process, so that a new shell prompt appears immediately after the command is entered.

Working with the Linux Command Prompt

Linux commands share a simple, common structure. This section describes their common structure and explains how you can obtain helpful information about the commands available to you.

Commands and Arguments

The general form of a shell command line is this:

```
command [options] [arguments]
```

The **command** determines what operation the shell will perform and the *options* and *arguments*—which, as indicated by the enclosing brackets, may or may not appear—customize, or fine-tune, the operation. Sometimes the **command** specifies a program file that will be launched and run; such a command is called an *external command*. Linux generally stores these files in */bin*, */usr/bin*, or */usr/local/bin*. System administration commands are generally stored in */sbin* or */usr/sbin*, which are included by default in the path of the root user. When a command specifies a program file, the shell passes any specified arguments to the program, which scans and interprets them, adjusting its operation accordingly.

However, some commands are not program files; instead they are built-in commands interpreted by the shell itself. One important way in which shells differ is in the built-in commands that they support. Later in this section, you'll learn about some of *bash*'s built-in commands.

The name of a Linux command almost always consists of lowercase letters and digits. Most commands let you specify options or arguments. However, in any given case, you may not need to do so. For example, typing the **w** command without options and arguments causes Linux to display a list of current users.

 Remember, Linux commands are case-sensitive; be sure to type each character of a command in the proper case.

Options modify the way that a command works. Many options consist of a single letter, prefixed by a dash. Often, you can specify more than one option; when you do so, you separate each option with a space or tab. For example, the **–h** option of the **w** command causes the output of the command to omit the header lines that give the time and the names of the fields:

```
[bill@home bill]$ w -h
```

The **w –h** command/option pair simply prints a list of users without the header lines.

Arguments specify filenames or other targets that direct the action of the command. For example, the **w** command lets you specify a username as an argument, which causes the command to list only logins that pertain to the specified user:

```
[bill@home bill]$ w bill
```

Some commands let you specify a series of arguments; you must separate each argument by typing a space or tab. For example, the following command prints a list of logins by the root user, without header lines:

```
[bill@home bill]$ w -h bill
```

When a command includes several arguments, a command may not fit on a single line. However, you can continue typing when you reach the end of a line, because the shell automatically wraps your input to the next line. If you find line wrapping disconcerting, you can type a backslash (\) at the end of a line, press **Enter**, and continue typing on the next line. The backslash is the shell's line continuation character; the shell sees lines joined by a backslash as though they were a single line.

Getting Help

Because Linux provides so many commands, and because Linux commands provide so many possible options, you can't expect to recall all of them. To help you, Linux provides the **man** and **apropos** commands, which let you access a help database that describes commands and their options.

Using man

Each Linux command is described by a special file called a *manual page*. The manual pages (or *manpages*) are stored in a group of subdirectories comprising a help database. To access this database, you use the **man** command, which resembles the MS-DOS **help** command. For example, to get help on using the **w** command, type:

```
[bill@home bill]$ man w
```

Figure 7-1 shows the resulting output, which the command displays one page at a time. Notice the colon prompt that appears at the bottom left of the screen. To page forward, press the **Space** key; to page backward, press the **B** key. To exit the **man** program, press the **Q** key.

Manpages are organized according to a common format. At the beginning of a manpage, you'll find the name of the page and the section of the database from which the page comes, shown in parentheses. For example, Figure 7-1 shows "W(1)"

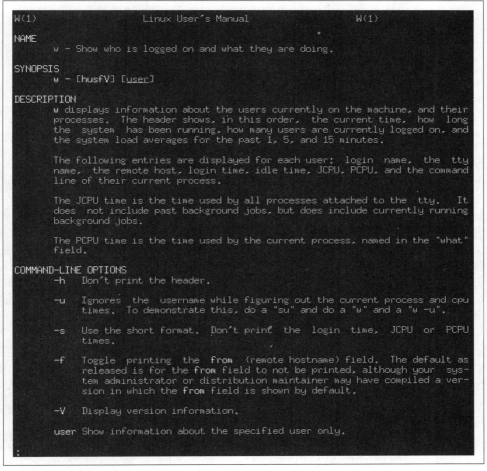

```
W(1)                    Linux User's Manual                    W(1)

NAME
      w - Show who is logged on and what they are doing.

SYNOPSIS
      w - [husfV] [user]

DESCRIPTION
      w displays information about the users currently on the machine, and their
      processes. The header shows, in this order, the current time, how  long
      the  system  has been running, how many users are currently logged on, and
      the system load averages for the past 1, 5, and 15 minutes.

      The following entries are displayed for each user:  login  name,  the  tty
      name,  the remote host, login time, idle time, JCPU, PCPU, and the command
      line of their current process.

      The JCPU time is the time used by all processes attached to the  tty.   It
      does  not  include past background jobs, but does include currently running
      background jobs.

      The PCPU time is the time used by the current process, named in the "what"
      field.

COMMAND-LINE OPTIONS
      -h   Don't print the header.

      -u   Ignores  the  username while figuring out the current process and cpu
           times.  To demonstrate this, do a "su" and do a "w" and a "w -u".

      -s   Use the short format.  Don't print  the  login  time,  JCPU  or  PCPU
           times.

      -f   Toggle  printing  the  from  (remote hostname) field. The default as
           released is for the from field to not be printed, although your  sys-
           tem administrator or distribution maintainer may have compiled a ver-
           sion in which the from field is shown by default.

      -V   Display version information.

      user Show information about the specified user only.
```

Figure 7-1. A typical manpage

in the upper-left and -right corners. This means that you're looking in section 1 of the manpage (the section pertaining to commands) for the **w** command. Table 7-4 describes the sections of the manual page database; most sections are primarily of interest to programmers. As a user and system administrator, you'll be interested primarily in sections 1 and 8.

Table 7-4. Manual Page Sections

Section	Description
1	Executable programs and shell commands
2	System calls (provided by the kernel)
3	Library calls (provided by system libraries)
4	Special files (for example, device files)

Table 7-4. Manual Page Sections (continued)

Section	Description
5	File formats and conventions
6	Games
7	Macro packages and conventions
8	System administration commands
9	Nonstandard kernel routines
N	Tcl/Tk commands

Next in the output is the name and a brief description of the command. Then there's a synopsis of the command, which shows the options and arguments that you can specify. Brackets enclose parts of a command that you can choose to include or omit. Next is a detailed description of the operation of the command, followed by a description of its options.

As you're learning your way around Linux, you may find it convenient to reserve a virtual console for running the **man** command. That way, you can enter commands in a separate virtual console, switching between consoles to refresh your recollection of the options and arguments of commands as you type them.

Using apropos

The **man** command searches the manual pages and displays detailed information about a specified command. The **apropos** command also searches the manual pages; however, it displays summary information about manpages that contain a specified keyword. The search is limited to the short description that appears at the beginning of each manpage. For example, typing the command:

```
[bill@home bill]$ apropos samba
```

will display a list of manpages containing the word *samba*, as shown in Figure 7-2.

The **apropos** command is useful when you don't recall the name of a Linux command. By typing a related keyword, you can obtain a list of commands and search the list for the command you need.

Using Commands That Work with Directories

Now that you understand the fundamentals of issuing Linux commands, you're ready to learn some commands that work with directories. Rather than simply reading this section, you should log in to your Linux system and try the commands for yourself. By doing so, you will begin to develop skill in working with shell commands.

Displaying the working directory

To display the current working directory, issue the **pwd** command. The **pwd** command requires no options or arguments.

```
utime              .(2)  - change access and/or modification times of an inode
utimes [utime]     (2)   - change access and/or modification times of an inode
wtimeout [curs_inopts] (3x) - curses input options
zdump              (8)   - time zone dumper
zic                (8)   - time zone compiler
XDeviceTimeCoord [XGetDeviceMotionEvents] (3x) - get device motion history
XTimeCoord [XSendEvent] (3x) - send events and pointer motion history structure
XtAddInput         (3x)  - register input, timeout, and workprocs
XtAddTimeout [XtAddInput] (3x) - register input, timeout, and workprocs
XtAppAddTimeOut    (3x)  - register and remove timeouts
XtAppGetSelectionTimeout (3x) - set and obtain selection timeout values
XtAppSetSelectionTimeout [XtAppGetSelectionTimeout] (3x) - set and obtain selection timeou
t values
XtGetMultiClickTime [XtSetMultiClickTime] (3x) - set and get multi-click times
XtGetSelectionTimeout (3x) - set and obtain selection timeout values
XtLastEventProcessed (3x) - last event, last timestamp processed
XtLastTimestampProcessed [XtLastEventProcessed] (3x) - last event, last timestamp processe
d
XtRemoveTimeOut [XtAppAddTimeOut] (3x) - register and remove timeouts
XtSetMultiClickTime (3x) - set and get multi-click times
XtSetSelectionTimeout [XtGetSelectionTimeout] (3x) - set and obtain selection timeout valu
es
t3d                (1)   - clock using flying balls to display the time
Benchmark          (3)   - benchmark running times of code
CPAN::FirstTime    (3)   - Utility for CPAN::Config file Initialization
Time::Local        (3)   - efficiently compute time from local and GMT time
Time::gmtime       (3)   - by-name interface to Perl's built-in gmtime() function
Time::localtime    (3)   - by-name interface to Perl's built-in localtime() function
Time::tm           (3)   - internal object used by Time::gmtime and Time::localtime
base               (3)   - Establish IS-A relationship with base class at compile time
fields             (3)   - compile-time class fields
lib                (3)   - manipulate @INC at compile time
timeit [Benchmark] (3)   - run a chunk of code and see how long it goes
timethese [Benchmark] (3) - run several chunks of code several times
timethis [Benchmark] (3) - run a chunk of code several times
[root@linux RPMS]# apropos samba
Samba [samba]      (7)   - A Windows SMB/CIFS fileserver for UNIX
lmhosts            (5)   - The Samba NetBIOS hosts file
make_smbcodepage   (1)   - Construct a codepage file for Samba
make_unicodemap    (1)   - Construct a unicode map file for Samba
smb.conf [smb]     (5)   - The configuration file for the Samba suite
smbpasswd          (5)   - The Samba encrypted password file
smbstatus          (1)   - report on current Samba connections
swat               (8)   - Samba Web Administration Tool
[root@linux RPMS]#
```

Figure 7-2. Output of the apropos command

```
[bill@home bill]$ pwd
/root
```

The **pwd** command displays the absolute pathname of the current working directory.

Changing the working directory

To change the working directory, issue the **cd** command, specifying the pathname of the new working directory as an argument. You can use an absolute or relative pathname. For example, to change the working directory to the */bin* directory, type:

```
[bill@home bill]$ cd /bin
[bill@home /bin]#
```

Notice how the prompt changes to indicate that */bin* is now the working directory.

You can quickly return to your home directory by issuing the **cd** command without an argument:

```
[bill@home /bin]# cd
[bill@home bill]$
```

Again, notice how the prompt changes to indicate the new working directory.

If you attempt to change the working directory to a directory that doesn't exist, Linux displays an error message:

```
[bill@home bill]$ cd nowhere
bash: nowhere: No such file or directory
```

Displaying directory contents

To display the contents of a directory, you use the **ls** command. The **ls** command provides many useful options that let you tailor its operation and output to your liking.

The simplest form of the **ls** command takes no options or arguments. It simply lists the contents of the working directory, including files and subdirectories (your own output will differ, reflecting the files present in your working directory):

```
[bill@home bill]$ ls
GNUstep             firewall            sniff
Xrootenv.0          linux               ssh-1.2.26
audio.cddb          mail                ssh-1.2.26.tar.gz
audio.wav           mirror              support
axhome              mirror-2.8.tar.gz   temp
conf                nlxb3181.tar        test
corel               openn               test.doc
drivec.img          scan                tulip.c
dynip_2.00.tar.gz   screen-3.7.6-0.i386.rpm  win98
```

Here, the output is presented in lexical (dictionary) order, as three columns of data. Notice that filenames beginning with uppercase letters appear before those beginning with lowercase letters.

A more sophisticated form of the **ls** command that includes the –l option displays descriptive information along with the filenames, as shown in Figure 7-3.

The first line of the output shows the amount of disk space used by the working directory and its subdirectories, measured in 1 KB blocks. Each remaining line describes a single file or directory. The columns are:

Type
> The type of file: a directory (d), or an ordinary file (-). If your system supports color, Linux displays output lines that pertain to directories in blue and lines that pertain to files in white.

Access modes
> The access mode, which determines which users can access the file or directory. You'll learn more about access modes, links, and groups in subsequent sections of this chapter.

Links
> The number of files or directories linked to this one.

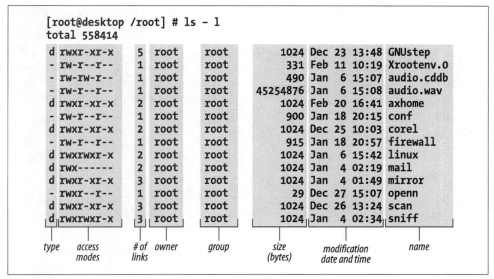

```
[root@desktop /root] # ls - l
total 558414
d rwxr-xr-x   5  root    root      1024  Dec 23 13:48  GNUstep
- rw-r--r--    1  root    root       331  Feb 11 10:19  Xrootenv.0
- rw-rw-r--    1  root    root       490  Jan  6 15:07  audio.cddb
- rw-r--r--    1  root    root  45254876  Jan  6 15:08  audio.wav
d rwxr-xr-x   2  root    root      1024  Feb 20 16:41  axhome
- rw-r--r--    1  root    root       900  Jan 18 20:15  conf
d rwxr-xr-x   2  root    root      1024  Dec 25 10:03  corel
- rw-r--r--    1  root    root       915  Jan 18 20:57  firewall
d rwxrwxr-x   2  root    root      1024  Jan  6 15:42  linux
d rwx------   2  root    root      1024  Jan  4 02:19  mail
d rwxr-xr-x   3  root    root      1024  Jan  4 01:49  mirror
- rwxr--r--    1  root    root        29  Dec 27 15:07  openn
d rwxr-xr-x   3  root    root      1024  Dec 26 13:24  scan
d rwxrwxr-x   3  root    root      1024  Jan  4 02:34  sniff
```

| type | access modes | # of links | owner | group | size (bytes) | modification date and time | name |

Figure 7-3. Output of the ls command

Group
> The group that owns the file or directory.

Size
> The size of the file or directory, in bytes.

Modification date
> The date and time when the file or directory was last modified.

Name
> The name of the file or directory.

If a directory contains many files, the listing will fill more than one screen. To view the output one screen at a time, use the following command:

```
[bill@home bill]$ ls -l | less
```

This command employs the pipe redirector, sending output of the **ls** subcommand to the **less** subcommand, which presents the output one screen at a time. You can control the operation of the **less** command with the following keys:

- **Space** moves you one page forward.
- **b** moves you one page back.
- **q** exits the program and returns you to the command prompt.

If you want to list a directory other than the working directory, you can type the name of the directory as an argument of the **ls** command. Linux displays the contents of the directory but does not change the working directory. Similarly, you can display information about a file by typing its name as an argument of the **ls** command. Moreover, the **ls** command accepts an indefinite number of arguments, so you can type a series of directories and filenames as arguments, separating each with one or more spaces or tabs.

When the name of a directory or file begins with a dot (.), the output of the **ls** command does not normally include the directory or file, because the file is *hidden*. To cause the output of the **ls** command to include hidden directories and files, use the –**a** option. For example, to list all the files and subdirectories in the current directory—including hidden ones—type:

```
[bill@home bill]$ ls -a -l
```

If you prefer, you can combine the –**a** and –**l** options, typing the command like this:

```
[bill@home bill]$ ls -al
```

A user's home directory generally includes several hidden files containing configuration information for various programs. For example, the *.profile* file contains configuration information for the Linux shell.

The **ls** command provides a host of additional useful options; see its manual page for details.

Creating a directory

You can create directories by using the **mkdir** command. Just type the name of the new directory as an argument of the command. Linux creates the directory as a subdirectory of the working directory. For example, this command creates a subdirectory named *office*:

```
[bill@home bill]$ mkdir office
```

If you don't want to create the new directory as a subdirectory of the working directory, type an absolute or relative pathname as the argument. For example, to create a directory named */root/documents*, type:

```
[root@desktop /root]# mkdir /root/documents
```

The name of a directory or file must follow certain rules. For example, it must not contain a slash (/) character. Directory names and filenames usually include letters (either uppercase or lowercase), digits, dots, and underscores (_). You can use other characters, such as spaces and hyphens, but such names present problems, because the shell gives them special meaning. If you simply must use a name containing special characters, enclose the name within single quotes ('). The quotes don't become part of the name that is stored on the disk. This technique is useful when accessing files on a Windows filesystem; otherwise, you'll have trouble working with files in directories such as *My Documents*, which have pathnames containing spaces.

Most MS-DOS filenames contain a dot, but most Linux filenames do not. In MS-DOS, the dot separates the main part of the filename from a part known as the extension, which denotes the type of the file. For example, the MS-DOS file *memo.txt* would contain text. Most Linux programs ignore file extensions, so Linux filenames don't require an extension. However, if you plan to send a file to someone using an operating system other than Linux, you should include an appropriate file extension, such as *.txt* for a text file.

Removing a directory

To remove a directory, use the **rmdir** command. For example, to remove *unwanted*, a subdirectory of the working directory, type:

```
[bill@home bill]$ rmdir unwanted
```

If the directory you want to delete is not a subdirectory of the working directory, remove it by typing an absolute or relative pathname.

You cannot use **rmdir** to remove a directory that contains files or subdirectories; you must first delete the files in the directory and then remove the directory itself.

Working with Files

Directories contain files and other directories. You use files to store data. This section introduces you to several useful commands for working with files.

Displaying the contents of a file

Linux files, like most Windows files, can contain text or binary information. The contents of a binary file are meaningful only to skilled programmers, but you can easily view the contents of a text file. Simply type the **cat** command, specifying the name of the text file as an argument. For example:

```
[root@desktop /root]# cat /etc/passwd
```

displays the contents of the */etc/passwd* file, which lists the valid system logons.

If a file is too large to be displayed on a single screen, the first part of the file will whiz past you and you'll see only the last few lines of the file. To avoid this, you can use the **less** command:

```
[root@desktop /root]# less /etc/passwd
```

This command displays the contents of a file in the same way the **man** command displays a manual page. You can use **Space** and the **b** key to page forward and backward through the file, and the **q** key to exit the command.

Removing a file

To remove a file, type the **rm** command, specifying the name of the file as an argument. For example:

```
[bill@home bill]$ rm badfile
```

removes the file named *badfile* contained in the working directory. If a file is located elsewhere, you can remove it by specifying an absolute or relative pathname.

Once you remove a Linux file, its contents are lost forever. Be careful to avoid removing a file that contains needed information. Better still, be sure to have a backup copy of any important data.

The –i option causes the **rm** command to prompt you to verify your decision to remove a file. If you don't trust your typing skills, you may find this option helpful. If you log in as the root user, Linux automatically supplies the –i option even if you don't type it.

Copying a file

To copy a file, use the **cp** command, specifying the name (or path) of the file you want to copy and the name (or path) to which you want to copy it. For example:

```
[root@desktop /root]# cp /etc/passwd sample
```

copies the */etc/passwd* file to a file named *sample* in the working directory.

If the destination file already exists, Linux overwrites it. You must therefore be careful to avoid overwriting a file that contains needed data. Before copying a file, use the **ls** command to ensure that no file will be overwritten; alternatively, use the –i option of the **cp** command, which prompts you to verify the overwriting of an existing file. If you log in as the root user, Linux automatically supplies the –i option even if you don't type it.

Renaming or moving a file

To rename a file, use the **mv** command, specifying the name (or path) of the file and the new name (or path). For example:

```
[bill@home bill]$ mv old new
```

renames the file named *old* as *new*. If the destination file already exists, Linux overwrites it, so you must be careful. Before moving a file, use the **ls** command to ensure that no file will be overwritten, or use the –i option of the **mv** command, which prompts you to verify the overwriting of an existing file. If you log in as the root user, Linux automatically supplies the –i option even if you don't type it.

The **mv** command can rename a directory but cannot move a directory from one device to another. To move a directory to a new device, first copy the directory and its contents and then remove the original.

Finding a file

If you know the name of a file but do not know what directory contains it, you can use the **find** command to locate the file. For example:

```
[bill@home bill]$ find . -name 'missing' -print
```

attempts to find a file named *missing*, located in (or beneath) the current working directory (.). If the command finds the file, it displays its absolute pathname.

If you know only part of the filename, you can surround the part you know with asterisks (*):

```
[bill@home bill]$ find / -name '*iss*' -print
```

This command will find any file whose name includes the characters *iss*, searching every subdirectory of the root directory (that is, the entire system).

Another command useful for finding files is **locate**. The **locate** command uses a database that is updated only daily. So it can't find recently created files, and it shows files that may have been recently deleted. But it operates much more quickly than the **find** command. To use the **locate** command, specify as the command's argument a string of characters, which need not be enclosed in quotes. The command lists all filenames in its database that contain the specified characters. For example, the command:

```
locate pass
```

lists all files containing the characters *pass*.

Printing a file

If your system includes a configured printer, you can print a file by using the **lpr** command. For example:

```
[root@desktop /root]# lpr /etc/passwd
```

sends the file */etc/passwd* to the printer. See Chapter 9 for information on configuring a printer.

If a file is lengthy, it may require some time to print. You can send other files to the printer while a file is printing. The **lpq** command lets you see what files are queued to be printed:

```
[root@desktop /root]# lpq
lp is ready and printing
Rank   Owner    Job  Files              Total Size
active root      155  /etc/passwd        1030 bytes
```

Each waiting or active file has an assigned print job number. You can use **lprm** to cancel printing of a file, by specifying the print job number. For example:

```
[root@desktop /root]# lprm 155
```

cancels printing of job number 155. However, only the user who requested that a file be printed (or the root user) can cancel printing of the file.

Working with compressed files

To save disk space and expedite downloads, you can compress a data file. By convention, compressed files are named ending in *.gz*; however, Linux doesn't require or enforce this convention.

To expand a compressed file, use the **gunzip** command. For example, suppose the file *bigfile.gz* has been compressed. Typing the command:

```
[bill@home bill]$ gunzip bigfile.gz
```

extracts the file *bigfile* and removes the file *bigfile.gz*.

To compress a file, use the **gzip** command. For example, to compress the file *bigfile*, type the command:

```
[bill@home bill]$ gzip bigfile
```

The command creates the file *bigfile.gz* and removes the file *bigfile*.

Sometimes it's convenient to store several files (or the contents of several subdirectories) in a single file. This is useful, for example, in creating a backup or archive copy of files. The Linux **tar** command creates a single file that contains data from several files. Unlike the **gzip** command, the **tar** command doesn't disturb the original files. To create a *tarfile*, as a file created by the **tar** command is called, issue a command like this:

```
tar -cvf tarfile files-or-directories
```

Substitute *tarfile* with the name of the tarfile you want to create and *files-or-directories* with a list of files and directories, separating the list elements by one or more spaces or tabs. You can use absolute or relative pathnames to specify the files or directories. By convention, the name of a tarfile ends with *.tar*, but Linux does not require or enforce this convention. Some people refer to tarfiles as *tarballs*, because they often contain multiple files.

For example, to create a tarfile named *backup.tar* that contains all the files in all subdirectories of the directory */home/bill*, type:

```
[bill@home bill]$ tar -cvf backup.tar /home/bill
```

The command creates the file *backup.tar* in the current working directory.

You can list the contents of a tarfile by using a command that follows this pattern:

```
tar -tvf tarfile | less
```

The | less causes the output to be sent to the **less** command, so that you can page through multiple pages. If the tarfile holds only a few files, you can omit | less.

To extract the contents of a tarfile, use a command that follows this pattern:

```
tar -xvf tarfile
```

This command expands the files and directories contained within the tarfile as files and subdirectories of the working directory. If a file or subdirectory already exists, it is silently overwritten.

The **tar** command provides a host of useful options; see its manpage for details.

It's common to compress a tarfile. You can easily accomplish this by specifying the options –**czvf** instead of –**cvf**. Compressed tarfiles are conventionally named ending with *.tgz*. To expand a compressed tarfile, specify the options –**xzvf** instead of –**xvf**.

The **tar** command doesn't use the ZIP method of compression common in the Windows world. However, Linux can easily work with, or even create, ZIP files. If you specified the MS-DOS Connectivity package group during installation, the installation program installed the *zip* package, which enables you to work with ZIP files. If you didn't select that package group, you can install the package manually by inserting Disc 1 of Red Hat Linux into your system's CD-ROM drive and issuing the following commands:

```
su -
mount -t iso9660 /dev/cdrom /mnt/cdrom -o ro
rpm -ivh /mnt/cdrom/RedHat/RPMS/zip-*.rpm
umount /mnt/cdrom
exit
```

To create a ZIP file that holds compressed files or directories, issue a command like this one:

zip -r *zipfile files_to_zip*

where *zipfile* names the ZIP file that will be created and *files_to_zip* specifies the files and directories to be included in the ZIP file.

To expand an existing ZIP file, issue a command like this one:

unzip *zipfile*

Working with links

Windows supports shortcuts, which let you refer to a file or directory (folder) by several names. Shortcuts also let you include a file in several directories or a subdirectory within multiple parent directories. In Linux, you accomplish these results by using the **ln** command, which links multiple names to a single file or directory. These names are called *symbolic links*, *soft links*, *symlinks*, or simply *links*.

To link a new name to an existing file or directory, type a command that follows this pattern:

ln -s *old new*

For example, suppose that the current working directory contains the file *william*. To be able to refer to this same file by the alternative name *bill*, type the command:

```
[bill@home bill]$ ln -s william bill
```

The **ls** command shows the result:

```
[bill@home bill]$ ls -l
lrwxrwxrwx  1 root     root            7 Feb 27 13:58 bill->william
-rw-r--r--  1 root     root         1030 Feb 27 13:26 william
```

The new file (*bill*) has type 1, which indicates it's a link, rather than a file or directory. Moreover, the **ls** command helpfully shows the name of the file to which the link refers (*william*).

If you omit the –s option, Linux creates what's called a *hard link*. A hard link must be stored on the same filesystem as the file to which it refers, a restriction that does not apply to symbolic links. The link count displayed by the **ls** command reflects only hard links; symbolic links are ignored. Hard links are seldom used, because soft links are more flexible.

Working with file permissions

As explained in Chapter 4, access permissions determine what operations a user can perform on a directory or file. Table 7-5 lists the possible permissions and explains the meaning of each. Recall from Chapter 4 that permissions work differently for directories than for files. For example, permission r denotes the ability to list the contents of a directory or read the contents of a file. A directory or file can have more than one permission. Only the listed permissions are granted; any other operations are prohibited. For example, a user who had file permission rw could read or write the *file* but could not execute it, as indicated by the absence of the execute permission, x. Look back to Figure 7-3 to see how the **ls** command displays permissions.

Table 7-5. Access Permissions

Permission	Meaning for a directory	Meaning for a file
r	List the directory.	Read contents.
w	Create or remove files.	Write contents.
x	Access files and subdirectories.	Execute.

The access modes of a directory of file consist of three permissions:

User/Owner
    Applies to the owner of the file

Group
    Applies to users who are members of the group assigned to the file

Other
    Applies to other users

The **ls** command lists the file access modes in the second column of its long output format, as shown in Figure 7-4. The column contains nine characters: the first three specify the access allowed the owner of the directory or file, the second three specify the access allowed users in the same group as the directory or file, and the final three specify the access allowed to other users (see Figure 7-5).

You set the access modes of a directory or file by using the **chmod** command, which has the following pattern:

```
chmod nnn directory-or-file
```

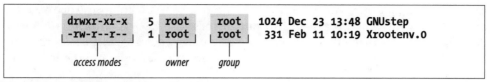

Figure 7-4. Access modes as shown by the ls command

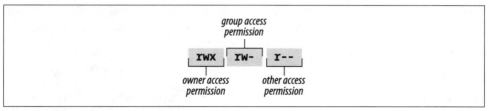

Figure 7-5. Access modes specify three permissions

The argument *nnn* is a three-digit number, which gives the access mode for the owner, group, and other users. Table 7-6 shows each possible digit and the equivalent access permission. For example, the argument **751** is equivalent to rwxr-x--x, which gives the owner every possible permission, gives the group read and execute permission, and gives other users execute permission.

Table 7-6. Numerical Access Mode Values

Value	Meaning
0	---
1	--x
2	-w-
3	-wx
4	r--
5	r-x
6	rw-
7	rwx

If you're the owner of a file or directory (or if you're the root user), you can change its ownership by using the **chown** command. For example, the following command assigns *newuser* as the owner of the file *hotpotato*:

```
[bill@home bill]$ chown newuser hotpotato
```

The owner of a file or directory (and the root user) can also change the group of a file. For example, the following command assigns *newgroup* as the new group of the file *hotpotato*:

```
[bill@home bill]$ chgrp newgroup hotpotato
```

The group you assign to a file or directory must have been previously established by the root user. The valid groups appear in the file */etc/group*, which only the *root* user can alter. The root user can assign each user to one or more groups. When you log on to the system, you are assigned to one of these groups—your *login group*—by default. To change to another of your assigned groups, you can use the *newgrp* command. For example, to change to the group named *secondgroup*, use the following command:

```
[root@desktop /root]# newgrp secondgroup
```

If you attempt to change to a group that does not exist or to which you have not been assigned, your command will fail. When you create a file or directory, it is automatically assigned your current group as its owning group.

Running programs

In Linux, as in MS-DOS and Windows, programs are stored in files. Often, you can launch a program by simply typing its filename. However, this assumes that the file is stored in one of a series of directories known as the *path*. A directory included in this series is said to be *on the path*. If you've worked with MS-DOS, you're familiar with the MS-DOS path, and the Linux path works much like it.

If the file you want to launch is not stored in a directory on the path, you can simply type the absolute pathname of the file. Linux then launches the program even though it's not on the path. If the file you want to launch is stored in the current working directory, type *./* followed by the name of the program file. Again, Linux will launch the program even though it's not on the path.

For example, suppose the program **bigdeal** is stored in the directory */home/bob*, which is the current directory and which happens to be on the path. You could launch the program with any of these commands:

```
bigdeal
./bigdeal
/home/bob/bigdeal
```

The first command assumes that the program is on the path. The second assumes that the program resides in the current working directory. The third explicitly specifies the location of the file.

Mounting and Unmounting Drives

To mount a device or partition, you use the **mount** command, which has the following pattern:

```
mount options device directory
```

The **mount** command provides many options. However, you can generally use the **mount** command without any options; consult **mount**'s manpage to learn about the available options.

The reason you can use the **mount** command without options is that the file */etc/fstab* describes your system's devices and the type of filesystem each is likely to contain. If you add a new device to your system, you may need to revise the contents of */etc/fstab* or specify appropriate options when you mount the device.

You must specify the device that you want to mount and a directory, known as the *mount point*. To make it convenient to access various devices, Linux treats a mounted device as a directory; mounting the device associates it with the named directory. For example, the following command is used to mount a CD-ROM:

```
[root@desktop /root]# mount -t iso9660 /dev/cdrom /mnt/cdrom -o ro
```

The file */dev/cdrom* is a link that points to the actual device file associated with your system's CD-ROM drive. The directory */mnt/cdrom* is created by the install program; this directory is conventionally used as the mounting point for CD-ROMs. The type of filesystem found on most CD-ROMs is **iso9660**, the value of the –**t** argument. The –**o** argument, **ro**, specifies that the filesystem is read-only, that is, it can be read but not written. The file */etc/fstab* can supply most of these arguments if they're omitted. Generally, you can mount a CD-ROM by issuing the abbreviated command:

```
mount /dev/cdrom
```

After the command has completed, you can access files and directories on the CD-ROM just as you would access ordinary files and directories on the path */mnt/cdrom*. For example, to list the top-level files and directories of the CD-ROM, simply type:

```
[root@desktop /root]# ls /mnt/cdrom
```

To mount an MS-DOS floppy disk in your *a:* drive, type:

```
[root@desktop /root]# mount -t msdos /dev/fd0 /mnt/floppy
```

To unmount a device, specify its mount point as an argument of the **umount** command. For example, to unmount a CD-ROM diskette, type:

```
[root@desktop /root]# umount /mnt/cdrom
```

Generally, only the root user can unmount a device. Moreover, a device can be unmounted only if it's not in use. For example, if a user's working directory is a directory of the device, the device cannot be unmounted.

If you can't unmount a device, check each terminal window and virtual console to see if one of them has a session that's using the device as its working directory. If so, either exit the session or change to a working directory that isn't associated with the device.

Formatting a Floppy Disk

Before you can write data on a floppy disk, you must format it. The Linux command to format a floppy disk is **fdformat**. Simply follow the command with an argument that specifies the floppy drive and the capacity of the floppy disk; the available arguments are listed in Table 7-7.

Table 7-7. Floppy Drive Designators

Designation	Meaning
/dev/fd0	3.5-inch disk in *a:* (1.44 MB)
/dev/fd0H1440	3.5-inch disk in *a:* (1.44 MB)
/dev/fd1	3.5-inch disk in *b:* (1.44 MB)
/dev/fd1H1440	3.5-inch disk in *b:* (1.44 MB)
/dev/fd1H2880	3.5-inch disk in *b:* (2.88 MB)

For example, to format a 1.44 MB floppy disk, log in as *root* and issue the command:

```
[root@desktop /root]# fdformat /dev/fd0H1440
```

Once you've formatted the floppy disk, you can place a filesystem on it. Floppy disks containing an MS-DOS filesystem are useful for transferring data between Windows and Linux. To place an MS-DOS filesystem on a formatted floppy disk, issue the command:

```
[root@desktop /root]# mkdosfs /dev/fd0
```

Once the floppy disk has been formatted and given a filesystem, you can mount it and then read and write it. Be sure you unmount the floppy disk before you remove it. Unmounting the floppy disk ensures that all pending data has been written to it; otherwise, the floppy disk may be unusable due to corrupt data.

Useful Linux Programs

This section presents several programs you may find helpful in working with your Linux system. You'll learn several commands that report system status, and you'll also learn how to use *pico*, a simple text editor.

Viewing System Information

Linux provides a number of commands that report system status. The most commonly used commands are shown in Table 7-8. These commands can help you troubleshoot system problems and identify resource bottlenecks. Although each command can be used without options or arguments, each supports options and arguments that let you customize operation and output; consult the appropriate manpage for details.

Table 7-8. Useful System Commands

Command	Function
df	Shows the amount of free disk space (in 1 KB blocks) on each mounted filesystem
du	Shows the amount of disk space (in 1 KB blocks) used by the working directory and its subdirectories
free	Shows memory usage statistics, including total free memory, memory used, physical memory, swap memory, shared memory, and buffers used by the kernel
ps	Shows the active processes (instances of running programs) associated with this login session; use the −a option to list all processes
top	Shows a continually updated display of active processes and the resources they are using; type the Q key to exit
uptime	Shows the current time, the amount of time logged in, the number of users logged in, and system load averages
users	Shows each login session
w	Shows a summary of system usage, currently logged-in users, and active processes
who	Shows the names of users currently logged in, the terminal each is using, the time each has been logged in, and the name of the host from which each logged in (if any)

Using the pico Editor

If you're working under X, you have access to a variety of GUI text editors. However, GUI text editors cannot be used from a virtual console. The *pico* editor is a simple text editor that you can think of as the Linux equivalent of the Windows Editor program, because it can be used in graphical or text mode. To start *pico*, simply type **pico** at the shell prompt, or if you want to edit a particular file, type **pico** followed by the name of the file (or the file's path, if the file is not in the working directory). For example, to edit the file *mydata*, type:

```
[bill@home bill]$ pico mydata
```

 If *pico* fails to start, you probably did not install the *pine* mailer package. You can install *pine* and *pico* by following the instructions for installing packages given in Chapter 8.

Figure 7-6 shows *pico*'s standard display. At the top of the display is a status line, which shows the version of the program and the name of the file being edited (or New Buffer, if the file is new). If the file has been modified, the upper-right corner of the display contains the word Modified. The bottom two lines of the display list the available editing commands. Most of the commands require you to type a control character, so that commands can be distinguished from characters you want to add to the buffer, as *pico*'s work area is termed. Typing an ordinary character inserts it at the current cursor position. You can use the cursor keys to move around the display; you can use the Delete or Backspace key to erase unwanted characters. Some commands use the third line from the bottom to report status and obtain additional input.

Figure 7-6. The pico editor

Table 7-9 summarizes *pico*'s commands. Notice that the command **Ctrl-G** accesses *pico*'s help system. You can access several of the commands by using function keys; for example, pressing **F1** has the same result as typing **Ctrl-G**.

Table 7-9. Summary of pico Commands

Command	Description
Ctrl-^	Mark the cursor position as beginning of selected text.
Ctrl-A	Move to the beginning of the current line.
Ctrl-B	Move backward one character.
Ctrl-C (F11)	Report the current cursor position.
Ctrl-D	Delete the character at the cursor position.
Ctrl-E	Move to the end of the current line.
Ctrl-F	Move forward one character.
Ctrl-G (F1)	Display help.
Ctrl-I	Insert a tab at the current cursor position.
Ctrl-J (F4)	Format the current paragraph.
Ctrl-K (F9)	Cut selected text.
Ctrl-L	Refresh the display.
Ctrl-N	Move to the next line.
Ctrl-O (F3)	Save the current buffer to a file.
Ctrl-P	Move to the previous line.
Ctrl-R (F5)	Insert an external file at the current cursor position.
Ctrl-T (F12)	Invoke the spelling checker.
Ctrl-U (F10)	Paste text at the current cursor position.
Ctrl-V (F8)	Move forward one page of text.
Ctrl-W (F6)	Search for text, neglecting case.
Ctrl-X (F2)	Exit *pico*, saving the edit buffer.
Ctrl-Y (F7)	Move backward one page of text.

## CHAPTER 8

Using the RPM Package Manager

This chapter explains the RPM Package Manager (RPM), a tool that facilitates installing, uninstalling, and upgrading software for your Red Hat Linux system. The chapter explains how to use RPM to find the package associated with an application and quickly and easily install the package. It also explains how to use RPM to upgrade packages and query the status of installed packages.

Packages

An RPM package (or more simply, an *RPM* or a *package*) is a file that contains executable programs, scripts, documentation, and other files needed by an application or software unit. RPM packages are generally named using a convention that lets you determine the name of the package, the version of the software, the release number of the software, and the system architecture for which the application is intended. Figure 8-1 shows how the components of a package name are arranged.

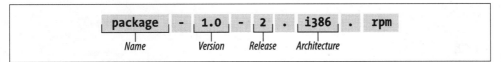

Figure 8-1. The structure of a package name

The rpm Command

RPM packages are built, installed, uninstalled, and queried with the **rpm** command. RPM package names generally end with a *.rpm* extension. **rpm** has several modes, each with its own options. The general format of the **rpm** command is:

> rpm [*options*] [*packages*]

The first option generally specifies the **rpm** mode (e.g., install, query, update, build, etc.); any remaining options pertain to the specified mode.

The **rpm** command has built-in FTP and HTTP clients. So, you can specify an *ftp://* or *http://* URL to identify an RPM package stored on a remote host.

Unless the system administrator has specially configured the system, any user can query the RPM database. Most other RPM functions require *root* privileges. Strictly speaking, it's not necessary for you log in as *root* to install an RPM package; however, your user account must be authorized to access and modify the files and directories required by the package, including the RPM database itself. Generally, the easiest way to ensure such access is by logging in as *root*.

General rpm Options

The following **rpm** options can be used with all modes:

--dbpath *path*
> Use *path* as the path to the RPM database.

--ftpport *port*
> Use *port* as the FTP port.

--ftpproxy *host*
> Use *host* as a proxy server for all transfers. Specified if you are FTPing through a firewall system that uses a proxy.

--help
> Print a long usage message (running **rpm** with no options gives a shorter usage message).

--justdb
> Update only the database; don't change any files.

--pipe *command*
> Pipe the **rpm** output to *command*.

--quiet
> Display only error messages.

--rcfile *filename*
> Use *filename,* not the system configuration file */etc/rpmrc* or *$HOME/.rpmrc,* as the configuration file.

--root *dir*
> Perform all operations within directory *dir*.

--version
> Print the version number of **rpm**.

–vv
> Print debugging information.

Finding Packages

A good place to look for interesting packages is Daniel Veillard's RPM repository, *http://rpmfind.net/linux/RPM*. Mirror sites are available for speedy access across North America and other parts of the world.*

The **rpmfind** utility can help you locate and download packages. You can find **rpmfind** on Disc 2 of Red Hat Linux. To install it, insert Disc 2 into your system's CD-ROM and issue the following commands:

```
su -
mount -t iso9660 /dev/cdrom /mnt/cdrom -o ro
rpm --replacepkgs -Uvh /mnt/cdrom/RedHat/RPMS/rpmfind-*.rpm
umount /mnt/cdrom
exit
```

To use **rpmfind**, type a command like this one:

```
rpmfind --apropos vnc
```

The command will search the RPM database on *rpmfind.net*, reporting the name of each package having a description that includes the letters *vnc*:

```
Loading catalog to /root/.rpmfinddir/fullIndex.rdf.gz
Searching the RPM catalog for vnc ...
1: ftp://ftp.redhat.com/pub/redhat/linux/7.0/en/os/i386
   /SRPMS/vnc-3.3.3r1-9.src.rpm
   vnc : Virtual Network Computing

etc.

Found 95 packages related to vnc
```

Often, **rpmfind** finds many packages. You should check for packages that have the appropriate architecture (i386). For best results, you should ignore packages other than those built for use with Red Hat Linux 7.*x*, which you can generally recognize by inspecting the URL.

To download and install a package, type a command like this one, which installs the *vnc* package:

```
rpmfind vnc
Installing vnc will require 88 KBytes

### To Transfer:
ftp://ftp.redhat.com/pub/redhat/linux/7.2/en/os/i386/RedHat/RPMS/
   vnc-3.3.3r2-18.i386.rpm
Do you want to download these files to /tmp [Y/n/a] ? :
```

The **rpmfind** utility prompts you to authorize download and installation of the files. If you decide you don't want to download the files, simply respond by typing **n**.

---

* For a complete list of mirrors, go to *http://rpmfind.net/linux/rpm2html/mirrors.html*.

Querying the RPM Database

You can query RPM's database, which lists the packages installed on your system. For example, to display a simple description of an installed package, use a command like this one:

```
rpm -q package
```

In this command, *package* is the name of the package you want RPM to describe. In response, RPM prints the package name, version, and release number.

Rather than use the –q option and the package name, you can use any of the following alternative options:

–a

    Causes RPM to display information about all installed packages

–f *file*

    Causes RPM to display information about the package that owns *file*

–p *packagefile*

    Causes RPM to display information about the package contained in *packagefile*

You can also tailor the output of an RPM query by specifying one or more of the following options:

–c

    Causes RPM to display a list of configuration files included in the package

–d

    Causes RPM to display a list of documentation files included in the package

–i

    Causes RPM to display the package name, description, release number, size, build date, installation date, vendor, and other information

–l

    Causes RPM to display the list of files that the package owns

–s

    Causes RPM to display the state of all the files in the package—normal, not installed, or replaced

For example, the command:

```
rpm -qid rhide
```

displays information about the *rhide* package, including a list of documentation files included in the package.

Installing a Package

To install a package, log in as *root* and issue the following command from a shell prompt:

```
rpm -ivh package
```

where *package* specifies the name of the file that contains the package. You can specify multiple packages, as long as you include a space to separate each package name from its neighbor. For example, the following command installs both the *pine* and *elm* packages from files in the current directory:

```
rpm -ivh pine-4.33-8.i386.rpm elm-2.5.3-11.i386.rpm
```

The options used with the **rpm** command include:

–i

This option specifies that RPM should install the package or packages given as arguments.

–h

This option specifies that RPM should print hash marks (#) as it installs the package as a visible indication of progress.

–v

The verbose option specifies that RPM should print messages that summarize its actions and progress.

Generally, RPM successfully installs the specified package. However, errors can occur. RPM may report:

- That the package is already installed
- That a package file conflicts with a file from another package
- A failed dependency

The next three sections explain how to resolve these errors.

Package Is Already Installed

If a package has already been installed, RPM will not overwrite the package without your permission:

```
# rpm -ivh bad-1.0-1.i386.rpm
bad package bad-1.0-1 is already installed
```

If you want to overwrite the package, add the **--replacepkgs** option to your command:

```
rpm -ivh --replacepkgs bad-1.0-1.i386.rpm
```

It may be more appropriate to update the package. Updating the package leaves its configuration files intact, whereas overwriting the package replaces the configuration files with files containing default options. An upcoming section shows you how to update a package.

Of course, it's also possible that you should do nothing. You may have attempted to install the package without first checking whether it's already installed and operational. In that case, you can use RPM to verify that the package is installed correctly and update or overwrite the package only if RPM reports problems.

To verify an installed package against a package file, issue the following command from a shell prompt:

`rpm -Vp` *package*

In the command, *package* specifies the name of the file that contains the package; for example, *basesystem-7.0-2.rpm*. In verifying a package, RPM compares the installed files with the original package contents. If RPM detects no discrepancies, no output will appear. Otherwise, RPM displays a line for each file that differs from the original package contents. Figure 8-2 shows the structure of such a line. The first eight characters of such a line report discrepancies; each character has the meaning described in Table 8-1. Following the list of discrepancies, you may see the letter *c*, which denotes that this is a configuration file. Finally, the filename appears.

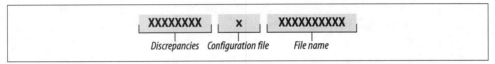

Figure 8-2. The structure of RPM's discrepancy report

Table 8-1. Package File Discrepancy Codes

Code	Meaning
.	No discrepancy
5	MD5 checksum discrepancy
D	Device discrepancy
G	Group discrepancy
L	Symbolic link discrepancy
M	Access mode or file type discrepancy
S	File size discrepancy
T	File modification time discrepancy
U	User discrepancy

The configuration files associated with a package are generally modified during installation and use, so it's not unusual for the content of configuration files to differ from that of the original files. You should generally ignore MD5 checksum and file size discrepancies that pertain to configuration files.

You can verify a package against the information recorded in the RPM database when the package was installed. To do so, issue a command of the form:

`rpm -V` *package*

Here, *package* specifies the name the package, for example, *basesystem*. Another form of the **rpm** command lets you verify packages that contain a specified file:

```
rpm -Vf path
```

In this form, *path* specifies the absolute pathname of the file. The output of this command is the same as that given earlier.

Conflicting File

Conflict is RPM's term for a situation in which two packages include one or more identically named files that have different contents. For example, suppose that package **a** contains a file named */etc/superconfig* having 12 lines and that package **b** contains a file named */etc/superconfig* having 13 lines. The two packages conflict, because the two instances of */etc/superconfig* are inconsistent.

In the event of a conflict, only one of the two conflicting packages is likely to work properly. If you instruct RPM to install a package and RPM finds that one or more of the package files conflict with existing files, RPM reports the conflict and terminates without installing the package:

```
# rpm -ivh bad-1.0-1.i386.rpm
bad /bin/badfile conflicts with file from good-1.0-1
```

In its report, RPM gives the name of the file and the name of the package that originally installed the file. You can use the **--replacefiles** option to force RPM to install the package:

```
rpm -ivh --replacefiles package
```

In response, RPM saves and then replaces any conflicting configuration files; it overwrites other types of files. However, using the **--replacefiles** option is a bit like hitting a malfunctioning mechanical device with a hammer. Sometimes, it's what you must do, but, more often, it merely causes damage. The better way to resolve a conflict is to decide which of the two conflicting packages you prefer. Then, delete the unwanted package and install the preferred one.

Failed Dependency

Packages are not always self-contained; some packages require that other packages be installed before they operate correctly. RPM can identify such dependencies. If you attempt to install a package before you install other packages it requires, RPM reports a "failed dependency" and terminates without installing the package:

```
# rpm -ivh bad-1.0-1.i386.rpm
failed dependencies:
    mefirst is needed by bad-1.0-1
```

To resolve a failed dependency, you should install the missing package (or packages) and then install the desired package. If you prefer, you can force *RPM* to install the package; however, the package may not operate correctly. To force package installation, specify the **--nodeps** option:

```
rpm -ivh --nodeps bad-1.0-1.i386.rpm
```

However, a forcibly installed package is unlikely to work correctly.

Determining the identity of the missing package responsible for the failed dependency can be challenging. The best way to do so is to install the Red Hat RPM database, contained in the package *rpmdb-redhat* that resides on Disc 2. To install the package, insert Disc 2 into your system's CD-ROM drive and issue the following commands:

```
su -
mount -t iso9660 /dev/cdrom /mnt/cdrom -o ro
rpm --replacepkgs -Uvh /mnt/cdrom/RedHat/RPMS/rpmdb-redhat-*.rpm
umount /mnt/cdrom
exit
```

The Red Hat RPM database describes every package included in Red Hat Linux 7.2. Once you've installed the package containing the Red Hat RPM database, you can query the database to discover the name of a package that satisfies a given dependency. For example, suppose you're trying to install the package *gnorpm* and RPM fails to do so, complaining that the library file *librpm.so.0* is needed but not installed. To discover the name of the related package, issue the command:

```
rpm --redhatprovides librpm.so.0
```

The RPM facility will print a message telling you that the needed file is found in the package *rpm-4.0.2-8*. Simply install that package and then try again to install *gnorpm*.

Uninstalling a Package

To uninstall a package, type a command like this one:

```
rpm -e package
```

In this command, *package* is the name of the package, not the name of the package file. The name should omit the architecture; it can also omit the package version or package version and release number. For example, you can erase the **pine** package by issuing either of the following commands:

```
rpm -e pine-4.33-8
rpm -e pine
```

If you attempt to uninstall a package on which another package depends, *RPM* will report a dependency error and terminate without uninstalling the package. You can force *RPM* to uninstall the package by using the **--nodeps** option:

```
rpm -e --nodeps package
```

However, doing so will probably cause the dependent package to cease working properly. Therefore, you shouldn't use the **--nodeps** option very often.

Updating a Package

When you update (upgrade) a package, RPM installs the new version of the software but attempts to leave your existing configuration files intact. You can update a package by using the –U option of the **rpm** command:

```
rpm -Uvh package
```

When you update a package, RPM automatically uninstalls the old version of the package before installing the new one.

 If no old version of the specified package exists, RPM simply installs the new version. Therefore, you can use the –U option to install or update a package; many Linux users avoid the –i option, always using the –U option instead. However, you should not use the –U option when installing a package containing an updated Linux kernel.

If RPM determines that your existing configuration files may be incompatible with those of the new version of the package, RPM will save a copy of the existing files. In that case, you need to examine the old and new files and determine what the proper configuration should be. The documentation that accompanies the package should assist you in this process.

If you attempt to update an existing package using an older version of the package, RPM will report an error and terminate without performing the update. To force RPM to perform the update, use the **--oldpackage** option:

```
rpm -Uvh --oldpackage package
```

Advanced RPM Techniques

Because you invoke the **rpm** command by using the shell, just as you do any other program, you can combine options and arguments to perform a variety of useful tasks. Consider the following examples:

rpm –Va
Verifies every installed package. You might find this command useful if you accidentally deleted some files. The output of the command would help you determine what packages, if any, suffered damage.

rpm –qf /usr/bin/mystery
Displays the name of the package that owns the specified file.

rpm –Vf /usr/bin/mystery
Verifies the package that owns the file */usr/bin/mystery*.

rpm –qdf /usr/bin/puzzle
Lists the documentation files associated with the package that owns the file */usr/bin/puzzle*. This could be helpful, for example, if */usr/bin/puzzle* is a program you're having difficulty using.

Gnome RPM

Gnome RPM (or *GnoRPM*) is an X-based, graphical interface to the Red Hat Linux RPM facility. You can use GnoRPM to:

- Query and verify installed packages
- Find and install new packages or upgrade existing packages
- Uninstall packages

GnoRPM is somewhat temperamental, tending sometimes to crash or produce odd results. But it works properly often enough to be useful, especially if you find the **rpm** command confusing.

Installing GnoRPM

If you installed the GNOME desktop during system installation, the installation procedure automatically installed GnoRPM by default. If you installed X but chose the KDE desktop rather than GNOME, you can manually install GnoRPM by inserting Disc 1 of Red Hat Linux in your system's CD-ROM drive and issuing the following commands:

```
su -
mount -t iso9660 /dev/cdrom /mnt/cdrom -o ro
rpm --replacepkgs -Uvh /mnt/cdrom/RedHat/RPMS/gnorpm-*.rpm
umount /mnt/cdrom
exit
```

Launching GnoRPM

You can launch GnoRPM from a terminal window by issuing the command:

`gnorpm &`

Or, depending on your desktop configuration, you may by able to launch GnoRPM from the GNOME or KDE menu. To do so, select Main Menu → Programs → System. → GnoRPM.

Shortly after you launch GnoRPM, its main window appears, as shown in Figure 8-3.

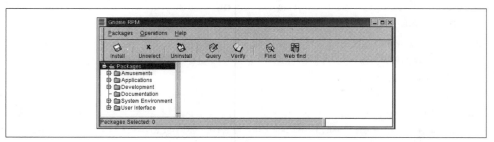

Figure 8-3. GnoRPM

The left half of the window contains a tree that represents the installed package hierarchy, organized by category. If you click on a subtree, the right half of the GnoRPM window displays the packages that reside in the subtree, as shown in Figure 8-4.

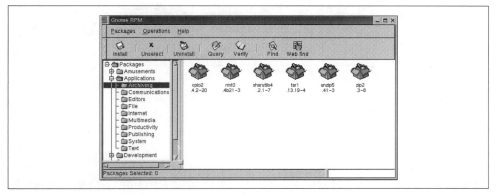

Figure 8-4. Selecting a package subtree

Querying, Verifying, and Uninstalling Packages

If you right-click on an icon representing a package, a pop-up menu lets you query, uninstall, or verify the package. You can also select these operations by clicking the appropriate icon in the toolbar. If you select the query item, the Package Info window, as shown in Figure 8-5, appears. As you can see, this window shows the same information as that provided by the **rpm –l** command. The top panel describes the package, and the bottom panel lists the files it contains.

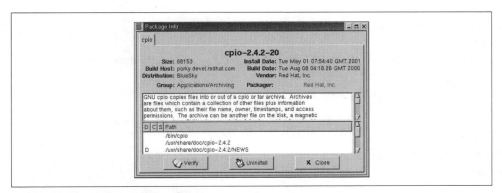

Figure 8-5. The Package Info window

If you select the Verify item, the Verifying Packages window, as shown in Figure 8-6, appears. As explained, verifying a package checks the files owned by the package against their original contents. Verifying a package can help you troubleshoot incorrect package operation. If a program isn't working correctly, you can verify its package. If the result shows that files have been inappropriately changed, you can repair the damage by reinstalling the package.

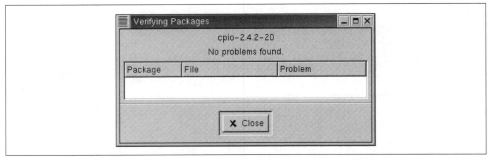

Figure 8-6. The Verifying Packages window

You can also use GnoRPM to query packages by their attributes by clicking on the Find icon on the toolbar. The Find Packages window, shown in Figure 8-7, appears. You can select the type of query you want to perform (for example, finding packages that contain a specific file) and provide the name of a file, group, or package. The following types of queries are supported:

Contains File
Lists packages containing a specified file, for example, */etc/passwd*

Are in the Group
Lists packages that are part of a specified group, for example, **System Environment/Base**

Provide
Lists the capabilities provided by the specified package

Require
Lists the packages and capabilities required by the specified package

Conflict with
Lists packages that conflict with the specified package

Match Label
Lists packages with names matching the specified text string

Clicking Find starts the query; the results appear in the text area.

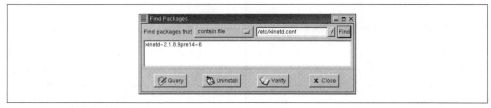

Figure 8-7. The Find Packages window

Installing and Upgrading Packages

To install or upgrade a package, click the Install icon on the toolbar. This launches the Install window, shown in Figure 8-8, which lets you choose the package files you want to install or upgrade. Using the Filter list at the top of the window, you can specify what package files you want to view; generally, the All But Installed Packages setting is appropriate, since you don't generally want to view packages that are already installed. Click the Add button to obtain the list of packages. GnoRPM searches a set of specified directories for packages and lists the packages. The later section titled "Configuring Gnome RPM" explains how to specify the list of directories that GnoRPM searches.

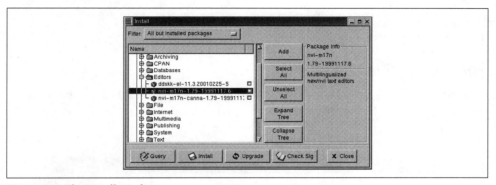

Figure 8-8. The Install window

Clicking on a package filename causes GnoRPM to display a brief description of the package. To specify packages to be installed or upgraded, set the checkbox appearing to the right of the package filename. Then click Install or Upgrade to begin the desired operation.

 If you have trouble accessing your CD-ROM drive when using GnoRPM, try turning off GNOME's CD-ROM autorun feature. To do so, select Main Menu → Programs → Settings → GNOME Control Center → CD Properties. Uncheck the checkbox that says "Automatically mount CD when inserted," then click OK.

Finding New Packages

GnoRPM can also help you find new packages. Click the Web Find button to launch the Rpmfind dialog box, shown in Figure 8-9. To operate the dialog box, type a search word in the text box at the top of the dialog box and click Search. GnoRPM searches a web database for packages related to the word you typed, listing matching packages in the left window. If you click on the name of a package, the dialog box displays a description of the package. Click Download to download the selected package or Install to download and install the selected package.

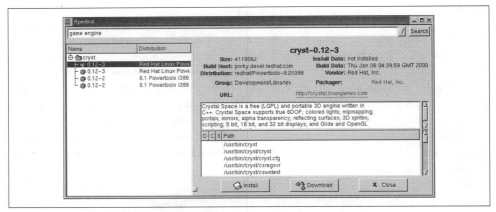

Figure 8-9. The Rpmfind dialog box

Configuring GnoRPM

GnoRPM provides several configuration options. To view these, select Operations →
Preferences. GnoRPM displays the Behavior tab of the Preferences dialog box, as
shown in Figure 8-10.

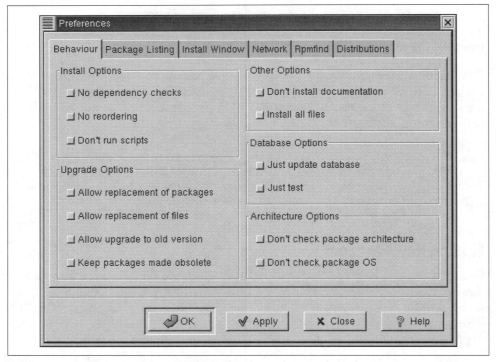

Figure 8-10. GnoRPM's Behavior tab, located in the Preferences dialog box

Generally, you should not modify the setting of the Behavior tab. The Package Listing tab lets you choose whether packages are shown as icons or text. You may prefer the textual display, which provides more information than the iconic display.

The Install Window tab, shown in Figure 8-11, lets you specify the directories that GnoRPM searches for new packages. Generally, the directory */mnt/cdrom/RedHat/ RPMS* appears on this list. If your CD-ROM drive is configured to use a different mount point, or if you want to access packages made available via NFS, you can use the Install Window tab to specify the directories you prefer.

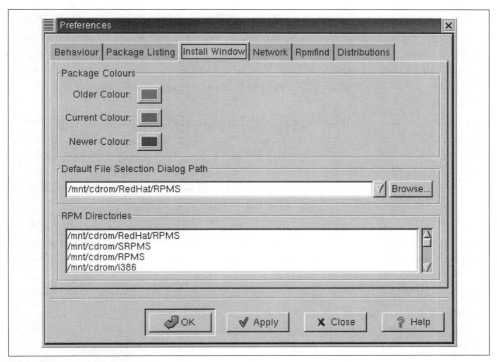

Figure 8-11. The Install Window tab

The Network tab is useful if you need to configure proxies to circumvent a local firewall. It lets you specify HTTP and FTP proxies and the user ID and password needed to access them.

The Rpmfind tab lets you specify the server used to search the Web for packages, called a metadata server. The default server is a host operated by Red Hat. You can specify a different server, if you prefer. However, bear in mind that some RPM packages may not be compatible with your Red Hat Linux system. Installing an incompatible package can result in system instability.

The Red Hat Network

Red Hat provides a service known as the Red Hat Network (*http://www.redhat.com/ products/network*), designed to help you keep your Red Hat Linux system up-to-date and secure. If you purchased the official release of Red Hat Linux, you're entitled to a 30-day subscription to the Red Hat Network for one system. You can purchase additional subscriptions for $19.95 per month, per system. Users of freely redistributed copies of Red Hat Linux, such as that included with this book, are not entitled to a free Red Hat Network subscription.

The Red Hat Network provides access to security alerts, bug fix alerts, and enhancement alerts published by Red Hat. Updated packages can be downloaded or automatically installed via the Red Hat Update Agent. The Red Hat Network would seem to be of significant benefit to administrators of multiple systems, who might otherwise have difficulty timely applying patches to close security loopholes and fix problems.

The Red Hat Network does have several limitations, at least as currently implemented. The version of Red Hat Update Agent shipped with Red Hat Linux 7.2 sometimes has difficulty updating the kernel; therefore, security and bug fixes that require installation of a new kernel sometimes cannot be performed automatically. The Agent can, however, download a package containing a new kernel, which can be manually installed by the system administrator.

Similarly, the Agent is not without its flaws. In one instance, the Agent automatically downloaded an updated version of itself. Unfortunately, the updated version broke some features, and a bug fix for the broken version was still not available several weeks after the incident.

This incident points up a general problem applicable to all automatic software update systems. Because humans who operate such systems are intrinsically error-prone, the software updates they supply are not invariably good. An automatic update could potentially render a system unusable, which may not be as happy a state as a somewhat out-of-date system. Moreover, automatic software update facilities may be vulnerable to security attack; using one may open your system to compromise. When deciding whether to use an automatic software update facility, be sure to consider both the risks and the benefits of its use. It may be preferable to configure the facility to download newly available packages for offline review and testing, rather than immediate installation.

## CHAPTER 9

Configuring and Administering Linux

This chapter equips you to perform common system administration tasks. It explains how you can override many configuration choices made during system installation. You'll learn how to add, delete, and modify user accounts and how to add and delete groups and change their membership. You'll also learn how to configure swap space and how to cause Linux to automatically mount filesystems on startup. Finally, you'll learn how to configure a printer and how to configure your system's sound adapter.

Configuring the Locale

During the installation procedure, you're asked to specify the languages that you want to use during system operation. Thereafter, you can specify a different language, which is referred to as a *locale*. A locale may include the characters (glyphs) used to display text written in the associated language, a keyboard layout used to type text in the associated language, and a spelling dictionary used to check text written in the associated language.

To specify the current locale, use the Locale Chooser, which you can access by selecting Main Menu → Programs → System → Locale Chooser. Figure 9-1 shows the Setting Default Locale dialog box that appears after a short interval. To specify a locale, select it and click OK.

Switching Desktops

During the installation procedure, you chose a default desktop, either GNOME or KDE. Thereafter, you can revise your choice by using the desktop switcher.

To do so, select Main Menu → Programs → System → Desktop Switching Tool. The Desktop Switcher dialog box, as shown in Figure 9-2, appears. In addition to GNOME and KDE, the Desktop Switcher lets you specify TWM (tiny window manager), a sparsely functional but highly efficient desktop. The checkbox labeled "Change only applies to current display" lets you restrict your choice of desktop to

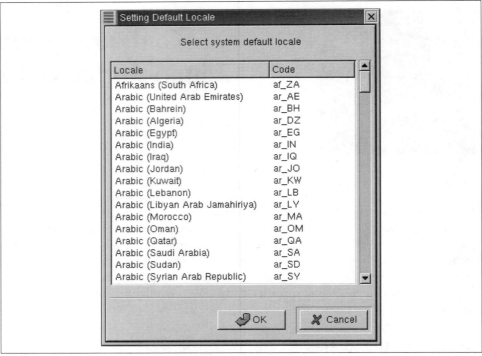

Figure 9-1. The Setting Default Locale dialog box

the current desktop, as indicated in the top line of the dialog box. This facility is useful if your system has been configured to allow remote users to log in via X, a topic not covered in this book.

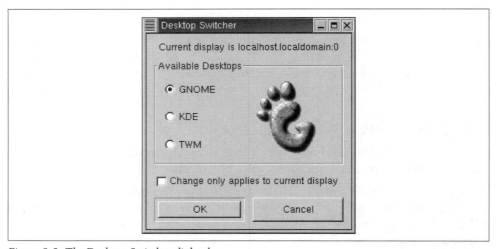

Figure 9-2. The Desktop Switcher dialog box

To specify a desktop, click the desired radio button and click OK. A dialog box appears, informing you that you must restart X for the selected desktop to appear. When you restart X, the selected desktop should appear.

User Mount Tool

Before you can access the contents of a filesystem, the filesystem must be mounted. When Linux boots, it automatically mounts one or more filesystems. However, you may need to mount other filesystems—particularly those associated with removable media such as CD-ROMs and floppies.

You can manually mount or unmount a filesystem by using the User Mount Tool. To launch the tool, select Main Menu → Programs → System → Disk Management. The User Mount Tool dialog box that appears is shown in Figure 9-3.

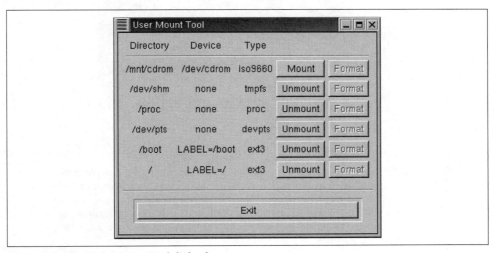

Figure 9-3. The User Mount Tool dialog box

To mount a filesystem, click Mount; to unmount a filesystem, click Unmount. The Format button is generally disabled. When it is enabled, you can use it to format a filesystem. A filesystem must be formatted before it can be used; however, formatting a filesystem destroys all data on it. So, you should generally format a filesystem only when preparing to mount media that have not been previously used.

Change Password

You can change the password associated with the current user account by using the Change Password Tool. To do so, select Main Menu → Programs → System → Change Password. A dialog box, shown in Figure 9-4, appears. Type the desired password and click OK. A second dialog box, as shown in Figure 9-5, appears. As instructed, retype the new password and click OK. A third dialog box appears, confirming that the password has been changed; click OK to dismiss it.

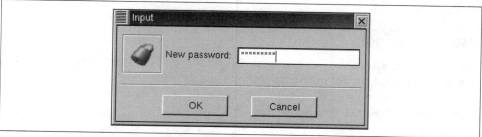

Figure 9-4. The Change Password dialog box

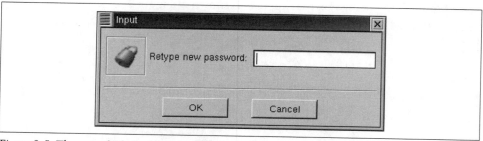

Figure 9-5. The second Change Password dialog box

 The system evaluates passwords and can determine if a password you specify is insecure. In such a case, it may prevent you from using the insecure password or, if you are the root user, it may merely inform you that the password is insecure. Unless your PC is physically secure and never connected to a network, you should generally choose only secure passwords.

Date/Time Properties

The Date/Time Properties Tool lets you perform a variety of operations. You can:

- Change the current date
- Change the current time
- Specify a host that provides time synchronization data via the Network Time Protocol
- Specify the time zone

To launch the Date/Time Properties Tool, select Main Menu → Programs → System → Date/Time Properties. Figure 9-6 shows the tool's user interface.

To set the current date and time, use the calendar control labeled Date and the text boxes labeled Time. Click OK to save your changes. To synchronize your system's

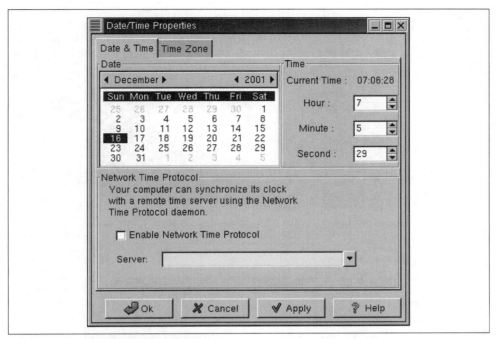

Figure 9-6. The Date/Time Properties dialog box

time to that of another system, check the box labeled Enable Network Time Protocol and specify the hostname or IP address in the text box labeled Server. Alternatively, you can select from among several preconfigured hostnames.

To change the time zone, click the Time Zone tab. The Time Zone pane, shown in Figure 9-7, appears. You can choose between a view of the world or any of six continents or subcontinents. Select the time zone by clicking on the map or by clicking an item in the list box. If you prefer to set your system's clock to UTC (formerly known as Greenwich Mean Time), check the box labeled System Clock Uses UTC. However, if your system is configured to boot multiple operating systems, enabling this option may cause incorrect operation of other operating systems.

Hardware Browser

The Hardware Browser Tool lets you view your system's hardware configuration, including CD-ROM and hard drives, network devices, and system devices. To launch the tool, select Main Menu → Programs → System → Hardware Browser. The tool spends a few seconds scanning your system's hardware and then presents the display shown in Figure 9-8.

Click in the left pane to select the device or device category you wish to view. Information pertaining to your selection appears in the right pane.

Figure 9-7. The Time Zone pane of the Date/Time Properties dialog box

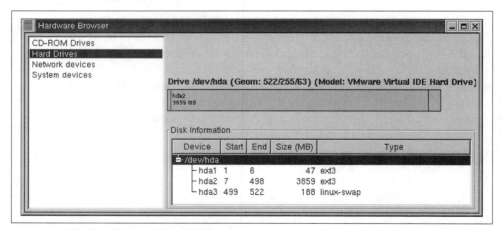

Figure 9-8. The Hardware Browser window

User and Group Administration

In this section, you'll learn how to use the User Manager Tool to perform common administrative tasks affecting users and groups. To launch the User Manager Tool, select Main Menu → Programs → System → User Manager. The Red Hat User Manager appears, as shown in Figure 9-9. The tool presents a scrollable list of user accounts (users) and displays the following information about each user account:

User Name
> The login name associated with the user account.

Primary Group
> The name of the primary user group associated with the user account. Accounts used by people rather than system processes generally have an associated primary group having the same name as the user account.

Full Name
> The name of the person or process owning the user account.

Login Shell
> The login shell assigned to the user account. Assigning */bin/false* or */sbin/nologin* prevents the user account from logging in.

Home Directory
> The home directory associated with the user account. When the user logs in, this directory is set as the current working directory.

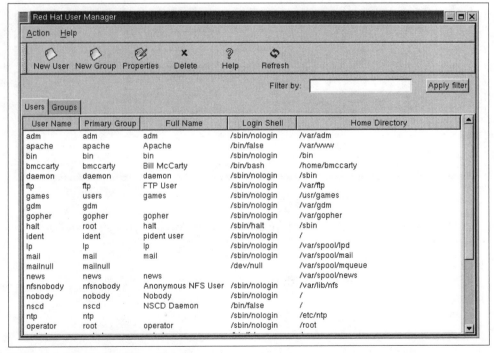

Figure 9-9. The Red Hat User Manager

When many user accounts are configured, it may be inconvenient to scroll through the list. You can use the text box labeled Filter By to display only user accounts having names matching a specified pattern. Type the pattern in the text box and click Apply Filter.

Modifying a user account

To modify a user account, click the desired account and click Properties. The User Properties dialog box, as shown in Figure 9-10, appears.

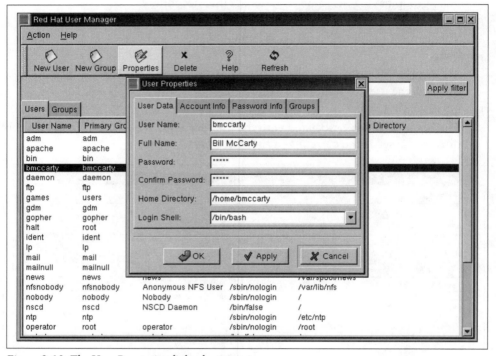

Figure 9-10. The User Properties dialog box

The User Data pane of the User Properties dialog box lets you view and change a variety of properties:

User Name
> The login name associated with the user account.

Full Name
> The name of the person or process owning the user account.

Password
> The password to be associated with the user account.

Confirm Password

The password to be associated with the user account. The password is specified twice in order to reduce the risk of assigning an incorrect password due to a typing error.

Home Directory

The home directory associated with the user account. When the user logs in, this directory is set as the current working directory.

Login Shell

The login shell assigned to the user account. Assigning */bin/false* or */sbin/nologin* prevents the user account from logging in.

The Account Info pane, shown in Figure 9-11, lets you specify a date on which a user account becomes unusable. Alternatively, you can use the text box labeled User Account Is Locked to immediately disable an account.

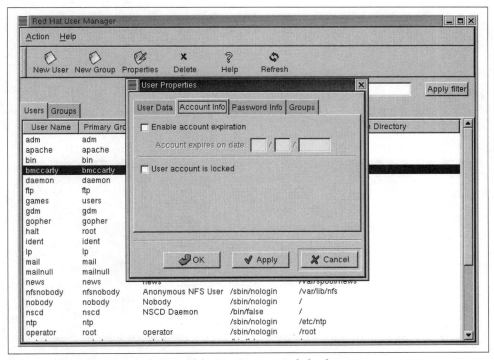

Figure 9-11. The Account Info pane of the User Properties dialog box

The Password Info pane, shown in Figure 9-12, lets you set password expiration options for the account. To do so, enable the checkbox labeled Enable Password Expiration. Then you can specify any of the following values:

Days Before Change Allowed

The number of days that must elapse before the user can change the password associated with the user account.

Days Before Change Required

After the specified number of days, the user must change the password associated with the user account.

Days Warning Before Change

This value is used in combination with the Days Before Change Required value. The user will be given advance notice of the need to change the password associated with the user account. The notification begins the specified number of days before the change must be made.

Days Before Account Inactive

After the specified number of days, the user account is disabled.

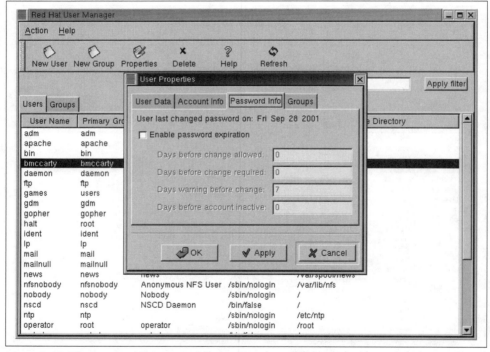

Figure 9-12. The Password Info pane of the User Properties dialog box

The Groups pane displays a series of checkboxes corresponding to user groups. To associate the user account with a group, check the box corresponding to the desired group.

Choosing a Secure Password

A cracker who manages to obtain a copy of your system's */etc/shadow* file may be able to discover your password by using a utility that tries to determine the clear text password corresponding to the encrypted password stored in the file. You can make the cracker's job more difficult by using one or more of the following techniques:

- Choose a password having a length of at least six characters.
- Choose a password that is not a dictionary word. For example, use a made-up word or a phrase rather than a dictionary word.
- Choose a password that includes uppercase and lowercase letters.
- Choose a password that includes digits as well as letters. However, don't merely follow a dictionary word by the digit 1 or use a similarly guessable scheme.
- Choose a password that includes one or more special characters, such as a dollar sign, pound sign, or underscore.

Password Expiration

Other things being equal, the longer a password is used, the greater the likelihood that it has been compromised. One way to protect users from password crackers is to require users to change their passwords regularly.

Some overly zealous system administrators require users to change their passwords every 30 days. Unless a system contains top secret data, such a short interval is unnecessary, amounting to what's called *password fascism*. You may find that requiring users to change their passwords every six months or every year is sufficient to avoid hacker invasion of user accounts.

Adding a new user

To create a new user account, click New User in the Red Hat User Manager dialog box. Doing so launches the Create New User dialog box, shown in Figure 9-13. When you create a new user account, you can specify the following values:

User Name
> The name of the user account to be created.

Full Name
> The name of the user who will use the account.

Password
> The password associated with the user account.

Confirm Password
> The password to be associated with the user account.

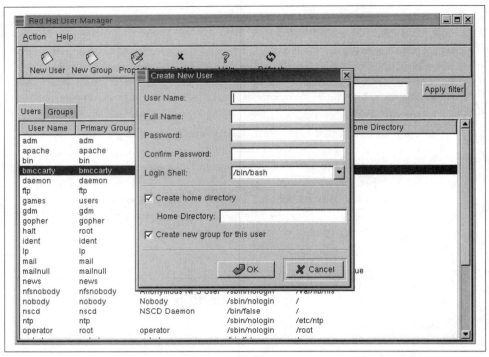

Figure 9-13. The Create New User dialog box

Login Shell

The login shell associated with the account. You should generally select */bin/ bash*.

Create Home Directory

You should generally check this box, so that a home directory is created.

Home Directory

This value is used only when Create Home Directory is enabled. The default value is generally acceptable.

Create New Group for This User

You should generally enable this checkbox, which causes automatic creation of a primary user group having the same name as the user account. When you've specified the desired values, click OK to create the user account.

Deleting a user account

To delete a user account, click on the desired account and click Delete. The user account is immediately deleted; no confirmation dialog box appears. Therefore, exercise care to ensure that the correct user account is highlighted before clicking Delete.

Configuring groups

You may recall from Chapter 4 that Linux uses groups to define a set of related user accounts that can share access to a file or directory. You probably won't find it necessary to configure group definitions very often, particularly if you use your system as a desktop system rather than a server.

To view the configured groups, launch the User Manager tool and click the Groups tab. The Groups pane, as shown in Figure 9-14, appears. Groups are shown in a scrollable list, similar to the way user accounts are shown.

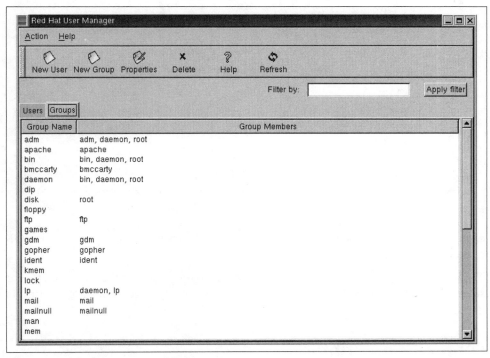

Figure 9-14. The Groups pane of the User Manager

To create a new group, click the New Group icon. The Create New Group dialog box, as shown in Figure 9-15, appears. The dialog box lets you specify the name of the new group. When you've specified the name of the new group, click OK to create the group.

To modify a group, click on the name of the group. The Group Properties dialog box, shown in Figure 9-16, appears. The Group Data pane of the dialog box lets you revise the name of the group. The Group Users pane contains a scrollable list of users; you can associate a user account with a group by enabling the checkbox adjacent to the username or dissociate a user account from a group by disabling the

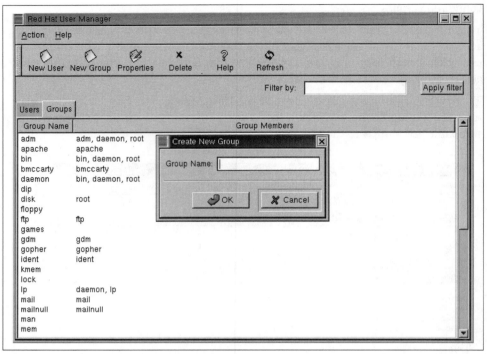

Figure 9-15. The Create New Group dialog box

checkbox adjacent to the username. When you've completed your changes, click OK to make them effective.

To delete a group, select the group in the Groups pane and click the Delete icon. The selected group is immediately deleted. So, before clicking Delete, be sure the proper group is highlighted.

Configuring a Printer

Before you can print from Red Hat Linux, you must configure a printer. Red Hat Linux supports local printers attached to your system's parallel port and remote printers that your system accesses via the network. Before you can configure a remote printer, you must first configure networking, as explained in Chapter 11.

To configure a local printer, launch the printer configuration tool by selecting Main Menu → Programs → Printer Configuration. The Printer Configuration Tool, as shown in Figure 9-17, appears.

First, create a new printer by clicking the New icon. The Add a New Print Queue wizard appears. Click Next to proceed. The Set the Print Queue Name and Type dialog box, as shown in Figure 9-18, appears.

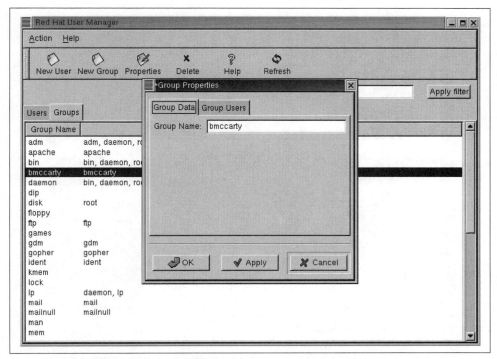

Figure 9-16. The Group Properties dialog box

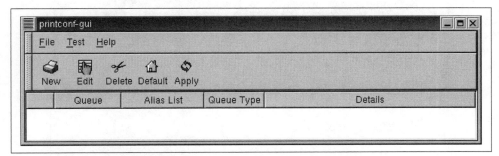

Figure 9-17. The printer configuration tool

Every print queue has a name. The default print queue has the name *lp*. Type **lp** or another print queue name of your choice in the text box labeled Queue Name. Select the Local Printer radio button and click Next. The Configure a Local Printer dialog box, as shown in Figure 9-19, appears.

The dialog box shows the parallel ports associated with your system. Linux numbers parallel ports starting with zero, so the port designated */dev/lp0* corresponds to the device known by Microsoft Windows as LPT1. Select the parallel port to which your printer is attached and click Next.

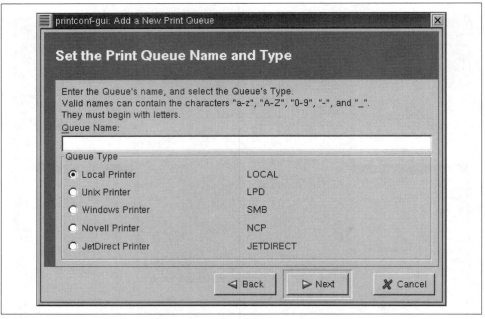

Figure 9-18. The Set the Print Queue Name and Type dialog box

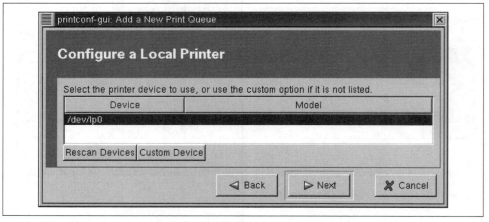

Figure 9-19. The Configure a Local Printer dialog box

The Select a Print Driver dialog box, as shown in Figure 9-20, appears. Select the make of your printer by clicking the triangle that appears at the left of its name. From the sublist that appears, select the model of your printer and choose a print driver, as shown in Figure 9-21. More than one driver may be available for your printer. Some drivers work better than others, so you'll eventually want to try each driver in order to locate the one that works best. For now, merely choose a driver arbitrarily. Then click Next.

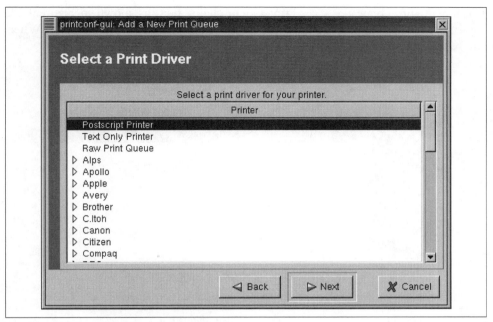

Figure 9-20. The Select a Print Driver dialog box

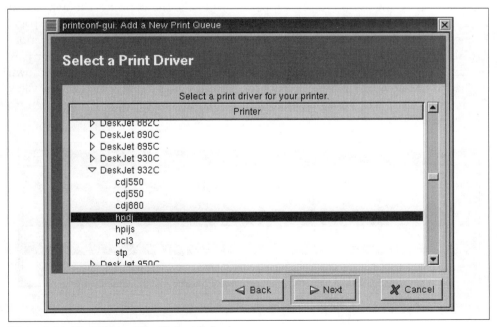

Figure 9-21. The Select a Print Driver dialog box

The Finish and Create the New Print Queue dialog box, as shown in Figure 9-22, appears. Check the information and use the Back button to correct any errors. When you're satisfied with your specifications, click Finish.

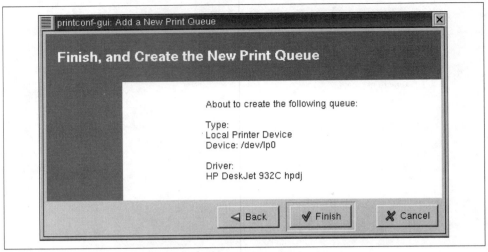

Figure 9-22. The Finish and Create the New Print Queue dialog box

The printer configuration tool reappears, with the new printer shown as in Figure 9-23. To verify the configuration, click Test and choose ASCII Text Testpage. Doing so sends a sample page to the printer so that you can verify correct operation. A dialog box invites you to save your configuration changes; click Yes, or your new printer configuration will be lost. The system then restarts the printer system, known as the *lpd* daemon, and informs you of the result by presenting a dialog box. Click OK to continue. Finally, a dialog box confirms that the sample page has been sent to the printer.

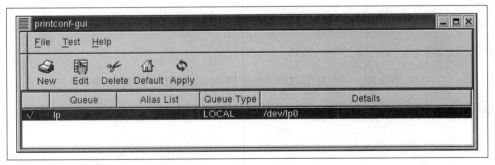

Figure 9-23. The printer configuration tool

If the sample page doesn't appear or appears incorrectly, select the printer and click Edit. Use the Edit Queue dialog box that appears, as shown in Figure 9-24, to select a different print driver or revise options associated with the current driver.

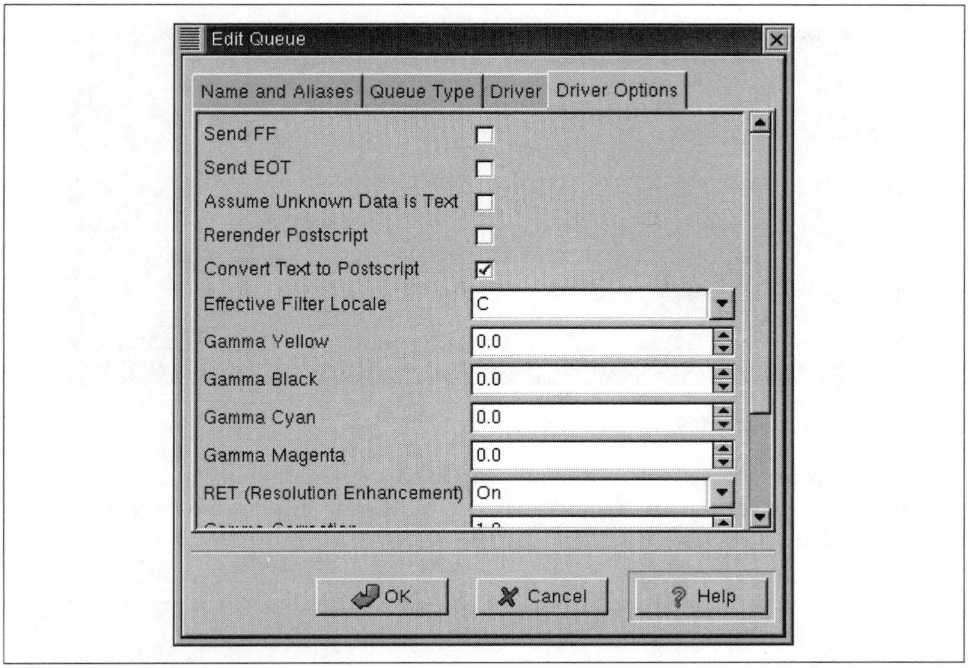

Figure 9-24. The Edit Queue dialog box

Configuring Sound

If your system includes a sound adapter supported by Red Hat Linux, you can use *sndconfig* to configure your adapter. If you're unsure whether your system's sound adapter is supported, check the Red Hat Linux hardware compatibility database at *http://hardware.redhat.com*. Several popular cards are not fully compatible with Red Hat Linux, so it's best to check the database before wasting time trying to configure incompatible hardware.

To configure your system's adapter, launch a terminal window and issue the following commands:

```
su -
sndconfig
```

The Sound Configuration utility's Introduction dialog box, as shown in Figure 9-25, appears. The utility has the same user interface as that used by the text-based Red Hat Linux installation program:

- Use the arrow keys to move from control to control.
- Use the **spacebar** to select an item, such as a checkbox.
- Use **Enter** to click a button.

Click the OK button and press **Enter** to continue.

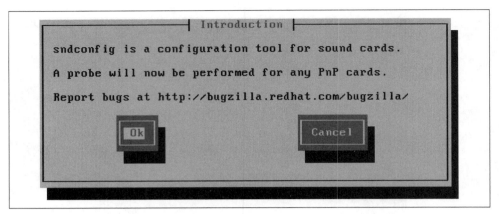

Figure 9-25. The Introduction dialog box

The utility probes your system, seeking supported sound adapters. If the probe fails, the utility announces the failure and lets you select your system's adapter from a list of supported adapters, as shown in Figure 9-26.

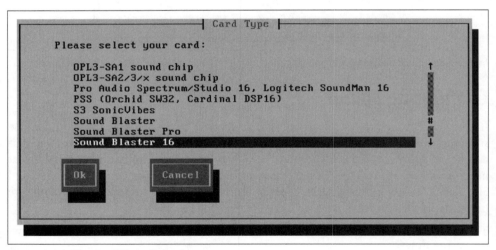

Figure 9-26. The Card Type dialog box

After a sound adapter has been identified, the utility may present a dialog box that lets you configure hardware options, such as that shown in Figure 9-27. To determine the proper settings, refer to your hardware documentation or information you collected from Microsoft Windows in Chapter 2 (see Table 2-1).

Next, the utility plays a sample sound, as explained by the Sound Card Test dialog box, shown in Figure 9-28.

If you hear the sound, you can exit the utility. If not, you can go back and select a different sound adapter. If you don't hear the sound, check that your speakers are

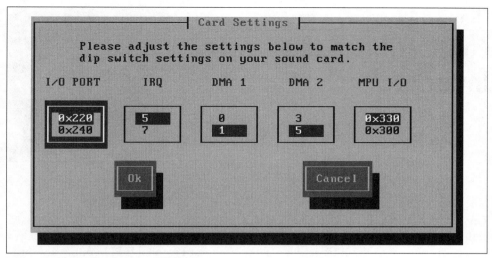

Figure 9-27. The Card Settings dialog box

Figure 9-28. The Sound Card Test dialog box

plugged in and, if necessary, powered on. Otherwise, you may spend time trying to reconfigure a sound adapter that's actually working fine.

If the utility suspects that your sound card includes a MIDI synthesizer, it presents a series of dialog boxes that let you configure the MIDI facility. These dialog boxes resemble those pertaining to audio.

CHAPTER 10

Connecting to the Internet

This chapter explains how to use Red Hat Linux to connect to the Internet via a dialup connection. First, it explains how to use *rp3*, an X-based program that makes it easy to connect to the Internet via a Point-to-Point Protocol (PPP) connection provided by an Internet service provider (ISP). The chapter also explains how to use *wvdial*, a related program that doesn't require X. Next, the chapter describes several popular network client applications available under Linux, including several web browsers and a graphical FTP client. Finally, the chapter gives some tips on how to configure Linux to work with your cable or DSL modem.

Configuring Your Modem Using rp3

Most ISPs provide a type of dialup connection known as a PPP connection. ISPs use a variety of dialogs to make a PPP connection. Often the most difficult part of configuring your computer to make a PPP connection is specifying dialog options consistent with those required by your ISP. Technical support representatives of many ISPs may not be especially helpful in explaining the necessary options to customers who use an operating system other than Windows.

The *rp3* program simplifies making a PPP connection. It transparently establishes the connection in much the same way as Windows Dial-up Networking. It understands a variety of possible dialogs used by ISPs. In most cases, it will analyze data sent by your ISP and respond with the proper data in the format required by the ISP.

Installing rp3

If you installed the GNOME and Dialup Workstation package groups, you've already installed *rp3* and the packages on which it depends. If not, you can use GnoRPM to install the *ppp*, *rp3*, and *wvdial* packages.

Configuring rp3

To configure *rp3*, start your preferred desktop environment, GNOME or KDE. Then, if you're using GNOME, select Programs → Internet → Dialup Configuration; if you're using KDE, select Internet → Dialup Configuration.

A wizard (Red Hat calls them "druids"), titled "Create a new Internet connection," as shown in Figure 10-1, appears. You can use the wizard to configure your modem and Internet accounts. To begin, click Next.

Figure 10-1. The "Create a new Internet connection" wizard

The Select Modem dialog box, shown in Figure 10-2, appears. Again, click Next to proceed.

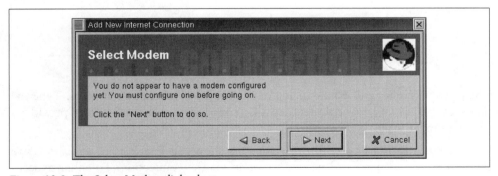

Figure 10-2. The Select Modem dialog box

A dialog box shows progress as *rp3* searches your system's devices to locate a modem. If the search is not successful, simply try again; sometimes *rp3* is unable to locate a modem on the first or second attempt. If *rp3* fails repeatedly, you should suspect that something is wrong with your modem. If it's an external modem, check the power and data cables. If it's an internal modem, check that any configuration switches or jumpers are properly set.

 If you can't locate the problem, it may be with your modem. Some modems, referred to as WinModems, require special drivers generally available only for Windows. Unfortunately, Red Hat's hardware database does not include many entries describing modems. As a rule of thumb, most external modems—except WinModems—are compatible with Linux. To learn more about your modem and its compatibility with Linux, see *http://www.linmodems.org* or Rob Clark's *WinModems Are Not Modems* page, *http://www.idir.net/~gromitkc/ winmodem.html.*

When the wizard finds your system's modem, the Modem Found dialog box, shown in Figure 10-3, appears. If you want to customize modem properties, click the radio button labeled "Modify this modem manually, or add a new modem" and click Next. Use the dialog box that appears to customize modem settings, such as baud rate and speaker volume. Then, whether you customized modem settings or not, click Next to proceed.

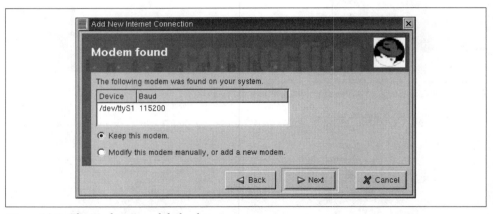

Figure 10-3. The Modem Found dialog box

The Phone Number and Name dialog box, shown in Figure 10-4, appears. Type the name by which you want to refer to this connection and the Internet provider's phone number. Click Next to proceed.

The User Name and Password dialog box, as shown in Figure 10-5, appears. Type the username and password needed to log in via the connection. To enhance security, the password is echoed as asterisks as you type it. Click Next to proceed.

The Other Options dialog box, shown in Figure 10-6, appears. Select your Internet provider from the list, or if your provider is not shown, select Normal ISP. Click Next.

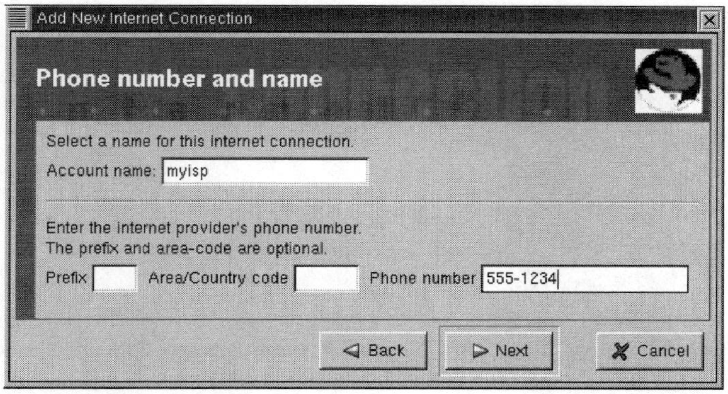

Figure 10-4. The Phone Number and Name dialog box

Figure 10-5. The User Name and Password dialog box

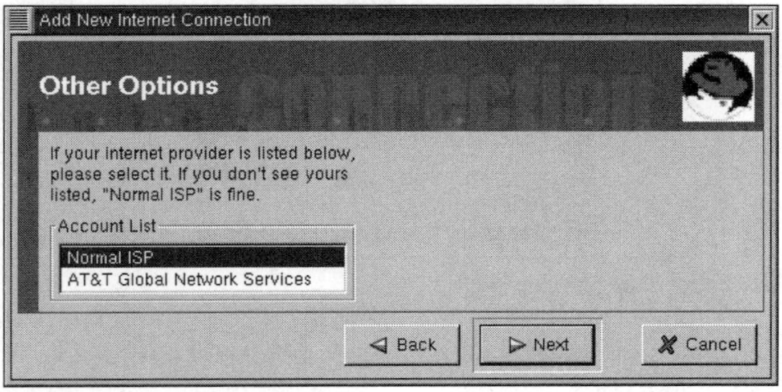

Figure 10-6. The Other Options dialog box

The Create the Account dialog box, shown in Figure 10-7, appears. Click Finish.

Once you've created an Internet connection, you're ready to connect to your ISP. The following section explains how to do so.

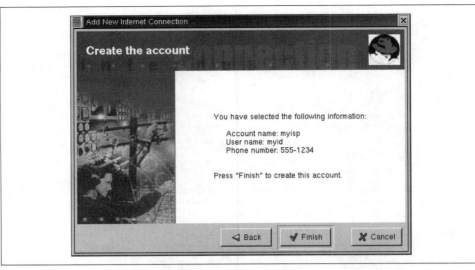

Figure 10-7. The Create the Account dialog box

Connecting to Your ISP

If you're using GNOME, you can connect to your ISP by selecting Main Menu →
Applets → Network → RH PPP Dialer; if you're using KDE, select Internet → RH PPP
Dialer. The Choose dialog box, as shown in Figure 10-8, appears and asks you to
choose an interface. Select the Internet connection you just created and click OK.

Figure 10-8. The Choose dialog box

The Change Connection Status? dialog box, as shown in Figure 10-9, appears. Click
Yes to initiate the connection.

Within a few seconds, you should hear a dial tone from your modem (if you have
sound enabled), and shortly thereafter the connection should be established. Once
connected, *rp3* launches a dialog box titled with the name of the Internet connection; if you're running GNOME, the dialog box may appear as a docked applet, so
you won't be able to view the dialog box's titlebar.

Figure 10-9. The Change Connection Status? dialog box

If *rp3* cannot open the Internet connection, you'll see a dialog box announcing the failure. In that case, you should check the phone number, username, and password you entered earlier. To do so, launch *rp3-config* and use the Edit button to view and correct the entries you made.

> If you hear your modem dialing but *rp3* doesn't succeed in establishing a connection, check the most recent messages in the system log by issuing the command:
>
> ```
> tail /var/log/messages
> ```
>
> You may find relevant messages that point you to the source of the problem.

Once *rp3* establishes the connection, you should be able to access the Internet. Try to ping an Internet host by issuing a command such as **ping www.redhat.com** in a terminal window.

If the command doesn't work, perhaps your connection isn't working. Or perhaps your ISP's PPP server failed to properly provide DNS information. Try pinging the IP address of a host you know to be available. For example:

```
ping -n 216.148.219.195
```

If pinging the IP address works, simply use Netconfig to revise your DNS configuration and you're set. Otherwise, you may have some difficulty getting the connection to work. Use the *ifconfig* and *route* commands to view your network configuration. If you can figure out the problem, again you're set. If not, you may be able to obtain help from your ISP or from participants in an Internet newsgroup, such as *linux.redhat* or *linux.redhat.misc*.

Terminating an Internet Connection

To terminate an Internet connection established by *rp3*, simply click the button in the upper-right corner of the dialog box or applet associated with the connection. A dialog box asking you to confirm your decision appears. Clicking Yes terminates the Internet connection.

Using wvdial

If you have *rp3* working perfectly, you may have little interest in exploring *wvdial*. However, in that case, you apparently don't realize that you're *already* using *wvdial*. As it happens, *rp3* is merely a GUI façade that overlays *wvdial*, which does the real work of establishing PPP connections. Here are three reasons you should consider learning more about *wvdial*:

- You can use *wvdial* even if X isn't working or isn't installed.
- You can use knowledge of *wvdial* to work around some problems and bugs affecting *rp3*.
- You can use *wvdial* in shell scripts of your own design. Chapter 13 includes an example script.

The /etc/wvdial.conf File

The most salient aspects of the relationship between *rp3* and *wvdial* are that *rp3-config* maintains the *wvdial* configuration file, */etc/wvdial.conf*, and that *rp3* establishes Internet connections described by that file.

To configure *wvdial*, become the root user and issue the following command:

```
wvdialconf /etc/wvdial.conf
```

This command analyzes your system and creates a template configuration file, */etc/wvdial.conf*. You must edit this file to specify the username and password your ISP expects.

 Running *wvdialconf* overwrites any configuration information stored by *rp3-config*; you should copy the */etc/wvdial.conf* file or make a note of its contents before running *wvdialconf*.

The contents of the template file look something like this:

```
[Dialer Defaults]
Modem = /dev/ttyS1
Baud = 115200
Init1 = ATZ
Init2 = ATQ0 V1 E1 S0=0 &C1 &D2 S11=55 +FCLASS=0
; Phone = <Target Phone Number>
; Username = <Your Login Name>
; Password = <Your Password>
```

Edit the last three lines of the file, deleting the leading semicolon and space and substituting the proper phone number, username, and password required to connect to your ISP. When you're done, your file should look something like this:

```
[Dialer Defaults]
Modem = /dev/ttyS1
Baud =  115200
```

```
Init1 = ATZ
Init2 = ATQ0 V1 E1 &C1 &D2 +FCLASS=0
Phone = 15625551100
Username = bill100
Password = donttell
```

Now, you're ready to make a connection by issuing the following command:

`wvdial &`

The command generates quite a bit of output, which makes further use of this virtual terminal distracting. The simplest solution is to switch to another virtual terminal by pressing **Alt-*n***, where *n* stands for the virtual terminal (17). Alternatively, you can direct the output of the command to a file, by typing this command in place of the one given earlier:

`wvdial 2>/tmp/wvdial.messages &`

Of course, you'll need to consult the file if something goes wrong with **wvdial**. Do so by using the *less* command:

`less /tmp/wvdial.messages`

Once your connection is up, you can browse the Web and access other Internet services, as described later in this chapter. For now, simply verify that your connection is working by issuing the command:

`ping www.redhat.com`

The *ping* command should report that echo packets were successfully received from the server. If not, check your name server configuration and other details, as described in the preceding section.

When you want to terminate the Internet connection, issue the command:

`killall wvdial`

If you prefer, you can use *rp3* to establish and terminate the Internet connection. When you build the */etc/wvdial.conf* file by using *rp3-config*, the file contains more sophisticated entries than those generated by *wvdialconf*. However, the simpler entries are sufficient to enable *rp3* to establish an Internet connection.

Web Browsers

Once you've established a PPP connection to the Internet, whether via *rp3* or *wvdial*, you can surf the Web using a browser. In addition to browsers written specifically for Unix and Linux, you can use Mozilla's web browser, which includes a mail client, newsgroup client, HTML editor, and other features. With the release of Red Hat 7.2, Mozilla is the default web browser under GNOME; however, Netscape Communicator is also available. This section surveys several popular Linux web browsers:

- Mozilla
- Netscape Navigator and Communicator

- Links
- Opera

Konqueror, which is the default file manager/web browser for KDE, is described in Chapter 6.

Mozilla

The Mozilla project aims to implement a fully functioned, open source web browser. Recent releases have begun to approach that goal. Figure 10-10 shows the same web page as the preceding figure, rendered by Mozilla rather than Konqueror. A few details differ, mainly because the web page includes dynamic content.

Figure 10-10. Mozilla running under Linux

If you installed GNOME or KDE and the *Mail/WWW/News* package group during system installation, Mozilla will be installed on your system.

Like Netscape Communicator, Mozilla appears in the GNOME and KDE menus. To launch Mozilla manually, issue the following command from an X terminal:

```
mozilla &
```

Netscape Navigator and Communicator

Netscape Navigator still rules the Linux world as it once ruled all platforms. However, Navigator doesn't look quite as good under X as it does on a Windows or Macintosh system, mainly because of the font technology used by X. That said, Navigator certainly looks much better than Links. Linux also supports Netscape Communicator, Navigator's big brother, which provides email and newsgroup access in addition to web browsing capabilities. No matter what you call it, Netscape's browser is a killer Linux X application. Figure 10-11 shows a typical web page rendered by Communicator.

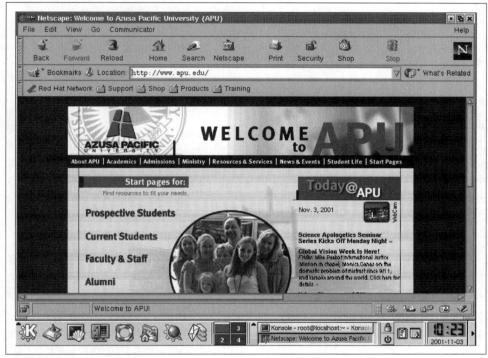

Figure 10-11. Netscape Communicator running under Linux

As you can see, the Linux version of Communicator is very similar to the Windows version. As such, you'll find configuring and using Communicator to be quite straightforward. To configure Communicator, choose Edit → Preferences. Then, specify your identity and that of your mail and newsgroup servers, along with any other special preferences you desire.

 If you installed GNOME or KDE during system installation, the installer includes Netscape Communicator in the build.

Both GNOME and KDE include Communicator on their menus, making it easy to launch. If you prefer to launch Communicator manually, you can issue the following command from an X terminal:

```
netscape-communicator &
```

Communicator is the simplest way to get email and news working under Linux, because its configuration dialog boxes closely resemble those of its Windows-based sibling: merely replicate your Windows-based Communicator settings under Linux and you're done. However, Linux supports many other email clients that you may wish to explore, such as:

- balsa
- elm
- kmail
- mutt
- pine

Links

Links is a text-based browser, meaning that it can be run from a command-line prompt and does not display images or graphics. Figure 10-12 shows a web page as viewed using Links. Because of its limitations, Links is useful mainly for displaying simple web pages. Links is automatically installed if you select the *Mail/WWW/News* package group during installation.

To use Links, specify the initial URL as a command-line argument, for example:

```
links http://www.oreilly.com
```

Opera

Opera is an interesting web browser developed in Norway by Jon S. von Tetzchner and Geir Ivarsøy and used by 1.5 million customers. Figure 10-13 shows a web page viewed using Opera. Opera Software ASA distributes Opera in two forms: a free version that displays banner ads and a version that cost $39 at the time of this writing. You can obtain Opera at *http://www.opera.com*.

Opera is available for several platforms, including Windows, Macintosh, and Linux. Opera's support for Cascading Style Sheets (CSS) and Extensible Markup Language (XML) are considered by many to surpass that of Internet Explorer and Netscape Navigator. Because of Opera's compactness and excellent XML support, its developers have entered into agreements to adapt Opera for use in cell phones and Personal Digital Assistants (PDAs). Partners in these endeavors include IBM, AMD, Ericsson, Psion, Qualcomm, Palm, and Screen Media.

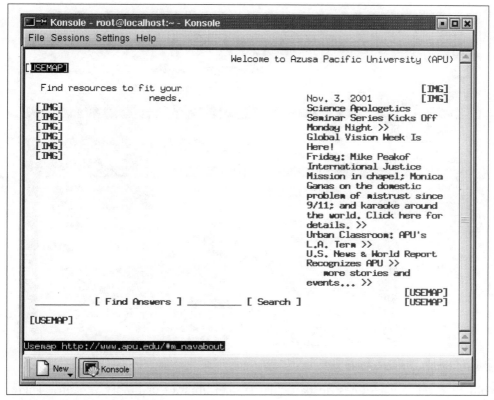

Figure 10-12. The Links web browser

Among Opera's features are the following:

- Opera's developers claim that it's the world's fastest browser.
- It offers accessibility features for users with visual and motor impairments.
- It is highly compliant with a variety of standards, including HTML, XML, HTTP, SSH, TLS, CSS1, CSS2, ECMAScript, JavaScript, and DOM.

The Windows version of Opera supports additional features including instant messaging, integrated search, presentation graphics, WML (Wireless Markup Language), integrated support for Java, and email.

Opera can be downloaded as a *deb*, *rpm*, or *tar.gz* file. If you plan to install Opera under Red Hat Linux, you'll find the *rpm* file the most convenient format. You can download Opera as a dynamically or statically linked binary. A dynamically linked binary depends on system libraries in much the same way many Windows programs depend on DLLs. Although the dynamically linked binary is smaller than the statically linked one and uses fewer system resources, you may prefer the statically linked

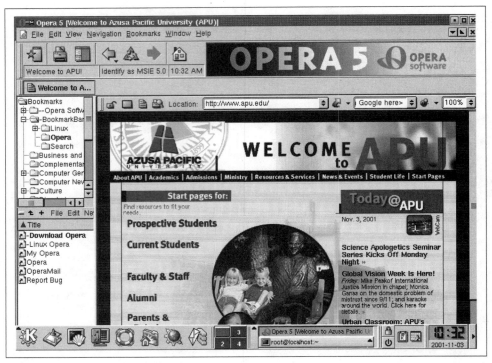

Figure 10-13. The Opera web browser

binary because it requires no particular system libraries or library versions. Therefore, installation of the statically linked binary is less likely to fail. Once you've
installed Opera, you'll find it on the GNOME or KDE menu; however, if you prefer,
you can launch Opera by issuing the command:

```
/usr/bin/opera
```

gFTP FTP Client

You can use your web browser to download files from an FTP server, but to upload
files you need an FTP client. The gFTP client, included with Red Hat Linux, is an
excellent choice, because its user interface resembles that of popular Windows FTP
clients, such as WS-FTP. Figure 10-14 shows the gFTP client.

If you selected GNOME during system installation, the installer included gFTP in
your build. Despite this GNOME-centricity, you can use gFTP with KDE.

gFTP appears on GNOME's menu. To manually launch gFTP, issue the following
command from an X terminal:

```
gftp &
```

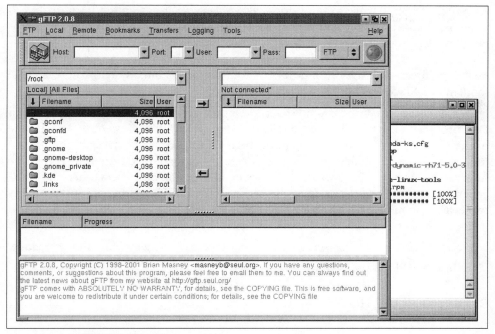

Figure 10-14. The gFTP FTP client

To connect to a remote system, choose Remote → Connect, identify the system's hostname, specify the appropriate username and password, and click on the Connect icon in the upper left of *gFTP*'s window. To upload a file, click on the name of the file in the local list box at the left of the window and then click on the right-pointing arrow. To download a file, click on the name of the file in the list box at the right of the window and then click on the left-pointing arrow. When you've transferred all your files, choose Remote → Disconnect or click again on the Connect icon.

> You can access an FTP server in command-line mode, if you prefer. Chapter 12 explains how to do so.

Configuring Linux to Use a Cable or DSL Modem

Several years ago, establishing home networks became popular, to allow the entire family to simultaneously surf the Web. Because of Linux's comprehensive TCP/IP networking facilities, Linux systems became popular as gateway routers to dialup, ISDN, cable, and DSL feeds.

As writer of the Newbies column for *Linux Magazine*,* I have often been invited to write a column on using Linux to establish such a configuration. While I've maintained such a home network for several years, I haven't been able to figure out how to write a short, 2000-word column—or, for that matter, a book chapter—that adequately addresses all the ins and outs of configuring a Linux system to use a cable modem or DSL connection.

Here's how the situation sizes up. First, the bad news. It seems that every cable and DSL provider has decided to set up client systems a different way. And almost none of the providers are Linux-friendly. But there's also good news. Despite the foregoing, you have a good chance of being able to use your Linux system to access the Internet via a cable or DSL modem. However, all that can be provided here are some general principles and pointers to further information. There are simply too many twists and too many rapidly changing turns to be able to do justice to particulars in a medium such as a book.

Some useful resources when setting up Linux to access a cable or DSL modem include:

Hal Burgiss' DSL HOWTO for Linux
   http://www.linuxdoc.org/HOWTO/DSL-HOWTO

David Fannin's DSL HOWTO for Linux
   http://www.linuxdoc.org/HOWTO/DSL-HOWTO/index.html

Paul Ramey's Red Hat Linux 6.X as an Internet Gateway for a Home Network
   http://www.linuxdoc.org/HOWTO/mini/Home-Network-mini-HOWTO.html

Vladimir Vuksan's Cable Modem Providers HOWTO
   http://www.oswg.org/oswg-nightly/oswg/en_US.ISO_8859-1/articles/Cable-Modem/Cable-Modem.html

Another solution, one that I personally recommend, is the use of a cable/DSL gateway router. Netgear and Linksys, among others, manufacture popular models. These inexpensive devices—often less than $100 retail—sit between your cable or DSL modem and your home network. Cable/DSL gateway routers generally provide a masquerading firewall and DNS proxy services. Better models have multiple ports so that you can connect several PCs without buying additional hubs or switches. Some recent models even provide a wireless LAN, though the ability to interface a Linux PC to the LAN is uncertain, owing to the possible lack of Linux drivers.

Because such devices are designed to work with as many cable and DSL configurations as possible, they work right out of the box most of the time. It's true that they provide no function that couldn't be provided—at least in principle—by a Linux PC. But they consume less power, occupy less space, make less noise, and require less configuration and administration than a Linux PC. I retired a quite venerable Pentium 166 Linux PC from cable modem gateway duty some months ago and have never regretted the decision.

---

* To read through my current and previous articles, go to *http://www.linux-mag.com/depts/newbies.html*.

## CHAPTER 11

Setting Up a Networked Workstation

Linux's greatest strength is its powerful and robust networking capabilities. The good news is that everything about Linux's networking setup is open to inspection and completely configurable. Nothing is hidden from the user, and no parameters are forced on you. The challenge is to get the most out of this setup.

Basic networking principles don't differ much between Windows and Linux, and indeed the principles aren't unfamiliar. This chapter begins with an overview of networking and then looks in more detail at Linux networking on a local area network (LAN). In the next chapter, you'll learn about setting up Internet services.

This chapter explains how to set up a LAN that includes a Linux Samba server, which lets Microsoft Windows and Unix systems access shared files and printers across the network. Samba not only lets you share files and printers, it can also be used to back up and restore files via the network. The chapter also explains how to use Neat (Red Hat's Network Administration Tool) to administer a simple LAN. Administering the network configurations of the hosts on even a modest network can be a headache. This chapter explains how to install and configure a DHCP server that lets you manage network configurations centrally, facilitating network administration.

Networking Overview

Most computers today handle network traffic much as the post office handles mail. Think, for example, of the steps involved in sending and receiving a letter. Your postal carrier must know where to drop off and where to pick up mail. So your home must have some kind of recognizable *interface*; we call this a mailbox. And whereas your postal carrier may know your neighborhood quite well, delivery in other areas will require other carriers. Mail is passed to these other carriers through a *gateway*; we call this the post office. Although you can think of the whole postal system as one big network, it's easier to understand if you think of it as a hierarchy of *subnetworks* (or *subnets*): the postal system is divided into states, states are divided into counties and cities with a range of Zip Codes, Zip Codes contain a number of streets, and each street contains a unique set of addresses.

Computer networking mirrors this model. Let's trace an email message from you to a coworker. You compose the message and click Send. Your computer passes the message to a network interface. This interface may be a modem by which you dial up an Internet service provider (ISP), or it may be via an Ethernet connection on a LAN. Either way, on the other side of the interface is a gateway machine. The gateway knows how to look at the address of the recipient on the email message and interpret that message in terms of networks and subnets. Using this information, the gateway passes the message to other gateways until the message reaches the gateway for the destination machine. That gateway in turn delivers the message via a recognizable interface (such as a modem or Ethernet link) to the recipient's inbox.

If you review this story, you can easily see which parts of networking you'll need to configure on your Linux system. You'll need to know the address of your machine. Just as the town name *Sebastopol* and the Zip Code *95472* are two different names for the same location, you may have both a name, called a *hostname*, and a number, called an *IP number* or *IP address*,* that serve as the address for your machine.

To translate between these two notations, you may need to know the address of a Domain Name Server (DNS). This is a machine that matches IP addresses with hostnames. You'll also need to know the address of a gateway machine through which network traffic will be routed. Finally, you'll need to be able to bring up a network interface on your system, and you'll need to assign a route from that interface to the gateway.

While all of this can seem complex, it really isn't any more complex than the postal system, and it functions in much the same way. Fortunately, Linux comes with tools to help you automate network configuration.

LAN Administration Using Neat

This section explains how to use Neat to configure TCP/IP networking. If your system is not part of a LAN, you won't generally need to perform the operations this section describes; establishing a PPP connection with your ISP generally configures your system's network settings automatically. However, if you wish to customize your system's network settings, or if you wish to better understand how Linux networking functions, you'll find this information helpful.

To launch Neat, choose Programs → System → Network Configuration from the GNOME main menu, or System → Network Configuration from the KDE main menu. The Network Configuration dialog box, as shown in Figure 11-1, appears.

---

* IP stands for Internet Protocol.

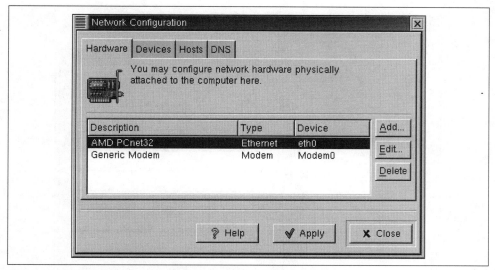

Figure 11-1. The Hardware tab of the Network Configuration dialog box

The dialog box has four tabs:

- Hardware
- Devices
- Hosts
- DNS

Each of these tabs is explained in a following section.

Configuring Hardware

The Hardware tab of the Network Configuration dialog box shows the network devices found in your system, including network adapters and modems. You can use the controls appearing on the tab to specify information pertaining to network devices. To do so, highlight the desired device and click Edit. A configuration dialog box appears. The format of the dialog box depends on the type of network device selected.

Figure 11-2 shows a dialog box associated with a network adapter. This dialog box lets you specify the IRQ, memory address, DMA port, and other information associated with the network adapter. The PCI bus of a modern PC can generally probe for this sort of information automatically. Consequently, you probably won't often find it necessary to use the Hardware tab. However, if your system is unable to detect an installed network device, you may be able to get the device working by entering the appropriate information in the configuration dialog box. To determine the proper information, inspect your system's Windows configuration and consult documentation associated with the network device.

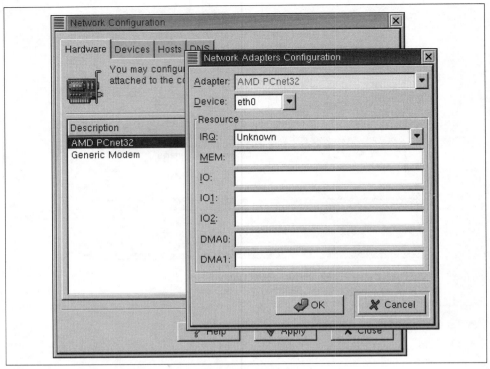

Figure 11-2. The Network Adapters Configuration dialog box

Configuring Devices

The Devices tab of the Network Configuration dialog box lets you configure network devices. Like the Hardware tab, it displays a list of devices. To configure a device, highlight the device and click Edit. A configuration dialog box appropriate to the type of the selected device appears. Figure 11-3 shows the Ethernet Device dialog box associated with a network adapter. The dialog box has three tabs, each of which is explained in a following subsection:

- General
- Protocols
- Hardware Device

General device options

The General tab of the Ethernet Device dialog box lets you perform the following operations:

Specify a nickname for the device
  By default, Ethernet devices have nicknames such as *eth0*, *eth1*, and so on. Generally, you should not change the nickname associated with an Ethernet device.

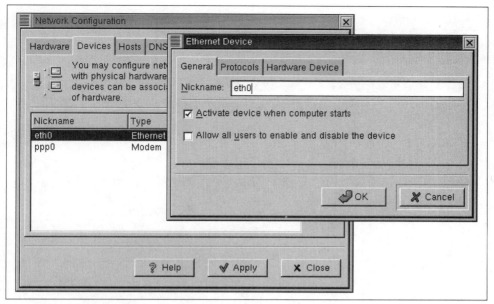

Figure 11-3. The General tab of the Ethernet Device dialog box

One circumstance in which you may wish to change the nickname occurs when you change the relative position of network adapters on your system's PCI bus. Doing so causes the device previously known as *eth0* to become known as *eth1* and vice versa. Rather than reconfigure networking, you can change the nickname associated with each device, so that the original network configuration is once again correct.

Specify that the device should be activated when the computer starts
Generally, Ethernet devices should be configured so that they're activated when the computer starts. You may wish to change this specification when troubleshooting or in order to temporarily deactivate a device.

Specify that any user can enable or disable the device
Generally, only the root user should be permitted to enable or disable a network device. The root user is presumed to be capable of exercising judgment that prevents, for example, unnecessarily disabling a device that other users are using.

However, you may wish to assign this privilege to trusted users who will exercise it appropriately. This is seldom necessary for Ethernet devices but may be useful for PPP devices. Allowing a user to enable a PPP device enables the user to establish an Internet connection without the assistance of the root user.

Device protocol options

The Protocols tab of the Ethernet Device dialog box lets you configure TCP/IP options pertaining to the device. To do so, highlight TCP/IP and click Edit. The TCP/IP Settings dialog box, as shown in Figure 11-4, appears.

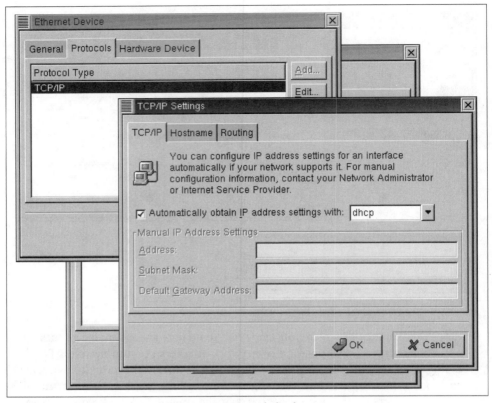

Figure 11-4. The TCP/IP tab of the TCP/IP Settings dialog box

The TCP/IP Settings dialog box has three tabs:

- TCP/IP
- Hostname
- Routing

Every Internet host has an associated identifier known as an IP address. As shown in Figure 11-4, the TCP/IP tab lets you specify how the IP address associated with the Ethernet device is obtained. If the device is associated with a network that includes a server that provides IP address information to clients, the IP address can be obtained automatically. To enable this feature, check the box labeled "Automatically obtain IP address settings with." Then, use the drop-down list box to specify the type of server, which can be any of the following:

- DHCP (Dynamic Host Configuration Protocol)
- Bootp (boot protocol)
- Dialup

You should consult your network administrator to determine whether the network includes an appropriate server and the type of server, if any. Generally, the server will use the DHCP protocol. Some Unix servers provide information via the Bootp protocol. The Dialup option is not appropriate for Ethernet adapters; however, it is often specified for PPP devices.

If no server is available, you can specify your system's IP address manually. Consult your network administrator to determine the proper values. Uncheck the box labeled "Automatically obtain IP address settings with" and specify the following information:

Address
Specify the IP address associated with the network adapter. An IP address consists of four numbers, separated by dots, for example, 192.168.1.1.

Subnet Mask
Specify the network mask that identifies the part of the adapter's IP address that represents the network address. If you're uncertain what value to use, try the value 255.255.255.0, which works in most cases.

Default Gateway Address
Specify the IP address of the system that forwards packets from the network to the outside world. If your system connects to the Internet via a dialup connection, leave this field blank.

If you're setting up your own network, you can use the IP numbers from 192.168.1.1 to 192.168.1.254 to identify your systems. These numbers are one of several sets of IP addresses set aside for private use.

Figure 11-5 shows the Hostname tab of the TCP/IP Settings dialog box. This tab lets you specify a hostname by which your system is known. The hostname you specify is known only to your system; unless you configure a DNS server, which is a demanding task, your system will be known to other systems only by its IP address.

The Hostname tab also lets you specify how your system obtains DNS information, which it uses to determine the IP address associated with a hostname. If a DHCP server on the network provides the IP address of a DNS server, you can check the box labeled "Automatically obtain DNS information from provider."

If your network connects to other local area networks, you must identify these networks in order to be able to access hosts on them. To do so, use the Routing tab of the TCP/IP Settings dialog box, shown in Figure 11-6.

To identify a local network, click Add. A dialog box lets you specify the IP address and subnet mask of the network and the IP address of the system that acts as the gateway to the network.

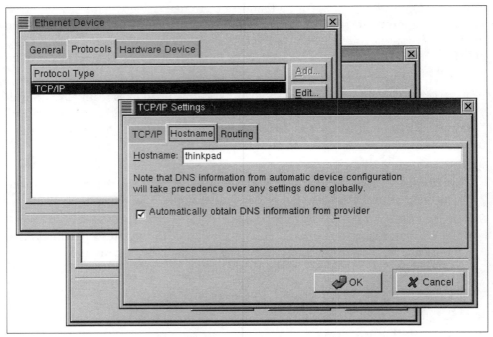

Figure 11-5. The Hostname tab of the TCP/IP Settings dialog box

Hardware device options

The Hardware Device tab of the Ethernet Device dialog box, shown in Figure 11-7, lets you specify special hardware device options. These options are seldom needed except in sophisticated network configurations.

It's possible to associate multiple IP addresses with a single network device. Addresses other than the primary address are called *aliases*. You can create an alias by checking the box labeled Enable Device Alias Support and specifying the device and alias.

You can also specify the hardware or Media Access Control (MAC) address associated with an Ethernet device, overriding the value specified at the time of manufacture. To do so, check the box labeled Use Hardware Address and specify the desired hardware address.

Configuring Hosts

Most systems attached to a network use DNS services to determine the IP address associated with a hostname. However, you can configure your system to determine the IP address associated with a hostname even when DNS services are not available. To do so, use the Hosts tab of the Network Configuration dialog box, shown in Figure 11-8.

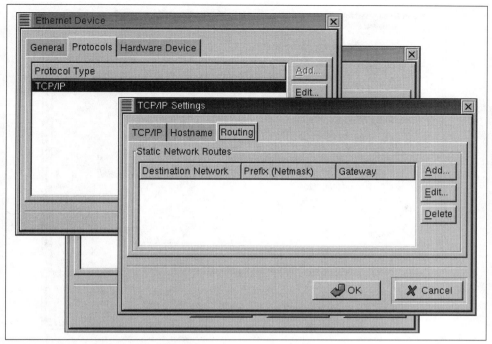

Figure 11-6. The Routing tab of the TCP/IP Settings dialog box

To specify host information, click Add and supply the IP address and name of the host. If desired, you can specify one or more aliases or abbreviated names for the host. By default, the host information includes an entry for the IP address 127.0.0.1, which is associated with the hostname *localhost*. You should not disturb this entry, which provides a way for your system to access its own network facilities.

Configuring DNS

The DNS tab of the Network Configuration dialog box, shown in Figure 11-9, lets you specify options that govern how your system determines IP addresses from hostnames. The tab lets you specify the following information:

Hostname
> The hostname of your system, including the domain name. By default, the hostname is *localhost.localdomain*. You should change this value only if your system has a hostname registered with a DNS server.

Domain
> The domain name of your system. By default, the domain name is *localdomain*. You should change this value only if your system has a hostname registered with a DNS server.

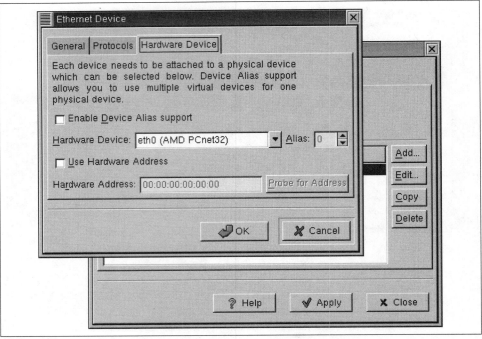

Figure 11-7. The Hardware Device tab of the Ethernet Device dialog box

Primary DNS

The IP address of the DNS server, if any, your system should use. If a DHCP server provides your system with its network configuration, you may omit this value.

Secondary DNS

The IP address of a backup DNS server, if any, that your system should use if the primary DNS server is unavailable. If a DHCP server provides your system with its network configuration, you may omit this value.

Tertiary DNS

The IP address of a second backup DNS server, if any, that your system should use if the primary and secondary DNS servers are unavailable. If a DHCP server provides your system with its network configuration, you may omit this value.

DNS Search Path

If you frequently access other hosts on your ISP's network, you should specify a search domain, for example, *oreilly.com*. Doing so enables you to refer to the host *abc.oreilly.com*, for example, as simply *abc*. To do so, type the domain name in the text box labeled Search Domain and click Add. If you like, you can specify multiple domains, which are searched in the order specified, from top to bottom. You can use the Up and Down buttons to reorder the domains.

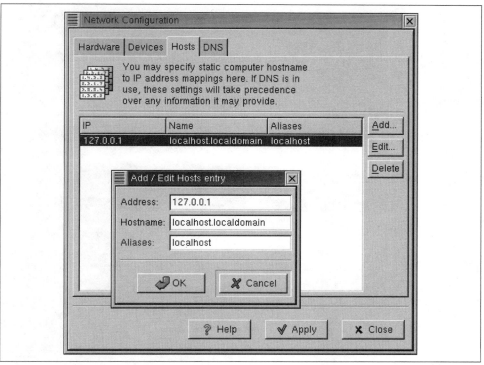

Figure 11-8. The Hosts tab of the Network Configuration dialog box and the Add/Edit Hosts Entry dialog box

Samba

Once you've set up a LAN, you're ready to provide services to hosts on the network. To provide printer and file sharing, Windows uses a facility known as the Server Message Block (SMB). This same facility is sometimes known as the Common Internet File System (CIFS), NetBIOS, or LanManager. Thanks to Andrew Tridgell and others, Linux systems provide support for SMB via a package known as Samba. Like SMB, Samba lets you:

- Authorize users to access Samba resources
- Share printers and files among Windows, OS/2, Netware, and Unix systems
- Establish a simple name server for identifying systems on your LAN
- Back up PC files to a Linux system and restore them

Samba has proven its reliability and high performance in many organizations. According to the online survey at *http://www.samba.org/pub/samba/survey/ssstats.html*, Bank of America is using Samba in a configuration that includes about 15,000 clients, and Hewlett-Packard is using Samba in a configuration that includes about 7,000 clients.

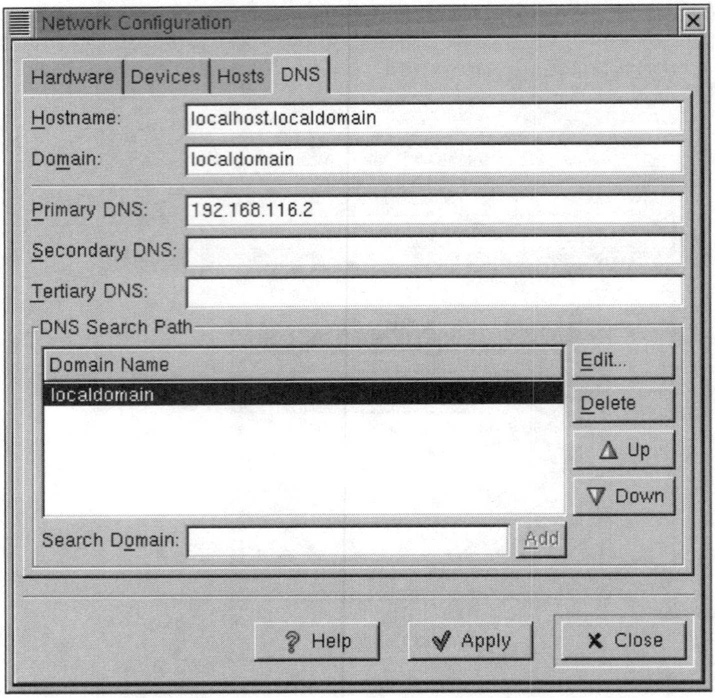

Figure 11-9. The DNS tab of the Network Configuration dialog box

Installing the Samba Server

If you've never installed and configured a network server, Samba is a good place to begin; its installation and configuration are generally simple and straightforward.

The Samba server includes the *nmbd* and *smbd* programs (which run as daemons), several utility programs, manpages and other documentation, and three configuration files: */etc/samba/smbusers*, */etc/samba/smb.conf*, and */etc/samba/lmhosts*. The *smbusers* file associates several user accounts that are special to Samba with Linux user accounts; for example, it associates the Samba user IDs, *administrator* and *admin*, with *root*. Generally, you don't need to change *smbusers*. Likewise, you don't generally need to revise *lmhosts*. You'll learn how to configure the *smb.conf* file shortly.

The simplest way to install Samba is to select it during system installation. However, if you failed to do so, you can install Samba by using GnoRPM to install the following packages:

- *samba*
- *samba-client*
- *samba-common*
- *samba-swat*

Configuring Samba

The */etc/samba/smb.conf* file lets you specify a variety of options that control Samba's operation. You can edit the file by using your favorite text editor; however, the Samba Web Administration Tool (SWAT) lets you view and change options using your web browser, which is generally much easier than using a text editor. The SWAT tool verifies the values of parameters you enter and provides online help.

To use SWAT, you must first configure *xinetd* to launch SWAT when you request it. To do so, issue the commands:

```
chkconfig xinetd on
chkconfig swat on
```

Then signal the *xinetd* process that you've modified one of its configuration files, by issuing the following command:

```
service xinetd reload
```

To access SWAT, point your browser to port 901; for example, you can use the URL *http://localhost:901*.

You can configure SWAT to accept connections from remote hosts. To do so, delete the line:

```
only_from = 127.0.0.1
```

from the /etc/xinted.d SWAT file. That deletion is not recommended, except perhaps for accessing SWAT from your LAN. Accessing SWAT remotely requires that your system's root password be sent over the network via HTTP, which cannot encrypt data. A cracker using a *packet sniffer* may discover the password and compromise your system. A packet sniffer is a program that lets its operator view packets sent across a network. If the packets are unencrypted or only weakly encrypted, the operator may be able to obtain user IDs, passwords, and other information contained in the packets.

Your web browser will prompt you for a user account and password; specify *root* as the user account and give the appropriate password. Figure 11-10 shows *SWAT*'s main menu, accessed by using the system's IP address in place of its hostname.

To configure your Samba server, click the following toolbar icons:

Home
Return to the main menu (shown in Figure 11-10). The main menu also provides convenient access to Samba documentation via the links in the body of the page.

Globals
Configure global Samba variables.

Shares
Configure file shares.

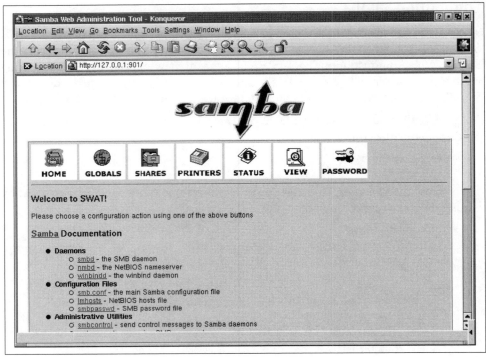

Figure 11-10. SWAT's main menu

Printers
Configure shared printers.

Status
View the status of the Samba server.

View
View Samba's configuration file, */etc/samba/smb.conf*.

Password
Add and delete users and change user passwords.

Configuring global variables

To configure global options, click the Globals button on the toolbar. Figure 11-11 shows the Global Variables page, and Table 11-1 describes the most important options. You can access additional options by clicking Advanced View. To change an option, select or type the desired value. When you've changed all the options you want to change, click Commit Changes, and the changes take effect.

Samba's main configuration file, */etc/samba/smb.conf*, is overwritten by SWAT. The specifications contained in the file are retained and shown as initial values; however, any comments in the file are deleted.

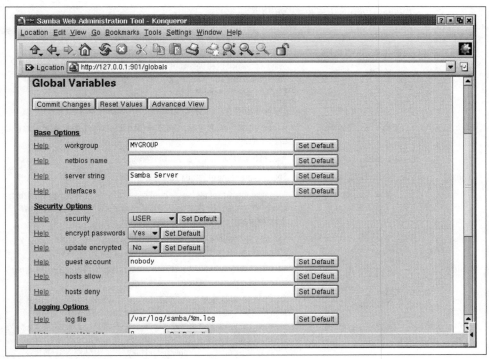

Figure 11-11. SWAT's Global Variables screen

Table 11-1. Samba's Global Variables

Option group	Option	Description
Base	workgroup	The workgroup name displayed when the server is queried by a client.
	netbios name	The NetBIOS name by which the server is known.
	server string	The text string displayed to describe the server.
	interfaces	The IP address(es) of the interface(s) through which Samba should listen. Each IP address is followed by a forward slash and a number that specifies the number of bits that pertain to the network portion of the IP address (usually 24), for example, 192.168.1.0/24. If this option is not set, Samba attempts to locate and automatically configure a primary interface. Samba lets you specify the interface name, rather than an IP address, if you prefer.
Security	security	Specifies how Samba authenticates requests for access to shared resources. The default value, *user*, is helpful when the Samba server and its clients have many common user accounts. The value *share* can be useful when few common user accounts exist, because it allows users to access shared resources without first logging in to the server. The value *server* lets another SMB server perform authentication on behalf of the server. The value *domain* specifies that the host is integrated within a Windows NT domain; it behaves similarly to the value *user*. You should generally use the default value.
	encrypt passwords	Specifies whether Samba will negotiate encrypted passwords, which are expected by Windows NT 4.0 SP3 and later, 98, Me, and 2000.

Table 11-1. Samba's Global Variables (continued)

Option group	Option	Description
	update encrypted	Allows automatic updating of an encrypted password when a user logs on using a nonencrypted password. This option is useful when migrating to encrypted passwords and should otherwise be set to No. It requires that Encrypt Passwords be set to No.
	guest account	The Linux user account used to provide services for guest users.
	hosts allow	A list of hosts that can access the server. If not specified, all hosts are permitted access.
	hosts deny	A list of hosts that cannot access the server.
Logging	log file	Specifies the name of Samba's log file.
	max log size	The maximum size of the log file in kilobytes (KB). When the specified size is exceeded, Samba begins a new log file. A value of 0 lets the log file grow indefinitely.
Tuning	socket options	Specifies TCP options that can improve performance. The default options are generally acceptable.
Printing	printing	Specifies how Samba interprets printer status information. Generally, *lprng* is an appropriate choice for a Linux system.
Browse	os level	Specifies the level at which Samba advertises itself for browse elections. A high number makes it more likely that Samba will be selected as the browser. The value 65 causes clients to prefer Samba to a Windows NT server. The default value is generally acceptable; unintentionally high values may cause browsing problems and may cause NT/2000 servers to become unstable.
	preferred master	Specifies whether Samba is the preferred master browser for its workgroup. Used with domain master = yes to force acceptance of the host as the master browser for its workgroup.
	local master	Specifies whether Samba will bid to become the local master browser on a subnet. Generally, the default value is acceptable.
	domain master	Specifies collation of browse lists across a Wide-Area Network (WAN). May result in strange behavior when a workgroup includes a Windows NT Primary Domain Controller (PDC). Generally, the default value is acceptable.
WINS	dns proxy	Specifies that Samba will use DNS to attempt to resolve unknown NetBIOS hostnames. Generally, the default value is acceptable.
	wins server	Specifies the IP address of the WINS server with which Samba should register itself, if any. This item should be specified whenever a network includes a WINS server.
	wins support	Specifies that Samba should act as a WINS server. Useful when the network includes several subnets. Do not specify this option for multiple systems of a single network. Generally, the default value is acceptable.

You probably won't need to make many changes to Samba's global variables. Setting the workgroup and netbios name is sufficient for most users. If your system has more than one network adapter card, you'll also need to set the interfaces variable.

If your network includes Windows 98/NT/2000 clients, you'll need to set encrypt passwords.

 If your system is attached to a cable modem or other interface that makes it available to other network users, you should specify security options that prevent unauthorized users from accessing your files or printer. For example, use the hosts allow option to restrict the hosts allowed to access your Samba server.

Configuring file share parameters

To establish and maintain file shares, use the Shares button on the toolbar. Figure 11-12 shows the Share Parameters page.

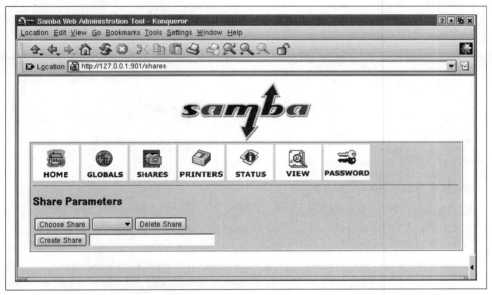

Figure 11-12. SWAT's Share Parameters screen

Red Hat Linux configures a default share, *homes*, which lets Linux users access their Linux */home* directory as a Samba share. You can create a new share by typing its name and clicking Create Share. To delete a share, choose the share name from the drop-down list and click Delete Share. To work with an existing share, choose it from the drop-down list and click Choose Share. When you click Choose Share, the page shown in Figure 11-13 appears. This page lets you view and change a variety of share options. Table 11-2 describes the available share options. You can access additional options by clicking Advanced View. As with the global options, you may not need to change many share options. Likely candidates for change are the comment, path, and read only options.

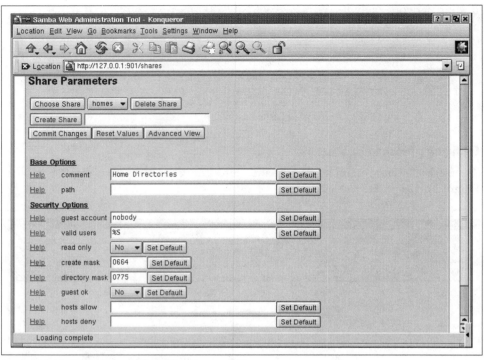

Figure 11-13. SWAT's expanded Share Parameters screen

Table 11-2. Samba File Share Options

Option group	Option	Description
Base	comment	The description displayed when the file share is queried by a client.
	path	The path that is shared by the server.
Security	guest account	The Linux user account used to provide services for guest users.
	valid users	Specifies users allowed to access the share.
	read only	Specifies whether the share can be written or is read-only.
	create mask	Specifies the permissions associated with created files, as an inverse value.
	directory mask	Specifies the permissions associated with created directories, as an inverse value.
	guest ok	Specifies whether guest access (access without a password) is allowed.
	hosts allow	A list of hosts that can access the file share. If not specified, all hosts are permitted access.
	hosts deny	A list of hosts that cannot access the file share.
Browse	browseable	Specifies whether the file share is visible in the list of shares made available by the server.
Miscellaneous	available	Specifies whether the share is available; by setting this option to No you can prevent access to the share.

Configuring printer share parameters

You configure printer share parameters in much the same way you configure shares. Begin by clicking the Printers toolbar button. You can use the page shown in Figure 11-14 to create a new printer share, delete a printer share, or modify an existing printer share.

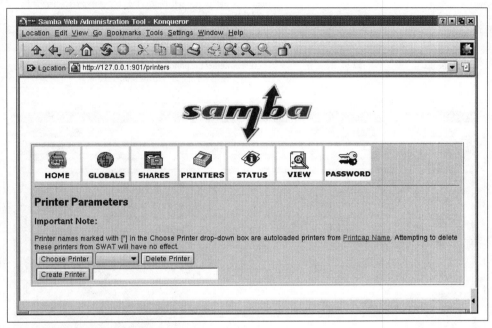

Figure 11-14. SWAT's Printer Parameters screen

If you select a printer from the drop-down list and click Choose Printer, the page shown in Figure 11-15 appears. Table 11-3 describes the available print share options. You can access additional options by clicking Advanced View. As with the global options and file share options, you may not need to change many printer share options. The comment option is the most likely to be changed.

Table 11-3. Samba Print Share Options

Option group	Option	Description
Base	comment	The description displayed when the printer share is queried by a client.
	path	The print spooling directory.
Security	guest account	The Linux user account used to provide services for guest users.
	guest ok	Specifies whether guest access (access without a password) is allowed.
	hosts allow	A list of hosts that can access the printer share. If not specified, all hosts are permitted access.
	hosts deny	A list of hosts that cannot access the printer share.

Table 11-3. Samba Print Share Options (continued)

Option group	Option	Description
Printing	printable	Specifies whether printing is permitted. If this option is set to No, clients may still be able to browse the printer share.
	printing	Specifies the type of printer interface used, which determines what commands Samba issues to control the printer; *lprng* is generally a good choice.
Browse	browseable	Specifies whether the printer share is visible in the list of shares made available by the server.
Miscellaneous	available	Specifies whether the printer share is available; by setting this option to No, you can prevent access to the printer share.

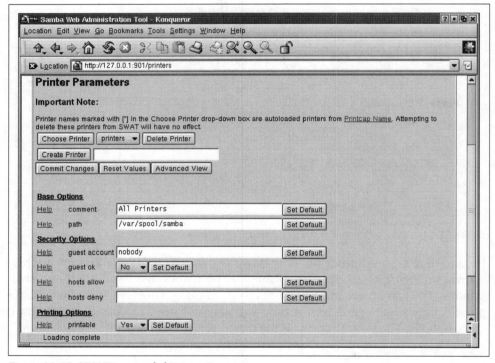

Figure 11-15. SWAT's expanded Printer Parameters screen

Viewing Samba Server Status

The Status button on SWAT's toolbar lets you view the status of the Samba server. The page shown in Figure 11-16 shows the following information about the status of your Samba server:

- The interval at which the page is refreshed, given in seconds
- The version of Samba and the status of the server daemons (*smbd* and *nmbd*)

- Any active connections
- Any active file and printer shares
- Any open files

Using the controls on the page, you can refresh the contents, set the auto refresh interval (in seconds), start and stop either daemon, and kill an active connection.

 It's generally better to start and stop Samba processes by using the script in */etc/rc.d/init.d*, as explained later in this chapter.

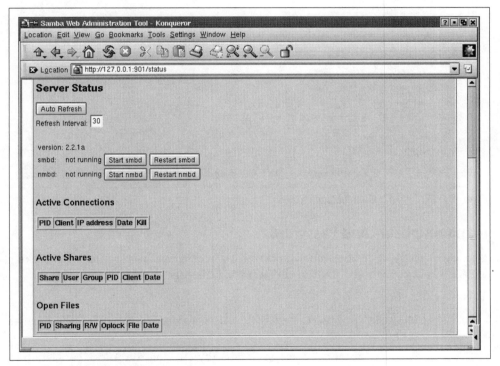

Figure 11-16. Samba's Server Status page

Viewing Samba Server Configuration

The View button on SWAT's toolbar lets you view the Samba server's main configuration file, */etc/samba/smb.conf* (shown in Figure 11-17). By default, the page shows only the basic configuration options; clicking Full View causes SWAT to display every configuration option.

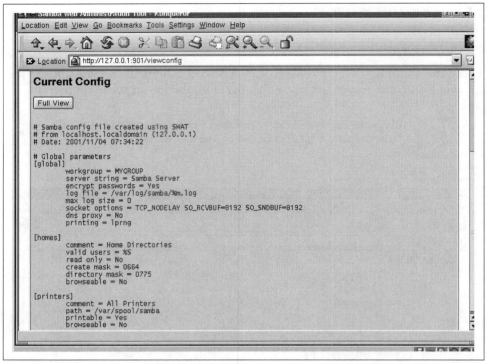

Figure 11-17. SWAT's Current Config screen

Managing Users and Passwords

You can specify user accounts authorized to access Samba resources by clicking SWAT's Password toolbar button and accessing the page shown in Figure 11-18.

This page lets you:

- Change the password associated with a user account (by clicking the Change Password button)
- Authorize a user account to access Samba (by clicking the Add New User button)
- Delete a user account (by clicking the Delete User button)
- Disable or enable a user account (by clicking the Disable User or Enable User buttons, respectively)

The user accounts that you specify on the Server Password Management page are those that your Samba server recognizes as authorized to access its resources.

The bottom part of the page, titled Client/Server Password Management, lets you change the password associated with a user account on a remote system running

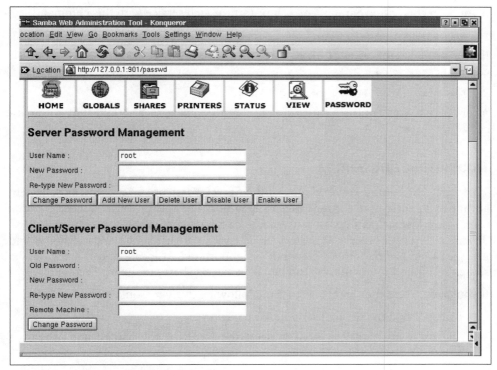

Figure 11-18. The Server Password Management page

Samba or SMB. Changing a password by using Client/Server Password Management is often more convenient than logging in to the remote host and using its password change facility.

Starting and Stopping Samba

After you've configured Samba, start the *smb* service by issuing the command:

```
service samba start
```

This command starts both the SMB and NMB (NetBIOS name server), services associated with Samba.

You can view the status of the *smb* service by issuing the command:

```
service samba status
```

If the service is running, the command should report the process IDs of Samba's *snmd* and *nmbd* processes.

To stop Samba, issue the command:

```
service samba stop
```

If you've reconfigured Samba, you can restart the *smb* service with this command:

```
service samba restart
```

If you want Samba to start automatically when you boot your system, issue this command:

```
chkconfig --level 345 smb on
```

Alternatively, you can use Neat to specify that the *smb* service should start automatically.

Troubleshooting Samba

To verify that Samba is working, use the Server Password Management screen to authorize a Linux user account to access Samba. For this purpose, choose a Linux user account that has the same username and password as an account on a Windows client. Log in to the Windows client using that username and password and use the Windows Explorer's Network Neighborhood to locate and use the Samba share. You'll find more information on using Samba shares in the next section.

If you can't access the share, consider the following likely reasons:

- You specified the wrong username or password.
- The username and password are not the same on the Samba and Windows hosts.
- You haven't authorized the user to access Samba.
- Networking isn't properly configured on the Samba or Windows host.

If you're unable to find the problem, consult the documentation that accompanies Samba. In particular, peruse the file *DIAGNOSIS.txt*, which resides in the */usr/share/ doc/samba-*/docs/textdocs* directory or its equivalent on your system. This file includes a step-by-step procedure for verifying the operation of your Samba server. When a step fails, you can consult the file to determine the likely causes and how to go about fixing the problem. Chances are, you'll be able to administer Samba without outside help, but if not, you'll find the participants in the *comp.protocols.smb* newsgroup to be helpful. Another resource is O'Reilly's *Using Samba*, by Robert Eckstein, David Collier-Brown, and Peter Kelly. Since the book was published under the Open Publication License (OPL), *Using Samba* is also available online in electronic form at *http://www.oreilly.com/catalog/samba/*.

Like any network server, Samba provides a wealth of options and facilities. If you thoroughly explore these facilities, you're likely to break your server. To avoid problems, you should keep a backup copy of your */etc/samba/smb.conf* file. Doing so can be as easy as issuing the following command after Samba is up and running:

```
cp /etc/samba/smb.conf /etc/samba/smb.conf.bak
```

Then, if your server ceases to work, you can restore your old configuration by issuing the command:

```
cp /etc/samba/smb.conf.bak /etc/samba/smb.conf
```

You'll also need to restart your system (or at least the Samba daemons).

Samba Client Configuration and Use

Once you've got your Samba server up and running, you can access it via Windows and Linux. This section shows you how to access the Samba server and also how to use your Samba server to create backups of important datafiles on client systems.

SMB clients are also available for most popular operating systems, including OS/2 and Mac OS (including Mac OS X). You shouldn't expect to have trouble getting them to work with Samba. If your client seems not to work, simply follow the procedure given in the troubleshooting section.

Windows Client

Windows 3.11, 9*x*, Me, and NT—including Windows 2000, which is an updated release of Windows NT—have built-in support for the SMB protocol, so systems running these operating systems can easily access your Samba server's resources. Under Windows 9*x*/NT, you can access Samba resources by using the Windows Explorer. Log on using a user account that's authorized to access Samba resources, then click Network Neighborhood, and you should see a subtree that corresponds to your workgroup. Click that subtree, and you should see a subtree that corresponds to your Samba server. By expanding the subtree, you can see the browseable file and printer shares that are available. You can easily drag and drop files to and from a shared directory, assuming your user account is permitted the necessary access.

To use a shared printer, click Start → Settings → Printers and then double-click Add Printer. The wizard will guide you through the setup procedure. Simply choose the Network Printer option and browse to select the desired printer. If you configured the printer share without the browseable option, you cannot browse and therefore must type the name of the printer share. To do so, type two backward slashes, followed by the name of your Samba server, followed by a single backslash, followed by the name of the printer share. For example, if you want to access a printer share named *lp* on the Samba server known as *SERVER*, you'd type *SERVER**lp*.

You can map a file share to a drive letter by using the Tools → Map Network Drive menu item of the Windows Explorer. Simply select an available drive letter and type the name of the file share, which consists of two backward slashes, followed by the name of your Samba server, followed by a single backslash, followed by the name of the file share. For example, if you want to access a file share named *db* on the Samba server known as *SERVER*, you'd type *SERVER**db*.

If you have difficulty connecting to your Samba server, follow the procedure given in the preceding section on troubleshooting.

Linux Client

The Samba package includes a simple SMB client that can access your Samba server and other SMB servers accessible to your system. To demonstrate that your client and server are working, log on using a user account that has Samba authorization and issue the following command:

```
smbclient -L localhost
```

You should see a list of the browseable shares available on your server. To query a different SMB server, issue the following command:

```
smbclient -L server
```

where *server* is the name of the SMB server you want to contact. Rather than logging on using an authorized user account, you can explicitly specify a user account by using this command form:

```
smbclient -L server -U userid
```

To actually access resources via SMB, use the following command form:

```
smbclient service -U userid
```

where *service* specifies the name of the SMB host and share and *userid* specifies the user account to be used. The name of the SMB host should be preceded by two backward slashes and followed by one backward slash, for example:

```
smbclient \\server\myshare -U mccartyb
```

If the SMB server accepts your request, the client displays a special prompt:

```
smb: dir>
```

where *dir* indicates the current working directory on the SMB server. To download a file from the server, issue the command:

```
get file
```

where *file* specifies the name of the file to be downloaded. To upload a file to the server, issue the command:

```
put file
```

where *file* specifies the name of the file. To list the contents of the current directory, issue the command:

```
dir
```

To enter a subdirectory, issue the following command, where *dir* specifies the name of the subdirectory:

```
cd dir
```

You can return to the parent directory by issuing the command:

```
cd ..
```

To exit the SMB client, issue the command **exit**. You can obtain a list of commands by issuing the command **help** or obtain help on a particular command by issuing the command:

```
help command:
```

where *command* specifies the command that you need help with.

If SWAT fails to suit your taste, several other utilities are available:

KSamba
> Available at *ftp://rpmfind.net/linux/dld/5.4/i386/RPMS/i386//ksamba-0.3.3-1. i386.rpm*, KSamba is a Samba client for use with KDE.

GnoSamba and Gnomba
> Red Hat provides the GNOME tools GnoSamba, which you can find at *ftp://ftp. redhat.com/pub/redhat/redhat-7.1-en/powertools/i386/RedHat/RPMS/GnoSamba-0.3.3-11.i386.rpm*, and Gnomba, which you can find at *ftp://ftp.redhat.com/pub/ redhat/redhat-7.1-en/powertools/i386/RedHat/RPMS/gnomba-0.6.2-4.i386.rpm*.

You can use the *smbprint* script included in the Samba package to print Linux files by using a printer share. However, you'll probably have to do some tweaking of configuration files and adjusting of shell scripts to get *smbprint* to work.

Using the Linux Samba Client for File Backup and Recovery

One of the more practical uses of the Linux SMB client is creating backup copies of files stored on a Windows system. To do so, simply share the drive or directory containing the files you want to back up. Using the Windows Explorer, right-click the drive or directory, click Properties, click the Sharing tab, and select the desired share options. Then, access the share from Linux using *smbclient*. Once you have the SMB prompt, move to the directory you want to back up and issue the SMB **tar** command:

```
smb: \> tar c backup.tar
```

The syntax of the SMB **tar** command resembles that of the **tar** command, though it supports only a handful of options. When you issue the SMB **tar** command with the **c** option, the files of the current directory and all its subdirectories will be backed up and stored in the file *backup.tar* on your Linux system. Of course, you can specify a filename other than *backup.tar* if you wish (although the *.tar* extension is required). Once you've created the backup file, you can write it to a tape, a writable CD-ROM, or other media. If your backup requirements are meager, it may be sufficient merely to have a copy of the file on both your Windows and Linux systems.

To restore a backup, move to the directory where you want the files restored and issue the SMB **tar** command:

```
smb: \> tar x backup.tar
```

The SMB client restores each file from the *backup.tar* file. Of course, you must have write access to the shared directory in order to be able to restore files.

Setting Up a DHCP Server

Managing the network configurations of the hosts on even a small network can be tedious. Administrators of large networks, including ISPs, have long used the DHCP service to centrally manage network configurations. Red Hat Linux includes a DHCP server that you can install in order to facilitate the management of your network. Hosts configured with DHCP clients can load their network configurations from the DHCP server at boot time, including such configuration items as:

- Hostname
- Domain name
- IP address
- Netmask
- Broadcast IP address
- Gateway IP address
- DNS server address

Installing the DHCP Server

Before installing the DHCP server, you should check whether your system's network adapter is properly configured to support DHCP. To do so, issue the **ifconfig** command, as follows:

```
[root@localhost]# ifconfig -a
eth0      Link encap:Ethernet  HWaddr 00:A0:CC:25:8A:EC
          inet addr:192.168.0.5  Bcast:192.168.255.255
            Mask:255.255.0.0
          UP BROADCAST RUNNING MULTICAST  MTU:1500  Metric:1
          RX packets:71910 errors:0 dropped:0 overruns:0
            frame:0
          TX packets:108334 errors:0 dropped:0 overruns:0
            carrier:0
          collisions:89 txqueuelen:100
          Interrupt:11 Base address:0x6000
```

If your system's network adapter is properly configured to support DHCP, the output of the **ifconfig** command will indicate that the adapter supports BROADCAST and MULTICAST. If the output doesn't include these specifications, you must reconfigure or replace the network adapter. Fortunately, it's rare that an adapter lacks these capabilities.

To set up a DHCP server, use GnoRPM to install the *dhcp* package. Then, configure the service as explained in the following section.

Configuring the DHCP Service

To configure the DHCP service, you must create the DHCP configuration file, */etc/dhcpd.conf*. Here's a simple configuration that you can use as a starting point:

```
default lease-time 64800;
max-lease-time     64800;

option domain-name-servers 192.168.0.1;
option domain-name         "oreilly.com";

subnet 192.168.0.0 netmask 255.255.255.0
{
  option subnet-mask        255.255.255.0;
  option broadcast-address  192.168.0.255;
  option routers            192.168.0.1;
  server-identifier 192.168.0.5;
  host sara
  {
    hardware ethernet  00:50:04:d2:3f:15;
    fixed-address      192.168.0.33;
    default-lease-time 86400;
  }

  range 192.168.0.50 192.168.0.254;
}
```

When a DHCP client obtains a network configuration from the server, it doesn't generally obtain the configuration permanently. Instead, a DHCP client is said to *lease* a configuration. The two lines at the top of the configuration file specify the default and maximum lease duration, in seconds. The figure 64800 (seconds) is equivalent to 18 hours. By choosing a relatively long lease time, a client will not generally need to renew its leased network configuration during a workday. You can choose a shorter or longer duration, as you prefer.

The next two lines specify information transmitted to clients as part of their network configurations:

domain-name-servers
> The DNS server IP address. More than one server can be specified. Each server is separated from its neighbor by a comma.

domain-name
> The domain name.

Next comes a group of lines—delimited with paired curly braces appearing in column 1—that define a network or subnetwork. In this case, the network defined has the IP address 192.168.0.0 with a netmask of 255.255.255.0. This means that the range of network addresses is from 192.168.0.0 to 192.168.0.255.

Hosts in this network share three parameters:

subnet-mask

> The network mask, which indicates by 1-bits the bit positions of the IP address associated with the network, rather than the host. Often, the network mask has the value 255.255.255.0.

broadcast-address

> The IP address of the network, with all 1-bits in the bit positions associated with the host address. Often, this means that the first three members of the dotted quad IP address appear, followed by the value 255.

routers

> The default gateway IP address.

The next set of lines define the network configuration for a particular host, named sara:

```
host sara
  {
    hardware ethernet  00:50:04:d2:3f:15;
    fixed-address      192.168.0.33;
    default-lease-time 86400;
  }
```

The host's network adapter has an Ethernet MAC address of 00:50:04:d2:3f:15. The Ethernet address is a unique code, assigned by the adapter's manufacturer, that serves to identify the adapter. When it queries the DHCP server, this adapter will be leased the IP address 192.168.0.33; the lease will have a duration of 24 hours (86400 seconds). This adapter will always receive this IP address, which is also known as a *static IP address*.

The next line defines a range of IP addresses:

```
range 192.168.0.50 192.168.0.254;
```

Hosts not assigned a static IP address will be leased an address within the specified range. Such an IP address is termed a *dynamic IP address*.

For more information about the *dhcpd.conf* file, see the associated manpage.

Starting the DHCP Service

Before starting the DHCP service for the first time, you must create the file that DHCP uses to store information on current leases. The file need not have any particular content; an empty file will do. To create the file, issue the following command:

touch /var/lib/dhcp/dhcpd.leases

Now, the DHCP service can be started. To do so, issue the command:

service dhcpd start

To verify that the DHCP service has started, issue the following command to view recent system log entries:

```
tail -40 /var/log/messages
```

You should see something like the following:

```
May  5 11:57:39 localhost dhcpd: Internet Software Consortium
   DHCP Server 2.0pl5
May  5 11:57:39 localhost dhcpd: Copyright 1995, 1996, 1997,
   1998, 1999 The Internet Software Consortium.
May  5 11:57:39 localhost dhcpd: All rights reserved.
May  5 11:57:39 localhost dhcpd:
May  5 11:57:39 localhost dhcpd: Please contribute if you find
   this software useful.
My  5 11:57:39 localhost dhcpd: For info, please visit
   http://www.isc.org/dhcp-contrib.html
May  5 11:57:39 localhost dhcpd:
May  5 11:57:39 localhost dhcpd: Listening on
   Socket/eth0/192.168.0.0
May  5 11:57:39 localhost dhcpd: Sending on
   Socket/eth0/192.168.0.0
May  5 11:57:39 localhost dhcpd: dhcpd startup succeeded
```

Now, boot a client configured to obtain its network configuration via DHCP. If you need help configuring a client to use DHCP, consult the next section. If the DHCP client and server are working, you should see system log messages that resemble the following:

```
May  5 11:59:40 localhost dhcpd: DHCPREQUEST for
   192.168.0.4 from 00:50:04:d2:3f:15 via eth0
May  5 11:59:40 localhost dhcpd: DHCPACK on 192.168.0.4 to
   00:50:04:d2:3f:15 via eth0
```

If you find that the DHCP server is not working, consult the file */usr/share/doc/dhcp-*/README*. Due to an error, this HTML file lacks the file extension *.html*. To view the file, first rename it, like so:

```
cd /usr/share/doc/dhcp-*
mv README README.html
```

Then view it with Links, Netscape Navigator, Konqueror, or some other web browser.

What often appears to be a problem with a DHCP server is most likely a problem with the DHCP client. If you have difficulty getting the DHCP service to work properly, configure the client as explained in the next subsection. Another common problem is configuring multiple DHCP servers on the same network. In order to avoid conflicts between servers, you should generally operate only a single DHCP server on your network.

You can use the **service** command to control the DHCP service. To stop the server, issue this command:

```
service dhcpd stop
```

To stop and restart the DHCP service, issue this command:

```
service dhcpd restart
```

This command reports the current status of the server:

```
service dhcpd status
```

If you want the DHCP service to start automatically when you boot your system, issue the command:

```
chkconfig --level 345 dhcpd on
```

Or use Neat to configure the service to start automatically.

Configuring DHCP Clients

To configure a Windows 9x client to use DHCP, select Start → Settings → Control Panel → Network → Configuration to open the TCP/IP Properties dialog box. Select the TCP/IP network component associated with the network adapter you want to configure and click Properties. Select the IP Address tab and choose "Obtain an IP address automatically." Then select the DNS tab and choose Disable DNS. This setting does not actually disable DNS; it merely configures the system to rely on DHCP to provide the IP address of the DNS server.

Next, select the Gateway tab and remove any installed gateways. Click OK to dismiss the TCP/IP Properties dialog box, and click OK again to dismiss the Network Properties dialog box. You can use a similar procedure to configure Windows NT/2000 clients.

Windows 9x lets you view leased network configuration information. To do so, run the program *winipcfg* and select the proper adapter. The program shows the Ethernet address, IP address, subnet mask, and default gateway associated with the client, if any. Click More to view additional information, such as hostname, DNS server IP address, and the lease expiration time. You can manually release or renew a lease by clicking Release or Renew.

Under Windows 2000, you can view similar information describing the network configuration by issuing the command:

```
ipconfig /all
```

To configure a Linux client to use DHCP, launch Neat: select Config → Networking → Client Tasks → Basic Host Information, and set the following options for the adapter:

- Enabled
- Config Mode DHCP

You can view the status of a DHCP lease on a Linux client by issuing the command:

```
/sbin/pump -s
```

To release and renew a lease, issue the command:

```
/sbin/pump -i eth0 -R
```

If the lease is associated with an adapter other than eth0, revise the command accordingly.

CHAPTER 12

Setting Up Internet Services

In the preceding chapters, you learned how to connect your Linux system to a local area network (LAN) or to the Internet via an Internet service provider (ISP). By doing so, you were able to access a plethora of services provided by others, including file transfers via FTP, web pages, email, and Telnet. In this chapter you'll learn how to set up several Linux Internet servers, including an FTP server, an Apache web server, an email (SMTP/POP) server, and a DNS server. You'll also learn how to implement a basic firewall to help protect your systems from unauthorized access via the Internet. These applications let you and others access data on your Linux system via the Internet. These applications will be most useful if your system is connected to the Internet 24/7. But, even if your connection is intermittent, you and others can access the services these applications provide whenever the connection is active.

Running an FTP Server

An FTP server lets you transfer files from one system to another via a network. When two computers are connected to the Internet, you can use FTP to transfer files from one to the other even though the computers are not directly connected.

An FTP server attempts to authenticate users that ask to use it. You can configure your FTP server to accept requests only from users who have an account on the system running the FTP server, or you can configure it to accept requests from anyone, via a facility known as *anonymous FTP*. It's fairly simple to install and configure an anonymous FTP server; however, crackers regularly exploit vulnerabilities in them, breaking into systems and causing manifold mischief. Because it's difficult to protect a system running anonymous FTP from attack, this section does not describe the process for installing and configuring anonymous FTP. Instead, we'll cover installing and configuring *wu-ftp* to support authenticated users.

Even ordinary FTP carries significant risk. FTP sends login passwords over the network as clear text. Anyone using a packet sniffer can discover passwords entered during an FTP session and use them to breach security. A more secure alternative is the Secure Shell (SSH) *scp* utility, described later in this chapter.

Installing and Starting the FTP Server

To install FTP, use GnoRPM to install the package *wu-ftpd*. To enable your FTP server, you must tell *xinetd* to respond to FTP requests. To do so, issue the command:

```
chkconfig wu-ftpd on
```

Testing the FTP Server

To test your FTP server, start an FTP client by issuing the following command:

```
ftp localhost
```

The FTP server should prompt you for a login user account name and password. If you correctly supply them, you should see the FTP prompt that lets you know the FTP server is ready to execute FTP subsystem commands. Type **quit** and press **Enter** to exit the FTP client.

 By default, FTP does not allow the root user to log in. You could modify this behavior, but doing so could compromise system security because FTP sends passwords across the network in an insecure manner.

Once your FTP server is working, try contacting it from a remote system. If you have a Windows machine, you can contact your server by using the built-in Windows FTP client that works similarly to the Linux FTP client, interpreting the same FTP subsystem commands. Open an MS-DOS Prompt window and type the command:

```
ftp server
```

where *server* specifies the hostname or IP address of your Linux server. Generally, once the FTP subsystem prompt is available, you should immediately issue the **binary** (or **bin**) command. This command specifies that files will be transferred verbatim; without it, executable files, documents, and other files that contain binary data will be scrambled when transferred.

When you're ready to actually transfer some files, use the FTP commands described in Table 12-1. Here's a typical FTP session that you can use as a model:

```
[mccartyb@athlon mccartyb]# ftp localhost
Connected to localhost.
220 athlon.localdomain FTP server (Version wu-2.6.1-16) ready.
Name (localhost:root): mccartyb
331 Password required for mccartyb.
```

```
Password:
230 User mccartyb logged in.
Remote system type is UNIX.
Using binary mode to transfer files.
ftp> bin
200 Type set to I.
ftp> ls
227 Entering Passive Mode (127,0,0,1,94,209)
150 Opening ASCII mode data connection for directory listing.
total 206490
-rw-r--r--   1 500      500           81560 May 10 16:06 01installing.jpg
-rw-r--r--   1 500      500           56611 May 10 16:34 02bootdisk.jpg
-rw-rw-r--  1 500      500          199853 Jan 28  2000 3c90x-1.0.0e.tar.gz
drwxr-xr-x  8 500      500            1024 Aug 31  2000 Desktop
drwxr-xr-x  2 500      500            2048 Aug  5  2000 KSnapshot
-rw-r--r--   1 500      500        36754977 Mar 31  2000 LearnRedHat.tgz
drwxr-xr-x  2 500      500            1024 Oct 30  2000 Samplifile
226 Transfer complete.
ftp> get 3c90x-1.0.0e.tar.gz
local: 3c90x-1.0.0e.tar.gz remote: 3c90x-1.0.0e.tar.gz
227 Entering Passive Mode (127,0,0,1,48,29)
150 Opening BINARY mode data connection for 3c90x-1.0.0e.tar.gz
(199853 bytes).
226 Transfer complete.
199853 bytes received in 0.0457 secs (4.3e+03 Kbytes/sec)
ftp> quit
221-You have transferred 199853 bytes in 1 files.
221-Total traffic for this session was 200480 bytes in 1 transfers.
221 Thank you for using the FTP service on athlon.localdomain.
```

FTP provides a very fast and reliable way for a Linux server to share files with other clients, without the need to install and configure Samba.

Table 12-1. Important FTP Commands

Command	Function
!command	Invokes a shell on the local system. You can use this command, for example, to obtain a listing of the current directory on the local system by issuing the !ls command, for a Unix system, or !dir, for a Microsoft system.
ascii	Specifies that files will be transferred in ASCII mode.
binary bin	Specifies that files will be transferred in binary mode, which performs no translation.
cd directory	Changes to the specified directory of the remote system.
delete file	Deletes the specified file from the remote system.
dir	Displays the contents of the current directory of the remote system.
get file	Retrieves the specified file from the remote system.
hash	Prints a series of hash marks (#) during file transfer (upload or download).
help	Displays command help information.
lcd directory	Changes to the specified directory of the local system.

Table 12-1. Important FTP Commands (continued)

Command	Function
mkdir *directory*	Creates the specified directory on the remote system.
put *file*	Stores the specified local file on the remote system.
pwd	Displays the current working directory on the remote system.
quit	Exits the FTP session and returns you to the shell prompt.
rmdir *directory*	Removes the specified directory from the remote system.

Running Apache

Installing and configuring the Apache web server is not much more difficult than installing an FTP server. Moreover, web servers tend to be more secure than FTP servers, so a web server may be a better way for you to publish files. Once your web server is up and running, other Internet users can view and download documents within the web-enabled directories on your Linux system. This section explains the installation and configuration of Apache, the most popular web server on the Internet.

The Tux Web Server

Red Hat 7.2 ships with Tux, a web server developed by Red Hat. Tux may be the fastest web server available. The secret of Tux's speed is that it is integrated with the Linux kernel, so the overhead involved in serving a web page is minimal.

However, don't toss Apache overboard just yet. Tux can serve only static HTML pages. It can't be used with server-side includes, PHP, or other popular methods of serving web pages whose content is determined when they're served. When Tux is asked to serve a dynamic page, it can hand off the request to Apache, so Tux and Apache can work together to rapidly serve static web pages yet provide the full power and flexibility of Apache.

Unless you're planning to establish a high-traffic web site, you won't need to be concerned with Tux, which is somewhat complicated to configure. To learn more about Tux, see *http://www.dell.ca/en/gen/topics/power_ps1q01-redhat.htm* and *http://www.redhat.com/docs/manuals/tux/TUX-2.1-Manual/*.

Installing Apache

To install Apache, use GnoRPM to install the following packages:

- *apache*
- *apache-manual*
- *apache-conf*

You'll find the *apache-manual* package on Disc 2 of Red Hat Linux 7.2. You may also need to install the *mm* package, which contains a library needed by Apache.

Strictly speaking, you do not need to install the *apache-manual* or *apache-conf* packages. However, you may find the Apache manual useful, and you'll probably find it easier to configure Apache using *apacheconf* than using a text editor.

Configuring Apache

Configuring a web server can be as easy or as difficult as you choose. Like other web servers, Apache provides seemingly countless options. As distributed with Red Hat Linux, Apache has a default configuration that generally requires only a little tweaking before use. Apache's configuration files reside in the directory */etc/httpd/conf*. For historical reasons that no longer apply, Apache has three configuration files:

- *access.conf*
- *httpd.conf*
- *srm.conf*

However, the only configuration file that's currently used is *httpd.conf*. As mentioned, the easiest way to perform a basic configuration of Apache is with the X-based tool, *apacheconf*. To configure Apache, choose Programs → System → Apache Configuration from the GNOME menu or choose System → Apache Configuration from the KDE menu. Alternatively, start X and launch *apacheconf* by issuing the following command in a terminal window:

apacheconf &

The main configuration screen, shown in Figure 12-1, appears.

The main configuration screen lets you specify the following:

Server Name
This is the hostname of your system. Often, this will be *www.domain.com*, where *domain.com* is the name of your domain.

Webmaster Email Address
Any messages concerning the web server will be sent to this address.

Available Addresses
This is the IP address (or addresses) on which the web server listens.

You should specify the Server Name and Webmaster Email Address. Unless your system has multiple network adapters or you want to run the web server on a nonstandard port (that is, a port other than 80), you don't need to modify the Available Addresses configuration item.

The Virtual Hosts tab, shown in Figure 12-2, lets you specify virtual hosts. Virtual hosting is a feature that lets you host multiple web sites with a single IP address. For example, both *www.myfirstsite.com* and *www.myothersite.com* could be hosted on

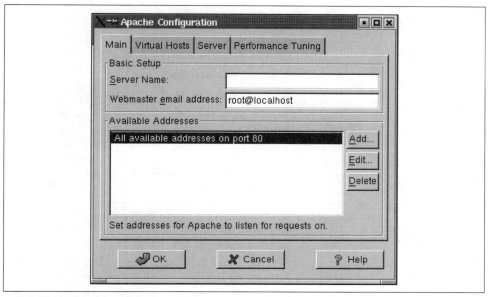

Figure 12-1. The main apacheconf screen

the same system using a single IP address. However, virtual hosting is not compatible with HTTP 1.0 browsers.

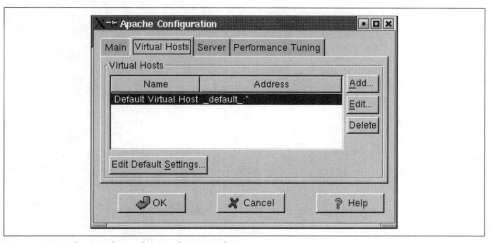

Figure 12-2. The apacheconf Virtual Hosts tab

The Server tab, shown in Figure 12-3, lets you specify the location of important files and directories and the user account and group used by Apache. You should not generally alter these configuration items.

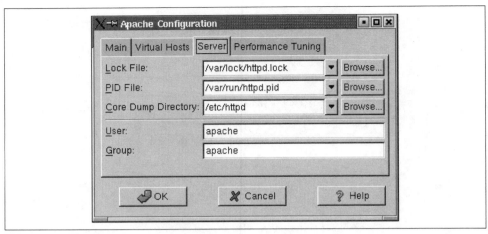

Figure 12-3. The apacheconf Server tab

The Performance Tuning tab, shown in Figure 12-4, provides access to configuration items that let you optimize Apache's performance. Unless your web server will see very heavy service, you should reduce the maximum number of connections. A value of 15 is more than appropriate for a personal web server.

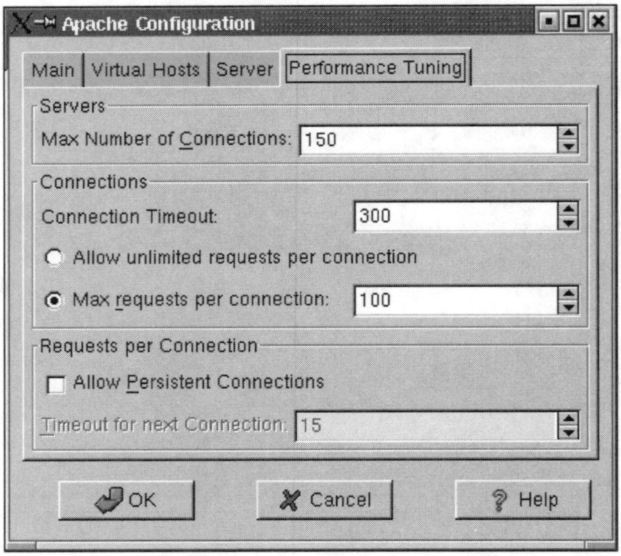

Figure 12-4. The apacheconf Performance Tuning tab

If you're interested in exploring the many other configuration options provided by Apache, see the Apache manual, which resides in */var/www/html/manual*. You can view the file with Links or another HTML browser. Also, see the Apache web site (*http://www.apache.org*), which includes a tutorial on Apache configuration.

Starting and Stopping Apache

Once you've configured your web server, you can start it by issuing the following command:

```
service httpd start
```

You can verify that the web server has started by issuing the command:

```
service httpd status
```

which should report that one or more processes are running, like so:

```
[root@athlon /root]# service httpd status
httpd (pid 658 657 656 649 648 647 646 645 641) is running...
```

If you installed the Links browser, you can use it to test your web server by issuing the following command:

```
links http://localhost
```

You should see a screen that resembles Figure 12-5.

If you prefer, you can view the start page with Netscape Navigator or Konqueror, both of which support the graphics embedded in the page. The result should resemble Figure 12-6.

Once you can access your web server locally, try accessing it from a remote computer. This should be as simple as forming a URL that includes the fully qualified hostname or IP address of your system (that is, the host and domain names), for example, *http://mysystem.mydomain*.

To stop Apache, issue the command:

```
service httpd stop
```

If you change Apache's configuration, you can restart the server with the command:

```
service httpd restart
```

If you want to start Apache automatically when you boot the system, issue the command:

```
chkconfig --level 345 httpd on
```

You can create HTML pages in */var/www/html*, owned by the *root* user account. These pages are accessible via the URL *http://www.domain.com*, where *domain.com* is the name of the host. Alternatively, users can create a *public_html* subdirectory within their home directory, for example, */home/joepublic/public_html*. There, they can publish files that are web-accessible. To access such files, use a special URL that consists of a tilde (~) followed by the name of the user account. For example, *http://www.domain.com/~joepublic* refers to the user *joepublic*'s web directory.

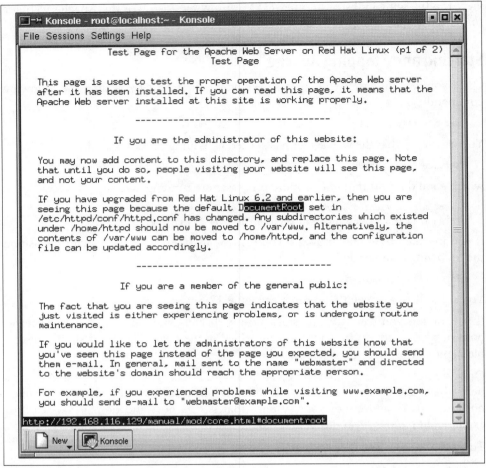

Figure 12-5. The Apache start page as viewed with Links

By default, a user's home directory and its subdirectories—including the *public_html* subdirectory—are not web-accessible. For the user *joepublic*'s web pages to be web-accessible, the *apache* user account or group must have execute access to the directories */home*, */home/joepublic*, and */home/joepublic/public_html*. Moreover, if automatic directory indexes are desired, the *apache* user account or group must have read access to the directory */home/joepublic/public_html*. The files themselves must be publicly readable.

If you have trouble accessing web pages on your server, check Apache's log files, which reside in the directory */etc/httpd/logs*. The log files may provide valuable clues to help you understand what's going wrong.

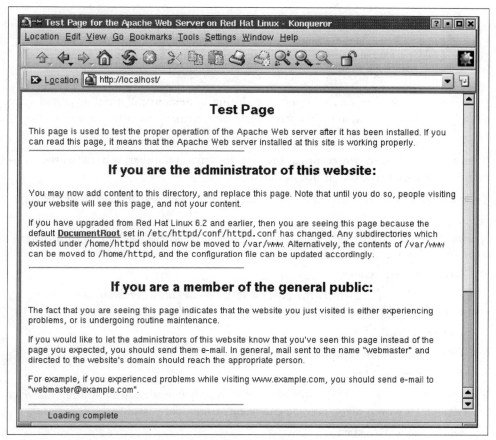

Figure 12-6. The Apache start page as viewed with Netscape Navigator

Configuring a Mail Server

Does your ISP prohibit email message attachments larger than 10 MB or impose other restrictions that you find cumbersome? Your Linux system can provide an email server that isn't subject to such arbitrary restrictions.

 Mail is one of the services that ISPs are least likely to tolerate, owing to the ongoing war against spam. Often, ISPs block the ports used by *sendmail* so customers cannot operate unauthorized mail servers. Check with your ISP before taking the time to set up a mail server.

The *sendmail* package is a powerful Mail Transfer Agent (MTA), which transfers email from one system to another.

Don't confuse *sendmail* and other MTAs with mail clients (sometimes called mail user agents), such as *pine* or *mutt*, which merely allow you to send and receive email. Mail clients communicate with MTAs, not with one another.

Depending on the options you selected during system installation, *sendmail* may already reside on your system. To check whether it's installed, issue the command:

```
rpm -q sendmail
```

If *sendmail* is installed, the command reports its version number; otherwise, the command reports that *sendmail* is not installed.

To install *sendmail*, use GnoRPM to install the *sendmail*, *sendmail-cf*, and *m4* packages.

sendmail starts automatically when you install it; to check the status of *sendmail*, issue the following command:

```
service sendmail status
```

The command should identify the process ID of *sendmail*. If *sendmail* is not running, you can start it by issuing the following command:

```
service sendmail start
```

You can stop *sendmail* by issuing the command:

```
service sendmail stop
```

You probably won't need to change *sendmail*'s hugely complex configuration file, */etc/sendmail.cf*. However, if you do, you can restart *sendmail* by issuing the command:

```
service sendmail restart
```

If you want *sendmail* to start automatically when your system boots, issue the command:

```
chkconfig --level 345 sendmail on
```

You can also use Linuxconf to configure *sendmail* to start automatically.

You should now be able to send and receive email. Test your server by sending yourself an email message:

```
[root@localhost /etc]# mail myself@domain.com
Subject: test message
This is a test.
.
Cc:
[root@localhost /etc]#
```

Once you know that the server is working, you can configure your favorite mail client to specify your own system as your mail server. For example, if you're using Netscape Navigator, select Edit → Preferences → Mail Servers. Make a note of the existing mail server settings, just in case something goes wrong. Then, change the incoming and outgoing mail server options to specify your Linux machine.

The *sendmail* service is capable of sending and receiving email. If you plan to receive email, your system should be continuously connected to the Internet. This means that you'll need a static IP address and a registered domain name. And, as explained earlier, you should also have an understanding ISP. Contact your ISP prior to setting up any web or mail server of your own.

By default, *sendmail* accepts connections only from the local host. To configure *sendmail* to accept connections from other hosts, you must edit the */etc/mail/sendmail.mc* file. Insert a hash mark (#) in column one of the line containing the term *DAEMON_OPTIONS* and the line containing *FEATURE(accept_unresolvable_ domains)* and then save the file. Then, issue the following commands:

```
m4 /etc/mail/sendmail.mc > /etc/sendmail.cf
service sendmail restart
```

The Secure Shell

The Secure Shell (SSH) lets you connect to a system from another system via TCP/IP and obtain a shell prompt, from which you can issue commands and view output in a secure fashion. If you are not familiar with SSH but are familiar with Telnet, SSH works similarly. SSH differs from Telnet in that conversations between SSH and its clients are sent in encrypted form so hackers cannot easily discover private information, including user account names and passwords.

Installing SSH

The SSH client lets you remotely log in to systems that provide an SSH server. It's likely that the installation procedure installed the SSH client for your use. To check whether it's installed, issue the command:

```
rpm -q openssh
```

If *openssh* is installed, the command reports its version number; otherwise, the command reports that *openssh* is not installed.

You can manually install the SSH client by using GnoRPM to install the following packages:

- *openssh*
- *openssh-clients*
- *openssh-askpass*
- *openssh-askpass-gnome*

To install the SSH server, use GnoRPM to install the *openssh-server* package.

Once installed, the SSH server should start automatically. To check the status of the SSH server, issue the command:

```
service sshd status
```

The command's output should report that the server is running. If not, you can manually start the server by issuing this command:

```
service sshd start
```

If you want to stop the SSH server, issue this command:

```
service sshd stop
```

 The SSH service has several configuration files, residing in */etc/ssh*. You don't have to modify them to get SSH running. If you're curious about them, view the *sshd* manpage.

Using SSH

To verify that the SSH server is properly running, you can access it via a client on the local system by issuing the following command:

```
ssh localhost
```

The client will attempt to log you onto the local system using your current user account and will prompt you for your password. If you supply the correct password, you should see a shell prompt, indicating that the client and server are functioning correctly. Type **exit** and press **Enter** to exit SSH.

To log on to a remote system, simply specify the hostname or IP address of the remote system in place of *localhost*. If you want to log in to a user account other than one named identically to the account you're using on the local system, issue the command:

```
ssh userid@host
```

where *host* is the hostname or IP address of the remote host and *userid* is the name of the user account you want to use. For example:

```
# ssh bmccarty@gonzo.apu.edu
```

You can use the SSH client's **scp** command to transfer files to or from a remote system running an SSH server. To transfer a file to a remote system, issue a command such as this one:

```
scp file userid @host:path
```

where *file* is the path of the file to be transferred, *host* is the hostname or IP address of the remote host, *path* is the directory to which the file should be transferred, and *userid* is your user account on the remote system. You can specify multiple files to be transferred if you like. For example:

```
# scp rhbook_rev.txt bmccarty@gonzo.apu.edu:bmcarty/files
```

You can use shell metacharacters to specify a set of files to be transferred. You can also specify the −r flag, which specifies that **scp** should recursively copy a directory rather than a file or set of files. For example, the following command copies an entire directory to the remote system:

```
scp -r Desktop bmccarty@gonzo.apu.edu:bmcarty/files
```

To transfer files from a remote system, issue a command based on this pattern:

```
scp userid @host:file path
```

where *host* is the hostname or IP address of the remote system, *file* is the path of the file to be transferred, *path* is the destination path of the file, and *userid* is your user account on the remote system. For example:

```
# scp bmcarty@ftp.ora.com:/outgoing/word98temp.doc /home/bmcarty/files
```

This command would log in the user *bmcarty* to *ftp.ora.com/outgoing*, retrieve the *word98temp.doc* file, and place it in his */home/bmcarty/files* directory.

SSH also provides the **sftp** command, which lets you transfer files in much the same way the **ftp** command does. The command has the following form:

```
sftp user@host
```

The command will prompt for the password associated with the specified user account. For example, to transfer files to and from the host *ora.com*, you could issue the following command:

```
sftp bmcarty@ora.com
```

After establishing a connection to the specified host, the **sftp** command presents a prompt that lets you enter commands similar to those supported by the **ftp** command. Use the **help** command to learn more about the supported commands.

Using a Windows SSH Client

To log on to your Linux system from a remote system via SSH, you must install an SSH client on the remote system. A suitable client for Windows is Simon Tatham's *PuTTY*, available at *http://www.chiark.greenend.org.uk/~sgtatham/putty*. Simply download *PuTTY* to any convenient directory (the *windows* directory is a good choice). The program doesn't have a setup script; you can run it by selecting Start → Run and typing **putty**; if the directory in which *PuTTY* resides is not on the execution path, you must type the drive, path, and filename. Alternatively, you can create a shortcut that spares you the trouble. Figure 12-7 shows *PuTTY*'s main screen.

To use *PuTTY* to connect to a host, specify the following information:

Hostname
    The hostname or IP address of the SSH server.

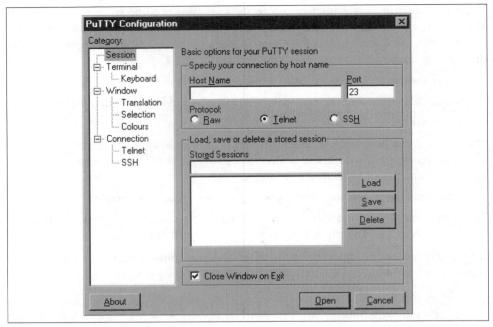

Figure 12-7. PuTTY's screen

Protocol
> You should select SSH. This causes *PuTTY* to automatically select port 22, the default SSH port. If the SSH server listens on a different port, specify the non-standard port by using the Port text box.

Click Open to make the connection to the specified host.

The left pane of *PuTTY*'s screen provides access to several configuration options, such as:

- Key mappings
- Character translations
- Selection, copy, and paste options
- Screen colors

Like most Telnet or FTP clients, *PuTTY* lets you save configurations so you can quickly connect to often-used hosts. Use the Load, Save, and Delete buttons to manage your list of hosts and associated configurations.

Protocol Tunneling

SSH lets you establish a network connection that you can use as a *Virtual Private Network (VPN)*, so called because traffic flowing over the connection is encrypted and therefore secure from eavesdroppers. This facility is known as *protocol tunneling* because the data that flows via the connection need not use the standard TCP/IP protocol; for example, the data might be encoded using Novell's IPX protocol.

Configuring and troubleshooting a VPN is not a task for a Linux newbie. However, if your Linux skills are growing and you desire a challenge, see Arpad Magosanyi's *VPN HOWTO*, available at *http://www.linuxdoc.org/HOWTO/mini/VPN.html*. Also see *Virtual Private Networks*, by Charlie Scott, Paul Wolfe, and Mike Erwin (O'Reilly & Associates, Inc.).

Configuring DNS

DNS maps hostnames to IP addresses and vice versa. Configuring DNS can be somewhat difficult. However, you can easily configure your Linux system as a *caching name server*. A caching name server remembers mappings it has recently fetched and can supply them to clients. Accessing a local or nearby caching name server is much faster than accessing a remote name server.

The Linux program that performs name resolution is the Berkeley Internet Name Daemon (BIND). BIND is sometimes referred to as *named* (pronounced *name dee*), an abbreviation for *name daemon*. So, the same facility is variously referred to as DNS, BIND, or *named*. Some Linux/Unix systems are configured to use a name server other than BIND; however, BIND is the most popular name server on the Internet.

To install BIND and configure it as a caching name server, use GnoRPM to install the *bind* and *caching-nameserver* packages.

To start the *named* service, issue the command:

```
service named start
```

To verify whether the service is running, issue the following command:

```
service named status
```

The command should report the process ID of the *named* server.

To use the *named* server, you must specify its IP address in the resolver configuration. To do so, launch the network configuration tool by choosing Programs → System → Network Configuration from the GNOME menu or System → Network Configuration from the KDE menu.

Make a record of the existing specification and then specify 127.0.0.1 as the IP address of the primary name server. Test your name server by pinging an Internet host:

```
ping www.apu.edu
```

A series of replies confirms that the name server is working. Press **Ctrl-C** to halt the pinging.

Implementing a Basic Firewall

Sometimes you may want a host to provide certain services to only local clients or clients on other hosts of a network that you control. If your network is connected to the Internet, you can use a *firewall* to prevent undesired access to services. A Linux firewall depends on certain kernel facilities to examine incoming and outgoing packets. Packets that fail to pass specified rules can be rejected, preventing undesired access to private services.

A related facility, known as *IP masquerading*, lets hosts on a network connect to the Internet via a host known as the *masquerading host*. All packets from the network seem to the outside host to have come from the masquerading host. IP masquerading lets you:

- Prevent outside access to services offered on a private network
- Hide the structure of private networks
- Conserve IP addresses by assigning freely usable reserved IP addresses to masqueraded hosts

Configuring the Firewall

At installation time, Red Hat Linux lets you configure a firewall for your system; however, you can reconfigure the firewall after installation. For a firewall to be secure and flexible, customization is almost always required. However, customizing a firewall requires an understanding of the ports and protocols used by each running service, an expertise that generally requires considerable time to achieve. To learn more about services, ports, and protocols, see the resources described at the end of this chapter.

To configure a firewall, issue the command:

```
lokkit -f
```

The main Firewall Configuration dialog box, as shown in Figure 12-8, appears. This dialog box lets you select the desired security level:

High
> The firewall admits only DNS and DHCP replies, which are generally necessary for normal system operation. The firewall prohibits active-mode FTP, Internet Relay Chat (IRC) file transfers, Real Audio playback, and Remote X clients. In addition, outside access to services is blocked, unless you use the Customize dialog box to make them available.

Medium
> The firewall blocks access to privileged ports (ports 0–1023), used by services such as FTP, SSH, *sendmail*, and HTTP. In addition, it blocks the NFS server port (2049). It blocks access to the local X Window System display and font server port by remote clients.

No Firewall

The firewall is disabled; remote clients can freely access services on your host.

 The loopback device, *lo*, is a trusted device under the high and medium security levels and therefore cannot be freely accessed. You may find it difficult to test service availability even from the system itself when you configure your system to operate under high or medium security.

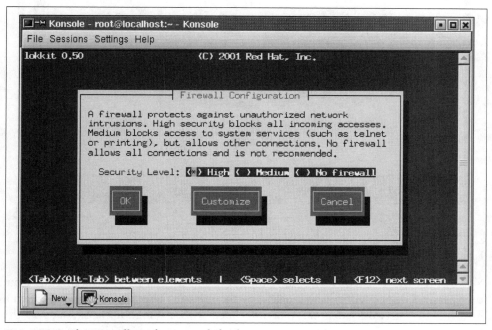

Figure 12-8. The Firewall Configuration dialog box

To customize the access permitted to remote clients, click on Customize. The Firewall Configuration—Customize dialog box, as shown in Figure 12-9, appears. You can use the Allow Incoming checkboxes to allow access to services that would otherwise be blocked by the medium or high security levels. If you want to allow access to a service other than one of the six listed, you can use the Other Ports text box. There, you can list the number (or name) of the port, followed by a colon and the port type (*tcp* or *udp*). The file */etc/services* lists the commonly agreed-upon port numbers and the associated services. For example, the IMAP mail service is associated with port 143 and both TCP and UDP port types. To permit access to IMAP, you could place the specification:

```
143:tcp,143:udp
```

in the Other Ports text box.

You can list as many ports as you like, separating each from its neighbor by a comma. It is possible to list ports by name, but since the names acceptable to the dialog box are not documented, it's better to use port numbers.

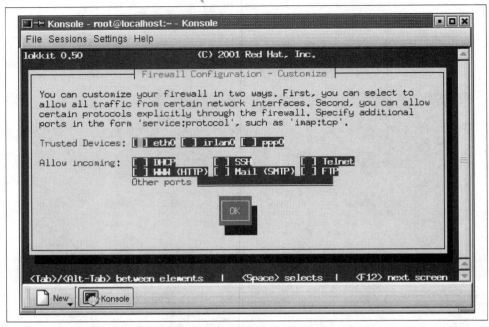

Figure 12-9. The Firewall Configuration—Customize dialog box

You can use the Trusted Devices checkboxes to specify that packets originating from the specified device will not be blocked by the firewall. This facility is useful when a host has two network adapters: one associated with a public network, such as the Internet, and another associated with a private network. By specifying the network adapter associated with the private network as a trusted device, you permit clients on the private network free access to services, while blocking clients on the public network from access other than that permitted by the firewall configuration.

Controlling the Firewall

To start the firewall, issue the command:

```
service ipchains start
```

To stop the firewall, issue the command:

```
service ipchains stop
```

To stop and then restart the firewall, so that a new firewall configuration can become effective, issue the command:

```
service ipchains restart
```

To view the current firewall policies, issue the command:

```
service ipchains status
```

The *ipchains* manpage describes the format in which the policies are listed.

To block outside access to all services, issue the command:

```
service ipchains panic
```

This command is handy if you suspect that an intrusion is in progress and you want to terminate the cracker's access immediately.

If you've manually revised the firewall by using the **ipchains** command, you can save the current firewall status by issuing the command:

```
service ipchains save
```

The next time the firewall is started, the saved firewall status will be restored.

To specify that the firewall should start automatically when the system is booted, issue the command:

```
chkconfig --level 2345 ipchains on
```

Configuring IP Masquerading

To configure IP masquerading, issue a command of the following form:

```
ipchains -A forward -i eth -s xxx.xxx.xxx.xxx/yy -j MASQ
```

where *eth* is the device associated with the network adapter that interfaces to the masqueraded network, *xxx.xxx.xxx.xxx* is the network address associated with the masqueraded network, and *yy* is the number of 1-bits in the netmask associated with the masqueraded network.

For example, if *eth0* is the network adapter associated with the masqueraded network *192.168.0.0* having a netmask of *255.255.255.0* (that is, 24 1-bits), you should add the following command:

```
ipchains -A forward -i eth0 -s 192.168.0.0/24 -j MASQ
```

Then, save the current firewall status by issuing the command:

```
service ipchains save
```

Network Security Tips

Anyone who administers a system connected to the Internet needs to know something about network security. It's not uncommon for systems connected to the Internet to be probed by would-be hackers several times daily. If a would-be hacker manages to detect a vulnerability, the hacker can often exploit it in a matter of seconds. Therefore, it's almost certain that a system administrator ignorant of network security will eventually suffer a system break-in.

Network security is a large and sophisticated topic that can be only cursorily surveyed in a book such as this. Concerned readers should consult books such as *Building Internet Firewalls*, by Elizabeth D. Zwicky, Simon Cooper, and D. Brent Chapman (O'Reilly & Associates, Inc.); *Computer Security Basics,* by Deborah Russell and G.T. Gangemi, Sr. (O'Reilly); and *Practical UNIX & Internet Security*, by Simson Garfinkel and Gene Spafford (O'Reilly).

If a sufficiently skilled hacker is intent on compromising a system you administer, the hacker will probably succeed. However, here are some tips that can help you avoid falling victim to amateur hackers:

- Establish a firewall that prevents outsiders from accessing services you don't need to make publicly available.

- Monitor security web sites and mailing lists so that you're aware of recent threats and the associated countermeasures. The CERT Coordination Center, *http://www.cert.org*, provides many useful resources.

- Apply bug fixes promptly, particularly those related to security. See Red Hat's errata page, *http://www.redhat.com/support/errata/rh72-errata.html*, for applicable fixes. To be informed of Red Hat Linux fixes when they're released, subscribe to the *redhat-watch-list* email list. To subscribe, visit *http://www.redhat. com/mailing-lists*.

## CHAPTER 13

Advanced Shell Usage and Shell Scripts

Like an MS-DOS Prompt window, the Unix shell is a command interpreter that lets you issue and execute commands. By means of the shell, you use and control your system. If you're accustomed to the point-and-click world of graphical user interfaces, you may question the value of learning to use the Linux shell. Many users initially find the shell cumbersome, and some retreat to the familiar comfort of the graphical user interface (GUI), avoiding the shell whenever possible. However, as this chapter explains, the shell unlocks the true power of Linux.

The Power of the Unix Shell

While it's true that the shell is an older style of interacting with a computer than the GUI, the graphical user interface is actually the more primitive interface. The GUI is easy to learn and widely used, but the shell is vastly more sophisticated. Using a GUI is somewhat like communicating in American Indian sign language. If your message is a simple one, like "We come in peace," you can communicate it by using a few gestures. However, if you attempted to give Lincoln's Gettysburg address—a notably short public discourse—you'd find your task quite formidable.[*]

The designer of a program that provides a GUI must anticipate all the possible ways in which the user will interact with the program and provide ways to trigger the appropriate program responses by means of pointing and clicking. Consequently, the user is constrained to working only in predicted ways. The user is therefore unable to adapt the GUI program to accommodate unforeseen tasks and circumstances. In a nutshell, that's why many system administration tasks are performed using the shell: system administrators, in fulfilling their responsibility to keep a system up and running, must continually deal with and overcome the unforeseen.

---

[*] American Sign Language, used to communicate with those who have a hearing impairment, is a much richer language than American Indian sign language. Unfortunately, programmers have not yet risen to the challenge of creating graphical user interfaces that are equally sophisticated.

The shell reflects the underlying philosophy of Unix, which provides a wide variety of small, simple tools (that is, programs), each performing a single task. When a complex operation is needed, the tools work together to accomplish the complex operation as a series of simple operations, one step at a time. Many Unix tools manipulate text, and since Unix stores its configuration data in text form rather than in binary form, the tools are ideally suited for manipulating Unix itself. The shell's ability to freely combine tools in novel ways is what makes Unix powerful and sophisticated. Moreover, as you'll learn, the shell is extensible: you can create *shell scripts* that let you store a series of commands for later execution, saving you the future tedium of typing or pointing and clicking to recall them.

The contrary philosophy is seen in operating systems such as Microsoft Windows, which employ elaborate, monolithic programs that provide menus, submenus, and dialog boxes. Such programs have no way to cooperate with one another to accomplish complex operations that weren't anticipated when the programs were designed. They're easy to use so long as you remain on the beaten path, but once you step off the trail, you find yourself in a confusing wilderness.

Of course, not everyone shares this perspective. The Usenet newsgroups, for example, are filled with postings debating the relative merits of GUIs. Some see the Unix shell as an arcane and intimidating monstrosity. But, even if they're correct, it's inarguable that when you learn to use the shell, you begin to see Unix as it was intended (whether that's for better or for worse).

When you are performing common, routine operations, a GUI that minimizes typing can be a relief, but when faced with a complex, unstructured problem that requires a creative solution, the shell is more often the tool of choice. Creating solutions in the form of shell scripts allows solutions to be stored for subsequent reuse. Perhaps even more important, shell scripts can be studied to quickly bone up on forgotten details, expediting the solution of related problems.

Filename Globbing

Before the shell passes arguments to an external command or interprets a built-in command, it scans the command line for certain special characters and performs an operation known as *filename globbing*. Filename globbing resembles the processing of wildcards used in MS-DOS commands, but it's much more sophisticated. Table 13-1 describes the special characters used in filename globbing, known as *filename metacharacters*.

Table 13-1. Filename Metacharacters

Metacharacter	Function
*	Matches a string of zero or more characters
?	Matches exactly one character

Table 13-1. Filename Metacharacters (continued)

Metacharacter	Function
[abc...]	Matches any of the characters specified
[a-z]	Matches any character in the specified range
[!abc...]	Matches any character other than those specified
[!a-z]	Matches any character not in the specified range
~	The home directory of the current user
~userid	The home directory of the specified user
~+	The current working directory
~-	The previous working directory

In filename globbing, just as in MS-DOS wildcarding, the shell attempts to replace metacharacters appearing in arguments in such a way that arguments specify filenames. Filename globbing makes it easier to specify names of files and sets of files.

For example, suppose the current working directory contains the following files: *file1*, *file2*, *file3*, and *file04*. Suppose you want to know the size of each file. The following command reports that information:

```
ls -l file1 file2 file3 file04
```

However, the following command reports the same information and is much easier to type:

```
ls -l file*
```

As Table 13-1 shows, the * filename metacharacter can match any string of characters. Suppose you issued the following command:

```
ls -l file?
```

The ? filename metacharacter can match only a single character. Therefore, *file04* would not appear in the output of the command.

Similarly, the command:

```
ls -l file[2-3]
```

would report only *file2* and *file3*, because only these files have names that match the specified pattern, which requires that the last character of the filename be in the range 2-3.

You can use more than one metacharacter in a single argument. For example, consider the following command:

```
ls -l file??
```

This command will list *file04*, because each metacharacter matches exactly one filename character.

Most commands let you specify multiple arguments. If no files match a given argument, the command ignores the argument. Here's another command that reports all four files:

```
ls -l file0* file[1-3]
```

 Suppose that a command has one or more arguments that include one or more metacharacters. If none of the arguments matches any filenames, the shell passes the arguments to the program with the metacharacters intact. When the program expects a valid filename, an unexpected error may result.

The tilde (~) metacharacter lets you easily refer to your home directory. For example, the following command:

```
ls ~
```

would list the files in your home directory.

Filename metacharacters don't merely save you typing. They let you write scripts that selectively process files by name. You'll see how that works later in this chapter.

Shell Aliases

Shell aliases make it easier to use commands by letting you establish abbreviated command names and by letting you prespecify common options and arguments for a command. To establish a command alias, issue a command of the form:

```
alias name='command'
```

where *command* specifies the command for which you want to create an alias and *name* specifies the name of the alias. For example, suppose you frequently type the MS-DOS command **dir** when you intend to type the Linux command **ls –l**. You can establish an alias for the **ls –l** command by issuing this command:

```
alias dir='ls -l'
```

Once the alias is established, if you mistakenly type **dir**, you'll get the directory listing you wanted instead of the default output of the **dir** command, which resembles **ls** rather than **ls –l**. If you like, you can establish similar aliases for other commands.

Your default Linux configuration probably defines several aliases on your behalf. To see what they are, issue the command:

```
alias
```

If you're logged in as *root*, you may see the following aliases:

```
alias cp='cp -i'
alias dir='ls -l'
alias ls='ls --color'
alias mv='mv -i'
alias rm='rm -i'
```

Notice how several commands are self-aliased. For example, the command **rm –i** is aliased as **rm**. The effect is that the –i option appears whenever you issue the **rm** command, whether or not you type the option. The –i option specifies that the shell will prompt for confirmation before deleting files. This helps avoid accidental deletion of files, which can be particularly hazardous when you're logged in as *root*. The alias ensures that you're prompted for confirmation even if you don't ask to be prompted. If you don't want to be prompted, you can issue a command like:

    rm -f *files*

where *files* specifies the files to be deleted. The –f option has an effect opposite that of the –i option; it forces deletion of files without prompting for confirmation. Because the command is aliased, the command actually executed is:

    rm -i -f *files*

The –f option takes precedence over the –i option, because it occurs later in the command line.

If you want to remove a command alias, you can issue the **unalias** command:

    unalias *alias*

where *alias* specifies the alias you want to remove. Aliases last only for the duration of a login session, so you needn't bother to remove them before logging off. If you want an alias to be effective each time you log in, you can use a shell script, which we'll discuss later in the chapter.

Using Virtual Consoles

You can use a terminal window to issue shell commands. However, you can issue shell commands even when X is not running or available. To do so, you use the Linux virtual console feature.

Linux provides six virtual consoles for interactive use; a seventh virtual console is associated with the graphical user interface. You can use special keystrokes to switch between virtual consoles. The keystroke **Alt-F***n*, where *n* is the number of a virtual console (1–6), causes Linux to display virtual console *n*. For example, you can display virtual console 2 by typing **Alt-F2**. You can view only a single console at a time, but you can switch rapidly between consoles by using the appropriate keystroke. The keystroke **Alt-F7** causes Linux to enter graphical mode using virtual console 7.

Virtual consoles also have a screensaver feature like that found on Windows. If a virtual console is inactive for an extended period of time, Linux blanks the monitor. To restore the screen without disturbing its contents, simply press the **Shift** key.

Logging In

To log in using a virtual console, type your user ID and press **Enter**. The system prompts you for the password associated with your account. Type the proper password and press **Enter**. To prevent anyone nearby from learning your password, Linux does not display your password as your enter it. If you suspect you've typed it incorrectly, you can either hit the **Backspace** key a number of times sufficient to delete the characters you've entered and type the password again or simply press **Enter** and start over. If you type the user ID or password incorrectly, Linux displays the message "login incorrect" and prompts you to try again.

When you've successfully logged in, you'll see a command prompt that looks something like this:

```
[bill@home bill]$
```

If you logged in as a user other than the root user, you'll see a prompt other than a hash mark (#); by default, you'll see a dollar sign ($). The prompt tells you that the Linux *bash* shell is ready to accept your commands.

Logging Out

When you're done using a virtual console, you should log out by typing the command **exit** and pressing **Enter**. When you log out, the system frees memory and other resources that were allocated when you logged in, making those resources available to other users.

When the system logs you out, it immediately displays a login prompt. If you change your mind and want to access the system, you can log in simply by supplying your username and password.

X and the Shell

You can configure your system to boot into nongraphical mode, if you prefer. If your video adapter is not compatible with X, you have no alternative but to do so. However, some Linux users prefer to configure their system to boot into nongraphical mode. A simple command lets such users launch an X session whenever they wish.

Configuring a Nongraphical Login

Linux provides several runlevels. Each runlevel has an associated set of services. For instance, runlevel 3 is associated with a text-based login and run level 5 is associated with an X-based, graphical login. Changing runlevels automatically starts and stops services associated with the old and new run levels.

You can determine the current runlevel by issuing the following command:

```
[bill@home bill]$ runlevel
```

The output of the command shows the previous and current runlevels. For example, the output:

```
3 5
```

indicates that the current run level is 5 and that the previous run level was 3.

To change the current runlevel, issue the **init** command. For example, to enter runlevel 3, issue the following command while logged in as *root*:

```
[bill@home bill]$ init 3
```

In response to this command, the system will start and stop services as required to enter runlevel 3.

The */etc/inittab* file specifies the default runlevel, which the system enters when booted. By changing the default run level to 3, you can configure your system to provide a nongraphical login when it boots. To do so, log in as *root* and load the */etc/inittab* file into the *pico* editor by issuing the command:

```
[bill@home bill]$ pico /etc/inittab
```

Find the line that reads:

```
id:5:initdefault:
```

Change the 5 to a 3:

```
id:3:initdefault:
```

Save the file and exit *pico*. The next time you boot your system, it will automatically enter runlevel 3 and provide a nongraphical login screen.

Starting and Stopping X from a Text-based Login

To start X from a text-based login, type the command:

```
startx
```

Your system's screen should briefly go blank and then you should see X's graphical desktop.

 If the screen is garbled or remains blank for more than about 30 seconds, your X configuration may be faulty. Immediately turn off your monitor or terminate X by pressing **Ctrl-Alt-Backspace**.

To quit X, press **Ctrl-Alt-Backspace**. This is a somewhat abrupt way of exiting X. Depending on the X configuration, you may be able to right-click the desktop and select Exit from the pop-up menu. This method is less abrupt than pressing **Ctrl-Alt-Backspace**, but it still falls short of ideal.

Shell Scripts

A shell script is simply a file that contains a set of commands to be run by the shell when invoked. By storing commands as a shell script, you make it easy to execute them again and again. As an example, consider a file named *deleter*, which contains the following lines:

```
echo -n Deleting the temporary files...
rm -f *.tmp
echo Done.
```

The **echo** commands simply print text on the console. The **–n** option of the first **echo** command causes omission of the trailing newline character normally written by the **echo** command, so both **echo** commands write their text on a single line. The **rm** command removes all files having names ending in *.tmp* from the current working directory.

You can execute this script by issuing the **sh** command, as follows:

```
sh deleter
```

 If you invoke the **sh** command without an argument specifying a script file, a new interactive shell is launched. To exit the new shell and return to your previous session, issue the **exit** command.

If the *deleter* file were in a directory other than the current working directory, you'd have to type an absolute path, for example:

```
sh /home/bill/deleter
```

You can make it a bit easier to execute the script by changing its access mode to include execute access. To do so, issue the following command:

```
chmod 555 deleter
```

This gives you, members of your group, and everyone else the ability to execute the file. To do so, simply type the absolute path of the file, for example:

```
/home/bill/deleter
```

If the file is in the current directory, you can issue the following command:

```
./deleter
```

You may wonder why you can't simply issue the command:

```
deleter
```

In fact, this still simpler form of the command will work, so long as *deleter* resides in a directory on your search path. You'll learn about the search path later.

Linux includes several standard scripts that are run at various times. Table 13-2 identifies these and gives the time when each is run. You can modify these scripts to operate differently. For example, if you want to establish command aliases that are available whenever you log in, you can use a text editor to add the appropriate lines to the *.profile* file that resides in your */home* directory. Since the name of this file begins with a dot (.), the **ls** command won't normally show the file. You must specify the **–a** option in order to see this and other hidden files.

Table 13-2. Special Shell Scripts

Script	Function
/etc/profile	Executes when the user logs in
~/.bash_profile	Executes when the user logs in
~/.bashrc	Executes when *bash* is launched
~/.bash_logout	Executes when the user logs out

 If you want to modify one of the standard scripts that should reside in your home directory but find that your */home* directory does not contain the indicated file, simply create the file. The next time you log in, log out, or launch *bash* (as appropriate) the shell will execute your script.

Input/Output Redirection and Piping

The shell provides three standard data streams:

stdin
> The standard input stream

stdout
> The standard output stream

stderr
> The standard error stream

By default, most programs read their input from stdin and write their output to stdout. Because both streams are normally associated with a console, programs behave as you generally want, reading input data from the console keyboard and writing output to the console screen. When a well-behaved program writes an error message, it writes the message to the stderr stream, which is also associated with the console by default. Having separate streams for output and error messages presents an important opportunity, as you'll see in a moment.

Although the shell associates the three standard input/output streams with the console by default, you can specify input/output redirectors that, for example, associate an input or output stream with a file. Table 13-3 summarizes the most important input/output redirectors.

Table 13-3. Input/Output Redirectors

Redirector	Function
>*file*	Redirects standard output stream to specified file
2>*file*	Redirects standard error stream to specified file
>>*file*	Redirects standard output stream to specified file, appending output to the file if the file already exists
2>>*file*	Redirects standard error stream to specified file, appending output to the file if the file already exists

Table 13-3. Input/Output Redirectors (continued)

Redirector	Function
&>*file*	Redirects standard output and error streams to the specified file
2>&1	Combines the standard error stream with the standard output stream
<*file*	Redirects standard input stream from the specified file
<<*text*	Reads standard input until a line matching *text* is found, at which point end-of-file is posted
cmd1 | cmd2	Takes the standard input of *cmd2* from the standard output of *cmd1* (also known as the *pipe* redirector)

To see how redirection works, consider the **wc** command. This command takes a series of filenames as arguments and prints the total number of lines, words, and characters present in the specified files. For example, the command:

```
wc /etc/passwd
```

might produce the output:

```
    22      26      790 /etc/passwd
```

which indicates that the file */etc/passwd* contains 22 lines, 26 words, and 790 characters. Generally, the output of the command appears on your console. But consider the following command, which includes an output redirector:

```
wc /etc/passwd > total
```

If you issue this command, you won't see any console output, because the output is redirected to the file *total*, which the command creates (or overwrites, if the file already exists). If you execute the following commands:

```
wc /etc/passwd > total
cat total
```

you will see the output of the **wc** command on the console.

Perhaps you can now see the reason for having the separate output streams stdout and stderr. If the shell provided a single output stream, error messages and output would be mingled. Therefore, if you redirected the output of a program to a file, any error messages would also be redirected to the file. This might make it difficult to notice an error that occurred during program execution. Instead, because the streams are separate, you can choose to redirect only stdout to a file. When you do so, error messages sent to stderr appear on the console in the usual way. Of course, if you prefer, you can redirect both stdout and stderr to the same file or redirect them to different files. As usual in the Unix world, you can have it your own way.

A simple way of avoiding annoying output is to redirect it to the null device file, */dev/ null*. If you redirect the stderr stream of a command to */dev/null*, you won't see any error messages the command produces. For example, the **grep** command prints an error message if you invoke it on a directory. So, if you invoke the **grep** command on the current directory (*) and the current directory contains subdirectories, you'll see unhelpful error messages. To avoid them, use a command like this one, which searches for files containing the text "localhost":

```
grep localhost * 2>/dev/null
```

Just as you can direct the standard output or error stream of a command to a file, you can also redirect a command's standard input stream to a file so the command reads from the file instead of the console. For example, if you issue the **wc** command without arguments, the command reads its input from stdin. Type some words and then type the end-of-file character (**Ctrl-D**), and **wc** will report the number of lines, words, and characters you entered. You can tell **wc** to read from a file, rather than the console, by issuing a command like:

```
wc </etc/passwd
```

Of course, this isn't the usual way of invoking **wc**. The author of **wc** helpfully provided a command-line argument that lets you specify the file from which **wc** reads. However, by using a redirector, you could read from any desired file even if the author had been less helpful.

 Some programs are written to ignore redirectors. For example, when invoked without special options, the **passwd** command expects to read the new password only from the console, not from a file. You can compel such programs to read from a file, but doing so requires techniques more advanced than redirectors.

When you specify no command-line arguments, many Unix programs read their input from stdin and write their output to stdout. Such programs are called *filters*. Filters can be easily fitted together to perform a series of related operations. The tool for combining filters is the *pipe*, which connects the output of one program to the input of another. For example, consider this command:

```
ls ~ | wc -l
```

The command consists of two commands, joined by the pipe redirector (|). The first command lists the names of the nonhidden files in the user's home directory, one file per line. The second command invokes **wc** by using the –l option, which causes **wc** to print only the total number of lines, rather than printing the total number of lines, words, and characters. The pipe redirector sends the output of the **ls** command to the **wc** command, which counts and prints the number of lines in its input, which happens to be the number of files in the user's home directory.

This is a simple example of the power and sophistication of the Unix shell. Unix doesn't include a command that counts the files in the user's home directory and doesn't need to do so. Should the need to count the files arise, a knowledgeable Unix user can prepare a simple script that computes the desired result by using general-purpose Unix commands.

Shell Variables

If you've studied programming, you know that programming languages resemble algebra. Both programming languages and algebra let you refer to a value by a name. And both programming languages and algebra include elaborate mechanisms for manipulating named values.

The shell is a programming language in its own right, letting you refer to variables known as *shell* or *environment variables*. To assign a value to a shell variable, you use a command that has the following form:

```
variable=value
```

For example, the command:

```
DifficultyLevel=1
```

assigns the value 1 to the shell variable named `DifficultyLevel`. Unlike algebraic variable, shell variables can have nonnumeric values. For example, the command:

```
Difficulty=medium
```

assigns the value `medium` to the shell variable named `Difficulty`.

Shell variables are widely used within Unix, because they provide a convenient way of transferring values from one command to another. Programs can obtain the value of a shell variable and use the value to modify their operation, in much the same way they use the value of command-line arguments.

You can see a list of shell variables by issuing the **set** command. Usually, the command produces more than a single screen of output. So, you can use a pipe redirector and the **less** command to view the output one screen at a time:

```
set | less
```

Press the spacebar to see each successive page of output. You'll probably see several of the shell variables described in Table 13-4 among those printed by the **set** command. The values of these shell variables are generally set by one or another of the startup scripts described earlier in this chapter.

Table 13-4. Important Environment Variables

Variable	Function
DISPLAY	The X display to be used; for example, localhost:0
HOME	The absolute path of the user's home directory
HOSTNAME	The Internet name of the host
LOGNAME	The user's login name
MAIL	The absolute path of the user's mail file
PATH	The search path (see next subsection)
SHELL	The absolute path of the current shell

Table 13-4. Important Environment Variables (continued)

Variable	Function
TERM	The terminal type
USER	The user's current username; may differ from the login name if the user executes the **su** command

You can use the value of a shell variable in a command by preceding the name of the shell variable by a dollar sign ($). To avoid confusion with surrounding text, you can enclose the name of the shell variable within curly braces ({}); it's good practice (though not necessary) to do so consistently. For example, you can change the current working directory to your */home* directory by issuing the command:

```
cd ${HOME}
```

Of course, issuing the **cd** command with no argument causes the same result. However, suppose you want to change to the */work* subdirectory of your home directory. The following command accomplishes exactly that:

```
cd ${HOME}/work
```

An easy way to see the value of a shell variable is to specify the variable as the argument of the **echo** command. For example, to see the value of the HOME shell variable, issue the command:

```
echo ${HOME}
```

To make the value of a shell variable available not just to the shell, but to programs invoked by using the shell, you must export the shell variable. To do so, use the **export** command, which has the form:

```
export variable
```

where *variable* specifies the name of the variable to be exported. A shorthand form of the command lets you assign a value to a shell variable and export the variable in a single command:

```
export variable=value
```

You can remove the value associated with a shell variable by giving the variable an empty value:

```
variable=
```

However, a shell variable with an empty value remains a shell variable and appears in the output of the **set** command. To dispense with a shell variable, you can issue the **unset** command:

```
unset variable
```

Once you unset the value of a variable, the variable no longer appears in the output of the **set** command.

The Search Path

The special shell variable PATH holds a series of paths known collectively as the *search path*. Whenever you issue an external command, the shell searches the paths that comprise the search path, seeking the program file that corresponds to the command. The startup scripts establish the initial value of the PATH shell variable, but you can modify its value to include any desired series of paths. You must use a colon (:) to separate each path of the search path. For example, suppose that PATH has the following value:

```
/usr/bin:/bin:/usr/local/bin:/usr/bin/X11:/usr/X11R6/bin
```

You can add a new search directory, say */home/bill*, by issuing the following command:

```
PATH=${PATH}:/home/bill
```

Now, the shell will look for external programs in */home/bill* as well as the default directories. However, the only problem is that the shell will look there last. If you prefer to check */home/bill* first, issue the following command instead:

```
PATH=/home/bill:${PATH}
```

The **which** command helps you work with the PATH shell variable. It checks the search path for the file specified as its argument and prints the name of the matching path, if any. For example, suppose you want to know where the program file for the **wc** command resides. Issuing the command:

```
which wc
```

will tell you that the program file is */usr/bin/wc* (or whatever other path is correct for your system).

Quoted Strings

Sometimes the shell may misinterpret a command you've written, globbing a filename or expanding a reference to a shell variable that you hadn't intended. Of course, it's actually your interpretation that's mistaken, not the shell's. Therefore, it's up to you to rewrite your command so the shell's interpretation is congruent with what you intended.

Quote characters, described in Table 13-5, can help you by controlling the operation of the shell. For example, by enclosing a command argument within single quotes, you can prevent the shell from globbing the argument or substituting the argument with the value of a shell variable.

Table 13-5. Quote Characters

Character	Function
' (single quote)	Characters within a pair of single quotes are interpreted literally, that is, their metacharacter meanings (if any) are ignored. Similarly, the shell does not replace references to shell or environment variables with the value of the referenced variable.
" (double quote)	Characters within a pair of double quotes are interpreted literally, that is, their metacharacter meanings (if any) are ignored. However, the shell does replace references to shell or environment variables with the value of the referenced variable.
` (backquote)	Text within a pair of backquotes is interpreted as a command, which the shell executes before executing the rest of the command line. The output of the command replaces the original backquoted text.
\ (backslash)	The following character is interpreted literally, that is, its metacharacter meaning (if any) is ignored. The backslash character has a special use as a line continuation character. When a line ends with a backslash, the line and the following line are considered part of a single line.

To see this in action, consider how you might cause the **echo** command to produce the output $PATH. If you simply issue the command:

```
echo $PATH
```

the **echo** command prints the value of the PATH shell variable. However, by enclosing the argument within single quotes, you obtain the desired result:

```
echo '$PATH'
```

Double quotes have a similar effect. They prevent the shell from globbing a filename but permit the expansion of shell variables.

Backquotes operate differently; they let you execute a command and use its output as an argument of another command. For example, the command:

```
echo My home directory contains `ls ~ | wc -l` files.
```

prints a message that gives the number of files in the user's */home* directory. The command works by first executing the command contained within backquotes:

```
ls ~ | wc -l
```

This command, as explained earlier, computes and prints the number of files in the user's directory. Because the command is enclosed in backquotes, its output is not printed; instead the output replaces the original backquoted text.

The resulting command becomes:

```
echo My home directory contains 22 files.
```

When executed, this command prints the output:

```
My home directory contains 22 files.
```

You may now begin to appreciate the power of the Linux shell: by including command aliases in your *bashrc* script, you can extend the command repertoire of the shell. And, by using filename completion and the history list, you can reduce the amount of typing it takes to enter frequently used commands. Once you grasp how to use it properly, the Linux shell is a powerful, fast, and easy-to-use interface that avoids the limitations and monotony of the more familiar point-and-click graphical interface.

But the shell has additional features that extend its capabilities even further. As you'll see in the next section, the Linux shell includes a powerful programming language that provides argument processing, conditional logic, and loops.

Understanding Shell Scripts

This section explains how more advanced shell scripts work. The information is also adequate to equip you to write many of your own useful shell scripts. The section begins by showing how to process a script's arguments. Then it shows how to perform conditional and iterative operations.

Processing Arguments

You can easily write scripts that process arguments, because a set of special shell variables holds the values of arguments specified when your script is invoked. Table 13-6 describes the most popular such shell variables.

Table 13-6. Special Shell Variables Used in Scripts

Variable	Meaning
$#	The number of arguments.
$0	The command name.
$1, $2, ... ,$9	The individual arguments of the command.
$*	The entire list of arguments, treated as a single word.
$@	The entire list of arguments, treated as a series of words.
$?	The exit status of the previous command; a value of 0 denotes a successful completion.
$$	The ID of the current process.

For example, here's a simple one-line script that prints the value of its second argument:

```
echo My second argument has the value $2.
```

Suppose you store this script in the file *second*, change its access mode to permit execution, and invoke it as follows:

```
./second a b c
```

The script will print the output:

```
My second argument has the value b.
```

Notice that the shell provides variables for accessing only nine arguments. Nevertheless, you can access more than nine arguments. The key to doing so is the **shift** command, which discards the value of the first argument and shifts the remaining values down one position. Thus, after executing the **shift** command, the shell variable $9 contains the value of the 10th argument. To access the 11th and subsequent arguments, you simply execute the **shift** command the appropriate number of times.

Exit Codes

The shell variable $? holds the numeric exit status of the most recently completed command. By convention, an exit status of zero denotes successful completion; other values denote error conditions of various sorts. You can set the error code in a script by issuing the **exit** command, which terminates the script and posts the specified exit status. The format of the command is:

> **exit** *status*

where *status* is a nonnegative integer that specifies the exit status.

Conditional Logic

A shell script can employ conditional logic, which lets the script take different action based on the values of arguments, shell variables, or other conditions. The **test** command lets you specify a condition, which can be either true or false. Conditional commands (including the **if**, **case**, **while**, and **until** commands) use the **test** command to evaluate conditions.

The test command

Table 13-7 describes some argument forms commonly used with the **test** command. The **test** command evaluates its arguments and sets the exit status to zero, which indicates that the specified condition was true, or a nonzero value, which indicates that the specified condition was false.

Table 13-7. Commonly Used Argument Forms of the test Command

Form	Function
-d *file*	The specified file exists and is a directory.
-e *file*	The specified file exists.
-r *file*	The specified file exists and is readable.
-s *file*	The specified file exists and has nonzero size.
-w *file*	The specified file exists and is writable.
-x *file*	The specified file exists and is executable.
-L *file*	The specified file exists and is a symbolic link.
f1 -nt *f2*	File *f1* is newer than file *f2*.

Table 13-7. Commonly Used Argument Forms of the test Command (continued)

Form	Function
f1 -ot *f2*	File *f1* is older than file *f2*.
-n *s1*	String *s1* has nonzero length.
-z *s1*	String *s1* has zero length.
s1 = *s2*	String *s1* is the same as string *s2*.
s1 != *s2*	String *s1* is not the same as string *s2*.
n1 -eq *n2*	Integer *n1* is equal to integer *n2*.
n1 -ge *n2*	Integer *n1* is greater than or equal to integer *n2*.
n1 -gt *n2*	Integer *n1* is greater than integer *n2*.
n1 -le *n2*	Integer *n1* is less than or equal to integer *n2*.
n1 -lt *n2*	Integer *n1* is less than integer *n2*.
n1 -ne *n2*	Integer *n1* is not equal to integer *n2*.
!	The NOT operator, which reverses the value of the following condition.
-a	The AND operator, which joins two conditions. Both conditions must be true for the overall result to be true.
-o	The OR operator, which joins two conditions. If either condition is true, the overall result is true.
\(... \)	You can group expressions within the test command by enclosing them within \(and \).

To see the **test** command in action, consider the following script:

```
test -d $1
echo $?
```

This script tests whether its first argument specifies a directory and displays the resulting exit status, a zero or a nonzero value that reflects the result of the test.

If the script was stored in the file *tester*, which permitted execute access, executing the script might yield results similar to the following:

```
$ ./tester /
0
$ ./tester /missing
1
```

These results indicate that the root directory (/) exists and that the */missing* directory does not.

The if command

The **test** command is not of much use by itself, but combined with commands such as the **if** command, it is useful indeed. The **if** command has the following form:

```
if command
then
  commands
else
 commands
fi
```

The command that usually follows **if** is a **test** command. However, this need not be so. The **if** command merely executes the specified command and tests its exit status. If the exit status is zero, the first set of commands is executed; otherwise, the second set of commands is executed. An abbreviated form of the **if** command does nothing if the specified condition is false:

```
if command
then
    commands
fi
```

When you type an **if** command, it occupies several lines; nevertheless, it's considered a single command. To underscore this, the shell provides a special prompt, called the *secondary prompt*, after you enter each line. You won't see the secondary prompt when entering a script using a text editor, or any other shell prompt for that matter.

As an example, suppose you want to delete a file, *file1*, if it's older than another file, *file2*. The following command would accomplish the desired result:

```
if test file1 -ot file2
then
  rm file1
fi
```

You could incorporate this command in a script that accepts arguments specifying the filenames:

```
if test $1 -ot $2
then
  rm $1
  echo Deleted the old file.
fi
```

If you name the script *riddance* and invoke it as follows:

riddance thursday wednesday

the script will delete the *thursday* file if that file is older than the *wednesday* file.

The case command

The **case** command provides a more sophisticated form of conditional processing:

```
case value in
    pattern1) commands ;;
    pattern2) commands ;;
    ...
esac
```

The **case** command attempts to match the specified value against a series of patterns. The commands associated with the first matching pattern, if any, are executed. Patterns are built using characters and metacharacters, such as those used to specify command arguments. As an example, here's a **case** command that interprets the value of the first argument of its script:

```
case $1 in
  -r) echo Force deletion without confirmation ;;
  -i) echo Confirm before deleting ;;
   *) echo Unknown argument ;;
esac
```

The command echoes a different line of text, depending on the value of the script's first argument. As done here, it's good practice to include a final pattern that matches any value.

The while command

The **while** command lets you execute a series of commands iteratively (that is, repeatedly) so long as a condition tests true:

```
while command
do
 commands
done
```

Here's a script that uses a **while** command to print its arguments on successive lines:

```
echo $1
while shift 2> /dev/null
do
   echo $1
done
```

Notice how the 2> operator is used to direct error messages to the device */dev/null*, which prevents them from being seen. You can omit this operator if you prefer.

The commands that comprise the **do** part of a **while** (or any other loop command) can include **if**, **case**, and even other **while** commands. However, scripts rapidly become difficult to understand when this occurs often. You should include conditional commands within other conditional commands only with due consideration for the clarity of the result. Don't forget to include comments in your scripts (with each commented line beginning with a #) to clarify difficult constructs.

The until command

The **until** command lets you execute a series of commands iteratively (that is, repeatedly) so long as a condition tests false:

```
until command
do
 commands
done
```

Here's a script that uses an **until** command to print its arguments on successive lines, until it encounters an argument that has the value *red*:

```
until test $1 = red
do
   echo $1
   shift
done
```

For example, if the script were named *stopandgo* and stored in the current working directory, the command:

```
./stopandgo green yellow red blue
```

would print the lines:

```
green
yellow
```

The for command

The **for** command iterates over the elements of a specified list:

```
for variable in list
do
   commands
done
```

Within the commands, you can reference the current element of the list by means of the shell variable *$variable*, where *variable* is the name specified following the **for**. The list typically takes the form of a series of arguments, which can incorporate metacharacters. For example, the following **for** command:

```
for i in 2 4 6 8
do
   echo $i
done
```

prints the numbers 2, 4, 6, and 8 on successive lines.

A special form of the **for** command iterates over the arguments of a script:

```
for variable
do
   commands
done
```

For example, the following script prints its arguments on successive lines:

```
for i
do
   echo $i
done
```

The break and continue commands

The **break** and **continue** commands are simple commands that take no arguments. When the shell encounters a **break** command, it immediately exits the body of the enclosing loop (**while**, **until**, or **for**) command. When the shell encounters a

continue command, it immediately discontinues the current iteration of the loop. If the loop condition permits, other iterations may occur; otherwise the loop is exited.

Periscope: A Useful Networking Script

Suppose you have a free email account such as that provided by Yahoo! You're traveling and find yourself in a remote location with web access. However, you're unable to access files on your home machine or check email that has arrived there. This is a common circumstance, especially if your business requires that you travel.

If your home computer runs Windows, you're pretty much out of luck. You'll find it extraordinarily difficult to access your home computer from afar. However, if your home computer runs Linux, gaining access is practically a piece of cake.

In order to show the power of shell scripts, this subsection explains a more complex shell script, *periscope*. At an appointed time each day, *periscope* causes your computer (which you must leave powered on) to establish a PPP connection to your ISP, which is maintained for about one hour. This provides you enough time to connect to an ISP from your hotel room or other remote location and then connect via the Internet with your home Linux system, avoiding long-distance charges. Once connected, you have about an hour to view or download mail and perform other work. Then, *periscope* breaks its PPP connection, which it will reestablish at the appointed time the next day.

Example 13-1 shows the *periscope* script file, which is considerably larger than any script you've so far encountered in this chapter. Therefore, we'll disassemble the script, explaining it line by line. As you'll see, each line is fairly simple in itself, and the lines work together in a straightforward fashion.

Example 13-1. The Periscope shell script

```
1   route del default
2   wvdial &
3   sleep 1m
4   ifconfig | mail username@mail.com
5   sleep 1h
6   killall wvdial
7   sleep 2s
8   killall -9 wvdial
9   killall pppd
10  sleep 2s
11  killall -9 pppd
12  echo "/root/periscope" | at 10:00
```

Here's the line-by-line analysis of the *periscope* script:

1. `route del default`

   This line is perhaps the most complex line of the entire script. The **route** command is normally issued by the system administrator. You've probably never issued the command yourself, because **neat** or another network configuration program has issued it on your behalf. The effect of the command is to delete the default network route, if any. The default route is the one along which TCP/IP sends packets when it knows no specific route to their specified destination. It's necessary to delete the default route because the **wvdial** program, which the script uses to establish its PPP connection, will not override an existing default route.

2. `wvdial &`

This line launches the **wvdial** program. As specified by the ampersand (&), the program will run in the background, so the script continues executing while **wvdial** starts up and runs.

3. `sleep 1m`

This line pauses the script for one minute, giving **wvdial** time to establish the PPP connection.

4. `ifconfig | mail` *username@mail.com*

This line runs the **ifconfig** command and mails its output to the specified user (you must replace *username@mail.com* with your own email address, which you can access remotely).

The **ifconfig** command produces output that looks something like this:

```
ppp0   Link encap:Point-Point Protocol
       inet addr:10.144.153.105  P-t-P:10.144.153.52 Mask:255.255.255.0
       UP POINTOPOINT RUNNING  MTU:552  Metric:1
       RX packets:0 errors:0 dropped:0 overruns:0
       TX packets:0 errors:0 dropped:0 overruns:0
```

You'll probably see other sections in the output that describe your Ethernet interface (*eth0*) and a loopback device (*lo*). The inet addr given in the command output (10.144.153.105) is the IP address of your computer. By mailing the output to yourself, you provide a simple way to discover your computer's IP address, which is likely to be different each time it connects to your ISP.

5. `sleep 1h`

This line causes the script to pause for an interval of one hour. You can easily change this interval to something more appropriate to your own needs.

6. `killall wvdial`

Now that the connection interval has elapsed, the last line terminates all executing instances of the **wvdial** program.

 Appendix D briefly describes the **killall** command and other possibly unfamiliar commands employed in this script.

7. `sleep 2s`

The script then pauses for two seconds, to ensure that **wvdial** has completely terminated.

8. `killall -9 wvdial`

   Under some circumstances, a program will ignore a termination request. This line deals with this possibility by sending a special code that compels a reluctant program to terminate without further delay.

9. `killall pppd`

   Behind the scenes, **wvdial** launches a program known as **pppd**, which actually establishes and manages the PPP connection. Another **killall** command is designed to terminate **pppd** if **wvdial** has failed to do so.

10. `sleep 2s`

    Again, the script pauses for a few seconds. This time, it does so to ensure that **pppd** has completely terminated.

11. `killall -9 pppd`

    And, again, the script uses the –**9** option to specify that any remaining instances of **pppd** should terminate immediately.

12. `echo "/root/periscope" | at 10:00`

    Finally, the script uses the **at** command to schedule itself for execution at 10:00 tomorrow. The **at** command reads one or more commands from its standard input and executes them at the time specified as an argument.

To try the script for yourself, you must have installed the **wvdial** program, as explained in Chapter 10. Place the script in the file */root/periscope*. Of course, you'll probably want to customize the script to specify an appointment time and duration of your own choosing. To start *periscope*, log in as *root* and issue the command:

   `(echo "/root/periscope" | at 10:00)&`

The parentheses cause the **&** operator to apply to the entire command, not just the **at**. When 10:00 a.m. (or any other time you specify) comes around, your Linux system should obediently dial your ISP and maintain the connection for the specified interval of time.

Using Periscope

At the appointed time, fire up your computer and access your email account. You should find a mail message that contains the **ifconfig** output giving your computer's current IP address. Now you can use *telnet* or an *ssh* client—your choice corresponds to the server you're running on your Linux system—to contact your computer and work for the remainder of the specified connection time. At the end of the connection time, your Linux system will sever its PPP connection and begin counting down until it's again time to connect.

Linux Directory Tree

Table A-1 describes the directories in the Linux directory tree.

Table A-1. The Linux Directory Tree

Directory	Description
/bin	Programs and scripts essential to system startup
/boot	Boot information, including the kernel
/dev	Device files
/etc	Configuration files
/home	Users' home directories
/lib	Libraries, modules, and other object files
/lib/modules	Loadable kernel modules
/lost+found	Recovered data from bad clusters
/mnt	Temporarily mounted filesystems
/proc	Kernel pseudo-directory that provides access to kernel information and configuration items
/root	System administrator's home directory
/sbin	System administration programs and scripts essential to system startup
/tmp	Temporary files, which are automatically deleted by Red Hat Linux
/usr/bin	Programs and scripts not essential to system startup
/usr/etc	Configuration files
/usr/games	Game files
/usr/include	C/C++ header files
/usr/lib	Libraries
/usr/local	Locally defined directory tree
/usr/sbin	System administration programs and scripts not essential to system start up
/usr/share	Shared files
/usr/share/doc	Documentation (formerly residing in */usr/doc*)
/usr/share/man	Manpages

Table A-1. The Linux Directory Tree (continued)

Directory	Description
/usr/src	Source files
/usr/src/linux	Linux kernel source
/usr/X11R6	X-related files
/var	Dynamic files, such as log files and spool files

For more information on the Linux directory tree, see the current version of the Linux Filesystem Hierarchy Standard (*http://www.pathname.com/fhs*). Red Hat Linux generally complies with that standard.

Principal Linux Files

Table B-1 describes the principal Linux files. You can use it, for example, to help you locate configuration files quickly.

Table B-1. Principal Linux Files

File(s)	Description
/boot/module-info	Module information for the Linux kernel
/boot/System.map	Map of the Linux kernel
/boot/vmlinuz	Linux kernel
/etc/aliases	Mail aliases
/etc/at.allow	User IDs of users allowed to use the **at** command
/etc/at.deny	User IDs of users forbidden to use the **at** command
/etc/auto.master	Configuration file for the *autofs* daemon, which automatically mounts filesystems
/etc/auto.misc	Automounter map file
/etc/bashrc	Systemwide functions and aliases for the *bash* shell
/etc/conf.modules	Aliases and options for loadable kernel modules
/etc/cron.daily/*	Daily *cron* jobs
/etc/cron.hourly/*	Hourly *cron* jobs
/etc/cron.monthly/*	Monthly *cron* jobs
/etc/cron.weekly/*	Weekly *cron* jobs
/etc/csh.cshrc	C shell initialization file
/etc/csh.login	C shell login file
/etc/default/useradd	Defaults for **useradd** command
/etc/DIR_COLORS	Directory listing colors
/etc/exports	NFS exported directories
/etc/filesystems	Supported filesystem types
/etc/fstab	Filesystems mounted or available for mounting
/etc/ftp*	FTP configuration files

Table B-1. Principal Linux Files (continued)

File(s)	Description
/etc/group	System group definitions
/etc/host.conf	Resolver configuration file
/etc/hosts	Map of IP numbers to hostnames
/etc/hosts.allow	Hosts allowed to access Internet services
/etc/hosts.deny	Hosts forbidden to access Internet services
/etc/httpd/access.conf	Web server configuration file
/etc/httpd/conf/*	Apache configuration files
/etc/httpd/httpd.conf	Web server configuration file
/etc/identd.conf	*identd* service configuration
/etc/inetd.conf	Configuration for the *inetd* daemon, which controls access to Internet services
/etc/initlog.conf	Logging configuration file
/etc/inittab	Configuration for the *init* daemon, which controls executing processes
/etc/issue	Linux kernel and distribution version
/etc/ld.so.conf	Shared library configuration file
/etc/lilo.conf	Loader (*lilo*) configuration file
/etc/login.defs	Options for **useradd** and related commands
/etc/logrotate.conf	Log rotation configuration file
/etc/logrotate.d/*	Scripts to rotate logs
/etc/lpd.conf	Printer configuration file
/etc/lpd.perms	Printer spooler permissions file
/etc/mail/*	*sendmail* configuration files
/etc/mailcap	*metamail* MIME information
/etc/man.config	*man* configuration file
/etc/mesa.conf	*mesa* configuration file
/etc/mime.types	MIME types
/etc/mime-magic*	Magic numbers for MIME data
/etc/minicom.users	User IDs allowed to use *minicom*
/etc/motd	Message of the day
/etc/mtab	Mounted filesystems
/etc/named.conf	BIND configuration file
/etc/nmh/*	*nmh* mail client configuration
/etc/nscd.conf	BIND cache configuration file
/etc/nsswitch.conf	Resolver configuration file
/etc/openldap/*	Open LDAP configuration files
/etc/pam.d/*	PAM configuration files
/etc/paper.config	Paper sizes

Table B-1. Principal Linux Files (continued)

File(s)	Description
/etc/passwd	User account information
/etc/pine.conf	Configuration of *pine* mail reader
/etc/ppp/*	PPP configuration
/etc/printcap	Printer options and capabilities
/etc/profile	Default environment for users of *bash* shell
/etc/profile.d/*	Shell initialization
/etc/protocols	Protocol names and numbers
/etc/pwdb.conf	*pwdb* library configuration
/etc/rc.d	Scripts for system and process startup and shutdown
/etc/rc.d/init.d/*	SysVinit scripts
/etc/rc.d/rc.local	Local startup script
/etc/rc.d/rc.sysinit	System initialization file
/etc/rc.d/rc?.d/*	Service start/stop scripts
/etc/rndc.conf	BIND control configuration
/etc/rpc	RPC program number database
/etc/rpm/*	RPM database and configuration files
/etc/samba/*	Samba configuration files
/etc/samba/codepages/*	Samba code pages
/etc/securetty	Secure tty configuration
/etc/security/*	PAM configuration files
/etc/sendmail.cf	*sendmail* configuration file
/etc/sensors.conf	*libsensors* configuration file
/etc/services	Standard service names and numbers
/etc/shadow	Secure user account information
/etc/skel	Skeleton files used to establish new user accounts
/etc/smb.conf	Configuration of *smb* (Samba) daemon
/etc/smbpasswd	Account information for Samba users
/etc/smbusers	User mappings for Samba
/etc/ssh/*	SSH configuration files
/etc/sysconfig/*	System configuration files
/etc/sysconfig/network-scripts/*	Network configuration files
/etc/sysctl.conf	*sysctl* configuration file
/etc/syslog.conf	System logging process configuration
/etc/termcap	Terminal capabilities and options
/etc/tux.mime.types	MIME types for Tux web server
/etc/updatedb.conf	*updatedb*/*locate* configuration file

Table B-1. Principal Linux Files (continued)

File(s)	Description
/etc/wvdial.conf	GNOME dialer configuration file
/etc/X11/applnk/*	X application shortcuts
/etc/X11/fs/config	X font server configuration
/etc/X11/gdm/*	GNOME display manager configuration
/etc/X11/prefdm	Display manager configuration file
/etc/X11/xdm/*	X display manager configuration file
/etc/X11/XF86Config	X configuration file
/etc/X11/xinit/Xclients	Default script for *xinit*
/etc/X11/xinit/xinitrc	X session initialization file
/etc/X11/Xmodmap	Key mappings used by *xdm* and *xinit*
/etc/xinetd.conf	*xinetd* configuration
/etc/xinetd.d/*	*xinetd* policy files
/etc/yp.conf	Yellow Pages (NIS) configuration file
/etc/ypserv.conf	Yellows Pages (NIS) server configuration file
/root/.bash_logout	*bash* logout script for system administrator
/root/.bash_profile	*bash* initialization script for system administrator
/root/.bashrc	*bash* options for system administrator
/root/.cshrc	C shell options for system administrator
/root/.tcshrc	C shell options for system administrator
/root/.Xresources	X resources for system administrator
/usr/lib/slrn/slrn.rc	*slrn* news reader configuration
/usr/share/config/*	Miscellaneous configuration files
/usr/share/fonts/*	Fonts
/usr/share/ssl/openssl.cnf	SSL certificate configuration
/usr/X11R6/lib/X11/app-defaults/*	X application defaults
/usr/X11R6/lib/X11/fonts/*	X fonts
/var/log/cron	Log of *cron* activity
/var/log/httpd/access_log	Log of web server access
/var/log/httpd/error_log	Log of web server errors
/var/log/lastlog	Last login log
/var/log/messages	System log
/var/named/	BIND configuration
/var/www/html/*	Web pages
/var/yp/*	Yellow Pages (NIS) configuration files

Managing the Boot Process

In this appendix, you'll learn more about how to boot a Linux system; in particular, you'll learn more about configuring your computer system to boot any of several operating systems. The appendix focuses on GNU GRUB, the Grand Unified Boot-loader, and *loadlin*, the most popular utilities for booting Linux systems.

Booting Linux

When you boot a PC, you cause it to execute a small program known as a *boot loader*. The purpose of the boot loader is to locate and read into memory the first stage of an operating system and transfer control to it. The operating system then locates and reads its remaining components as needed.

The simplest way to boot Linux is by using a floppy diskette. By doing so, you're able to leave the boot information on your hard drive untouched, ensuring that you can still boot Microsoft Windows or another operating system stored on the same hard drive. Moreover, some operating systems and virus protection programs prevent modification of the boot information on your hard drive. By booting from a floppy diskette, you avoid several potential problems.

However, many users find booting from a floppy disk slow or inconvenient. You don't have to boot Linux from a floppy diskette; you can boot it in any of several other ways. The two most popular alternatives are by using GRUB, which replaces the boot loader stored on your hard drive, or *loadlin*, which lets you first boot DOS and then boot Linux from DOS.

This chapter cannot describe the entire range of issues involved in booting Linux. Much of the information in this chapter is taken from several Linux HOWTOs that contain additional useful information on booting Linux:

- *BootPrompt-HOWTO*
- *CD-Writing-HOWTO*
- *CDROM-HOWTO*
- *Ethernet-HOWTO*

- *Ftape-HOWTO*
- *Hardware-HOWTO*
- *Multi-Disk-HOWTO*
- *PCI-HOWTO*
- *PCMCIA-HOWTO*

Boot Floppies

Even if you don't want to boot Linux from a floppy diskette, you should create and keep on hand a Linux boot floppy. If something goes wrong with your system, preventing you from booting in the normal way, you may be able to boot your system by using the floppy. Then, you can diagnose and repair the problem and get back to business as usual.

Creating a Boot Floppy

The Red Hat install program gives you the option of creating a boot diskette when you install Linux. You should exercise this option each time you install Linux, so that you have a fresh boot floppy containing software consistent with that stored on your hard drive.

However, you can easily create a boot diskette after the installation is complete. To do so, insert a blank floppy diskette into your system's floppy drive. Log on as *root* and issue the following command:

```
/sbin/mkbootdisk version
```

For *version*, supply the version number of your kernel. If you don't recall the version, simply access an unused virtual console. There you'll see the default Red Hat login prompt, which includes the version number of the kernel, for example, 2.4.2.

The **mkbootdisk** command creates a boot floppy that uses the same kernel running when the command is issued. It also configures the boot floppy to load any necessary SCSI modules, so that your SCSI drives will be accessible after booting from the floppy.

Another way to create a boot disk is from the GUI. In GNOME, use Main Menu → Programs → System → Create a boot disk, or in KDE, use Main Menu → System → Create a boot disk after inserting a blank floppy disk in the drive.

Using a Boot Floppy

Insert the boot floppy into your system's floppy drive. If your system is turned off, power up your system. If your system is turned on, first shut down the active operating system in the proper manner, then restart the system. Linux should then boot from the floppy.

To use your boot floppy, your system's CMOS must be configured to allow booting from the floppy drive. If your system boots from its hard drive even when the boot floppy is present, you must change your system's CMOS configuration. The relevant option is generally named Boot Sequence, Boot Order, or something similar. The value you want is generally labeled *A:*, *C:*, or something similar. Consult your system's documentation for further information.

The GRUB Loader

Most PCs can be booted from a floppy drive or hard drive; many recently manufactured computers can be booted from a CD-ROM drive. The first sector of a disk, diskette, or partition is known as the *boot sector*. The boot sector associated with a disk or diskette (the first sector of the disk or diskette) is known as the *Master Boot Record (MBR)*. In order for a diskette or disk to be bootable, it must contain a boot loader, which can reside in:

- The boot sector of the floppy diskette
- The MBR of the first hard disk or the first CD-ROM drive, if the PC supports booting from a CD-ROM
- The boot sector of a Linux filesystem partition on the first hard disk
- The boot sector of an extended partition on the first hard disk

GRUB is a sophisticated boot loader that can load Linux, Microsoft Windows 3.*x* and 9*x*, and other popular operating systems. Most users install GRUB on the MBR of their system's first hard disk. That way, when the system is started, it boots GRUB, which can be used to load Linux, Microsoft Windows, or another operating system.

Unless you direct otherwise, the Red Hat Linux installation procedure automatically installs GRUB. So you don't need to install GRUB; you just need to configure it.

Similarly, when you boot by using GRUB, you can also boot parameters to control the boot process; you can specify GRUB's boot parameters by selecting an operating system from GRUB's menu and pressing **e**. In response, GRUB displays an editor screen that shows the commands associated with the selected operating system, as shown in Figure C-1.

Commands that can be used in the editor screen are listed in Table C-1.

Table C-1. GRUB Editor Commands

Command	Meaning
b	Boot the currently selected operating system.
e	Edit the currently selected GRUB command.
c	Open a screen for interactively entering and executing GRUB commands.
o	Enter a new command after the currently selected command.
O	Enter a new command before the currently selected command.

Table C-1. GRUB Editor Commands (continued)

Command	Meaning
d	Delete the currently selected command.
Esc	Return to the main GRUB menu.

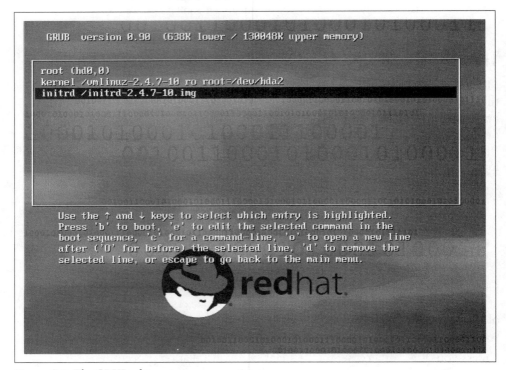

Figure C-1. The GRUB editor screen

The principal GRUB commands are:

chainloader
> Used to load a Microsoft operating system, including DOS, Windows 3.*x*, 9*x*, NT, or 2000.

initrd
> Specifies the file containing an initial RAM disk used in loading Linux. This command is necessary, for instance, when booting Linux from a SCSI drive.

kernel
> Specifies the file containing the Linux kernel to be booted.

root
rootnoverify
> Specifies the partition to be mounted as the root partition. The *root* command causes the filesystem to be verified before the partition is mounted.

GRUB refers to hard disks using the syntax (hd*n*), where *n* specifies the device number assigned by the system BIOS. For example, (hd0) refers to the first hard drive. Partitions are designated by the related syntax (hd*n*,*m*), where *m* is the number of the partition. For example, (hd1,0) refers to the first partition of the second hard drive.

GRUB can refer to the disk blocks that comprise a file by using a special syntax known as a *blocklist*. A blocklist consists of a comma-separated list of block ranges, each of which consists of a starting block number, followed by a plus sign (+), followed by the number of blocks in the range. For example, the blocklist 0+1,10+20 refers to a block range beginning at block 0 and including 1 block and a block range beginning at block 10 and including 20 blocks.

If the starting block number of a block range is omitted, the block range is implied to begin with block 0. For example, the block range +1 begins at block 0 and includes 1 block.

A blocklist can appear after a reference to a partition; if no partition is identified, the partition identified by the preceding root command is implied. For example, in the entry:

```
root (hd0,0)
chainlist +1
```

the blocklist +1 is implicitly associated with (hd0,0) and is equivalent to the blocklist (hd0,0)+1.

A typical GRUB entry for booting Linux resembles the following:

```
root (hd0,7)
kernel /boot/vmlinuz-2.2.17 root=/dev/hda8
```

This entry boots the specified kernel residing on partition 7 of the first hard drive, mounting partition 8 as the root partition. Linux boot parameters, such as those described in the later section titled "Boot Parameters," can be specified by using the *kernel* command.

If the kernel requires access to special drivers residing on a RAM disk, a RAM disk can be identified as in this entry:

```
root (hd0,7)
kernel /boot/vmlinuz-2.4.9-2 ro root=/dev/hda8
initrd /initrd-2.4.9-2.img
```

Notice that the name of the RAM disk file is specified as though the file resides in the root directory, whereas it actually resides in the */boot* directory. This is necessary because GRUB initially mounts the */boot* filesystem, as specified in the preceding root command. The mounted filesystem is treated by GRUB as its root filesystem.

A typical GRUB entry for booting a Microsoft operating system has this form:

```
rootnoverify (hd0,0)
chainloader +1
```

This entry boots the Microsoft operating system residing on partition 0 of the first hard drive. The blocklist +1 points to the first block of the root partition. Microsoft operating systems place their boot file at this location.

To boot your system, GRUB uses your system's BIOS, which may not be able to load a Linux kernel (or other program) stored beyond cylinder 1023 of your hard drive. Booting a kernel stored beyond cylinder 1023 requires a motherboard that supports *logical byte addressing* (LBA). Most motherboards manufactured in the last several years are supposed to support LBA. Unfortunately, some motherboards that claim to support LBA do not. If you're installing Linux on a preexisting hard drive, you may not be able to place your Linux kernel in an appropriate location. In that case, you won't be able to use GRUB to boot your system.

To learn more about GRUB, see the following resources:

- The manpage for GRUB
- The GRUB home page, *http://www.gnu.org/software/grub*
- The *Multiboot-with-GRUB* mini HOWTO, *http://www.redhat.com/mirrors/LDP/ HOWTO/mini/Multiboot-with-GRUB.html*

The loadlin Loader

Another way of booting Linux is by using *loadlin*, an MS-DOS program that can load a Linux kernel. To load Linux, *loadlin* relies on MS-DOS rather than your system's BIOS; therefore, *loadlin* can load a kernel stored beyond cylinder 1023. More generally, it can load a kernel from any filesystem or location accessible to MS-DOS.

However, *loadlin* cannot be run from a DOS Prompt window within Windows 3.*x* or 9*x*. You must start your system in MS-DOS mode in order for *loadlin* to work. By making the proper entries to your *config.sys* file, you can create a convenient boot menu that lets you boot MS-DOS, Windows, or Linux. Because Windows 2000 does not provide an MS-DOS mode, you cannot use *loadlin* with Windows 2000.

Installing loadlin

The *loadlin* program is found in the */dosutils* directory of the Red Hat Linux CD-ROM (Disc 1). The *loadlin* program must have access to the file containing the Linux kernel you want to boot. The easiest way to get this file onto your Windows system is to boot Linux, make sure the Windows filesystem that corresponds to the Windows C: drive is mounted, and copy the kernel file. The following commands assume that your Windows filesystem is mounted as */mnt/c* and that you want to store the kernel in the directory *c:\linux*:

```
mkdir /mnt/c/linux
cp /boot/vmlinuz /mnt/c/linux/vmlinuz
```

The *loadlin* program needs to know the identity of your Linux root partition. To learn the name of the root partition, issue the command:

```
mount
```

The command reports all the mounted devices:

```
/dev/hda2 on / type ext2 (rw)
none on /proc type proc (rw)
/dev/hda1 on /boot type ext2 (ro)
none on /dev/pts type devpts (rw,mode=0622)
/dev/hdc on /mnt/cdrom type iso9660 (ro)
```

The root partition is the partition mounted as /. Here, it's */dev/hda2*. Make a note of the partition name. Then, boot your Microsoft Windows system and copy the file *loadlin.exe* from the */dosutils* directory to a convenient location on your hard drive.

Using loadlin

To test *loadlin*, restart your Windows system in MS-DOS mode, by choosing Start → Shut Down, choosing Restart in MS-DOS Mode from the Shut Down Windows dialog box that appears, and clicking on OK. When the MS-DOS prompt appears, change to the directory containing *loadlin* and issue the command:

```
loadlin c:\linux\vmlinuz root=/dev/hdxn ro
```

where */dev/hdxn* is the root partition of your Linux system, which you earlier recorded. If your Linux files are stored in a directory other than *linux*, you must adjust the command's first argument appropriately. Your Linux system should boot. If it does not, check your work and try again.

Configuring loadlin

Once you're satisfied that *loadlin* works with your system, you can configure your system so that using *loadlin* is more convenient. Microsoft Windows supports a simple boot menu that will let you decide whether to boot Linux or Windows. To create such a boot menu, boot Windows and use *Notepad* to add the following lines to the top of your *config.sys* file:

```
[menu]
menuitem=Linux, Boot Linux
menuitem=Win95, Boot Windows 95
menudefault=Linux, 15

[linux]
shell=c:\linux\loadlin.exe @c:\linux\bootopts.txt

[win95]
```

If you're using Windows 3.*x* or Windows 98 rather than Windows 95, change the file accordingly.

The *config.sys* file is located in the root directory of the *C:* drive. If your system has no *config.sys* file, create one using the lines given.

Now, add the following lines to the top of your *autoexec.bat* file:

```
goto %config%
:win95
```

The *autoexec.bat* file is located in the root directory of the *C:* drive. If your system has no *autoexec.bat* file, create one using the lines given.

Finally, use *Notepad* to create the file *bootopts.txt* in the *linux* directory. The file should have contents similar to the following:

```
c:\linux\vmlinuz root=/dev/hdxn ro
```

Be sure to substitute the name of your Linux root partition for the placeholder xn. You can specify additional options if you like. The next section introduces you to the most popular ones.

Now when you boot your system, you'll see a convenient menu that lets you type a digit to choose which operating system you want to boot.

Another convenient way to use *loadlin* with Windows 95 (but not Windows 98) is to create a program shortcut that switches your system to MS-DOS mode and runs *loadlin*. Launch the dialog box for creating the shortcut by right-clicking on the desktop and clicking on New → Shortcut. The dialog box lets you specify the contents of the *autoexec.bat* and *config.sys* files. The former should be empty, and the latter should contain the line:

```
shell=c:\linux\loadlin.exe @c:\linux\bootopts.txt
```

Boot Parameters

Boot parameters are specified using a three-part directive that includes the name of the parameter and an optional list of options, which consists of an equal sign (=) followed by a comma-separated list of option values

No spaces may appear in the directive. As an example, the following directive specifies the identity of the Linux root partition:

```
root=/dev/hda1
```

You can specify multiple directives by separating them with a space. For example, the following specifies the identity of the Linux root partition and that the root partition is initially mounted read-only, so that a thorough check of its filesystem can be performed:

```
root=/dev/hda1 ro
```

Most directives are interpreted by the kernel, though GRUB is also capable of processing directives. If you specify a directive that neither the kernel nor GRUB understands (assuming you're using GRUB), a directive that includes an equal sign is passed to the init process as an environment variable. You learned about environment variables in Chapter 7. A nonkernel directive that doesn't include an equal sign is passed to the *init* process. An example of this usage is specifying the directive single, which causes *init* to start your system in single-user mode:

```
root=/dev/hda1 ro single
```

General Boot Arguments

Table C-2 describes some of the most popular and useful boot arguments. These arguments apply to your system as a whole; in subsequent sections, you'll learn about other boot arguments that apply to specific devices or functions. In addition to boot arguments previously introduced, the table describes the reserve argument, which is helpful in avoiding system memory conflicts.

Table C-2. Selected General Boot Arguments

Argument	Description and options
init=	Specifies arguments passed by the kernel to the init process.
mem=	Specifies the amount of physical memory available to Linux; lets you instruct Linux to avoid high memory areas used by some systems for BIOS or caching. You can specify the amount as a hexadecimal number or as a decimal number followed by k or M, denoting kilobytes or megabytes, respectively.
reserve=	Specifies I/O ports that must not be probed. The port number is specified by using a hexadecimal number, and the range is specified by using a decimal number. For example, reserve=0x320,32 specifies that I/O ports 320-33f must not be probed.
ro	Initially mounts the root filesystem in read-only mode, so that a more effective filesystem check can be done.

root=	Identifies the root filesystem:
	
	/dev/fd*n*
	    Floppy disk *n* (0 or 1)
	
	/dev/hd*xn*
	    Partition *n* of IDE drive *x* (a to d)
	
	/dev/sd*xn*
	    Partition *n* of SCSI drive *x* (a to e)

rw	Initially mounts the root filesystem in read/write mode; does not perform a filesystem check.
vga=	Specifies the default display mode set before booting. Specifying vga=ask will cause *lilo* to list the available video modes. You can then specify the desired mode in place of ask. (This argument is interpreted by *lilo* and will have no effect if another loader is used.)

RAM Disk Boot Arguments

Table C-3 describes four boot arguments used in working with RAM disks. You won't likely need to specify any of these, but knowing about them may help you understand boot specifications written by others, including those used by Red Hat Linux.

Table C-3. Selected RAM Disk Arguments

Argument	Description and options
load_ramdisk=	Specifies that a RAM disk is not to be loaded (0) or is to be loaded (1).
prompt_ramdisk=	Specifies whether to provide a prompt instructing the user to insert a floppy containing a RAM disk (1) or provide no such prompt (0).
ramdisk_size=	Specifies the amount of RAM to be allocated to a RAM disk. If not specified, the default is 4 MB.
ramdisk_start=	Specifies the offset (in disk blocks from the start of the boot media) of the RAM disk data; lets a kernel and RAM disk data occupy the same floppy disk.

SCSI Host Adapter Boot Arguments

Table C-4 describes the most often used boot arguments related to SCSI host adapters. Table C-5 describes the options used by the SCSI host adapter boot arguments and other boot arguments.

Table C-4. Selected SCSI Host Adapter Arguments

Argument	Description and options
advansys=	Advansys SCSI host adapter: *iobase,[iobase,[iobase,[iobase]]]*[a]
aha152x=	Adaptec aha151x, ada152x, aic6260, aic6360, and SB16-SCSI SCSI host adapters: *iobase[,irq[,scsi_id[,reconnect[,parity]]]]*
aha1542=	Adaptec aha154x SCSI host adapter: *iobase[,buson,busoff[,dmaspeed]]*
aic7xxx=	Adaptec aha274x, aha284x, aic7xxx SCSI host adapters: *extended,no_reset*
AM53C974=	AMD AM53C974-based SCSI host adapters: *scsi-id,dev_id,dmaspeed,offset* See the file *linux/drivers/scsi/README.AM53C974*.
buslogic=	BusLogic SCSI controller Many options are available. See the *BootPrompt-HOWTO*.
eata=	EATA SCSI host adapter: *iobase,[iobase,[iobase,[iobase]]]*
fdomain=	Future Domain SCSI controller: *iobase,irq[,scsi_id]*
in2000=	Always SCSI host adapter The driver for the Always SCSI controller accepts options in somewhat different format than other drivers. See the *Boot Prompt-HOWTO*.

Table C-4. Selected SCSI Host Adapter Arguments (continued)

Argument	Description and options
max-scsi-luns=	Specifies the maximum number of SCSI logical units to be probed; lets you avoid probing devices that might lock up the SCSI bus.
ncr5380=	NCR 5380-based SCSI host adapters: *iobase,irq,dma* *membase,irq,dma*
ncr53c400=	NCR 53c400-based SCSI host adapters: *iobase,irq,pio* *membase,irq,pio*
ncr53c406a=	NCR 53c406a-based SCSI host adapters: *iobase,irq,pio* *membase,irq,pio*
pas16=	Pro Audio Spectrum SCSI host adapter: *iobase,irq*
ppa=	Iomega parallel port SCSI adapter for ZIP drive: *iobase,speed_high,speed_low,nybble*
st0x=	Seagate ST-0x SCSI host adapter: *membase,irq*
t128=	Trantor T128 SCSI host adapter: *membase,irq*
tmc8xx=	Future Domain TMC-8xx and TMC-950 SCSI host adapters: *membase,irq*
u14-34f=	Ultrastor SCSI host adapter: *iobase,[iobase,[iobase,[iobase]]]*
wd7000=	Western Digital WD7000 SCSI host adapter: *irq,dma,iobase*

a Don't include the square brackets in your boot argument; they merely indicate which options must be present.

For example, from Table C-4 you can learn that Adaptec aha154x SCSI host adapters use a boot argument having the form:

iobase[,buson,busoff[,dmaspeed]]

Table C-5 helps you understand the form of the *iobase* option and the other italicized options. The *iobase* option, for example, lets you specify the I/O port associated with the SCSI host adapter. For example, you can specify a boot argument for an Adaptec aha154x SCSI host adapter by writing only an *iobase* option; the remaining options are optional. However, as indicated by the square brackets, if you include a *buson* option, you must include a *busoff* option. Similarly, to include the *dmaspeed* option, you must include each of the other options. Here's an example of a complete boot argument:

aha1542=0x300,11,4

Table C-5. Selected Boot Prompt Options

Option	Description and options
busoff	The interval (number of microseconds) during which the device will relinquish the ISA bus, specified as a decimal integer, for example, 4.
buson	The interval (number of microseconds) during which the device will dominate the ISA bus, specified as a decimal integer, for example, 11.
ctl	The I/O port used for control, specified as a hexadecimal number, for example, 0x300.
cyl,head,sect	The geometry of the storage device, specified as three integers denoting the number of cylinders, heads, and sectors, respectively.
dev_id	A SCSI device with which the host adapter communicates, specified as a decimal integer, for example, 2.
dma	The DMA (direct memory access) channel by used by the device, specified as a decimal integer, for example, 3.
dmaspeed	The rate (in MB/sec.) at which DMA transfers are performed, specified as a decimal integer, for example, 5.
extended	Whether extended translation for large disks is enabled (1) or not (0).
magic_number	Whether the driver attempts to work, even if the firmware version is unknown (79); other values are ignored.
no_reset	Whether the driver should reset the SCSI bus when setting up the host adapter at boot (1) or not (0).
iobase	An I/O port, specified as a hexadecimal number, for example, 0x300.
irq	A hardware interrupt number, specified as a decimal integer, for example, 5.
is_pas_card	Whether a Pro Audio Spectrum (PAS) card is used; otherwise, do not specify this option.
membase	The base address of a memory region used for memory-mapped I/O, specified as a hexadecimal number, for example, 0x2000.
parity	Whether the SCSI host adapter uses parity (1) or does not use parity (0).
pio	Whether insl and outsl multibyte instructions (1) or inb and outb single-byte instructions (0) are used.
reconnect	Whether the SCSI host adapter is allowed to disconnect and reconnect (1) or holds a connection until the operation is complete (0).
scsi_id	The ID by which the SCSI host adapter identifies itself, specified as a decimal integer, for example, 7.

To determine a proper value for options described in Table C-5, you must often know something about the hardware structure of your system. The procedures described in Chapter 2 will help you.

IDE Hard Drive and CD-ROM Boot Arguments

Table C-6 describes the most commonly used boot arguments associated with IDE hard drives and CD-ROM drives. Refer to Table C-7 to determine the form of the italicized options.

Table C-6. Selected IDE Hard Drive Arguments

Argument	Description and options
hdx=	IDE hard drive or CD-ROM (*x* denotes the physical device and must be a letter from a to h):
	autotune Specifies that the driver should attempt to tune the interface to the fastest possible mode and speed
	cdrom Specifies that the drive is a CD-ROM drive
	cyl,head,sect Specifies the geometry of the drive
	none Specifies that the drive is not present—do not probe
	noprobe Specifies that the driver should not probe for the device
	nowerr Specifies that the `WRERR_STAT` bit should be ignored on this drive
ide0=	IDE hard drive or CD-ROM:
	ali14xx Probe for and support the alil4xx interface.
	cmd640_vlb Probe for and support the cmd640 chip (required for controllers using a VLB interface).
	dtc2278 Probe for and support the dtc2278 interface.
	ht6560b Probe for and support the ht6560b interface.
	qd6580 Probe for and support the qd6580 interface.
	umc8672 Probe for and support the umc8672 interface.
idex=	IDE hard drive or CD-ROM (*x* specifies the physical device and must be a digit from 0 to 3):
	autotune Specifies that the driver should attempt to tune the interface to the fastest possible mode and speed
	iobase Specifies the I/O port used by the drive
	iobase,ctl Specifies the I/O port and control port used by the drive
	iobase,ctl,irq Specifies the I/O port, control port, and IRQ used by the drive
	noautotune Specifies that the driver should not attempt to tune the interface for fastest mode and speed
	noprobe Specifies that the driver should not probe for the device
	serialize Specifies that I/O operations should not be overlapped

Non-IDE CD-ROM Drive Boot Arguments

Table C-7 describes the most common boot arguments for non-IDE CD-ROM drives. Refer to Table C-5 to determine the form of the italicized options.

Table C-7. Selected CD-ROM Arguments

Argument	Description and options
aztcd=	Aztech CD-ROM: *iobase*[,*magic_number*][a]
cdu31a=	Sony CDU-31A or CDU-33A CD-ROM: *iobase*,[*irq*[,*is_pas_card*]
sonycd535=	Sony CDU-535 CD-ROM: *iobase*[,*irq*]
gscd=	Goldstar CD-ROM: *iobase*
isp16=	ISP16 CD-ROM: [*port*[,*irq*[,*dma*]]][[,]*drive_type*]
mcd=	Mitsumi CD-ROM: *iobase*,[*irq*[,*wait_value*]]
optcd=	Optical Storage CD-ROM: *iobase*
cm206=	Phillips CD206 CD-ROM: [*iobase*][,*irq*]
sjcd=	Sanyo CD-ROM: *iobase*[,*irq*[,*dma_channel*]]
sbpcd=	SoundBlaster Pro CD-ROM: *iobase*,*type*

[a] Don't include the square brackets in your boot argument; they merely indicate which options must be present.

Floppy Drive Boot Arguments

A few systems require special boot arguments to best use their floppy drives. Table C-8 describes the most common boot arguments related to floppy drives. Floppy drives that are not well behaved may malfunction if you specify the daring option, which you should use only with care. For additional boot arguments related to floppy drives, see */usr/src/linux/Documentation/floppy.txt*.

Table C-8. Selected Floppy Disk Arguments and Options

Argument and option	Description
floppy=asus_pci	Specifies that only units 0 and 1 are allowed, to work around problem with BIOS of certain ASUS motherboards.
floppy=daring	Specifies that the floppy controller is well behaved, allowing more efficient operation.
floppy=0,daring	Specifies that the floppy controller may not be well behaved (default).
floppy=thinkpad	Specifies that the system is an IBM ThinkPad.
floppy=no_unexpected_ interrupts or floppy=L40SX	Specifies that a message should be printed when an unexpected interrupt is received. This is required by IBM L40SX laptops in certain video modes.

Bus Mouse Boot Arguments

Two boot arguments provide bus mouse support. The first supports the Microsoft bus mouse:

    msmouse=*irq*

The second supports any non-Microsoft bus mouse:

    bmouse=*irq*

Each argument accepts a single option specifying the IRQ associated with the mouse.

Parallel Port Printer Boot Arguments

The Linux printer driver claims all available parallel ports. If you want to access a device other than a printer attached to a parallel port, you must instruct the printer driver to reserve only the ports associated with printers. To do so, use the lp boot argument, which takes as its options a list of ports and IRQs used to support printers. For example, the following boot argument specifies two printers:

    lp=0x3bc,0,0x378,7

The first printer is on port 0x3bc and the second is on port 0x378. The first printer uses a special IRQ-less mode known as polling, so its IRQ is specified as 0. The second printer uses IRQ 7.

To disable all printers, specify lp=0.

Loadable Ethernet Drivers

Early versions of Linux used a so-called monolithic kernel. At that time, Linux distributions typically included several kernels, offering support for a variety of devices that might be needed to boot and install a Linux system. Devices not needed to boot and install a system—so-called special devices—had second-class status. To access special devices, users had to compile customized kernels that included support for those devices. When adding a device to a system, users often had to compile a new kernel, which was something of an inconvenience.

More recent versions of Linux feature a modular kernel, which allows drivers to be dynamically loaded on command. This makes it much easier than before to configure your Linux system to support Ethernet cards and other special devices. Red Hat Linux is generally able to configure your primary Ethernet card automatically, by probing for it during installation of Linux.

However, the autoprobe doesn't always succeed. Moreover, if you have more than one Ethernet card, the installation program sets up only the first card it finds. To set up additional cards, you need to know a bit about Linux's loadable modules.

Dynamically Loading a Modular Driver

To dynamically load a modular driver, issue the following command:

```
modprobe driver
```

where *driver* specifies the module to be loaded. As an example, the command:

```
modprobe ne2k-pci
```

loads the modular driver for the PCI-based NE2000 Ethernet card.

To find out what network adapters are supported by Red Hat Linux or to find out what driver to use with a particular adapter, see the Red Hat Linux Hardware Compatibility List, *http://hardware.redhat.com*.

When a driver is loaded, it generally probes to locate the supported device. In case an autoprobe fails, most drivers let you specify the I/O port and IRQ by using a command like the following:

```
modprobe ne2k=pci io=0x280 irq=11
```

Some cards support additional options; these are documented in the file */usr/src/linux/Documentation/networking/net-modules.txt*.

Loading Modular Drivers at Boot Time

The Linux kernel automatically loads modules specified in the module configuration file, */etc/.modules.conf*. So, once you've determined the proper module and options required by your Ethernet card, you can add a line or two to the module configuration file so that your card will be made ready to operate each time you boot your system.

The **alias** directive associates a logical module name with an actual module. Logical module names specify types of devices; for example, eth0 specifies the first Ethernet card in a system, and eth1 specifies the second Ethernet card in a system. Suppose your system includes two Ethernet cards: a non-PCI-based NE2000 and an SMC EtherPower, which is based on DEC's TULIP chip. You could use the following directives to automatically load these modules at boot time:

```
alias eth0 ne
alias eth1 tulip
```

If a driver requires options, you can specify them by using an options directive, which has the following form:

```
options driver argument=value[,value,...]
               argument=value[,value,...] ...
```

For example, you might specify the I/O port and IRQ used by the NE2000 card like this:

```
options ne io=0x280 irq=12
```

Most ISA modules accept parameters like io=0x340 and irq=12 on the *insmod* command line. You should supply these parameters to avoid probing for the card. Unlike PCI and EISA devices, ISA devices sometimes cannot be safely autoprobed.

Administering Modular Drivers

The **lsmod** command, which takes no arguments, lists the loaded modular drivers. To unload a modular driver, specify the driver as the argument of the **modprobe** command and specify the **–r** argument. For example, to remove the ne driver, issue the command:

```
modprobe -r ne
```

To unload every unused module—that is, every module not associated with an operational device—invoke the **rmmod** command and specify the **–a** argument:

```
rmmod -a
```

You can't remove a module that's in use; therefore, you must shut down the device before removing it. To shut down an Ethernet device, you can use *neat*. Or you can issue the following command:

```
ifconfig ethn down
```

where ethn specifies the logical device (for example, eth0 or eth1).

Installing and Configuring X

Getting a proper X Window System up and running used to be a real challenge on Linux, almost a rite of passage. Today, device drivers are available for a much wider array of hardware, and configuration tools to assist in the setup process have greatly improved. While still tricky at times—especially with unusual hardware—X setup and configuration is no longer the daunting process it once was.

The easiest way to install and configure X is to install the X Window System component during the Linux installation procedure. If you omitted the X Window System component, you should consider redoing the installation procedure, as this may be the simplest way to install X. But if it's not practical to redo the installation procedure, you can use the information in this section to manually install and configure X.

 You should exercise due care while configuring X to run on your system. If you incorrectly or incompletely configure X, your system can be permanently damaged. In particular, if you configure your monitor for a refresh rate that exceeds its capacity, you can damage the monitor. Older fixed-frequency monitors are particularly susceptible to such damage. The author and publisher have taken pains to make this appendix clear and accurate, but our efforts don't ensure that the procedure presented here will work correctly with your hardware. Consequently, the author and publisher cannot be held responsible for damages resulting from a faulty installation or configuration of X.

If you have a card or monitor of unknown manufacture or model and feel that you must guess, at least start with a narrow range of middle values and gradually expand that range to see if you can find a value that works. Don't let a monitor that displays an unstable or garbled image run any longer than the time it takes you to cut power to the monitor.

Installing X

If you followed the instructions in Chapter 3 and the installation procedure went smoothly, you've already installed X on your system. However, sometimes the installation procedure is unable to properly install and configure X. Or, you may accidentally delete one or more files needed by X. In such cases, it's handy to know how to manually install X.

To manually install the packages needed to run X, insert Disc 1 of Red Hat Linux into your system's CD-ROM drive and issue the following commands:

```
su -
mount -t iso9660 /dev/cdrom /mnt/cdrom -o ro
cd /mnt/cdrom/RedHat/RPMS
rpm -Uvh --replacepkgs \
  libtiff-*.rpm \
  switchdesk-* \
  gtk+-*.rpm \
  gnome-libs-*.rpm \
  imlib-1*.rpm \
  ORBit-*.rpm \
  netpbm-* \
  libungif-*.rpm \
  qt-*.rpm \
  gdk-pixbuf-*.rpm \
  xinitrc-*rpm \
  Mesa-*.rpm \
  libmng-*.rpm \
  XFree86-100dpi-fonts-*.rpm \
  XFree86-75dpi-fonts-*.rpm \
  XFree86-tools-*.rpm \
  XFree86-twm-*.rpm \
  XFree86-xdm-*.rpm \
  XFree86-4*.rpm \
  Xaw3d-*.rpm \
  Xconfigurator-*.rpm
cd
umount /mnt/cdrom
exit
```

Be careful to type the commands correctly. A single mistyped character can cause a command to fail, possibly without warning.

Next, insert Disc 2 of Red Hat Linux into your system's CD-ROM drive and issue the following commands:

```
su -
mount -t iso9660 /dev/cdrom /mnt/cdrom -o ro
cd /mnt/cdrom/RedHat/RPMS
rpm -Uvh --replacepkgs \
  XFree86-3DLabs-*.rpm \
  XFree86-8514-*.rpm \
  XFree86-AGX-*.rpm \
  XFree86-doc-*.rpm \
  XFree86-I128-*.rpm \
  XFree86-Mach32-*.rpm \
  XFree86-Mach64-*.rpm \
  XFree86-Mach8-*.rpm \
  XFree86-Mono-*.rpm \
```

```
  XFree86-P9000-*.rpm \
  XFree86-S3-*.rpm \
  XFree86-S3V-*.rpm \
  XFree86-SVGA-*.rpm \
  XFree86-VGA15-*.rpm \
  XFree86-W32-*.rpm
cd
umount /mnt/cdrom
exit
```

 Depending on the packages you've installed, RPM may not be able to install the specified packages, owing to unsatisfied dependencies. If this is the case, read the section in Chapter 8 that explains how to install and use the *rpmdb-redhat* package. That package will help you identify the packages needed to satisfy the dependencies.

To install a set of packages providing a basic GNOME environment, insert Disc 1 of Red Hat Linux into your system's CD-ROM drive and issue the following commands:

```
su -
mount -t iso9660 /dev/cdrom /mnt/cdrom -o ro
cd /mnt/cdrom/RedHat/RPMS
rpm -Uvh --replacepkgs \
  gnome-core-*rpm \
  control-center-*.rpm \
  rep-gtk-*.rpm \
  pygnome-libglade-*.rpm \
  pygtk-libglade-*.rpm \
  fortune-mod-*.rpm \
  sawfish-*.rpm \
  xloadimage-*.rpm \
  libglade-*.rpm \
  xscreensaver-*.rpm \
  librep-*.rpm \
  libxml-*.rpm
cd
umount /mnt/cdrom
exit
```

To install a set of packages providing a basic KDE environment, insert Disc 1 of Red Hat Linux into your system's CD-ROM drive and issue the following commands:

```
su -
mount -t iso9660 /dev/cdrom /mnt/cdrom -o ro
cd /mnt/cdrom/RedHat/RPMS
rpm -Uvh --replacepkgs \
  arts-*.rpm
  kdebase-*.rpm \
  kdelibs-*.rpm \
  kdesupport-*.rpm \
  lm_sensors-*.rpm
cd
umount /mnt/cdrom
exit
```

The GNOME and KDE packages identified provide a very sparse desktop environment. So you'll probably want to install additional GNOME or KDE packages. A good way to identify some candidates is by studying the file */RedHat/base/comps* on Disc 1 of Red Hat Linux. Look for the section titled GNOME or KDE and examine the packages listed there. Then, use the techniques explained in Chapter 8 to install the desired packages.

Configuring X

If you followed the instructions in Chapter 3 and the installation procedure went well, X has already been configured. In that case, you don't need to perform the procedure given in this section. However, sometimes the installation procedure doesn't go well. In that case, you can use the procedure given in this section to configure X rather than redoing the installation procedure.

A configuration file named */etc/X11/XF86Config* or */etc/X11/XF86Config-4* controls the operation of X. As explained later in this chapter, you can edit this file using *pico* or another text editor (such as vi or Emacs), but it's much easier to use Xconfigurator, which asks a few questions about your system and then builds the file for you. To launch Xconfigurator, log in as root and type the command:

```
Xconfigurator --expert
```

Xconfigurator displays its opening screen, shown in Figure D-1. The configuration process that ensues is very similar to the one performed by the install program, but as you'll see, there are a few minor differences.

The biggest difference is that, unlike the install program, Xconfigurator's user interface is entirely text-based. You can't use the mouse to point or click. Instead, you must use the **Tab** and arrow keys to move the cursor and the **space**bar or **Enter** key to "click" buttons.

To begin the configuration process, use the **Tab** key to select the OK button and press **Enter**.

Xconfigurator overwrites the contents of the *XF86Config* file. If you already have a working X setup, you should create a backup copy of *XF86Config* before running Xconfigurator.

As shown in Figure D-2, Xconfigurator probes your system to determine the characteristics of your video card. The probe may fail. If so, don't fret; Xconfigurator will allow you to specify the card installed in your system. Likewise, if Xconfigurator's probe found an incorrect card, you can override the probe's result in the next dialog box, shown in Figure D-3.

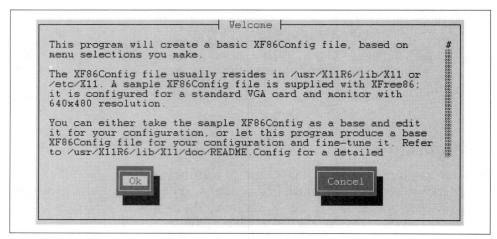

Figure D-1. The Xconfigurator Welcome dialog box

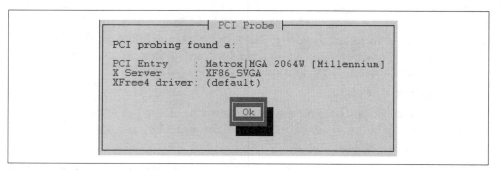

Figure D-2. The PCI Probe dialog box

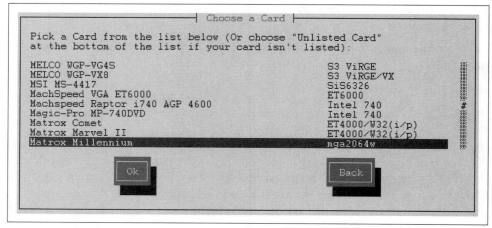

Figure D-3. The Choose a Card dialog box

In the Choose a Card dialog box, you can choose from hundreds of popular video adapters. Use the up and down arrow keys to select an adapter. To quickly move to the neighborhood of your adapter, type the first letter of the manufacturer's name. If your adapter is not listed, choose Unlisted Card. This prompts Xconfigurator to display the Pick a Server dialog box, shown in Figure D-4.

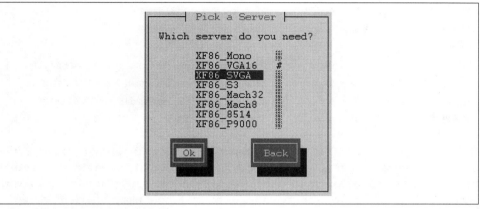

Figure D-4. The Pick a Server dialog box

An X server provides the interface between X and your video adapter. An X server might be more aptly termed a *video driver*. The most basic X servers include:

XFree86-Mono

A server that supports monochrome (black-and-white) monitors. The server runs with standard VGA graphics cards and supports a resolution of 640 × 480 or better.

XFree86-VGA16

A server that supports standard VGA cards and monitors, providing the standard 16 VGA colors. This server works with nearly all VGA and SVGA cards, but only in low resolution and with few colors.

XFree86-SVGA

A server that supports most SVGA cards, including the Trident 8900 and 9400, Cirrus Logic, C&T, ET4000, S3 ViRGE, and others.

However, XFree86 also includes a variety of servers for accelerated graphics cards, as shown in Table D-1.

The list of available Linux drivers for advanced graphics cards expands regularly. For a complete list, check relevant online resources, such as those at *http://www.xfree86.org*.

Table D-1. X servers for Accelerated Graphics Cards

Package	Server	Supported cards and chipsets
XFree86-8514	*XF86_8514*	IBM 8514/A and other compatible cards
XFree86-AGX	*XF86_AGX*	All AGX cards
XFree86-I128	*XF86_I128*	#9 Imagine 128 (including Series II) cards
XFree86-Mach32	*XF86_Mach32*	ATI cards using the Mach32 chipset
XFree86-Mach64	*XF86_Mach64*	ATI cards using the Mach64 chipset
XFree86-Mach8	*XF86_Mach8*	ATI cards using the Mach8 chipset
XFree86-P9000	*XF86_P9000*	Diamond Viper and other P9000 cards (excluding cards using the 9100)
XFree86-S3	*XF86_S3*	#9 cards, most Diamond cards, some Orchid cards, and others
XFree86-S3V	*XF86_S3V*	Cards using the S3 ViRGE chipset, including the DX, GX, and VX
XFree86-W32	*XF86_W32*	ET4000/W32 cards, excluding standard ET4000 cards

If you can't decide which X server is appropriate for your card, select the SVGA server, since most monitors support SVGA. Later, you can try other drivers that may provide accelerated video. On the other hand, if you can't get your monitor to work with the SVGA server, you can try either of the still more basic X servers, *XFree86-VGA16* or *XFree86-Mono*.

After you specify the desired server, Xconfigurator displays the Monitor Setup dialog box, shown in Figure D-5. If you can't find your monitor in that list, select the Custom option; Xconfigurator will then let you specify your monitor's characteristics.

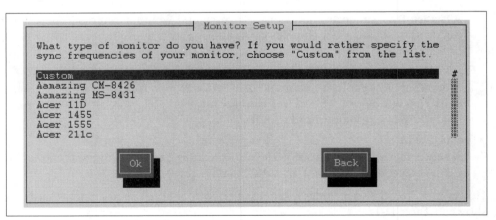

Figure D-5. The Monitor Setup dialog box

If you specified Custom, the Custom Monitor Setup dialog box, shown in Figure D-6, appears.

As the dialog box explains, two parameters are needed to configure your monitor: the vertical refresh rate and horizontal sync rate. You can find these values by:

- Consulting your monitor's documentation

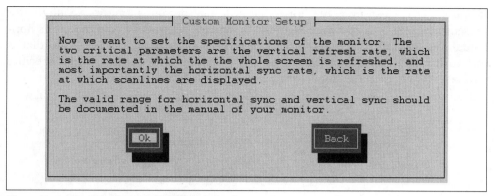

Figure D-6. The Custom Monitor Setup dialog box

- Viewing the monitor manufacturer's web support page
- Posting a question to the newsgroup *comp.os.linux.setup*
- Contacting the monitor manufacturer's technical support group and requesting the information

 Often, otherwise similar monitor models have significantly different horizontal sync rates. It is crucial that you accurately determine the horizontal sync rate of your monitor. You can permanently damage your monitor if you configure X to use an inappropriate horizontal sync rate.

If you earlier specified a custom monitor setup, Xconfigurator next displays a second Custom Monitor Setup dialog box (Figure D-7). This dialog box asks you to choose the proper horizontal sync rate for your monitor. If you're uncertain of your monitor's characteristics, choose a conservative value, such as Standard VGA or Super VGA 800 × 600. If you want to type specific values for the sync rates, select Custom.

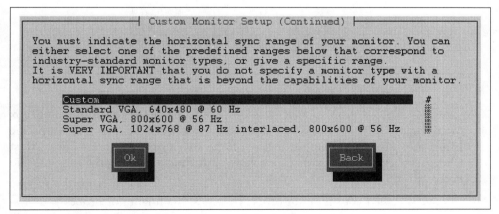

Figure D-7. The second Custom Monitor Setup dialog box

If you selected Custom as the horizontal sync rate of your monitor, Xconfigurator presents a dialog box, shown in Figure D-8, that lets you specify your monitor's horizontal and vertical sync rates. Interlaced video modes provide a sync rate that is approximately double the specified rate; if your monitor's documentation specifies two rates for an interlaced mode, specify the higher of the two rates.

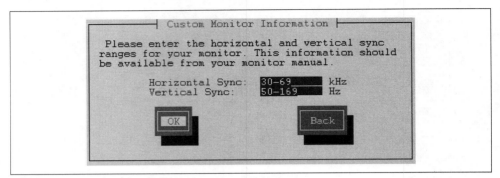

Figure D-8. The Custom Monitor Information dialog box

Xconfigurator may ask you to specify the amount of memory installed in your video adapter by presenting a dialog box like that shown in Figure D-9. If so, specify the proper amount of memory, select the OK button, and press **Enter**.

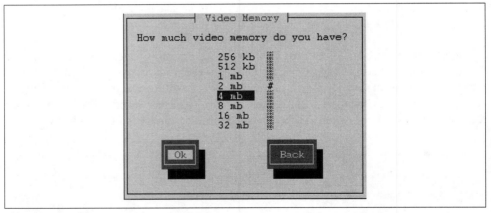

Figure D-9. The Video Memory dialog box

Xconfigurator will ask you to specify a Clockchip, by presenting the dialog box shown in Figure D-10. Unless you know that your video adapter has a specific Clockchip, select No Clockchip Setting, select the OK button, and press **Enter**. Most video adapters, even those with Clockchips, will function correctly with the No Clockchip setting.

After you've specified your monitor or its sync rates, Xconfigurator probes your system to discover additional video characteristics. It displays the dialog box shown in

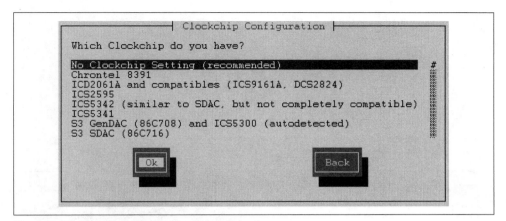

Figure D-10. The Clockchip Configuration dialog box

Figure D-11 before initiating the probe. Select the Probe button and press **Enter** to begin the probe. Your screen may flicker or blink while Xconfigurator probes your system. If you're retrying a failed attempt to configure X and know that the probe will not succeed, avoid the probe by selecting the Skip button and pressing **Enter**.

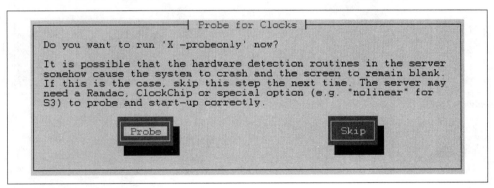

Figure D-11. The Probe for Clocks dialog box

If the probe fails, Xconfigurator displays the dialog box shown in Figure D-12. In that case, Xconfigurator makes some guesses concerning remaining configuration items and continues.

After Xconfigurator probes your system, it displays the dialog box shown in Figure D-13. The dialog box displays the default video mode or modes in which X will operate. Table D-2 shows the relationship between color depth and the number of displayed colors. You can use the Tab key to move from column to column and the **up** and **down** arrow keys to move within a column. To select a mode, press the **Spacebar**. You can select modes in multiple columns; you can even select multiple modes in a column. However, you shouldn't select modes other than those supported by your video adapter and monitor.

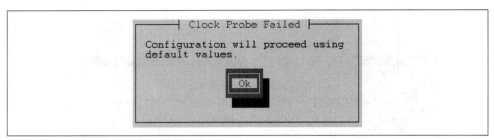

Figure D-12. The Clock Probe Failed message box

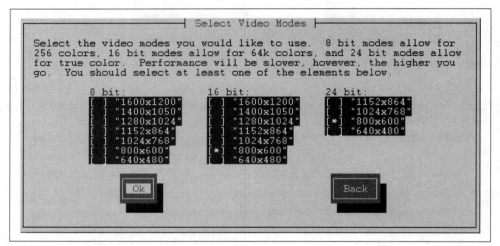

Figure D-13. The Select Video Modes dialog box

Table D-2. Color Depth and Number of Colors

Color depth	Number of colors
8 bit	256
16 bit	Thousands
24 bit	Millions

Xconfigurator now asks permission to start X in order to test your configuration, as shown in Figure D-14. Normally, you should test your X configuration to make sure everything has been set properly. You can test the X configuration by selecting the OK button and pressing **Enter**.

If Xconfigurator cannot start X, it displays the message box shown in Figure D-15. The message box lets you return to previous steps, modify the values of configuration items, and try again.

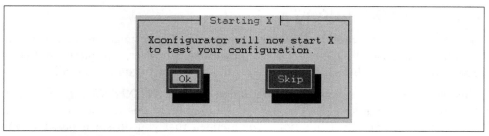

Figure D-14. The Starting X dialog box

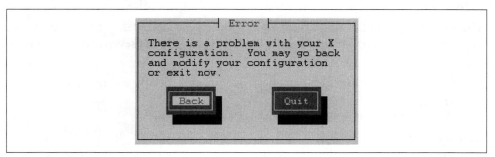

Figure D-15. The Error message box

 It's worth noting that it could take you several attempts to configure X properly if you don't have all of the appropriate information about your monitor and video card.

When X starts, you'll see a small dialog box that asks you to whether you can read its message. Use your mouse and click on Yes to dismiss the dialog box.* You'll need to do so within 10 seconds or Xconfigurator will assume X failed.

 This time limit is intended to avoid damage to your video hardware if the configuration is incorrect; however, some hardware can suffer damage even during such a brief interval.

After you respond that you can read the dialog box, Xconfigurator presents another dialog box, asking whether you'd like to automatically start X the next time you boot your system; answer Yes or No, according to your preference. For the purpose of this book, however, you should select the Yes option. Xconfigurator then presents its final dialog box, which explains that X has been successfully installed. Select the Ok button and press **Enter** to exit Xconfigurator.

---

* Yes, you can finally use your mouse again at this step of the X configuration process—but only on this one screen.

Manually Configuring X

Generally, you won't need to manually configure X. The installation procedure and Xconfigurator generally configure X automatically. However, automatic configuration sometimes fails. In that case, it's handy to know how to configure X manually.

This section explains a typical X configuration file, */etc/X11/XF86Config*, of the sort created by Xconfigurator. You can use the information in this section to tweak your X configuration. However, it's not recommended that you do so; if possible, you should use Xconfigurator to generate your system's X configuration file. The real value of this section is in helping you understand how X works.

The X configuration file, like almost all Linux configuration files, is a text file and can be viewed or edited by using a text editor. The typical file has seven main sections:

Files
> This section identifies files that specify colors and specify or contain fonts.

ServerFlags
> This section specifies flags that control X server operation.

Keyboard
> This section specifies the keyboard.

Pointer
> This section specifies the mouse or other pointing device. Unlike Windows, X cannot be used without a pointing device.

Monitor
> This section specifies the monitor.

Device
> This section specifies the video adapter.

Screen
> This section specifies the X display, by referencing monitor and device specifications and providing additional specifications.

Several of the sections can appear multiple times in the X configuration file. For example, a system with multiple video adapters could have multiple Device sections in its X configuration file. The XF86Config manpage describes the contents of the X configuration file in detail. However, it describes a newer file format than that used by Xconfigurator; the older format is still accepted, but not documented. The following subsections give an overview of the file.

Files Section

Here is an excerpt from a typical Files section. The lines beginning with a hash mark (#) are comments and are not processed by X. Only two configuration items—RgbPath and FontPath—are present.

```
Section "Files"

    # The location of the RGB database. Note, this is the name of the
    # file minus the extension (like ".txt" or ".db"). There is normally
    # no need to change the default.

        RgbPath "/usr/X11R6/lib/X11/rgb"

    # Multiple FontPath entries are allowed (they are concatenated together)
    # By default, Red Hat 6.0 and later now use a font server independent of
    # the X server to render fonts.

        FontPath    "unix/:7100"

EndSection
```

RgbPath gives the path of a file that contains names for commonly used colors. The actual name of the file is *rgb.txt*, not merely *rgb*. Here is an excerpt from the file:

```
255 250 250             snow
248 248 255             ghost white
248 248 255             GhostWhite
245 245 245             white smoke
245 245 245             WhiteSmoke
```

The file uses three numbers to represent a color, via the so-called RGB color scheme. The numbers represent the amount of red, green, and blue in a color. The numbers range from 0 to 255. The RGB value 0,0,0 corresponds to black, whereas the RGB value 255,255,255 corresponds to white. The color called snow is very nearly white.

FontPath can specify paths containing font files. However, Red Hat Linux uses the X Font Server. So, instead of font paths, what appears is merely a reference to the font server, which operates on port 7100.

ServerFlags Section

The typical ServerFlags section contains nothing but comments. Here's an example:

```
Section "ServerFlags"

    # Uncomment this to cause a core dump at the spot where a signal is
    # received. This may leave the console in an unusable state, but may
    # provide a better stack trace in the core dump to aid in debugging
    #NoTrapSignals

    # Uncomment this to disable the <Crtl><Alt><BS> server abort sequence
    # This allows clients to receive this key event.
    #DontZap

    # Uncomment this to disable the <Crtl><Alt><KP_+>/<KP_-> mode switching
    # sequences. This allows clients to receive these key events.
    #DontZoom

EndSection
```

Keyboard Section

The Keyboard section specifies the configuration items related to the keyboard. As explained by the comments in the Keyboard section, you can use keyboard configuration items to alter the operation of control keys, such as the Alt key. You can also specify the model and layout of the keyboard. However, you'll likely need to install special fonts to be able to use variant keyboard types. Therefore, it's much easier to use Xconfigurator than to attempt to hack the configuration file.

Here's a typical Keyboard section:

```
Section "Keyboard"

    Protocol    "Standard"

    # When using XQUEUE, comment out the above line, and uncomment the
    # following line
    #Protocol   "Xqueue"

    AutoRepeat  500 5

    # Let the server do the NumLock processing. This should only be
    # required when using pre-R6 clients
    #ServerNumLock

    # Specify which keyboard LEDs can be user-controlled (eg, with xset(1))
    #Xleds       1 2 3

    #To set the LeftAlt to Meta, RightAlt key to ModeShift,
    #RightCtl key to Compose, and ScrollLock key to ModeLock:

    LeftAlt         Meta
    RightAlt        Meta
    ScrollLock      Compose
    RightCtl        Control

# To disable the XKEYBOARD extension, uncomment XkbDisable.

#     XkbDisable

# To customise the XKB settings to suit your keyboard, modify the
# lines below (which are the defaults).  For example, for a non-U.S.
# keyboard, you will probably want to use:
#    XkbModel    "pc102"
# If you have a US Microsoft Natural keyboard, you can use:
#    XkbModel    "microsoft"
#
# Then to change the language, change the Layout setting.
# For example, a German layout can be obtained with:
#    XkbLayout   "de"
# or:
#    XkbLayout   "de"
#    XkbVariant  "nodeadkeys"
#
```

```
# If you'd like to switch the positions of your capslock and
# control keys, use:
#     XkbOptions   "ctrl:swapcaps"

# These are the default XKB settings for XFree86
#     XkbRules     "xfree86"
#     XkbModel     "pc101"
#     XkbLayout    "us"
#     XkbVariant   ""
#     XkbOptions   ""

    XkbKeycodes      "xfree86"
    XkbTypes         "default"
    XkbCompat        "default"
    XkbSymbols       "us(pc101)"
    XkbGeometry      "pc"
    XkbRules         "xfree86"
    XkbModel         "pc101"
    XkbLayout        "us"
EndSection
```

Pointer Section

The Pointer section specifies the mouse or other pointing device. The most important configuration items are Protocol and Device. Here's a typical Pointer section:

```
Section "Pointer"
    Protocol     "Microsoft"
    Device       "/dev/mouse"

# When using XQUEUE, comment out the above two lines, and uncomment
# the following line.

#     Protocol "Xqueue"

# Baudrate and SampleRate are only for some Logitech mice

#     BaudRate 9600
#     SampleRate 150

# Emulate3Buttons is an option for 2-button Microsoft mice
# Emulate3Timeout is the timeout in milliseconds (default is 50ms)

    Emulate3Buttons
    Emulate3Timeout     50

# ChordMiddle is an option for some 3-button Logitech mice

#     ChordMiddle

EndSection
```

The Protocol configuration item specifies the protocol used by the pointing device. Most modern PC mice, including recent Logitech mice, use the Microsoft protocol. However, other protocols are supported, including:

- PS/2
- BusMouse
- Various serial mouse protocols

To learn more about mouse protocols supported by X, view the file */usr/X11R6/lib/ X11/doc/README.mouse*, which is part of the *XFree86-doc* package.

The Device configuration item simply specifies the device file associated with the pointing device.

If you have a two-button mouse, you should generally specify the Emulate3Buttons configuration item, which lets you simulate pressing a middle mouse button by simultaneously pressing the left and right mouse buttons.

Monitor Section

The Monitor section contains several important configuration items. Several Monitor sections can be present, one for each of several monitors. Here's an example configuration:

```
Section "Monitor"

    Identifier  "ViewSonic 17GS"
    VendorName  "Unknown"
    ModelName   "Unknown"

# HorizSync is in kHz unless units are specified.
# HorizSync may be a comma separated list of discrete values, or a
# comma separated list of ranges of values.
# NOTE: THE VALUES HERE ARE EXAMPLES ONLY. REFER TO YOUR MONITOR'S
# USER MANUAL FOR THE CORRECT NUMBERS.

    HorizSync   30-69

# VertRefresh is in Hz unless units are specified.
# VertRefresh may be a comma separated list of discrete values, or a
# comma separated list of ranges of values.
# NOTE: THE VALUES HERE ARE EXAMPLES ONLY. REFER TO YOUR MONITOR'S
# USER MANUAL FOR THE CORRECT NUMBERS.

    VertRefresh 50-160

# Modes can be specified in two formats. A compact one-line format, or
# a multi-line format.

# These two are equivalent

#    ModeLine "1024x768i" 45 1024 1048 1208 1264 768 776 784 817 Interlace
```

```
#      Mode "1024x768i"
#         DotClock    45
#         HTimings    1024 1048 1208 1264
#         VTimings    768 776 784 817
#         Flags       "Interlace"
#      EndMode

# This is a set of standard mode timings. Modes that are out of monitor spec
# are automatically deleted by the server (provided the HorizSync and
# VertRefresh lines are correct), so there's no immediate need to
# delete mode timings (unless particular mode timings don't work on your
# monitor). With these modes, the best standard mode that your monitor
# and video card can support for a given resolution is automatically
# used.

<lines omitted>

# 800x600 @ 100 Hz, 64.02 kHz hsync
Modeline  "800x600"     69.65  800  864  928 1088    600  604  610  640 -HSync -VSync
# 800x600 @ 56 Hz, 35.15 kHz hsync
ModeLine "800x600"       36    800  824  896 1024    600  601  603  625
# 800x600 @ 60 Hz, 37.8 kHz hsync
Modeline "800x600"       40    800  840  968 1056    600  601  605  628 +hsync +vsync
# 800x600 @ 72 Hz, 48.0 kHz hsync
Modeline "800x600"       50    800  856  976 1040    600  637  643  666 +hsync +vsync
# 800x600 @ 85 Hz, 55.84 kHz hsync
Modeline "800x600"     60.75   800  864  928 1088    600  616  621  657 -HSync -VSync

<lines omitted>

EndSection
```

The following lines:

```
Identifier   "ViewSonic 17GS"
VendorName   "Unknown"
ModelName    "Unknown"
```

serve to identify the monitor. Only the `Identifier` configuration item is important; it's used to refer to the monitor.

The following lines:

```
HorizSync    30-69
VertRefresh  50-160
```

give the horizontal and vertical sync rates for the monitor. Sometimes, Xconfigurator will pick a value that's not quite right. Tweaking these values can turn a nonworking X configuration into a working one. Be sure, however, to specify only values consistent with the capabilities of your monitor; otherwise, you may damage it.

Perhaps the most important configuration item in the `Monitor` section is the `ModeLine`. Typically, there are many `ModeLine` entries, at least one for each video mode supported by the monitor. The example `Monitor` section shows only a handful of typical entries.

The format of a ModeLine entry is:

```
ModeLine name clock horizontal vertical options
```

The parameters have the following meanings:

name
: An arbitrary name assigned to the entry

clock
: The horizontal sync rate of the related video mode

horizontal and *vertical*
: Four numbers each, representing the timing of the sync pulses

options
: Can include a variety of options

Most monitors can use the Video Electronics Standards Association (VESA) modes that Xconfigurator includes in the configuration file it generates. If your monitor isn't cooperative, you have several alternatives:

- Download the latest XFree86 distribution from *http://www.xfree86.org*. There, you can find two files that give ModeLines for monitors or show you how to determine your own:
  - *modeDB.txt, which gives entries for many monitors*
  - *VideoModes.doc*, which explains how to determine ModeLine values
- Use the program **xvidtune** to generate one or more suitable ModeLine entries. See the program's manpage for more information.

Device Section

The Device section specifies the video adapter. Multiple device sections can be present. Here's a typical Device section:

```
# Device configured by Xconfigurator:

Section "Device"
    Identifier  "Matrox Millennium"
    VendorName  "Unknown"
    BoardName   "Unknown"
    #VideoRam    4096
Option    "sw_cursor"
    # Insert Clocks lines here if appropriate.
EndSection
```

The Identifier configuration item assigns a name to the Screen section that contains it. The VendorName and BoardName configuration items are unimportant. The VideoRam configuration item specifies the amount of video memory installed on the device; it is generally commented out, since X can probe for the values of most configuration items in the Device section. The Option configuration item is used to specify a variety of options needed to support video adapter features.

Screen Section

A typical X configuration file contains multiple Screen sections. Each section specifies a combination consisting of a monitor, video adapter, and X server. Here's a typical section:

```
# The Colour SVGA server

Section "Screen"
    Driver      "svga"
    Device      "Matrox Millennium"
    Monitor     "ViewSonic 17GS"
    DefaultColorDepth   16
    Subsection "Display"
        Depth       16
        Modes       "1280x1024" "1152x864" "1024x768" "800x600"
        ViewPort    0 0
    EndSubsection
    Subsection "Display"
        Depth       24
        Modes       "1152x864" "1024x768" "800x600"
        ViewPort    0 0
    EndSubsection
    Subsection "Display"
        Depth       32
        Modes       "1152x864" "1024x768" "800x600"
        ViewPort    0 0
    EndSubsection
EndSection
```

The Driver configuration item identifies the X server. Possible values are:

Mono
> For the non-VGA drivers of the XF86_Mono and XF86_VGA16 servers

SVGA
> For the XF86_SVGA server

VGA2
> For the XF86_Mono server

VGA16
> For the XF86_VGA16 server

Accel
> For the remaining, accelerated X servers

The Device and Monitor configuration items refer back to entries in the Device and Monitor sections.

The remaining configuration items specify video modes. These give the default color depth and the resolutions permissible for each video mode.

Linux Command Quick Reference

The following list describes some of the most useful and popular Linux commands. Consult the manpage for each command to learn about additional arguments and details of operation.

adduser *userid*

Creates a new *userid*, prompting for necessary information (requires root privileges).

alias name=*'command'*

Defines name as an alias for the specified command.

apropos *keyword*

Searches the manual pages for occurrences of the specified keyword and prints short descriptions from the beginning of matching manual pages.

at *time*

at –f *file time*

Executes commands entered via STDIN (or by using the alternative form, the specified file) at the specified time. The time can be specified in a variety of ways; for example, in hour and minute format (*hh:mm*) or in hour, minute, month, day, and year format (*hh:mm mm/dd/yy*).

atq

Displays descriptions of jobs pending via the **at** command.

atrm *job*

Cancels execution of a job scheduled via the **at** command. Use the **atq** command to discover the identities of scheduled jobs.

bg

bg *jobs*

Places the current *job* (or by using the alternative form, the specified jobs) in the background, suspending its execution so that a new user prompt appears immediately. Use the **jobs** command to discover the identities of background jobs.

cal *month year*

Displays a calendar for the specified month of the specified year.

cat *files*

Displays the contents of the specified files.

cd

cd *directory*

Changes the current working directory to the user's home directory or the specified directory.

chgrp *group files*

chgrp –R *group files*

Changes the *group* of the specified *files* to the specified group. The alternative form of the command operates recursively, changing the group of subdirectories and files beneath a specified directory. The group must be named in the */etc/groups* file, maintained by the **newgroup** command.

chmod *mode files*

chmod –R *mode files*

Changes the access mode of the specified files to the specified mode. The alternative form of the command operates recursively, changing the mode of subdirectories and files beneath a specified directory.

chown *userid files*

chown –R *userid files*

Changes the owner of the specified files to the specified *userid*. The alternative form of the command operates recursively, changing the owner of subdirectories and files beneath a specified directory

clear

Clears the terminal screen.

cmp *file1 file2*

Compares two files, reporting all discrepancies. Unlike the **diff** command, **cmp** can compare multiple files and binary files.

cp *file1 file2*

cp *files directory*

cp –R *files directory*

Copies a file to another file or directory or copies a subdirectory and all its files to another directory.

date

date *date*

Displays the current date and time or changes the system date and time to the specified value, of the form *MMddhhmmyy* or *MMddhhmmyyyy*.

df

Displays the amount of free disk space on each mounted filesystem.

diff *file1 file2*

Compares two files, reporting all discrepancies. Similar to the **cmp** command, though the output format differs.

dmesg

Displays the messages resulting from the most recent system boot.

du

du *directories*

Displays the amount of disk space used by the current directory (or the specified directories) and its (their) subdirectories.

echo *string*

echo –n *string*

Displays the specified text on the standard output stream. The **–n** option causes omission of the trailing newline character.

fdformat *device*

Formats the media inserted in the specified floppy disk drive. The command performs a low-level format only; it does not create a filesystem. To create a filesystem, issue the **mkfs** command after formatting the media.

fdisk *device*

Edits the partition table of the specified hard disk.

fg

fg *jobs*

Brings the current *job* (or the specified *jobs*) to the foreground.

file *files*

Determines and prints a description of the type of each specified file.

find *path* **–name** *pattern* **–print**

Searches the specified *path* for files with names matching the specified *pattern* (usually enclosed in single quotes) and prints their names. The **find** command has many other arguments and functions; see the online documentation.

finger *users*

Displays descriptions of the specified *users*.

free

Displays the amount of used and free system memory.

ftp *hostname*

Opens an FTP connection to the specified host, allowing files to be transferred. The FTP program provides subcommands for accomplishing file transfers; see the online documentation.

grep *pattern files*

grep –i *pattern files*

grep –n *pattern files*

grep –v *pattern files*

Searches the specified *files* for text matching the specified *pattern* (usually enclosed in single quotes) and prints matching lines. The **–i** option specifies that matching is performed without regard to case. The **–n** option specifies that each line of output is preceded by the filename and line number. The –v option reverses the matching, causing nonmatched lines to be printed.

gzip *files*
gunzip *files*
Expands or compresses the specified *files*. Generally, a compressed file has the same name as the original file, followed by *.gz*.

head *files*
Displays the first several lines of each specified file.

hostname
hostname *name*
Displays (or sets) the name of the host.

info
Launches the GNU Texinfo help system.

init *runlevel*
Changes the system runlevel to the specified value (requires *root* privileges).

insmod *module*
Dynamically loads the specified *module* (requires *root* privileges).

ispell *files*
Checks the spelling of the contents of the specified files.

jobs
Displays all background jobs.

kill *process_ids*
kill –l
kill –signal *process_ids*
Kills the specified processes, prints a list of available signals, or sends the specified processes the specified signal (given as a number or name).

killall *program*
killall –signal *program*
Kills all processes that are instances of the specified program or sends the specified signal to all processes that are instances of the specified program.

less *file*
Lets the user peruse a *file* too large to be displayed as a single screen (page) of output. The **less** command, which is more powerful than the **more** command, provides many subcommands that let the user navigate the *file*. For example, the spacebar moves forward one page, the **b** key moves back one page, and the **q** key exits the program.

links *URL*
Views the specified web page.

ln *old new*
ln –s *old new*
> Creates a hard (or soft) link associating a new name with an existing file or directory.

locate *pattern*
> Locates files with names containing the specified pattern. Uses the database maintained by the **updatedb** command.

lpq
> Displays the entries of the print queue.

lpr *files*
> Displays the specified *files*.

lprm *job*
> Cancels printing of the specified print queue entries. Use **lpq** to determine the contents of the print queue.

ls
ls *files*
ls –a *files*
ls –l *files*
ls –lR *files*
> Lists (nonhidden) files in the current directory or the specified files or directories. The –**a** option lists hidden files as well has nonhidden files. The –**l** option causes the list to include descriptive information, such as file size and modification date. The –**R** option recursively lists the subdirectories of the specified directories.

mail
> Launches a simple mail client that permits sending and receiving email messages.

man *title*
man *section title*
> Displays the specified manpage.

mkdir *directories*
mkdir –p *directories*
> Creates the specified *directories*. The –**p** option causes creation of any *parent directories* needed to create a specified directory.

mkfs –t *type device*
> Creates a filesystem of the specified *type* (such as *ext3* or *msdos*) on the specified *device* (requires *root* privileges).

mkswap *device*
> Creates a Linux swap space on the specified hard disk partition (requires *root* privileges).

more *file*

Lets the user peruse a *file* too large to be displayed as a single screen (page) of output. The **more** command provides many subcommands that let the user navigate the file. For example, the spacebar moves forward one page, the **b** key moves back one page, and the **q** key exits the program.

mount

mount *device directory*

mount –o *option* **–t** *type device directory*

Displays the mounted devices or mounts the specified device at the specified mount point (generally a subdirectory of */mnt*). The mount command consults */etc/fstab* to determine standard options associated with a device. The command generally requires root privileges. The –o option allows specification of a variety of options, for example, *ro* for read–only access. The –t option allows specification of the filesystem type (for example, *ext3*, *msdos*, or *iso9660*, the filesystem type generally used for CD–ROMs).

mv *paths target*

Moves the specified files or directories to the specified *target*.

newgroup *group*

Creates the specified *group*.

passwd

passwd *user*

Changes the current user's password or that of the specified *user* (requires *root* privileges). The command prompts for the new password.

pico

pico *file*

Launch **pico** to edit the specified *file*, if any.

ping –n *ip_address*

ping *host*

Sends an echo request via TCP/IP to the specified *host*. A response confirms that the host is operational.

pr *files*

Formats the specified *files* for printing, by inserting page breaks and so on. The command provides many arguments and functions.

ps

ps –aux

Displays the processes associated with the current *userid* or displays a description of each process.

pwd

Displays the absolute path corresponding to the current working directory.

reboot

Reboots the system (requires *root* privileges).

reset

Clears the terminal screen and resets the terminal status.

rm *files*
rm –f *files*
rm –i *files*
rm –if *files*
rm –rf *files*

Deletes the specified *files* or (when the –r option is specified) recursively deletes all subdirectories of the specified files and directories. The –f option suppresses confirmation; the –i option causes the command to prompt for confirmation. Because deleted files cannot generally be recovered, the –f option should be used only with extreme care, particularly when used by the *root* user.

rmdir *directories*
rmdir –p *directories*

Deletes the specified empty *directories* or (when the –p option is specified) the empty directories along the specified path.

scp *host1:file host2:*

Copies *file* from *host1* to *host2*, via SSH.

shutdown *minutes*
shutdown –h *minutes*
shutdown –r *minutes*

Shuts down the system after the specified number of *minutes* elapses (requires *root* privileges). The –r option causes the system to be rebooted once it has shut down. If the –r option is absent, the system is halted and powered off; the –h option also halts and shuts down the system. Alternatively, **now** can be used instead of *minutes*, which forces an immediate reboot or halt of the system.

sleep *time*

Causes the command interpreter to pause for the specified number of seconds.

sort *files*

Sorts the specified *files*. The command has many useful arguments; see the online documentation.

split *file*

Splits a *file* into several smaller files. The command has many arguments; see the online documentation.

ssh *host* **–l** *userid*

Logs in to *host* via SSH, using the specified *userid*.

su

su *user*

su –

su – *user*

Changes the current *userid* to root or to the specified *userid* (the latter requires *root* privileges). The – option establishes a default environment for the new *userid*.

swapoff *device*

Disables use of the specified *device* for swapping (requires *root* privileges).

swapon *device*

Enables use of the specified *device* for swapping (requires *root* privileges).

sync

Completes all pending input/output operations (requires *root* privileges).

tail *file*

tail –f *file*

tail –n *file*

Displays the last several lines of the specified *files*. The –**f** option causes the command to continuously print additional lines as they are written to the *file*. The –**n** option specifies the number of lines to be printed.

talk *user*

Launches a program that allows a chatlike dialog with the specified *user*.

tar cvf *tar_file files*

tar zcvf *tar_file files*

Creates a tar *file* with the specified name, containing the specified files and their subdirectories. The **z** option specifies that the tarfile will be compressed.

tar xvf *tar_file*

tar zxvf *tar_file*

Extracts the contents of the specified *tarfile*. The **z** option specifies that the tarfile has been compressed.

telnet *host*

Opens a login session on the specified *host*.

time

Times the execution of a job.

top

Displays a display of system processes that's continually updated until the user presses the **q** key.

touch *file*

Changes *file* access time. If the specified *file* does not exist, the command creates an empty (new) file.

traceroute *host*
> Uses echo requests to determine and print a network path to the *host*.

umask *mask*
> Specifies default permissions assigned to created directories and files.

umount *device*
> Unmounts the specified filesystem (generally requires *root* privileges).

uname –a
> Displays information about the system.

unzip *file*
> Unzips a compressed file.

uptime
> Displays the system uptime.

w
> Displays the current system users.

wall
> Displays a message to each user except those who've disabled message reception. Type **Ctrl–D** to end the message.

wc *files*
> Displays the number of characters, words, and lines in the specified *files*.

who
> Displays information about system users.

zip *file*
> Compresses the specified *file*.

Table E-1 identifies Linux commands that perform functions similar to MS-DOS commands. The operation of the Linux command is not generally identical to that of the corresponding MS-DOS command. See the index to this book or the Linux online documentation for further information about Linux commands.

Table E-1. MS-DOS Commands and Related Linux Commands

MS-DOS	Linux
ATTRIB	chmod
CD	cd
CHKDSK	df, du
DELTREE	rm –R
DIR	ls –l
DOSKEY	(built–in; no need to launch separately)
EDIT	pico, vi, and so on
EXTRACT	tar
FC	cmp, diff

Table E-1. MS-DOS Commands and Related Linux Commands (continued)

MS-DOS	Linux
FDISK	fdisk
FIND	grep
FORMAT	fdformat
MORE	more
MOVE	mv
SORT	sort
START	at, bg
XCOPY, XCOPY32	cp

Glossary

Absolute path
See *Path*.

Access mode
An attribute of a file or directory, which determines what operations a user may perform on the file or directory.

Alias
An alternative name for a command.

Argument
A parameter that controls the operation of a program or command.

Background
A background program does not interact with the user. See *Foreground*.

BIOS (Basic Input/Output System)
The program built into a computer to control its operation, especially the booting of an operating system. Most computers let the user configure various BIOS options by means of a special screen or set of screens.

Boot diskette
A diskette that contains the parts of an operating system needed to start the operating system.

Boot sector
A sector that contains a loader program for starting an operating system.

Browser
A client program that operates under user control, especially a web client.

Client
A program that makes a request (generally via a network) of a server.

Command interpreter
A program that accepts commands and executes (interprets) them.

Daemon
A program that runs in the background, that is, without user interaction.

Desktop
A work environment provided by a graphical user interface, generally including a video monitor background, a screensaver, and one or more taskbars and icons.

Distribution
A combination of a Linux kernel, a suite of Unix-like command programs, and other software for installing and maintaining a Linux system.

DNS (Domain Name Server)
A computer that translates hostnames to IP addresses on behalf of requesting clients.

Dotted quad notation
A form of representing a 32-bit IP address, consisting of four numbers from 0 to 255, each separated from the others by a dot.

EIDE (Enhanced Integrated Drive Electronics)
An incremental improvement of the IDE standard for hard drives, designed to better accommodate large-capacity drives.

Ethernet

A standard for sending data packets across networks, focused on the electronic signaling issues.

Foreground

A foreground program runs and interacts with the user. See *Background*.

FTP (File Transfer Protocol)

A protocol for transferring data files across a TCP/IP network.

GNU

GNU stands for "GNU's Not Unix" and refers generally to software distributed under the GNU Public License (GPL).

GPL (GNU Public License)

The GNU Public License provides for free access to software published under its terms. Users are allowed to copy, modify, and redistribute GPL software, provided that the GPL is maintained.

Graphical user interface (GUI)

A graphical user interface is a program that lets the user interact with a computer system in a highly visual manner, with a minimum of typing. Graphical user interfaces usually require a high-resolution display and a pointing device, such as a computer mouse.

Hidden file

A file with a name that begins with a dot (.). Such files are not listed by the **ls** command unless a special argument (–a) is specified.

Home directory

A directory provided for the personal files and directories of a user.

Host

A computer attached to a network.

Hostname

A name by which a host is known to other hosts on a network.

HTML

Hypertext Markup Language is the form in which web documents are transmitted and interpreted by browsers.

IDE

A popular standard for internal hard drives and CD-ROM drives of IBM-compatible systems.

Internet

A relatively loose federation of computer networks that permits data to be widely transferred among computers.

IP number

A number that identifies a host, corresponding to a network interface associated with the host.

Kernel

The part of an operating system that contains the most primitive functions upon which other, more sophisticated functions depend.

Kill

To terminate a process.

LILO

A program often used to load the Linux kernel from a hard drive or boot diskette.

Manpage

A document that describes a Unix command or file, readable by using the **man** command.

Master Boot Record (MBR)

The first sector of a hard drive, which by convention contains a loader program for starting an operating system.

Mount

To make a filesystem available for use.

Operating system

A program that provides a user interface and an application interface (which makes it possible for application programs to run) and manages computer system resources.

Option

A command argument that takes one of a small number of values. Command arguments that specify files (for example) are not options.

Package

A file that contains a set of related files that can be installed as a unit.

Partition
An area of a hard disk, generally allocated to a specific operating system (though perhaps usable by multiple operating systems).

Path
A path denotes the location of a file or directory. The path is an absolute path if it gives the complete path, beginning with the root directory and including every subdirectory. Otherwise, the path is a relative path.

PPP
Point-to-Point Protocol, the most popular way of connecting a computer to the Internet via a dialup modem.

Process
An instance of a running program.

Prompt
A character or series of characters displayed by a command interpreter to inform the user that execution of a command has been completed and the interpreter is ready to accept a new command.

Relative path
See *Path*.

root
The specially privileged user ID used to perform Unix system administration.

Root directory
The unique directory that has no parent directory. All other directories are children of the root directory or its subdirectories.

Route
A path along which data packets move from host to host across a network.

Runlevel
The operating mode of a Unix system, for example, single-user, multiuser without networking, or multiuser with networking.

Script
A series of commands, stored in a file for subsequent or repeated execution.

SCSI
A popular standard for internal and external hard drives and other peripherals.

Search path
A series of directories automatically searched by a command interpreter in order to locate the program file that corresponds to a command to be executed.

Server
A program that responds to client requests, which are generally transmitted over a network.

Shell
A command interpreter.

Swap file
A disk file or partition used to temporarily store information when system memory runs low.

Symbolic link
A filesystem entity that lets you associate an alternative name with a file or directory.

System administrator
The user who installs, configures, and otherwise maintains the software (and possibly the hardware) associated with a computer system.

TCP/IP (Transmission Control Protocol/Internet Protocol)
A standard method of sending data packets across a computer network, focused on the routing and connection issues.

Terminal
A combination of a keyboard and monitor, which together provide the capability to interact with a computer system.

Telnet
A protocol for establishing a login session via TCP/IP on a remote system.

Text editor
A program that lets you create and modify the contents of text files.

User ID
The unique identifier associated with a system user.

Window manager

A program that manages a graphical user interface, determining the appearance of windows (by providing standard elements such as titlebars, for example) and determining the response to operations such as clicking on the desktop.

Working directory

The directory that is implicitly combined with a relative path reference to determine the corresponding absolute path reference.

X

A sophisticated and powerful graphical user interface implemented on a variety of computer platforms.

X server

A program that implements X for some platform and type of video hardware.

Index

Symbols

\ (backslash)
   command line, 120
   MS-DOS, 71
$ (dollar sign), in shell variables, 257
/ (forward slash)
   defined, 71
   in filenames, 126
| (pipe redirector), 255
/ (root) partition, 42

A

AbiWord, 95
absolute pathnames, 72
accelerated graphics cards, XFree86
     servers, 297
access mode, 73
   defined, 323
   ls command, 124
access permissions, 73
accounts
   modifying, 162–165
   user accounts, 68
adapters, sound, 173
Additional Language Support screen, 48
addresses, Apache web server, 228
adduser command, 312
administration
   groups, 167
     new, 167
   LANs, Neat and, 192–200

modular drivers, 291
users
   deleting, 166
   new, 165
alias command, 312
aliases, 198, 290
   command, 248
   defined, 323
   root, 248
   self-aliased commands, 249
   Unix shell, 248
anonymous FTP, 224
Anonymous FTP Server package group, 55
Apache web server, 227
   configuration, 228
   HTML pages, 231
   installation, 227
   Links browser, 231
   log files, 232
   performance, 230
   starting/stopping, 231
   virtual hosts, 228
applets, 92
   GNOME, 85
     downloading, 89
   launcher applets, 85
apropos command, 122, 312
arguments, 323
   boot arguments, 283
     bus mouses, 289
     CD-ROMs, 286
     floppy drives, 288
     IDE hard drives, 286

We'd like to hear your suggestions for improving our indexes. Send email to *index@oreilly.com*.

arguments, boot arguments *(continued)*
  parallel ports, 289
  RAM disks, 284
  SCSI host adapters, 284
 command line, 119
 shell scripts, 260
at command, 312
atq command, 312
atrm command, 312
audio cards, Sound and Multimedia package
  group, 53
Audio Mixer, 79
authentication
 configuration, 50
 FTP servers, 224
Authoring and Publishing package group, 55

B

background, 323
 jobs, displaying, 315
 placing jobs in, 312
backups, Samba, 217
bash shell, 116
 built-in commands, 119
 command completion, 118
 Command Line Interface (CLI), 116
 command-line format, 119
 commands, 116
 filename completion, 118
 history list, 117
 terminal window, 116
Bell Labs, Multics and, 4
bg command, 312
BIND (Berkeley Internet Name
  Daemon), 239
BIOS (Basic Input/Output System), 323
 GRUB, booting and, 280
 motherboards, 14
blocklists, GRUB, 279
boot arguments
 bus mouses, 289
 CD-ROMs, 286
 floppy drives, 288
 IDE hard drives, 286
 parallel ports, 289
 RAM disks, 284
 SCSI host adapters, 284
boot disk
 creating, 31, 58, 276
 defined, 323
 GNOME, 276

mkbootdisk command, 276
 using, 276
boot filesystem, mounting, 279
boot loader, 275
 configuration, 44
 GRUB Loader, 277
 kernel parameters, 46
boot parameters, 282
/boot partition, 28, 41
 allowable drives, 41
 filesystems, type, 41
 mount point, 41
 size, 41
boot sectors, 277
 defined, 323
booting
 boot disk, creating, 276
 boot loaders, 275
 CD-ROM, 31
 floppy disk, 14, 275
 GRUB, 275
 installation program, 32
 loadln utility, 45, 275, 280
 messages, displaying, 314
 rebooting, 318
 virus protection software and, 275
bootloader (LILO), 22
BootPrompt-HOWTO, 275
break command, 265
broadcast option, network configuration, 47
browsers (see web browsers)
BSD (Berkeley Systems Division) Unix, 5
built-in commands, 119
bus mouses, boot arguments, 289
buttons, installation interface, 35

C

C programming language, 4
cable modems, configuration, 189
caching name server, configuration, 239
cal command, 312
calendar, displaying, 312
canceling jobs, 312
capplets, GNOME, 92
case command, 263
case sensitivity, commands, 119
cat command, 127, 313
cd command, 123, 313
CD Player, 79
CD-ROM drives, 14
 configuration information, 19

CDROM-HOWTO, 275
CD-ROMs, 70
  boot arguments, 286
  burning, Sound and Multimedia Support
      package group, 53
  installing from, 31
CD-Writing-HOWTO, 275
chainloader command (GRUB), 278
changing directories, 313
characters, displaying number, 320
chatting, 319
checkboxes, installation interface, 34
chgrp command, 313
chmod command, 132, 313
chown command, 313
CIFS (Common Internet File System), 201
Classic X Window System package group, 52
clear command, 313
CLI (Command Line Interface), 10, 116
client configuration, Samba, 215
clients
  defined, 323
  DHCP, configuration, 222
  Linux client, Samba, 216
clipboard, KDE panel, 104
clock
  GNOME applet, 86
  KDE panel, 103
Clockchip Configuration dialog box,
     Xconfigurator, 301
Clockchip, Xconfigurator, 300
CMOS, floppy drive booting, 277
cmp command, 313
color depth, video, 302
command completion, bash shell, 118
command interpreter
  defined, 323
  pausing, 318
Command Line Interface (CLI), 10
command-line format
  arguments, 119
  command prompt, 119, 120
  options, 119
commands
  aliases, 248
  bash shell, 116
  built-in, 119
  case sensitivity, 119
  correcting typing errors, 117
  directories and, 122
  external, 119
  firewalls, 242

FTP servers, 225
GRUB, 277, 278
  issuing, x
  man pages, 120, 312
  options, 324
  self-aliased, 249
  shell, 116
  system administration, 119
  system information, 136
  system status, 136
  (see also specific command names)
comparing files, 313
  diff command, 313
  discrepancies, 313
complex operations, Unix shell, 246
compressed files, 129, 320
  expanding, 315, 320
  ZIP files, 131
conditional logic, shell scripts, 261
config.sys file, 19, 281
configuration
  Apache web server, 228
  authentication, 50
  boot loader, 44
  cable modems, 189
  caching name server, 239
  collecting information, 14, 19
  date/time, 158
  desktop, 155
  DHCP clients, 222
  DHCP server, 219
  DNS, 239
  DSL modems, 189
  Enlightenment window manager, 89
  filesystem mounting, 157
  firewalls, 48, 240
  glyphs, 155
  GNOME, 90
  GnoRPM, 152
  groups, 160–168
  hardware, 159
  IP masquerading, 243
  KDE, 107–111
  keyboard, 155
  language, 48
  loadln, 281
  locale, 155
  mail servers, 233
  modem, rp3, 176–179
  mouse, 36
  Netscape Communicator, 185
  network devices, 194

configuration *(continued)*
    networks, 46–48
        devices, 194
        DNS, 199
        hardware, 193
        hosts, 198
    nongraphical login, 250
    passwords, 157
    printers, 168, 172
        local, 168
        parallel ports, 169
        queues, new, 168
    rp3, 177
    runlevels, 250
    Samba, 203
        client configuration, 215
        viewing configuration, 211
    sound, 173
    system clock, 49
    users, 160–168
    video, 56
        custom graphics, 60
        monitor, 59
    wvdial, 182
    X Window System, 295
        manual, 304–311
        troubleshooting, 61
        Xconfigurator, 295
conflicting files, RPM, 145
consoles, virtual (see virtual consoles)
continue command, 265
Control Panel, KDE
    configuration, 108
    desktop, 101
Control Panel, Windows 95/98, 17
copying
    files, 128, 313
        Nautilus, GNOME, 88
    subdirectories, 313
    text, X Window System, 77
copylefting, 6
correcting command typing errors, 117
cost, 9
cp command, 128, 313
current working directory, 71
cursor
    input focus, 33
    installation interface, 33
Custom installation, 23
cylinders, hard disks, 24

D

daemons, 323
data organization, 68
data protection, 23
data storage, 9
databases, RPM, 142
date command, 313
date/time
    configuration, 158
    displaying, 313
    GNOME applet, 86
    system clock configuration, 49
    time zone, 159
Date/Time Properties Tool, 158
Debian GNU/Linux, 8
deleting
    directories, 127, 318
    files, 127, 318
        Nautilus, GNOME, 88
    partitions, 28, 43
    users, 166
dependency, packages, 145
desktop, 89
    computer sales, 2
    default, 155
    defined, 323
    environments, 22, 79
        GNOME, 79, 81–99
        KDE, 80, 100–115
    pager, 78
    switching, 155
    systems, Linux as, 3
Desktop icon, KDE panel, 103
Desktop Switching Tool, 155
developers, 4
Device Manager, Windows 95/98, 17, 19
Device section, X configuration, 310
devices, 69
    enabling/disabling, 195
    Ethernet, nicknames, 194
    mounting, 74, 317
    networks
        configuration, 194
        protocols, 195
    partitions, 69
    startup and, 195
    swapping, disabling, 319
df command, 313

DHCP server, 47, 218
  configuration, 219
    clients, 222
  installation, 218
  starting, 220
DIAGNOSIS.txt file, Samba, 214
dialog boxes, installation interface, 33
Dialup Support package group, 54
diff command, 313
Digital Equipment Corporation, X Window
        System and, 75
directories, 70, 71
  / (slash) in filename, 126
  changing, 313
  commands, 122
  creating, 126, 316
  deleting, 127, 318
  displaying contents, 124
  /dosutils, 280
  dot (.) in names, 126
  home directory, 71, 324
  moving, 317
  on the path, 134
  ownership, 133
  pathnames, 72
  removing, 127
  root, 325
  subdirectories, copying, 313
  working directory, 71, 326
    absolute path, 317
    changing, 123
    displaying, 122
directory tree, 71, 269
disabling devices, 195
disk drives, fixed, 26
Disk Drives icon, Windows 95/98, 17
Disk Druid, 38, 39
  editing partitions, 43
  resetting partitions, 44
disk space, 14
  free, 313
  used, displaying, 314
disks
  boot disk creation, 276
  formatting, 314
distributions, 4, 8
  defined, 323
dmesg command, 314
DNS (Domain Name Server), 192
  configuration, 199, 239
  defined, 323

DNS Name Server package group, 55
  network configuration, 48
DocBook, 55
documentation, system configuration, 14, 19
dollar sign ($), in shell variables, 257
domain, DNS configuration, 199
DOS (see MS-DOS)
DOSKEY editor, 117
/dosutils directory, 280
dot (.) in naming conventions, 126
dots within pathnames, 73
dotted quad notation, 323
downloading
  Linux, 3
  packages, 141
drag and drop operations, GNOME, 89
drawers (GNOME desktop), 91
drive icons, GNOME, 82
Drive icons, KDE desktop, 102
drive letters, 24
  partitions, 40
drivers
  Ethernet, loadable drivers, 289
  graphics cards, 297
  modular
    adminstration, 291
    loading at boot time, 290
    loading dynamically, 290
  video driver, 297
DSL modems, configuration, 189
du command, 314
dual boot, 12, 22
dynamically linked libraries, Opera, 187

E

echo command, 314
  shell variables, 257
echo requests, 317
  paths, host, 320
editing partitions, 43
editors
  GRUB, 277
  pico, 137
    launching, 317
EIDE (Enhanced Integrated Drive
        Electronics), defined, 323
EISA system bus, 14
elm, 79
Emacs package group, 55

email
   mail command, 316
   Messaging and Web Tools package
         group, 54
enabling devices, 195
Enlightenment window manager, 77
   configuring, 89
environment variables, 256
environments, desktop (see desktop
         environments)
Ethernet
   defined, 324
   device nicknames, 194
   drivers, loadable, 289
   Ethernet Device dialog box, 194
   Ethernet-HOWTO, 275
   MAC (Media Access Control), 198
Everything package group, 55
exit code, 261
expanding compressed files, 315, 320
expiring passwords, 165
exporting shell variables, 257
external commands, 119

F

failed dependency, packages, 145
FAT (file allocation table), 24
Favorites, GNOME, 84
fdformat command, 136, 314
fdisk command, 314
fdisk utility, 25
   partitions and, 39
   unused partitions, 28
features, 9
fg command, 314
file command, 314
file compression, expanding files, 315
file managers, 89
   GNOME access, 82
   Konqueror, 104
   Nautilus, GNOME, 87
file permissions, 73, 132
file recovery, Samba, 217
file sharing
   Samba, 207
   Windows File Server package group, 54
filename completion, bash shell, 118
filename globbing, shell, 246
filename metacharacters, 246
filenames
   dot (.) in, 126
   slash (/) in, 126

files, 70
   access time, 319
   comparing, 313
   compressed, 129, 320
   contents, displaying, 127, 313
   copying, 128, 313
      Nautilus, GNOME, 88
   deleting, 127, 318
      Nautilus, GNOME, 88
   displaying, 316
      end lines, 319
   finding, 128
   formatting, printing, 317
   gz, 129
   hidden, 126, 324
   large
      displaying, 317
      less command, 315
   listing, 316
   modes, changing, 313
   moving, 128, 317
      Nautilus, GNOME, 87
   names, links, 316
   ownership, 133
      changing, 313
   permissions, 73
   printing, 129
   queuing for printing, 129
   removing, 127
   renaming, 128
      Nautilus, GNOME, 88
   sorting, 318
   splitting, 318
   swap files, 325
   tar files, 319
   transferring to remote system, 236
   type, 314
   ZIP files, 131
Files section, X configuration, 304
filesystems, 24, 70
   creating, 316
   floppy disks, 70, 136
   journal, 71
   mounting, 157
   operating systems and, 2
   type
      / partition, 42
      /boot partition, 41
      swap partition, 43
   types, 70
   unmounting, 320
   (see also partitions)

filters, 255
find command, 128, 314
Find Packages window, GnoRPM, 150
finger command, 314
fips utility, 29
firewalls, 240
   commands, 242
   configuration, 48, 240
fixed disk drives, 26
floppy disks
   boot disk, 14, 275, 276
      Boot Disk Creation screen, 58
      creating, 31
   filesystems, 70
   formatting, 136, 314
floppy drive boot arguments, 288
folder contents, Nautilus and, 87
for command, 265
foreground, 324
   jobs, moving to, 314
formatting
   files for printing, 317
   floppy disks, 136, 314
   partitions, 24
free command, 314
free disk space, displaying, 313
free operating systems, 3
free software, 5
   copylefting, 6
Free Software Foundation (FSF), 5
Ftape-HOWTO, 275
FTP (File Transfer Protocol), 324
   ftp command, 314
   opening connection, 314
   rpm command, 140
   servers, 55, 224
      anonymous connection, 224
      authentication, 224
      commands, 225
      installation, 225
      packet sniffers, 225
      root user, 225
      testing, 225
      wu-ftp, 224
   sites, 14
   (see also gFTP)

G

games, 79
   GNOME, 79
   KDE, 80

Games and Entertainment package
      group, 55
Gateway option, network configuration, 47
gateways, networks, 191
gEdit, 80
General Electric, Multics and, 4
geometry of hard disks, 24
gFTP, 79, 188
Ghostview, 79
GIMP (GNU Image Manipulation
      Program), 54, 79, 96
global variables, Samba, 204–207
glossary, 323, 326
glyphs, configuration, 155
GNOME, 22, 79
   boot disk creation, 276
   capplets, 92
   clock, 86
   configuration, 90
   drag and drop, 89
   Favorites, 84
   logging out, 81
   login, 62
   main menu, 91
   multimedia applications, 79
   Nautilus, 85, 86
   package installation, 294
   pager, 86
   preferences, 84
   Programs icon, 84
   resources, 98
   rp3 configuration and, 177
   Server Configurator, 84
   session awareness, 79
   Start Here, 92
   System Settings icons, 84
   themes, 94
GNOME desktop, 81, 89
   drive icons, 82
   Help Viewer, 86
   Home Directory, 82
   pop-up menus, 82
   Trash icon, 85
GNOME Office, 95–98
   AbiWord, 95
   GIMP, 96
   Gnumeric, 95
GNOME package group, 53
GNOME panel, 85
   applets, 85
   drawers, 91
   launchers, 90

GNOME panel (continued)
  main menu, 85
  Mozilla launcher, 86
  Start Here, 85
  Task list, 86
GNOME Terminal, 86, 89
  shell commands, 89
GNOME User's Guide, 86
GNOMEdesktop, 81
GnoRPM, 148
  Apache server installation, 227
  BIND installation, 239
  configuration, 152
  finding new packages, 151
  installation, 148
    packages, 151
  launching, 148
  ppp package and, 176
  querying packages, 149
  rp3 package and, 176
  Samba installation, 202
  SSH installation, 235
  uninstalling packages, 149
  upgrading packages, 151
  verifying packages, 149
  wvdial package and, 176
Gnumeric, 80
  GNOME Office, 95
GPL (GNU Public License), 6, 324
Grand Unified Boot Loader (see GRUB)
Graphical Interface (X) Configuration
      screen, 56
graphical login, failed, 65
graphical user interface (see GUI)
Graphics and Image Manipulation package
      group, 54
graphics cards
  drivers, 297
  XFree86 servers, 297
  (see also video cards/video adapters)
graphics, custom configuration, 60
grep command, 314
Group access, 74
Group permission, 132
groups, 73
  administration, 160–168
  changing, 313
  configuration, 167
  creating, 317
  ls command, 125
  new, 167

package groups, 52
root and, 133
GRUB (Grand Unified Boot Loader), 275
  blocklists, 279
  configuration, 44
  editor commands, 277
  installation, 277
  MBR and, 277
  passwords, 46
GRUB (Grand Unified Boot Loader),booting
      and, 275
GRUB Loader, 277
GUI (graphical user interface), 7, 22, 245,
      324
  Classic X Window System package
      group, 52
  X Window and, 8
gunzip command, 129, 315
gz files (compressed), 129
gzip command, 129

H

hard disks
  configuration information, 19
  cylinders, 24
  geometry, 24
  GRUB reference, 279
  installation
    new, 28
    preparation, 23
  LBA, 25
  organization of, 24
  partition information, 25
  sectors, 25
  space, 14
  structure, 24
hard links, 132
hardware
  configuration, 159
    networks, 193
  networks, options, 198
  variations, operating system and, 1
Hardware Browser Tool, 159
hardware requirements, 13
  disk space, 14
  hard disk, 14
  motherboards, 14
Hardware-HOWTO, 275
head command, 315
header, displaying, 315
heads, hard disk, 24

Help
  installation, 65
  installation interface, 35
Help Viewer, GNOME, 86
hidden files, 126, 324
hide button, KDE panel, 104
High security, firewalls, 240
history list, bash shell, 117
history of Linux, 4
  timeline, 7
Home Directory
  GNOME desktop, 82
  KDE desktop, 101
home directory, 71, 324
home directory icon (GNOME), 82
host
  defined, 324
  naming, 315
host configuration, networks, 198
hostname, 324
  DNS configuration, 199
  DNS information and, 197
  IP addresses, 192
  network configuration, 47
hostname command, 315
HOWTOs
  BootPrompt-HOWTO, 275
  CDROM-HOWTO, 275
  CD-Writing-HOWTO, 275
  Ethernet-HOWTO, 275
  Ftape-HOWTO, 275
  Hardware-HOWTO, 275
  Multi-Disk-HOWTO, 275
  PCI-HOWTO, 275
  PCMCIA-HOWTO, 275
HTML (Hypertext Markup Language), 324
HTML pages, Apache web server, 231

I

IDE, defined, 324
IDE hard drives, boot arguments, 286
If, 17
if command, 262
ifconfig command
  Internet connection, 181
  periscope, 267
info command, 315
init command, 315
initrd command (GRUB), 278
input focus
  cursor, 33
  windows, 75

input/output
  completing operations, 319
  piping, 253
  redirection, 253
insmod command, 315
installation, 13
  Apache web server, 227
  boot floppy, 31
  booting installation program, 32
  CD-ROM, 31
  DHCP server, 218
  FTP servers, 225
  GnoRPM, 148
  GRUB, 277
  hard disk, 23
  hardware requirements, 13
  Help, 65
  information collection, 14
  interface, 32
    keyboard type, 36
    missing, 33
  KOffice, 112
  mouse configuration, 36
  new disk drives, 28
  packages, 52, 57, 143
    GnoRPM, 151
  partition creation, 38
  partitionless, 27
  preparation, 13
  Red Hat install utility, 28
  resource guides, 66
  rp3, 176
  Samba, 202
  sendmail, 234
  sound adapter, 17
  SSH, 235
  starting process, 31
  types, 22
    selecting, 37
  virtual consoles, monitoring and, 35
  Workstation, 22
  X Window System, 292
    GNOME packages, 294
    KDE packages, 294
interfaces, 4, 7
  installation, 33
    keyboard type, 36
  installation process, 32
  ISP connection, 180
  networks, 191
Internet, 11
  defined, 324

Internet connections
    failure, rp3 and, 181
    ISPs, 180–181
    PPP, rp3 and, 176
    termination, 181
    wvdial, 182
iobase option, SCSI host adapter boot
        arguments, 285
IP addresses
    aliases, 198
    hostname, 192
    network configuration, 47
IP masquerading, 240
    configuration, 243
IP numbers, defined, 324
IRDA (infrared data interconnection), 22
    Laptop Support package group, 53
ISA system bus, 14
ispell command, 315
ISPs (Internet Service Providers), connecting
        to, 180–181
issuing commands, x
It, 107

J

jobs, background, 315
jobs command, 315
Joy, Bill (Sun Microsystems), 5

K

kbdconfig command, 36
KDE, 22, 80, 100
    configuration, 107–111
    Control Panel configuration, 108
    installation, 294
    KOffice, 80
        installation, 112
    Konqueror, 104–106
    licensing, 80
    login, 63
    main menu, 111
    multimedia applications, 79
    resources, 114
    rp3 configuration and, 177
    themes, 110
KDE Control Center, configuration and, 109
KDE desktop, 100–102
KDE package group, 53
KDE Panel, 102–104

KDE Terminal, 106
kernel, 6
    defined, 324
    monolithic, 289
    parameters, 46
    partitions, 40
kernel command (GRUB), 278
Kernel Development package group, 55
keyboard
    command editing, bash shell, 117
    configuration, 155
    installation interface, 36
    operations with, 77
    operations, X, 75
Keyboard section, X configuration, 306
keystrokes, virtual consoles, 35
keywords
    apropos command, 312
    descriptions, 312
Kfract, 80
kill a process, 324
kill command, 315
killall command, 315
Kmedia, 80
Kmines, 80
Kmix, 80
Konqueror, 104–106
Korganizer, 104
Kpoker, 80
Ktetris, 80
Kview, 80

L

LAN (Local Area Network) administration,
        Neat, 192–200
language configuration, 48
Laptop Support package group, 53
large disk support, 26
launch icons, KDE panel, 103
launcher applets, 85
launchers, GNOME panel, 90
launching
    GnoRPM, 148
    KOffice applications, 112
    programs, 134
LBA (logical block addressing), 25
leasing configuration, DHCP, 219
Legacy Application Support package
        group, 55
less command, 315

licensing, 2
  copylefting, 6
  KDE, 80
LILO (Linux loader) utility, 22, 324
lines, displaying number, 320
links
  file references, 131
  ls command, 124
  symbolic, 325
Links browser, 186
  Apache web server and, 231
links command, 315
Linux
  commands, x
    quick reference, 312, 321
  distributions, 4, 8
  downloading, 3
  features, 9
  history of, 4, 6
  operating system comparisons, 3
  performance, 9
  pronunciation, 2
  purchasing, 3
  reasons to use/not use checklist, 10
  releases, 6
  resources for further information, 3, 12
  running concurrently with Windows
    applications, 12
  Unix and, 3
  versions of, 6
Linux Documentation icon, KDE
    desktop, 101
Linux Documentation Project, xvii
Linux Filesystem Hierarchy Standard web
    site, 270
Linux Web Ring web site, xvii
list boxes, installation interface, 34
listing files, 316
ln command, 131, 316
loading
  modular drivers
    at boot time, 290
    dynamically, 290
  modules, 315
loadln utility, 275, 280
  booting and, 45
  configuration, 281
  testing, 281
  Windows 95 and, 282
local printers
  configuration, 168
  Printing Support package group, 52

locale
  configuration, 155
  glyphs, 155
locate command, 129, 316
log files, Apache web server, 232
logical structure, partitions, 24
login, 62
  GNOME, 62
  graphical, failed, 65
  KDE, 63
  nongraphical, 250
  SSH, 318
  telnet, 319
  text-based, starting/stopping X, 251
  virtual consoles, 249
logout
  GNOME, 81
  KDE, 104
  virtual console, 250
lpq command, 129, 316
lpr command, 129, 316
lprm command, 316
ls command, 124, 316
lsmod command, 291

M

MAC (Media Access Control), 198
mail command, 316
mail servers
  configuration, 233
  MTA (Mail Transfer Agent), 233
main menu
  GNOME, 91
    panel, 85
  KDE, 111
    panel, 103
main window, installation interface, 32
man command, 120, 316
manpages (manual pages), 120, 324
  apropos command and, 122
  commands, 312
  displaying, 316
manual configuration, X, 304–311
MBR (Master Boot Record), 277
  defined, 324
  GRUB, 44
MD5 passwords, 51
Medium security, firewalls, 240
memory
  displaying used and free, 314
  motherboard, 14

Messaging and Web Tools package
 group, 54
metacharacters
 file transfer and, 237
 filename characters, 246
MIDI synthesizers, configuration and, 175
minieditor, shell, 117
MIT (Massachusetts Institute of
 Technology), 7
 Multics and, 4
 X Window System, 75
mkbootdisk command, 276
mkdir command, 126, 316
mkfs command, 316
mkswap command, 316
modems
 configuration
  cable modems, 189
  DSL modems, 189
  rp3, 176–179
  rp3 installation, 176
  troubleshooting, installation, 178
  WinModems, 178
modes, changing, 313
modification date, ls command, 125
modprobe command, 291
modular drivers
 administration, 291
 loading
  at boot time, 290
  dynamically, 290
modules, loading, 315
monitor
 configuration, 59
 vertical refresh rate, 59
 VESA, 310
Monitor section, X configuration, 308
Monitor Setup dialog box,
 Xconfigurator, 298
monochrome monitor support, 297
monolithic kernel, 289
more command, 317
motherboards, 14
mount command, 134, 317
 root partition, 281
mount points, 135
 / partition, 42
 /boot partition, 41
 /swap partition, 43
mounted devices, reporting, 281

mounting
 boot filesystem, 279
 defined, 324
 devices, 74, 317
 filesystems, 157
mounting/unmounting devices, 134
mouse, 75
 configuration, 36
 configuration information, 19
 right-clicking, 77
 X Window System, 77
  copying text, 77
  pasting text, 77
mouseconfig command, 37
moving
 directories, 317
 files, 128, 317
  Nautilus, GNOME, 87
Mozilla web browser, 79, 86, 184
MS-DOS, 10
 loadln and, 275
 prompt, 10, 76, 116
 Prompt Window, bash shell and, 116
MTA (Mail Transfer Agent), 233
Mult-Disk-HOWTO, 275
Multics (Multiplexed Information and
 Computing Service), 4
multimedia adapters, configuration
 information, 19
mv command, 128, 317

N

named (BIND), 239
names, ls command, 125
Nautilus, GNOME, 85
 copying files, 88
 deleting files, 88
 moving files, 87
 renaming files, 88
NcFTP, 79
Neat, 192–200
NetBIOS, starting, 213
netmask, network configuration, 47
Netscape Navigator and Communicator, 185
 GNOME support for, 79
network adapter cards, configuration
 information, 19
network applications, GNOME, 79
Network Configuration screen, 46

Network Managed Workstation package
   group, 55
Network Support package group, 53
networking
   configuration, 46–48
   devices
      configuration, 194
      protocols, 195
   DHCP servers, configuration and, 47
   DNS, configuration, 199
   Ethernet, 324
   firewalls, configuration, 48
   gateways, 191, 192
   hardware configuration, 193
   hardware options, 198
   host configuration, 198
   interfaces, 191
   overview, 191–192
   routing, 197
   Samba, 201
   security, 243
   subnetworks, 191
newgroup command, 317
News Server package group, 54
newsgroups, Messaging and Web Tools
      package group, 54
NFS File Server package group, 54
NFS (Network File System) servers, 14
nicknames, Ethernet devices, 194
NMB, starting, 213
nmbd daemon, 202
No Firewall security, 240
nongraphical login, 250
notation, dotted quad notation, 323
NTFS filesystem, 9

O

office suites
   GNOME Office, 95–98
   KOffice, 80, 111–114˙
Online Help, installation interface, 35
openssh, 235
Opera web browser, 186
operating systems
   defined, 324
   filesystems and, 2
   free, 3
   hardware variations and, 1
   licenses, 2
   Linux, 3
   overview, 1–10

sales of for desktop computers, 2
   types available, 2
options, commands, 324
   command line, 119
organizing data, 68
Other access, 74
Other permission, 132
output stream, text display, 314
owners, 73
   access permission, 74
   files, 313
ownership of files and directories, 133

P

package groups, 52
packages
   conflicting files, 145
   defined, 324
   dependency, 145
   downloading, 141
   GnoRPM
      installation, 151
      new, 151
      upgrading, 151
   installation, 52, 57, 143
   overwriting, 143
   Red Hat Package Manager, 139
   rmp command, 139
   RPM and, 139
   uninstalling, 146
   updating, 147
   verification, 144
   X Windows, manual installation, 293
   XFree86, 75
packet sniffers, FTP servers, 225
pagers, 78
   GNOME, 86
   KDE panel, 103
parallel ports, 169
   boot arguments, 289
parameters
   boot parameters, 282
   kernel, 46
parent directories, creating, 316
partition table, editing, 314
partitionless installation, 27
PartitionMagic, 29
partitions, 24
   / (root) partition, 42
   boot, 28
   boot partition, 41

partitions *(continued)*
  defined, 325
  deleting, 28, 43
  devices, 69
  Disk Druid, 38
  drive letters, 40
  editing, 43
  fdisk utility and, 39
  formatting, 24
  free space, Windows Explorer, 29
  GRUB reference, 279
  installation and, 38
  kernel, 40
  logical structure, 24
  new, 40
  partitioning with Disk Druid, 39
  resetting, Disk Druid, 44
  root, mount command, 281
  root partition, 42
  saving changes, 44
  shrinking, 29
  splitting, 29
  swap partitions, 40, 43
  unused, 28
  viewing information, 25
  (see also filesystems)
passwd command, 317
passwords
  changing, 157, 317
  choosing secure, 165
  configuration, 157
  expiring, 165
  GRUB, 46
  MD5, 51
  root user, 50
  Samba, 212
  security, 158, 165
pasting text, X Window System, 77
pathnames
  absolute, 72
  dots in, 73
  relative, 72
paths, 134
  defined, 325
  relative path, 325
  rpm command, 140
  search path, 258, 325
pausing command interpreter, 318
PCI system bus, 14
PCI-HOWTO, 275
PCMCIA Laptop Support package group, 53
PCMCIA-HOWTO, 275

pending jobs, 312
performance, 9
  Apache web server, 230
periscope script, 266
permissions
  access permissions, 73
  default, 320
  file permissions, 132
  files, 73
physical structure (hard disks), 24
pico command, 317
pico editor, 137
  launching, 317
pine, 79
ping command, 317
pinging, 181
pipe operator, 125
piping, 253
Pointer section, X configuration, 307
pointing devices
  X Window System, 75
  (see also mouse)
pop-up menus, 77
  GNOME, 82
  X, 76
PostgreSQL database, 55
PPP (Point-to-Point Protocol)
  defined, 325
  rp3 and, 176
  wvdial and, 182
pr command, 317
preferences, GNOME, 84
preparation for Linux installation, 13
Primary DNS, network configuration, 48
print queue
  listing entries, 316
  new, 168
print sharing
  Samba, 209
  Windows File Server package group, 54
printer configuration, 168, 172
  local printers, 168
Printer Configuration Tool, 168
printing
  canceling, 316
  files, 129
  formatting files, 317
  queuing files, 129
Printing Support package group, 52
Probe for Clocks dialog box,
      Xconfigurator, 301

processes
    defined, 325
    displaying, 317, 319
    killing, 315
programming languages, 4
Programs icon, GNOME, 84
programs, launching, 134
Project Athena, 7
prompts
    defined, 325
    MS-DOS, 76
pronunciations, 2
protecting data, 23
protocol tunneling, 238
protocols
    devices, 195
    PPP, 325
ps command, 317
pseudodevices, 69
publications, 3
publishing tools, 55
purchasing Linux, 3
PuTTY SSH client, 237
pwd command, 122, 317

Q

querying RPM databases, 142
queuing files to print, 129
quick reference for Linux commands, 312,
    321
quote characters, shell, 258
quoted strings, 258

R

radio buttons, installation interface, 34
RAID (Redundant Array of Inexpensive
    Disks), 9
RAM disks
    boot arguments, 284
    GRUB, 279
RAM (random access memory), 14
read/write heads, hard disk, 24
reboot command, 318
rebooting, 318
recovery, Samba, 217
Red Hat Linux, 2
    FAQ (Frequently Asked Questions), xvii
    (see also entries at Linux)
Red Hat Network, 154
Red Hat Update Agent, 154
redirection, 253

Redundant Array of Inexpensive Disks
    (RAID), 9
relative path, 325
relative path names, 72
remote access (see periscope script)
remote printers, Printing Support package
    group, 52
remote systems, SSH file transfer, 236
removing directories, 127
removing files, 127
renaming files, 128
    Nautilus, GNOME, 88
reset command, 318
resetting partitions, Disk Druid, 44
resources
    books, 3
    GNOME, 98
    GNOME User's Guide, 86
    installation, 66
    KDE, 114
    Linux Documentation Project
        guides, xii–xiii
    Linux Journal, xiv
    Linux Magazine, xiv
    Linux Systems Labs, xiii
    Linux User Groups (LUGs), xvii
    mailing lists, xvi
    modem configuration, 190
    Open Source Writers Guild, xiii
    Red Hat web site, xi
    Specialized Systems Consultants, Inc.
        (SSC), xiii
    Usenet newsgroups, xiv–xvi
    web sites, xvii–xviii
        Red Hat, xi
RGB color scheme, 305
right mouse button, 77
Ritchie, Dennis (Bell Labs), 4
rm command, 127, 318
rmdir command, 127, 318
root, 50, 68
    aliases, 248
    boot disk creation, 276
    defined, 325
    FTP servers, 225
    groups and, 133
root command, GRUB, 278
root directory, 71
    defined, 325
    subdirectories and, 72
root partition, mount command, 281
rootnoverify command (GRUB), 278

route command
   Internet connection, 181
   periscope, 266
route, defined, 325
Router/Firewall package group, 55
routing, 197
rp3
   configuration, 177
   connection failure, 181
   installation, 176
   termination, 181
   wvdial, 182
rpm command, 139
   packages installation, 143
RPM (Red Hat Linux Package Manager), 139
   advanced techniques, 147
   conflicting files, 145
   databases, querying, 142
   installing packages, 143
   package dependency, 145
   uninstalling packages, 146
   updating packages, 147
rpmfind utility, 141
runlevels, 250
   defined, 325
   value, changing, 315

S

Samba, 201
   backups, 217
   client, 216
   configuration, 203
     client, 215
     viewing, 211
   file recovery, 217
   file sharing, 207
   global variables, 204–207
   installation, 202
   passwords, 212
   print sharing, 209
   Server Password Management, 214
   server status, viewing, 210
   starting/stopping, 213
   troubleshooting, 214
   users, 212
   Windows and, 215
scp command, 318
Screen section, X configuration, 311
screensaver icon, KDE panel, 104
screensaver, virtual consoles, 249

scripts
   defined, 325
   shell scripts, 251, 260
     argument processing, 260
     conditional logic, 261
     periscope, 266
scrollbars, X Window System, 77
SCSI (Small Computer Serial Interface)
   defined, 325
   host adapters, boot arguments, 284
search engine for Linux information, xvii
search path, 258, 325
searches, 314, 316
   find command, 128
   grep command, 314
   locate command, 129
Secondary DNS, network configuration, 48
secondary prompt, shell, 263
sectors, hard disks, 25
security
   firewalls, 240
   IP masquerading, 240
   networks, 243
   passwords, 158, 165
self-aliased commands, 249
sendmail package, 233
Server Configurator, GNOME, 84
Server installation type, 23
Server Password Management, Samba
     and, 214
server platform, Linux as, 3
ServerFlags section, X configuration, 305
servers
   Apache web server, 227
   caching name server, 239
   defined, 325
   DHCP, 218
     configuration, 219
     installation, 218
     starting, 220
   DNS, 239
   FTP, 224
   Linux as, 9
   mail servers, 233
   Samba
     installation, 202
     status, 210
   TCP/IP and, 196
   Tux web server, 227
   X server, 297, 326
   XFree86-Mono, 297

XFree86-SGVA, 297
XFree86-VGA16, 297
session awareness, GNOME, 79
sharing files, Samba, 207
sharing printers, Samba, 209
shell, 10
  aliases, 248
  command prompt, 119
  commands, 116
  defined, 325
  metacharacters, 237
  minieditor, 117
  piping, 253
  quote characters, 258
  quoted strings, 258
  redirection, 253
  secondary prompt, 263
  SSH, 235
  X Windows and, 250
shell scripts, 251, 260
  argument processing, 260
  conditional logic, 261
  periscope, 266
  Unix, 246
shell variables, 256
  echo command and, 257
  exit codes, 261
  exporting, 257
  PATH, 258
shellfilename globbing, 246
shrinking partitions, 29
shutdown command, 318
signals, listing, 315
Slashdot web site, xviii
sleep command, 318
slrn, 79
SMB (Server Message Block), 201
SMB shared volume, 14
smbd daemon, 202
sndconfig (sound), 173
sniffers, 203
  FTP servers, 225
SNMP (Simple Network Management
      Protocol), 55
soft links, 131
software
  copylefting, 6
  free, 5
  PartitionMagic, 29
Software Development package group, 55

software distribution, 6
Software in the Public Interest, Inc., 8
sort command, 318
sorting files, 318
sound adapter, installation and, 17
Sound and Multimedia package group, 53
sound cards, 19
sound configuration, 173
Sound Configuration utility, 173
spelling, 315
split command, 318
splitting partitions, 29
SQL Database Server package group, 55
ssh command, 318
SSH (Secure Shell), 235
  client installation, 237
  file transfer to remote system, 236
  installation, 235
  protocol tunneling, 238
  testing, 236
  VPN, 238
Stallman, Richard, 5
Start Here icon, GNOME, 83, 85, 92
starting/stopping
  Apache web server, 231
  X, text-based login, 251
statically linked libraries, Opera, 187
STDIN, command execution, 312
stdin (Unix input), 255
stdout (Unix output), 255
strings, quoted strings in shells, 258
su command, 319
subdirectories
  copying, 313
  root directory and, 72
subnetworks, 191
SVGA cards, XFree86-SVGA server, 297
swap files, 325
swap partitions, 40, 43
swap space, creating, 316
swapoff command, 319
swapon command, 319
swapping devices, disabling, 319
SWAT (Samba Web Administration
      Tool), 203
switching desktops, 155
symbolic links, 131
  defined, 325
symlinks, 131
sync command, 319

system
    administration commands, 119
    information display, 320
        commands for viewing, 136
    uptime display, 320
system administrator, 325
system buses, 14
system clock, configuration, 49
System Properties dialog box, 17
System Settings icons, GNOME, 84
system shutdown, 318
system status
    commands for viewing, 136
    w command, 116
System V, 5

T

tail command, 319
talk command, 319
tar command, 130, 319
tarfiles
    creating, 319
    listing contents, 130
task list
    GNOME, 86
    KDE panel, 103
TCP/IP (Transmission Control
        Protocol/Internet Protocol)
    defined, 325
    networking, 11
    servers and, 196
    settings, 196
Telnet, 325
telnet command, 319
terminal
    defined, 325
    resetting, 318
terminal window, 76
    bash shell and, 116
terminating Internet connection, 181
terminating X Window, 76
test command, 261
testing
    FTP servers, 225
    SSH, 236
TeX, 55
Texinfo (GNU), 315
text boxes, installation interface, 34
text editors
    defined, 325
    pico, 137

themes
    GNOME, 94
    KDE, 110
Thompson, Ken (Bell Labs), 4
thumbnails, pagers, 78
time command, 319
time (see date/time)
time zone, 159
timeconfig command, 49
timeline of Linux history, 7
timing job execution, 319
top command, 319
Torvalds, Linus, 1
touch command, 319
traceroute command, 320
tracks, hard disk, 24
Trash icon
    GNOME, 85
    KDE desktop, 102
trees, directory tree, 269
troubleshooting
    Samba, 214
    X Window System configuration, 61
Trusted Devices, firewall configuration, 242
Tux web server, 227
TWM (tiny window manager), 155
Type column, ls command, 124

U

umask command, 320
umount command, 320
uname command, 320
uninstalling packages, 146
Unix, 4, 11
    BSD, 5
    GNU, 5
    Linux and, 3
Unix shell, 245
    complex operations and, 246
    shell scripts, 246
unmounting devices, 134
until command, 264
unused partitions, 28
unzip command, 320
updating packages, 147
upgrading packages, GnoRPM, 151
uptime command, 320
URLs, Linux, xvii
user accounts, 68
    configuration, 50

User ID, 325
User Manager tool, configured groups, 167
User Mount Tool, 157
User Properties dialog box, 162
userid
    adduser command, 312
    changing, 319
User/Owner access, 74, 132
users
    account modification, 162–165
    administration, 160–168
    deleting, 166
    description, displaying, 314
    device enabling/disabling, 195
    displaying, 320
    information display, 320
    listing, 116
    messages to, 320
    new, adding, 165
    Samba, 212
UTC (Universal Coordinate Time), 49
utilities
    fdisk, 25
    fips, 29
    loadln, 275, 280
        mounting, 281
    rpmfind, 141
    Sound Configuration, 173
Utilities package group, 55

V

variables
    environment variables, 256
    exit codes, 261
    global, Samba, 204–207
    shell variables, 256
Verifying Packages window, GnoRPM, 149
version number, boot disk creation, 276
vertical refresh rate, monitor, 59
VESA (Video Electronics Standards
        Association), 310
    system bus, 14
VGA cards, XFree86-VGA16 server, 297
video
    color depth, 302
    configuration, 56
        custom graphics, 60
        monitor, 59
    monitor, 59
video cards/video adapters, 19
    memory, Xconfigurator, 300
video drivers, 297

Video Memory dialog box,
        Xconfigurator, 300
video modes, X Window System, 76
virtual consoles, 249
    installation monitoring, 35
    login, 249
    logout, 250
    XWindow System, 76
virtual desktops
    GNOME, 86
    X Window System, 78
virtual hosts, Apache web server, 228
virtual terminal, wvdial and, 183
virus protection, booting and, 275
VPN (Virtual Private Network), 238

W

w command, 116, 320
wall command, 320
wc command, 320
    redirection and, 254
web browsers, 183
    defined, 323
    Links, 186
    Mozilla, 184
    Netscape, 185
    Opera, 186
web pages, viewing with links
        command, 315
Web Server package group, 55
web servers
    Apache, 227
    Tux, 227
web sites, xvii
    Linux distributions, 8
    Linux Filesystem Hierarchy
        Standard, 270
which command, PATH shell variable, 258
while command, 264
who command, 320
wildcards (see filename globbing)
window managers, 78, 326
    Enlightenment, 89
    GNOME, 89
    X Window System, 8
Windows 95/98
    configuration information collection, 17
    dual boot with Linux, 22
Windows applications
    running concurrently with Linux, 12
    WINE emulation and, 12

Windows Compatibility/Interoperability
    package group, 55
Windows Explorer, partition free disk
    space, 29
Windows File Server package group, 54
Windows MS-DOS prompt, 76
Windows, Samba and, 215
WINE, 12
WinModems, 178
WML (Wireless Markup Language), Opera
    browser, 187
words, displaying number, 320
working directory, 71
    absolute path, 317
    changing, 123
    defined, 326
    displaying, 122
Workstation installation type, 22
wu-ftp, 224
wvdial
    configuration, 182
    Internet connection, 182
    periscope, 267

X

X Consortium, 7, 75
X servers, 297, 326
X Window System, 7, 75
    configuration, 295
        manual, 304–311
        troubleshooting, 61
    defined, 326
    input focus, 75
    installation, 292
        KDE packages, 294
        packages, 293

keyboard operations, 75
mouse, 77
    copying text, 77
    pasting text, 77
pop-up menus, 76
scrollbars, 77
shell and, 250
starting/stopping from text-based
    login, 251
terminating, 76
video modes, switching, 76
virtual consoles, 76
virtual desktop, 78
window managers, 8, 78
X Window System package group, 53
X-Chat, 79
Xconfigurator, 295
    Clockchip Configuration dialog box, 301
    Monitor Setup dialog box, 298
    Probe for Clocks dialog box, 301
    video adapter memory, 300
    video, color depth, 302
    Video Memory dialog box, 300
XFree86 package, 75
XFree86 Project, 7, 75
XFree86-Mono server, 297
XFree86-SVGA server, 297
XFree86-VGA16 server, 297
XML (eXtensible Markup Language), Opera
    browser, 186

Z

zip command, 320
ZIP files, 131

About the Author

Bill McCarty is associate professor of management information systems in the School of Business and Management of Azusa Pacific University, Azusa, California, and was previously associate professor of computer science, in which capacity he taught for ten years in Azusa Pacific's Master of Applied Computer Science program.

Bill holds a Ph.D. in the management of information systems from the Claremont Graduate University, Claremont, California, and worked for 15 years as a software developer and manager.

Colophon

Our look is the result of reader comments, our own experimentation, and feedback from distribution channels. Distinctive covers complement our distinctive approach to technical topics, breathing personality and life into potentially dry subjects.

The cover image of a man wearing a wide-brimmed hat is a 19th-century engraving from *Marvels of the New West: A Vivid Portrayal of the Stupendous Marvels in the Vast Wonderland West of the Missouri River*, by William Thayer (The Henry Bill Publishing Co., Norwich, CT, 1888).

Leanne Soylemez was the production editor and proofreader for *Learning Red Hat Linux*. Norma Emory was the copyeditor. Catherine Morris and Jane Ellin provided quality control. Johnna VanHoose Dinse wrote the index.

Hanna Dyer designed the cover of this book, based on a series design by her and Edie Freedman. Emma Colby and Melanie Wang produced the cover layout with QuarkXPress 4.1 using Adobe's ITC Garamond font.

David Futato designed the interior layout. The chapter opening images are from the Dover Pictorial Archive, *Marvels of the New West*, and *The Pioneer History of America: A Popular Account of the Heroes and Adventures*, by Augustus Lynch Mason, A.M. (The Jones Brothers Publishing Company, Cincinnati, OH, 1884). Neil Walls converted the files from Microsoft Word to FrameMaker 5.5.6 using tools created by Mike Sierra. The text font is Linotype Birka; the heading font is Adobe Myriad Condensed; and the code font is LucasFont's TheSans Mono Condensed. The illustrations that appear in the book were produced by Robert Romano and Jessamyn Read using Macromedia FreeHand 9 and Adobe Photoshop 6. The tip and warning icons were drawn by Christopher Bing.

Whenever possible, our books use a durable and flexible lay-flat binding.